Consent and Coe

Sex and Marriage in Ancient

and Medieval Societies

Consent and Coercion to Sex and Marriage in Ancient and Medieval Societies

Edited by Angeliki E. Laiou

Dumbarton Oaks Research Library and Collection
Washington, D.C.

Library of Congress Cataloging-in-Publication Data

Consent and coercion to sex and marriage in ancient and medieval societies
/ edited by Angeliki E. Laiou.
    p.   cm.
    Includes bibliographical references and index.
    ISBN 0-88402-213-7
    1. Rape—Europe—History.   2. Seduction—Europe—History.
3. Marriage law—Europe—History.   4. Violence (Law)—Europe—
History.   5. Consent (Law)—Europe—History.   6. Sex customs—
Europe—History.   I. Laiou-Thomadakis, Angeliki E.
KJC8550.C66   1993
306.7—dc20   93-3070
                                                         CIP

Contents

Introduction

The papers published in this volume deal with the role of consent—free, circumscribed, or coerced—in the formation of marriage links, and in sexual relations, whether within marriage or outside it, in ancient and medieval European societies. It must be stressed from the outset that the focus is neither on marriage, ancient or medieval (on which many excellent studies have been written), nor on sexual relations in ancient and medieval Europe (which is also a topic engendering much scholarship), but specifically on consent, its meaning, its implications, and the effects of its absence. The volume is the result of a colloquium, organized by Diana Moses and myself, which took place at Dumbarton Oaks in February 1992. For both of us, the specific topic of consent to sexual activity or marriage is inscribed within a much broader research interest in the role of consent in other areas of social relations in Rome and Byzantium respectively. We have decided to examine first the role of consent in marriage and sexual relations because these aspects of the question are the ones in which the statements of contemporaries are more conscious than for any other aspects. I cannot deny, as well, that modern concerns with such issues sharpen one's sensitivity and pose questions that would otherwise remain unexamined. The problems treated in this volume, however, were real problems, present in and sometimes debated by the societies in question.

Every society, including our own, addresses in some way the question of free and circumscribed consent: all societies place limits on individual consent, and some value it less than others; many societies accept a certain degree of coercion as valid. What varies, and is therefore historically significant, is the weight that each society places on individual consent, the limits it imposes upon it, and the validity it recognizes to measures or acts of coercion. Surely these constitute basic aspects of each society, and to some degree define it; the importance of the matter is immediately recognizable when one raises it in connection with political institutions and mores. One must, however, be careful, especially with the question of consent to sexual and marital relations. It is easy and seductive to approach the matter in a reductionist way; yet what matters deeply in one society does not matter in another, and resemblances are sometimes real and sometimes superficial. That is why a comparative approach is particularly useful as far as this topic is concerned. The papers published here on various aspects of the role of consent reveal an evolution in the concept itself, as well as differences and similarities in the way in which various ancient and medieval societies approached it.

For example, the influence of Christianity and the Christian church in matters of sexual morality and in the pertinent legislation has traditionally been stressed by scholars, even if the evidence is sometimes intuitive. At the same time, the scholarship of the last few decades has pointed out the fact that some of the moral imperatives that used to be identified with Christianity were already present in the Roman Empire, and in a pagan milieu. More generally, the late Antique period is now considered to be a formative time in matters concerning the family and public and private morality. Christianity had a tremendous impact, both institutional and moral, but it was different at various times and in various societies, as the papers published here reveal. It is not by accident that a number of the papers on the Western and Byzantine Middle Ages quote or refer to 1 Cor. 7:2–4: "To avoid fornication, let every man have his own wife, and let every woman have her own husband. Let the husband render unto the wife due benevolence; and likewise also the wife unto the husband. The wife hath not power of her own body, but the husband; and likewise also the husband hath not power of his own body, but the wife." Equally important, the use each society made of these and other Christian precepts was far from uniform.

As a second example, it is intriguing to examine whether certain concepts, such as rape or the marital debt, that we find in many societies have a universal definition or significance, or whether they have profoundly different definitions and import.

The investigation of the issues we are undertaking deals somewhat more extensively with the question of the consent of the woman than with that of the man. Certainly, when it comes to marriage, the role of the consent of both the future bridegroom and the future bride can be, and is here, examined. Certainly also in homosexual relationships between men, the question arises of the consent of male partners. Finally, in sexual relations within marriage, especially in a Christian setting, the consent of both partners is at issue. But in heterosexual relations that were adulterous, or outside of marriage, the man was the actor, and the question of his consent almost never arose; the consent of the woman becomes the central point in such relations, for it was not a given, and the problem then arises of how people dealt with her consent and where they placed the limits of free consent.

The issues treated in this volume being of considerable complexity, it would be hazardous to summarize them here. A few general points might, however, be usefully made. First, one should note that consent as a differentiating factor in establishing categories of sexual relations and crimes is limited by other factors. Among them, one might mention the concepts of honor and shame, which may apply to the act of intercourse itself; one could also mention social status, as well as incapacities or protections (the protection of age, for example, for those in prepubescence), which render consent irrelevant. These factors operate differently in different societies. The question of consent seems to loom large in imperial Rome and in Christian societies, less so in ancient Greece. Second, where consent *is* an important issue, a number of related questions come to the fore: when is consent clearly free, and does it matter; can it be freely withdrawn once it has been freely given; what is the measure, validity, weight of coerced consent, and what are its consequences, especially for the person coerced? These questions are addressed in a number of the papers, which make it clear that the answers were by no means universal or constant. Finally, there is, always, the problem of the relationship between law, ideology, and social practice. The complex interplay between normative rules and behavior is examined from a variety of viewpoints.

This volume is in many ways the result of a collaborative effort. Some time ago, after I had started to work on the topic of consent as it is formulated in Byzantine society, I became acquainted with the work of Diana Moses on the Roman period. The discussions we had helped me a great deal in clarifying my thoughts. In the fall term of 1991, Diana Moses and I offered, at Dumbarton Oaks, a seminar on free, coerced, and circumscribed consent in Rome and Byzantium, and at the same time planned the colloquium. The formulation of the *problématique,* of both the seminar and the colloquium, is in many ways due to Diana Moses. We are both grateful to the scholars who agreed to address these questions and to the audience of the colloquium, who participated in fruitful discussion. I should also like to thank my colleague, Henry Maguire, who selected the illustrations for the volume and wrote the captions for the illustrations accompanying Part I and Part III.

Angeliki E. Laiou

Part One

Ancient Greece and Rome

A centaur seizes a Lapith woman at the wedding feast of Perithous and Hippodameia. Sculptures from the western pediment of the Temple of Zeus at Olympia, ca. 465–460 B.C. *(Courtesy of Editions Gallimard, Paris)*

Consent and Sexual Relations in Classical Athens

DAVID COHEN

I

The modern law of rape and adultery relies upon a clear-cut distinction between these offenses. The central criterion which distinguishes them is that of consent. Indeed, rape is defined as sexual intercourse without the consent of the victim. In some jurisdictions, physical force is an additional element of the offense, in others it is an evidentiary matter which helps to establish lack of consent but is not itself a required element. Though ancient Athenian law to some extent utilizes these categories, the general picture is not quite so neat. Indeed, the picture is complicated by several additional factors: (1) slavery, (2) the limited right of women to dispose of their sexual capacities and the interest of the male members of their family in limiting the ways in which they do, and (3) pederasty. Of course, in a good deal of modern legislation the category of the traditional crime of sodomy also skews the picture, for there consent is also not an issue. Indeed, it is only in the last decade or two that many American jurisdictions have moved to render the structure of sexual offenses more coherent by making consent and force the determinative criteria regardless of the sex of the parties to the act.

In discussions of sexual violence in Athenian law, scholars have tended to focus upon societal attitudes toward rape and seduction.[1] Such a classification depends, of course, upon the criterion of consent as the factor which distinguishes the two offenses. However, the nature of Athenian conceptualizations of consent and of their role in shaping the contours of judicial and extra-judicial regulation of sexuality have received scant attention. Although it is doubtless correct to assume that consent plays a central role in distinguishing offenses like rape, adultery, and seduction, it may also be misleading to assume that such categories are as clear-cut and transparent as in modern law. Indeed, although in Athenian law the category of consensual versus non-consensual intercourse is clearly important, to some extent it may be conceptually useful to speak of a spectrum of coercive and non-coercive conduct potentially regulated by the law, where violence is at one end, free consent at the other, and a number of gradations of non-consensual and consensual relations lie in between. This paper, then, seeks to explore this spectrum of coercive and non-coercive sexual conduct so as to map the varied normative responses which are felt to be appropriate in different contexts.

II

Consent in heterosexual contexts largely centers on the distinction between rape and adultery. Seduction of maidens plays only a small role in sources other than New Comedy. The early age of marriage and the possibility of close supervision of pubescent girls in an urban environment most likely account for the scant references to cases of seduction as opposed to the many accounts of adultery. New Comedy, on the other hand, typically portrays maidens as victims of rape, in circumstances where the element of physical force is explicitly underscored. For slaves the issue was not *their* consent but that of their owner. Indeed, it was precisely this lack of ability to consent freely which was often described as distinguishing sexual relations with a slave, a distinction which was often seen as making these relations less satisfying (see, e.g., Xenophon, *Hiero* 1.27–37, *Oeconomicus* 10). For free women their consent determined whether the act was adultery or rape, but for purposes of the law of justifiable homicide this distinction was irrelevant and the consent of the *kurios* and family was the crucial fact.

---

[1] See most recently the not very illuminating treatment by E. Harris, "Did the Athenians Regard Seduction as Worse Than Rape?" *Classical Quarterly* 40 (1990), 370–77.

Adultery, however, had severe legal consequences for the woman, which rape did not. The varying importance of this distinction depending upon the legal context has to do with the confusion between the two statutes read to the judges in Lysias' oration, *On the Murder of Eratosthenes* (1.30–36). In defending the cuckolded husband, Euphiletus, on a charge of homicide brought by the family of the deceased adulterer, Lysias cites two laws which, he claims, justify the killing.[2] One statute refers to circumstances in which adultery was the determinative legal category which gave rise to specific legitimate acts of self-help. It probably provided that an adulterer taken in the very act could, under certain circumstances, be killed by the husband, or could be taken to the officials responsible for the summary treatment of such offenders.[3] The other is a probably earlier statute in which undifferentiated illicit intercourse gave rights *tout court* to a murderous response.[4] This latter statute is preserved in an oration of Demosthenes (23.53–57) and provides that, "If a man kills another unintentionally in an athletic contest, or overcoming him on the road, or unwittingly in battle, or in intercourse with his wife, or mother, or sister, or daughter, or concubine kept for the procreation of free children, then he shall not on this account go into exile as a homicide." As its general language indicates, this statute does not distinguish between rape, adultery, and seduction: from the standpoint of the law of justifiable homicide which protects the family's right to avenge its honor through self-help, the distinctions between these offenses are meaningless. On the other hand, the first statute cited by Lysias appears to deal with specific procedures for

---

[2] For a detailed examination of the law of adultery and of the legal context of this oration, see David Cohen, *Law, Sexuality and Society: The Enforcement of Morals in Classical Athens* (Cambridge, 1991), chap. 5. See also Eva Cantarella's assessment of these views in "*Moicheia:* Reconsidering a Problem," in M. Gagarin, ed., *Symposion 1990* (Cologne, 1991).

[3] Lysias 1.28–29. That is, the adulterer was treated as a member of the category of offenders known as *kakourgoi*. These offenders were subject to summary procedures which might include immediate execution. See Cohen, *Law, Sexuality and Society,* chap. 5, for an explanation of why the law to which Lysias refers here must have been that governing *kakourgoi*.

[4] Lysias (1.32) is apparently referring to the law of justifiable homicide when he says: "You hear, gentlemen, how the Court of the Areopagus itself, to which has been assigned . . . the trial for suits of murder, has expressly stated that whoever takes this vengeance on an adulterer caught in the act with his spouse shall not be convicted of murder."

the adulterer taken in the act. The existence of these two overlapping statutes is part of the confusion which underlies Lysias' defense of Euphiletus.

In undertaking his comprehensive rethinking of Athenian law, Plato resolves this confusion through a more straightforward treatment of justifiable homicide: "The man who forcibly violates a free woman or boy shall be slain with impunity by the person thus violently outraged, or by his father or brother or sons. And should a man discover his wedded wife being violated, he shall be guiltless if he kills the violator" (*Laws* 874c). As is clear from the statutory language, Plato's formulation applies only to intercourse accomplished by force. He relegates adultery, which lacks the element of coercion, to the realm of relatively minor offenses which do not permit self-help or require extreme penalties. Thus Plato's law of justifiable homicide sharply restricts self-help by excluding cases where the woman consents to the intercourse and including only acts of forcible rape. The lack of consent of the husband or male members of the family is no longer by itself sufficient to sanction the use of deadly force.

The reference to the rape of boys in Plato's statute indicates that in Athens, as today, children were regarded as potential objects of sexual aggression. In general, in both heterosexual and homosexual contexts, coerced sexual relations with male or female children, even without physical violence, is regarded as *hubris* and will give rise to retaliatory responses, whether legal or extra-legal. Several authors speak at length of the particular situation of an autocrat who can compel the sexual compliance of the children of his subjects.[5] Consent of the victims here seems not to be a central issue, and there appears to be little concern, for example, whether a ruler gains his will by force, non-physical coercion, or other kinds of inducements. The main point is that the *kurioi* of the children do not consent to the transaction. Thus, in a long passage in *Politics,* Aristotle advises rulers above all to avoid two kinds of *hubris:* corporal punishment of free men and sexual abuse of boys and girls (*Politics* 1315a15–28). These two forms of *hubris* should be shunned because they are most likely to cause attempts at revenge by the outraged families.

It is important to note here that there is no suggestion that this *hubris* must *necessarily* be accomplished by actual *physical* violence or assault. In-

---

[5] E.g., Aristotle, *Politics* 1315a15–28; Isocrates, *Nicocles* 36.5; Demosthenes 17.4.

deed, whether physical violence is used seems largely irrelevant as does the issue of consent of the victim. The mere fact of the sexual relations will give rise to retaliatory responses without precise inquiries into the state of mind of the victim. The point is that the hubristic tyrant exercises a coercive force to gain his pleasure at the expense of the dishonored boy or girl, and therefore also at the expense of the honor of her or his family. If, for Aristotle, the underlying motivation of hubristic behavior is the affirmation of one's superiority by disgracing or humiliating another person (*Rhetoric* 1378b20, 1374a13), one arena in which to find such affirmation is in sexual relations. If the sexual relation arises from an act of power rather than passion, then it is necessarily a relation of domination where the boy or girl submits to *hubris* and the disgrace it entails.[6] For this reason, Aristotle advises the tyrant to claim that he acted out of passion and then to grant public honors to his victims. This, it is hoped, will assuage the desire for revenge on the part of their families. Aristotle intends these remarks to extend beyond his immediate discussion of the sexual exploitation of minors, for in *Politics* 1311b19 a man who comes to believe that he submitted to someone who was not motivated by passion regards himself as the object of *hubris*.[7]

It appears here that we may have a fairly clear distinction between the hubristic satisfaction to be gained through non-consensual intercourse (that is, through the satisfaction of asserting one's power at the expense of another's humiliation and dishonor) and a different kind of satisfaction where passion and not sheer domination is the motivation. This is supported by passages like Xenophon's description of the dilemma of the tyrant who desires the satisfaction of obtaining sexual favors through the consent of the other:

[6] This should indicate, *pace* D. Halperin, J. Winkler, and others, that for Aristotle such sexual relations did not *necessarily* turn solely on an axis of domination and submission, activity and passivity. See e.g., D. Halperin, *One Hundred Years of Homosexuality* (New York, 1989), 24–40, 62–71; J. Winkler, *The Constraints of Desire* (London, 1990), 45–70.

[7] Cf. *Politics* 1311b2 and 1315a24. The same point arises in other contexts and helps to explain what it is about passion that eliminates the hubristic quality of the conduct, namely, the absence of the intent to assert oneself through the infliction of harm, humiliation, or disgrace. This intentional quality is nicely illustrated in *Anabasis* 5.5.16.2, where the men are said to take provisions not from *hubris* but from necessity. The same constellation appears in Thucydides 4.98.5, where soldiers say they drank holy water not from *hubris* but because of necessity.

> How say you Hiero? Do you deny that a tyrant may feel deep passion for a boy? Then do you not love Dailochus, whom they call most fair?
>
> Simonides, the explanation is this: I desire to get from him not what I may have for the asking, but that which a despot should be the last to take. . . . I desire of Dailochus just that which human nature may drive us to ask of the fair. But what I long to get, I very strongly desire to obtain by his goodwill, and with his consent; but I think I could sooner desire to do myself injury than to take it from him by force. For to take from an enemy against his will is the greatest of all pleasures, but favors from a loved one are very pleasant only when he consents.

This passage, of course, is informed by an antithesis between consensual intercourse, which is positively valued, and non-consensual intercourse, which is valued as appropriate for an enemy but not a beloved. The passage conflates the issue of actual force, for in one part Hiero says the favors are his for the asking (because of the implicit power of his position as tyrant), but in another he refers to violence (*bia*) and to the way one treats an enemy against his will. Clearly, Xenophon recognizes that force may be implicit and that perhaps the most insidious form of coercion is one where the victim must give the appearance of "willingly" submitting. Contemporary legal treatments of the role of force and threat in the law of rape often lack this subtlety. One might question, of course, the reasons for the classical Athenian preoccupation with the sexual sovereignty of the tyrant.[8] Certainly it may be that the potential role of each Athenian citizen as a sexual tyrant in his relations with slaves, prostitutes, wives, and others may have rendered this problem more acute than real concern about the domestic travails of actual tyrants. Already then, the apparently clear dichotomy of consensual and non-consensual sexual transaction appears to be more troubled than might first appear. As we will see, the problematic nature of homoerotic relations makes even clearer the complex nature of this dichotomy.

While I argued above that Aristotle's description of the monarch's or tyrant's hubristic sexual transactions did not conceptually require actual physical violence or coercion, numerous passages unequivocally do use *hubris* and its cognates to refer to rape. These include references to the fate of

---

[8] See, e.g., Polus' and Callicles' admiration for tyranny in Plato's *Gorgias* 471a–d, 483d–484c.

women and children in war as well as in other settings (e.g., Isocrates *Paneg.* 114.3, *Arch.* 36.6, *Epis.* 102; Thucydides 8.74.3.6, 8.86.3.6; Hyperides, *Funeral Speech* 8.14, 12.31, 12.35; Demosthenes 19.309; 23.56.2,5; Dinarchus, *Demosthenes* 19.6, and cf. 23.7 ff; Herodotus 3.80, 4.114; Aristotle, *N.E.* 1115a23, *Rhetoric* 1314b, 1315a15–20, 1373a35; Lysias 29.98.6). The lack of consent is implicit in the description. Dinarchus (*Dem.* 23.7), for example, enumerates three cases where sexual wrongdoers were punished by death. As he tells the court:

> You are the people who for crimes far smaller than those Demosthenes committed have inflicted on men severe and irrevocable penalties. It was you who killed Menon the miller, because he kept a free boy from Pellene in his mill. You punished with death Themistius of Aphidna because he committed *hubris* against the Rhodian lyremaker at the Eleusinian festival and Euthymachus because he put the Olynthian girl in a brothel.

In the description of only one of these cases does he explicitly mention the crime as *hubris*, but the context perhaps indicates that all three cases fell into this category.[9] The three cases involved very different kinds of conduct, all of which were non-consensual. The second case, and perhaps the first as well, may have involved straightforward rape, but in the absence of more information we cannot say a great deal about them. The third clearly involves the dishonoring of a free woman by treating her as a slave and subjecting her to prostitution. In any event, at least some of these cases appear to have been based upon sexual misconduct extending beyond violent rape, but involving non-consensual acts which dishonored the victim.

On the other hand, Plato's law of justifiable homicide in cases of rape, quoted above, is more explicit. The statutory formulation uses the passive of *hubrizein* to describe what the victim has suffered at the hands of the assailant, who may be killed with impunity. It is significant, however, that the act constituting the offense itself is described not by *hubrizein* but rather by *bia-*

---

[9] Further indication that this is *hubris* is his comparison with Demosthenes, who he says caused Theban women and children to be distributed among the barbarians' tents. In 19.6 he explicitly refers to this as *hubris* committed against "free bodies" (*ta eleuthera somata*). On sexuality and the law of *hubris* in general, see David Cohen, "Sexuality, Violence, and the Athenian Law of *Hubris*," *Greece and Rome* (1991), 171–88.

zomai. This use of *hubrizein*, it would seem, describes the intentional sexual dishonoring of the victim, not the physical violence used to accomplish it. This suggestion finds further support in the formulation Plato uses to describe the victim's right to kill the aggressor, where he refers to the victim as having suffered *hubris* "by force" (*upo te tou hubristhentos bia*). This statutory language also seems to indicate that it is necessary to spell out that all hubristic sexual transactions do not constitute rape, only those acts of intercourse accomplished by actual violence. Here the lack of consent of the woman appears constitutive of the offense. As pointed out above, the Athenian statute of justifiable homicide contains no such strictures and thus cannot distinguish between rape, adultery, and seduction, that is, between consensual and nonconsensual intercourse.

Indeed, from the standpoint of sexual honor, both rape and adultery against one's wife stain a man's reputation (though to differing degrees). Both constitute *hubris* against the woman and her husband, despite the fact that the woman consents to one and not to the other.[10] In Lysias' *On the Murder of Eratosthenes,* where the wife is portrayed as not only consenting to but actively engineering the adultery, the aggrieved husband repeatedly refers to the *hubris* of the adulterer against him.[11] The consent of the woman, which in modern law leads to the exculpation of the adulterer, here has no such effect, though it does produce particular legal consequences for all the parties involved: the adulterer is treated as a *kakourgos* and subject to specified forms of self-help and summary procedures; the husband must divorce the woman; the woman suffers severe civic disabilities. A woman's consent, like a man's, thus has important legal consequences. The speaker's lengthy argument about the way men regard adultery as worse than rape because of this consent, and hence punish it more severely, is largely specious and should not be taken seriously in its characterization of the law (Lysias 1.32–36). The defect in his argument is that he compares legal categories which are utterly distinct and have no real relation to one another: a private action for damages (from rape) and lethal self-help inflicted on an adulterer pursuant to a statute classifying certain offenses as warranting summary procedures. The problem is that such

---

[10] In the language of a 4th-century marriage contract from Elephantine (L. Mitteis, *Chrestomatie,* no. 283, p. 317), the sexual transgressions of the wife bring shame (*aischune*) to her husband, and this constitutes *hubris* against her.

[11] Lysias 1.4,17,25.

self-help was also permissible in cases of rape under the law of justifiable homicide discussed above. Further, rape was also prosecutable as *hubris* and hence also punishable by death. Thus Lysias' argument is a typical rhetorical trick, comparing incomparable things, though it does accurately identify important elements of the ideology of adultery (1.33). Here it is the deceitful consent of the woman which the speaker portrays as threatening to undermine the *oikos* by making patrimony and descent uncertain.

III

In homoerotic contexts, hubristic conduct includes similar gradations of violent, coercive, and consensual behavior. The discussion above of rape and sexual coercion by tyrants referred to women and boys as the victims. Plato's law of justifiable homicide in the case of rape also explicitly enumerated boys as victims falling within its scope. Perhaps more interesting, however, are the discussions of *hubris* in consensual homoerotic relations. On the one hand, boys may suffer *hubris*. Such *hubris* can take the form of violent rape but may also involve consensual relations. Thus, claims Aristotle (*N.E.* 1148b30), those subjected to *hubris* in childhood may acquire the disposition toward intercourse with men.[12] This attribution of *hubris* does not arise merely because the victim is a child. For example, when accusing Androtion of selling his favors, Demosthenes (22.58) says that Androtion suffered hubristic and abusive behavior from those men who did not love him but could pay his price. It is not that he does not consent when he sells his favors. Rather, because the sexual transaction is not based upon any sort of mutual attachment, the active partner, for his own gratification, subjects Androtion to behavior which is abusive, demeaning, and dishonoring. That is, Androtion consents to conduct to which any honorable free man should never consent.

Though Demosthenes' characterization of Androtion suggests that the intercourse involved *hubris* because it was for pay and not for love, other passages do not make this distinction. Xenophon, for example (*Mem.* 2.1.30), says that using men as women is to commit *hubris* against them.[13]

---

[12] And see also 1148b29.

[13] See also Thucydides (8.45.2), who claims that the Athenians keep the pay of the navy low so that the sailors will not weaken their bodies by engaging in *hubris*.

The same passage refers to the partners as *philoi,* so the basis of the attribution of *hubris* cannot arise from the mercenary quality of the relationship. Rather, for Xenophon it is the fact that a man is being sexually used as a woman which renders the conduct of the active partner hubristic. Here the description of the act as *hubris* arises from the view that a man is always dishonored by adopting the submissive sexual role of a woman. Plato, of course, refers to such a switch in sexual roles as unnatural (*Phaedrus* 250e5, *para phusin,* and cf. *Laws* 836e, 841d, and cf. 837c). Though Plato's description of such relations as "against nature" is often dismissed as idiosyncratic, Aeschines also describes Timarchus as having wronged his body with the *hamartemata* of a woman. In doing so, claims Aeschines, he has committed *hubris* against himself *para phusin.* Such a sentiment surely also underlies the statement of Xenophon with which this discussion began. In the sexual sphere, then, *hubris* may characterize the act of the person who demands the submission which dishonors. As a passage in Plato's *Symposium* puts it, the *erastes* who desires the body of the *eromenos* is *hubristes* and *poneros* (182a–183e). In such a case the victim is the passive object who "suffers *hubris*" and hence is dishonored. Further, as these latter passages indicate, individuals may also inflict *hubris* upon themselves by freely consenting to sexual behavior which dishonors them.

Apart from the problems explored above, the circumstances of Athenian pederasty, paradigmatically involving an adult male and an adolescent or preadolescent boy, render the legal situation particularly problematic. In Athenian law, as in most other ancient and modern legal systems, young males of an age to attract pederastic courtship, conventionally before the growth of the first beard, are legal minors. That is, they are incapable of entering into legal transactions and are subject to the authority of their father. In the absence of parental authority, their affairs are managed by a guardian until they come of age. Further, most legal systems carry over this legal incapacity into the sphere of criminal law. In particular, females below a certain age are seen as incapable of consenting to sexual intercourse. This lack of the capability of meaningful consent renders as rape what might otherwise have been seduction. Modern legal systems have clearly defined such occurrences as statutory rape, a variety of rape defined not by the lack of consent, but rather solely by the age of the minor and the fact of intercourse. We have no evidence of a statutory rape provision in Athens, but the problem must nonetheless have presented itself as it would in any system of criminal law where a man de-

fends himself against an accusation of raping a youth or maiden by claiming
that the child consented. I would suggest that in Athens the law of *hubris,*
which explicitly includes children within its scope, provided one of the principal means of regulating such situations.

While Athenian girls seem to have been closely supervised by their families in a way which would tend to diminish their vulnerability to seducers or
rapists, the same is not the case with boys.[14] Indeed, attractive boys might
find themselves the object of considerable male attention from an early stage
of their development. While strict laws protected them at school and well-to-
do parents provided *paidagogai* to ward off predatory males, there were
clearly other opportunities for courtship and seduction. The question which
the foregoing discussion of statutory rape raises is, "How old did an Athenian
boy have to be so as to render his consent effective?" Clearly, it seems unlikely that an Athenian prosecuted with the rape of, say, a ten-year-old *eromenos* would have had great success with the plea that the boy consented. On
the other hand, a boy of sixteen or seventeen, while nonetheless legally a
minor, might have been seen to be in a different position so that his consent
might negate an accusation of rape. Surely, however, when blithely stating
the orthodox view that there was absolutely no legal prohibition against un-
remunerated consensual intercourse between an adult and a younger *eromenos,* one must remember that at some age the consent of the boy would be
viewed as nugatory. Exactly what that age was we cannot say, but Aeschines
clearly acknowledges the existence of such a category. Indeed, in *Against
Timarchus* (139.2) he explicitly states that a young boy cannot give meaningful consent. Therefore, he continues, the lawgiver imposed chastity upon the
eromenos until he comes of age.

This discussion of the age of consent centers upon the notion of statutory
rape. The law of *hubris,* however, adds another dimension to this discussion,
for, as was seen above, it includes not only rape but consensual sexual trans-

---

[14] As Campbell's study of the Sarakatsani indicates, this was probably less true
in rural settings. See J. C. Campbell, *Honour, Family, and Patronage* (Oxford, 1964),
200–202, 269–71. Hence biblical and Assyrian law distinguish between rape in the
town and rape in the fields, where the woman's outcry cannot be heard. Menander, of
course, indicates the exceptional possibilities which religious festivals represented for
men to seduce or rape young women who were otherwise closely supervised. For full
references see Cohen, *Law, Sexuality and Society,* chap. 5.

actions as well. In other words, when prosecuting a man for dishonoring a youth by sexually using him "as a woman" (to use Aeschines' and Xenophon's category), the fact of the degrading behavior and not the consent would be primary. This is clearly indicated by the foregoing discussion of consensual hubristic relations. Moreover, in cases where the victim was well below the age of legal consent, his acquiescence would probably have been even more insignificant. That is, in a prosecution brought by the boy's father for the damage to the boy's reputation and honor, the boy's consent would no more negate the hubristic quality of the sexual intercourse than did the consent of Timarchus to the degrading conduct which men were thought necessarily to have demanded of him. Presumably, the younger the *eromenos*, the more difficult it would have been to construct a valid defense to the aggrieved father's accusation. At the same time, however, there would be powerful disincentives to bringing such prosecutions which would publicize the dishonor of one's son. Of course, in the absence of actual prosecutions (except for the case of *hubris* against the boy referred to by Dinarchus), much of this discussion must remain speculative.

University of California, Berkeley

Seduction and Rape in Greek Myth

MARY R. LEFKOWITZ

In this paper I will attempt to challenge the common assumption that Greek mythology effectively validates the practice of rape and approves of the violent mistreatment of women. Instead, I will argue that in the case of myths involving the unions of gods and goddesses with mortal men and women, we should talk about abduction or seduction rather than rape, because the gods see to it that the experience, however transient, is pleasant for mortals. Moreover, the consequences of these unions are usually glorious for the families of the mortals involved, despite and even because of the suffering that individual members of the family may undergo.

Stories about abduction of women play a central role in the "canon" of ancient Greek literature: the Trojan War was fought to bring back Helen from Troy, after the Trojan prince Paris had abducted her from her husband's home in Sparta. The fifth-century Greek historian Herodotus begins his history of the dissension (διαφορή) between the Greeks and the barbarians by recounting myths of how they abducted (ἁρπάζειν) each other's women (1–2.2).[1] According to these myths, after Phoenicians abducted (ἁρπάσαι) Io, Greeks abducted the princess Medea from Colchis; then the Trojan prince Paris decided he could get away with abducting Helen from Sparta (3.1). The Greeks showed that they took such matters seriously by sending an expedition to Troy. But the Persians, although they acknowledged that abductions were "the

---

[1] Cf. J. Gould, *Herodotus* (New York, 1989), 64.

17

work of unjust men," nonetheless refused to take action, because (as they said), "it's clear that the women wouldn't have been abducted if they hadn't been willing" (εἰ μὴ αὐταὶ ἐβούλοντο, 1.4.2).

As Herodotus makes clear, by contrasting the attitude of the Greeks toward abductions with those of the barbarians, Greeks, in responding to or avenging a case of rape, are not interested in whether or not the women gave their consent, so much as with the question of *honor*.[2] The Greek attitude toward women is both more strictly moralistic and more protective: Persians adopt a laissez-faire attitude, letting the women do what they want, without attempting to get revenge; Greeks not only take revenge, but (at least in the case of Helen) seek to retrieve the women. The difference emerges clearly in the case of the first of the abductions in Herodotus' list, that of Io. According to the traditional Greek version, which Herodotus does not tell because his audience knew it (2.1), Io's lover was the god Zeus. Instead, Herodotus first tells the Persian version of the story, that Io was carried off by Phoenician merchants.[3] A little later he gives what he calls the Phoenician version: they agree that they took Io to Egypt, but deny that they abducted her, claiming instead that she had had sexual relations with the captain of the merchant ship and decided to go away with the Phoenicians when she discovered she was pregnant, out of respect for (αἰδεομένη) her parents (5.1–2)—in other words, they didn't bother to take revenge because she had consented to her "abduction."

In contrast to these pragmatic barbarian versions, the Greek accounts of these same abductions emphasize the involvement of the gods: Io was seduced by Zeus; in the *Iliad,* although Helen regretfully admits that she "followed" Paris to Troy (ἑπόμην, 3.174), she puts some of the blame for her

---

[2] Such confrontations are a typical Herodotean device for conveying abstract ideas; whether they have any historical basis is another question. Cf. S. West, "Herodotus' Portrait of Hecataeus," *Journal of Hellenic Studies* 111 (1991), 151.

[3] Although the point of such rationalization is to give human beings full responsibility for their actions, S. Flory, *The Archaic Smile of Herodotus* (Detroit, 1987), 25–28, conjectures that Herodotus may be making fun here of rationalizing historians such as Hecataeus. For contemporary criticism of myths of seduction by gods, cf. Euripides (*Heracles* 1341–46), with precedents in Xenophanes (21A32.24–25 I 122 Diels-Kranz [hereafter D-K]), Antiphon the sophist (87B10 II p. 340 D-K, cf. Anaxagoras 59B12 II p. 37). Cf. M. R. Lefkowitz, "Commentary on Vlastos," *Proceedings of the Boston Area Colloquium in Ancient Philosophy* 5 (1991), 239–46.

seduction by Paris on the goddess Aphrodite, who brought her to Paris in fulfillment of her vow to give him the most beautiful woman in the world.[4] Even though it is clear in the *Iliad* that Helen gave her consent and feels guilty about it (3.172–76), the Greek generals, like the Greeks in Herodotus' account, insist on talking about it as if it were abduction or rape. Nestor says that the army cannot return to Greece "before one of us has slept with a Trojan man's wife, in order to avenge Helen's struggles and groans" (τείσασθαι δ' Ἑλένης ὁρμήματά τε στοναχάς τε, 2.356).[5] For rhetorical purposes, if not for the sake of Menelaus' honor (cf. 2.590), the generals must imply that Helen was abducted by force, against her will, and that her abduction was a crime against her husband and his allies.

In Greek myth, apparently, seduction was regarded as a serious crime, if (and this distinction is important) the seduction occurred in the house of the woman's husband or a male relative. In that case, the seduction or abduction from the house was taken as seriously as murder, since the relatives of the victim sought to kill the seducer. According to legend, the poet Hesiod was killed by two brothers who believed that Hesiod had seduced their sister while he was staying in their house; when the charge later proved to be false, the brothers themselves were sacrificed to the gods of hospitality and the sister hanged herself.[6]

But if in myth and legend Greek men were determined to avenge abduction and seduction from the woman's home, how can it be that the Greeks condoned or even applauded such behavior on the part of their gods? As I will now try to show, the gods do not rape or abduct mortal women from their

---

[4] Cf. *Il.* 3.401, where Helen asks Aphrodite where she will take her next (ἄξεις); Paris' gift from Aphrodite was "painful lust" (μαχλοσύνη ἀλεγεινή, 24.30). On Boston skyphos 13.186, Paris leads her off by the wrist (see below, note 27), in the presence of Aphrodite and Peitho (holding a flower, cf. below, note 40); cf. R. G. A. Buxton, *Persuasion in Greek Tragedy: A Study of Peitho* (Cambridge, 1982), 45–46.

[5] Aristarchus preferred to understand the line as meaning that the struggles and groans were undertaken by the Greeks on behalf of Helen (i.e., as an objective rather than subjective genitive). Cf. G. S. Kirk, *The Iliad: A Commentary* (Cambridge, 1985), ad loc.

[6] *Contest of Homer and Hesiod*, ed. T. W. Allen, *Homeri Opera* V (Oxford, 1912; repr. 1969), 224–46; cf. M. R. Lefkowitz, *The Lives of the Greek Poets* (Baltimore, 1981), 7.

father's or husband's homes. Rather, women are *seduced* by gods, usually outside of their homes; and the women give their consent, at least initially.

The distinction between rape (or forcible abduction) and voluntary seduction needs to be made with some care and emphasis, since these seductions by gods are often classified as "rape" in modern literature. E. Keuls in her provocative book, *The Reign of the Phallus,* speaks of male gods going on "raping expeditions."[7] P. M. C. Forbes Irving, in his book on metamorphoses, observes that "women are continually being punished in myth for being raped."[8] In a volume of essays devoted to the subject of rape in literature, F. Zeitlin, in an interesting article on "Configurations of Rape in Greek Myth," includes in her discussion of rape the myths of erotic pursuit by the gods.[9] But natural as it might seem in our own time to classify as rape all acts of sexual aggression by males (mortal or immortal) against females and younger males, the Greeks in their law codes distinguished between rape and seduction. As the founding myth of the court of the Areopagus suggests, rape provided sufficient justification for homicide: according to the story, it was there that the god Poseidon prosecuted the god Ares for the murder of his son Halirrhothius. Ares had killed Halirrhothius because he had raped Ares' daughter Alcippe, but the court acquitted Ares.[10]

Rape and seduction are regarded as equally serious crimes in Athenian law and in the Gortyn code.[11] In Lysias' speech about the murder of Eratosthenes, the defendant, Euphiletus, argues that seduction is the more serious crime; but this is a case of special pleading to help justify murder in the case of adultery that took place with the wife's full consent.[12] Rape, as defined in

[7] E. Keuls, *The Reign of the Phallus* (New York, 1985), 50.

[8] P. M. C. Forbes Irving, *Metamorphosis in Greek Myth* (Oxford, 1990), 69.

[9] F. Zeitlin, "Configurations of Rape in Greek Myth," in *Rape,* ed. S. Tomaselli and R. Porter (Oxford, 1986), 122–51.

[10] Apollodorus 3.14.2, Suda s.v. Ἄρεως πάγος (I 348 Adler); cf. R. Parker, *Miasma* (Oxford, 1983), 378.

[11] Cf. Demosthenes, *Against Aristocrates* 23.53, 55, where motive is not a factor; if someone kills a man having intercourse with his wife (ἐπὶ δάμαρτι) or mother or sister or daughter, or with a concubine kept for the purpose of bearing legitimate children, the homicide is justifiable.

[12] Cf. esp. E. M. Harris, "Did the Athenians Regard Seduction as a Worse Crime Than Rape?" *Classical Quarterly* 40 (1990), 370–77, with addendum by P. G. McC. Brown, "Athenian Attitudes to Rape and Seduction," ibid. 41 (1991), 533–34, *contra* (e.g.) C. Carey, ed., *Lysias: Selected Speeches* (Cambridge, 1989), 80.

the Gortyn code (ii.4), explicitly involves violence (κάρτει οἴπειν, i.e., κράτει οἴφειν).[13] The fine for rape of a free woman is the same as that for seduction in the house of a father, brother, or husband, 100 staters, whereas the fine for seduction in another man's house is only 50 staters (ii.21–24). The scale of fines in the code suggests that rape and seduction are equally serious crimes if the woman in question is married; but if she is not, the seriousness of the crime depends upon whether or not she gives her consent.[14]

But violence is not a characteristic of female mortals' encounters with the gods, at least in the heroic age; gods do not usually violate the laws of hospitality of a male relative's home; nor do they concern themselves with married women, unless the marriage has not been consummated. Instead, the encounters between gods and mortal women usually take place in beautiful settings, outside of the woman's home, while she is unmarried. Even though the encounters between gods and mortal women are almost always of short duration, they have lasting consequences not only for the females involved but for civilization generally, since the children born from such unions are invariably remarkable, famous for their strength or intelligence, or both. Whether we moderns choose to approve of it or not, most women in archaic Greek epic, perhaps because they believe that the gods exist and do not question the historicity of their mythology, tend to cooperate in their seduction.

Epic audiences clearly enjoyed hearing genealogies of heroes and races that derived from the unions of a god with a mortal woman; naturally any descendant would boast of such an origin. Like Achilles himself, two of his captains both have gods as fathers. In *Iliad* 16 the story of one of these, Eudorus, is told in some detail:

> a girl's child (παρθένιος), whom Polymele bore, beautiful in the dance, the daughter of Phylas; strong Argeiphontes (i.e., Hermes) fell in love with her (ἠράσατο) when he caught sight of her among the girls performing the choral dance to Artemis of the golden arrow, of the hunting cry, and straightway Hermes went into the women's quar-

---

[13] Cf. also κάρτει δαμάσαιτο, "deflower," ii.10–11. οἴφειν is "forthright," but perhaps not quite so offensive as Attic βινεῖν; cf. D. Bain, "Six Greek Verbs of Sexual Congress," *Classical Quarterly* 51 (1991), 72–74.

[14] R. Sealey, *Women and Law in Classical Greece* (Chapel Hill, N.C., 1990), 71–74.

ters and slept with her in secret, and he gave her a glorious son Eudorus, an excellent runner and swift fighter. (*Iliad* 16.180–86)

Polymele was not disgraced by her association with Hermes, even though the
seduction took place in her father's house; on the contrary, after Eudorus was
born, she was married to Echecles, who gave many wedding gifts for her,
and her father raised Eudorus as his own child. It is significant that when the
god falls in love with her "among the girls performing the choral dance"—
that is, at a time when she would be on display for mortal suitors—one of
these in fact marries her after the birth of her son by the god.[15]

Homer does not say whether or not Polymele invited or eagerly received
Hermes' attentions; the god "catches sight of her," literally, "sees her with his
eyes" (ὀφθαλμοῖσιν ἰδών, 182); did they exchange glances? When on vase
paintings gods are portrayed in pursuit of mortal women, there is emphasis
on the persuasive power of the god's glance; the woman moves away from
him but looks back, as if drawn to him.[16] Since there is no mention of violence, and Hermes and Polymele made love "in secret" (λάθρηι) in the wom-
en's quarters, the implication is that she did not strenuously resist the god's
attentions. There is, however, an explicit case of eagerness on the part of the
mortal woman in the catalogue of women in *Odyssey* 11; this is the story of
Tyro, the first woman Odysseus sees after he speaks to his mother:

> she was said to be the daughter of blameless Salmoneus, and she said
> that she was the wife of Cretheus son of Aeolus. She fell in love with
> (ἠράσσατο) divine Enipeus who was the most beautiful of rivers
> flowing on the earth, and she frequented the beautiful streams of En-
> ipeus. But the Holder of the Earth, the Shaker of the Earth Poseidon
> made himself resemble Enipeus, and slept with her in the mouth of
> the eddying river. And a dark shining wave stood over them like a
> mountain, arched over them, and it hid the god and the mortal

[15] Cf. the discussion in S. Lonsdale, *Dance and Ritual Play* (Baltimore, 1993).

[16] On the importance of eye contact, cf. Buxton, *Persuasion in Greek Tragedy,*
84, 112–13, and on the meeting of the glances of male and female on vase paintings
depicting erotic pursuit, see C. Sourvinou-Inwood, *Reading Greek Culture* (Oxford,
1991), 69. Cf. also NY 06.1021.149/ARV 523., 2, characterized by Keuls, *Reign of
the Phallus,* 50, as "Poseidon and Hermes on a raping expedition together." See also
the Niobid painter's Boreas and Oreithyia, Brunswick 1908.3 = S. Kaempf-
Dimitriadou, *Die Liebe der Götter in der Attischen Kunst des 5. Jahrhunderts v. Chr.*
(Bern, 1979), 38, no. 364.

woman. And when the god had completed his acts of love (φιλοτή-σια ἔργα), he took her hand (ἐν δ' ἄρα οἱ φῦ χειρί) and spoke and called her by name: "rejoice, lady, in our love (φιλότητι), and as the year comes round you will bear glorious children, since the beds of the gods are not infertile; and you must care for them and cherish them. Now go home and keep this to yourself and do not tell my name; but I am Poseidon the Shaker of the Earth." And with these words he went down under the swelling sea. And she became pregnant and bore Pelias and Neleus. (236–54)

Tyro in this story clearly feels intense physical passion (ἠράσσατο) for the god Enipeus, and wants to attract his attention. But because she spends so much of her time beside him away from her home, where she would be protected, she attracts the attention of a more powerful god, Poseidon. Poseidon does not use force to compel her to have intercourse with him; rather, he assumes the form of the god whom she explicitly desires, Enipeus.[17] Then he takes her into the river's stream and creates a setting that offers not only privacy but a magical splendor, with a dark shining wave like a mountain.[18] He touches her hand,[19] calls her by name, and speaks to her—the poet uses a formulaic line that introduces speech to a close associate (so Ares to Aphrodite in *Odyssey* 8.291). He tells her who he really is and that she will bear twin sons. Again, as in the case of Polymele's tryst with Hermes, Tyro's encounter with Poseidon brings no disgrace, because afterwards she is married to her uncle, the hero Cretheus.

In the cases of both Polymele and Tyro, the god has only this one encounter with her, and then disappears. Heartless as this may seem, it is characteristic of every kind of encounter mortals have with gods, no matter how close their relationship. A god will send a dream; he/she will appear in disguise and give instructions to a mortal, as Aphrodite does to Helen in *Iliad* 3 or Athena to Telemachus in *Odyssey* 1. Even Thetis does not linger in conversation with her son Achilles. In Homer, at least, the gods' female consorts

[17] Cf. the story of Demeter Fury at Thelpusa in Arcadia. Poseidon wanted to have intercourse with Demeter, who turned herself into a mare; when he saw that she had tricked him, he turned himself into a stallion and mated with her (Paus. 8.25.5).

[18] On the translation of πορφύρεος as "dark, shining" rather than "purple," cf. O. J. Schrier, "Love with Doris," *Mnemosyne* 32 (1979), 316–22.

[19] Like eye contact (cf. above, note 16), the touching of hands is a sign of consensual intimacy; cf. Sourvinou-Inwood, *Reading Greek Culture*, 68–69.

do not complain that the gods behaved like gods. Even as a ghost in Hades, two generations after her death, when Tyro explains to Odysseus who she is, it is her encounter with the god that makes her remarkable. The next woman Odysseus sees is Antiope, "who boasted that she spent the night in the arms of Zeus, and bore two sons, Amphion and Zethos" (*Odyssey* 11.261–62). Homer does not tell the rest of her story; but even though we know from other sources that she suffered great hardship because of her liaison with Zeus, what she boasts of to Odysseus is the one night that she spent with the god and the two sons she bore as a result of it.[20]

Liaisons between gods, heroes, and mortals appear to have been the subject of an entire epic, which was attributed to the poet Hesiod but was almost certainly written more than a century after his death. Only fragments of this poem survive, but we know that Tyro's story was told again in this so-called *Catalogue of Women*, this time with emphasis on Tyro's beauty and a much longer speech by Poseidon about her children and their descendants (frags. 30–42 Merkelbach-West [hereafter M-W]). A long papyrus fragment relates the story of another of Poseidon's liaisons, this time with Mestra, the daughter of Erysichthon: "the god took (ἐδάμασσε) her in Cos," having brought her, although she was capable of turning herself into the shape of different animals, "far away from her father across the wine-dark sea" (fr. 43a.55–57 M-W). After she bears a son she marries a mortal, Glaucus, and the catalogue of her descendants is given.

Nothing is said in the poem about whether Mestra consented or desired this union, though her life with her father could not have been easy: he had an insatiable appetite and, to pay for food, would sell Mestra in one of her animal forms, and then she would turn back into human form and escape (cf. 11.31–33). Poseidon's attentions at least provide her with a means of transport to the east, where a husband awaited her, and with additional honor. But the gods have ways of making their approaches welcome.[21] A summary of a

---

[20] Apollodorus 3.5.5.

[21] Cf. also one of the few surviving lines from Aeschylus' *Amymone*. Amymone, one of the Danaids, had gone out to look for water and was about to be raped by a satyr when she was rescued by Poseidon, who says: "you are fated to be my partner, and I am fated to be your partner (σοὶ μὲν γαμεῖσθαι μόρσιμον, γαμεῖν δ' ἐμοί)" (S. Radt, *Tragicorum Graecorum Fragmenta*, IV, 2d ed. [Göttingen, 1977], fr. 13 [hereafter *TrGF*]); cf. Kaempf-Dimitriadou, *Liebe der Götter*, 48.

later section of the poem describes how Zeus fell in love with Europa while she was gathering flowers, and changed himself into a bull and "breathed from his mouth the scent of saffron" (ἀπὸ τοῦ στόματος κρόκον ἔπνει, fr. 140); thus he was able to deceive her and carry her off on his back to Crete, where he had intercourse with her. After that she had famous children and lived with the king of Crete.

In what survives of the Hesiodic catalogue, the poet does not describe how the women involved in these liaisons felt about the experiences.[22] But since the Athenian tragic poets gave their women characters ample opportunity to speak, we can at least know what the poets imagined that the women might have said in retrospect about their encounters with gods, since of course no such incident could have been presented on the tragic stage. Only scraps of two plays about Sophocles' *Tyro* survive, but we have enough of the prologue of Aeschylus' *Kares* (or *Europa*) to see that Europa was very proud of her relationship with Zeus; she boasts of her fertility, since it is unusual for a woman to give birth to triplets rather than to one child or a set of twins as the result of a single encounter with the god:[23]

> There was a flourishing meadow to welcome the bull; such was the trick that Zeus devised, by staying where he was, to steal me from my father without a struggle. And after that: I shall tell the whole story in a few words. A mortal woman united with a god, I exchanged the honored state of maidenhood, and was joined to the common owner of my children (παίδων δ' ἐζύγη ξυνάονι). In three travails I endured the pains of women, and the noble seed of the father could not reproach the field, that it refused to bring forth. I started with the greatest of these offspring, by giving birth to Minos.

Again, a meadow with flowers proves to be an irresistible attraction for a young girl, and again the god uses a deception (κλέμμα, 2) in order to carry her off.

Although the philosopher Xenophanes complained that Homer and He-

---

[22] There is no question that the males enjoyed these erotic encounters; cf. Dioscurides' epigram about how, as the result of being in Doris' "garden," he has become "immortal" (ἄνθεσιν ἐν χλοεροῖς ἀθάνατος γέγονα, *Anthologia Palatina* 5.55 = 1484 G-P; cf. Schrier, "Love with Doris," 309–12).

[23] Here I follow the text of H. Lloyd-Jones, ed. and trans., "Appendix," in *Aeschylus*, ed. H. Weir Smyth, Loeb Classical Library (Cambridge, Mass., 1971), 599–603; cf. *TrGF* fr. 99.1–11.

siod sang about the unlawful actions of the gods, their lying (κλέπτειν), adultery, and deluding of one another (21 F 12 D-K), ordinarily people thought that when gods were involved, the ends justified the means. It was a different, reprehensible matter if a mortal used a ruse or disguise to deceive a young girl: he would be punished. An amusing example of such a case, perhaps based on the plot of a lost comedy, is preserved in a fragment of a novel, probably from the second century A.D. Since in Troy at that time young women who were about to be married dedicated their virginity to the river Scamander, the hero of the story, Cimon, crowned himself with reeds and hid in a bush: when the girl he was after, Callirhoe, asked the river to receive her virginity, he jumped out of the bush and said "I who am Scamander receive it with pleasure and take you, Callirhoe, in order to bestow great benefits on you" (*Epist. Aeschines* 10.4–5, pp. 38–39 Hercher). But when the next day Callirhoe's nurse discovered what had happened, Cimon had to leave town in a hurry.[24]

Why do the gods visit their mortal consorts only once, and never return again, even to offer encouragement or comfort? It is this failure to return, to care about their mortal partners and mortal children, that a chorus of Athenian women complain about in Euripides' *Ion,* when their queen Creusa describes how she has been neglected by the god Apollo, and has lost the son she bore to him and abandoned many years before:

> the son of Zeus [Apollo] shows that he does not remember, and did not beget the common fortune of children for my queen [Creusa] in her household, but produced a bastard child, doing Aphrodite another favor. (1099–1106)

The *Ion* is the only extant play which explicitly scrutinizes, rather than simply accepts, the pattern of divine behavior toward mortal partners.[25] Ion, before he discovers that he himself is Creusa's lost child by Apollo, raises the ques-

---

[24] Cf. S. Trenkner, *The Greek Novella in the Classical Period* (Cambridge, 1958), 133–34; C. Schwegler, *De Aeschinis quae feruntur epistolis,* diss. (Giessen, 1913), 16–17; for analogous *rites de passage,* cf. M. P. Nilsson, *Griechische Feste von religiöser Bedeutung* (Stuttgart, 1913), 365. My thanks to Prof. Rebecca Hague for the reference to this story.

[25] Cf. Aesch., *Dict.* fr. 47a17–20, where Danae claims that although Zeus is responsible, she has paid the penalty, and Eur., *Heraclid.* 718–19, where Alcmene briefly raises the question of Zeus' responsibility to her.

tion of why gods are not held liable for seduction and adultery like mortal men:

> if—though it will not happen, but for the sake of argument—you gods paid the penalty to mortals for violating marriages, you and Poseidon and Zeus the ruler of heaven would empty your temples by paying the fines for your wrongdoing. (444–47)

Creusa makes the charge of irresponsibility even more explicit:

> to this light I shall speak in reproach against you, son of Leto. You came to me, with your hair shining with gold, when I was gathering saffron petals in the folds of my gown, to reflect the golden light in their flowering. You grasped the pale wrists of my arms and you led me to a bed in the cave, while I cried out "mother," a lover god granting a favor for shameless Cypris. And I in my misfortune bore you a son, and out of fear for my mother I threw him on your bed, where you had lain with me in my misfortune, in my sadness on our sad bed. Alas, and now he is gone, stolen, a feast for the birds, my child and yours, you wretch, and you play the lyre and sing your paeans. (881–902)

As mortals, we instinctively sympathize with Creusa. But before we criticize the god, we must be precise about the nature of his crime. First of all, he did not use force.[26] Like Europa, Creusa was away from home, in a meadow, gathering flowers. Like Poseidon when he appeared to Tyro, the god appears to her as she would like to see him, with his hair sparkling with the gold she has sought to collect in her lap with the petals of her flowers. The god takes her by the wrists, employing the gesture used in the marriage ceremony (χεῖρ' ἐπὶ κάρπωι) to lead away (ἄγειν) the bride.[27] Again, as Poseidon did for Tyro, Apollo takes Creusa to a private place.

Did Creusa give her consent? Certainly not at first, since she called out to her mother, though it is also true that she does not try to escape. But

---

[26] It is not "rape"; cf. J. M. Bremer, "The Meadow of Love and Two Passages in Euripides' *Hippolytus*," *Mnemosyne* 28 (1975), 268–80, 274, also noted by A. P. Burnett, *Euripides: Ion* (Englewood Cliffs, N.J., 1970), 85–86, rightly; cf. also her "Human Resistance and Divine Persuasion in Euripides' *Ion*," *Classical Philology* 57 (1962), 89–103, 95–96, unfairly criticized by A. N. Michelini, *Euripides and the Tragic Tradition* (Madison, Wis., 1987), 269 note 166.

[27] On the gesture, see esp. I. Jenkins, "Is There Life after Marriage?" *Bulletin of the Institute of Classical Studies* 30 (1983), 139–40.

certainly afterwards she regrets the encounter; she calls herself unfortunate, sad, and even their bed was "sad." But the reason for her sorrow is not regret that she had intercourse with the god, but that he abandoned her and her son. The god behaved according to the epic pattern, except that he failed to inform his mortal partner fully of what would happen in the future to her child. In the *Odyssey* and in the *Catalogue,* the god tells the women who their children will be and that they will be famous. But Creusa discovers her child's fate and destiny only after many years, and then after much suffering and misapprehension of the facts.[28]

It would have been easier on Creusa if her father, like Polymele's, had been prepared to raise the god's son as his own.[29] But the god sees that all comes out well in the end, and Creusa, once she knows that Ion is her son and will be a famous hero, acknowledges the god has not abandoned them (1609–10). But why didn't the god let her know what would happen? Because, as Creusa begins to realize at the end of the play, and the goddess Athena confirms, acting on Apollo's behalf, the god had planned to let her know her son's identity when they were safely back in Athens. Apollo does not appear himself ex machina at the end of the play, not because he is ashamed of his actions, but in order that "criticism not arise between them about what happened previously" (1558). Whatever Creusa's resentments against him, the god also has reason to complain of Creusa; after all, she nearly murdered his son and ruined his first plans for his future.[30]

So it seems that the encounters between mortal women and gods, however beautiful they seem at the moment and however attractive the attentions of the god, are not only brief and singular, but often followed by a long interval of suffering and neglect. Creusa has been childless for years, and certain that her son by Apollo is dead. When Zeus asked the maiden Marpessa to choose between the mortal Idas, who had abducted her, and Apollo, who wanted to kill Idas and carry her off himself, Marpessa chose the mortal,

[28] M. R. Lefkowitz, *Women in Greek Myth* (Baltimore, 1986), 32–33.

[29] Or like Polydore, whose husband Borus raised her son by the river Spercheus as his own, *Il.* 16.175–77, or Evadne, whose father wisely inquired from the oracle of Delphi about his daughter's pregnancy, and so learned that the child was Apollo's (Pindar, *Ol.* 6.35–57). But other women were less fortunate, e.g., Alope (murdered by her father after he discovered she had borne a son by Poseidon), Leucothoe (buried alive by her father), and Danae (confined in a brazen tower, cf. below).

[30] Cf. Burnett, "Human Resistance," 94.

Idas, because Apollo would abandon her in her old age.[31] The other gods treat their women no better: Tyro was persecuted by her husband's second wife, Sidero.[32] Antiope was forced to abandon her twin sons Zethus and Amphion; she married a mortal man, but he was murdered by her uncle, and she was persecuted by her uncle and his wife. Even Europa complains that she never sees two of her sons and lives in fear that she will lose "everything" if her son Sarpedon dies at Troy (*TrGF* fr. 99.14, 23). As the old men in the chorus remind Antigone, "Danae suffered too . . . although she cherished the seed of Zeus that flowed in gold" (Sophocles, *Antigone* 945–50).[33] The moments of glory in these women's lives are memorable but brief: their seduction, the promise of their sons' fame, being reunited with their sons after a long separation. But that is the nature of human life as the ancient Greeks saw it: "in a moment delight flowers for mortals, and in a moment it falls to the ground, shaken by a stern decree"—so Pindar of a (male) victor in the games (*Pyth.* 8.92–94).[34]

Such flowers of delight, even if short-lived, are preferable for mortals to the alternative possibility, which is unrelieved suffering.[35] Why then do some mortal women resist the advances of the gods? In the *Prometheus Bound,* the maiden Io refuses to obey dreams that tell her to go to the meadow where Zeus awaits her (645–54); then for reasons that she does not explain, but which Prometheus attributes to Hera's jealous hatred (592), Io is turned into a cow and tormented by a gadfly. After they have seen Io in her transformed and maddened state, the chorus of the *Prometheus* says:[36]

> never, never, may you see me sharing a bed with Zeus; may I never be approached by a bridegroom who is one of the gods from heaven.

---

[31] Apparently this was a story told by Simonides in one of his poems, 563 PMG = Σ *Il.* 9.557–58 II 518–19 Erbse.

[32] Some aspects of her suffering were vividly described in Sophocles' *Tyro;* cf. frags. 658, 659 Radt.

[33] Cf. Forbes Irving, *Metamorphosis,* 69: "in myth women are continually punished for being raped [sic]," citing Leucothoe, Psamathe, Alope, Arne, Danae, along with Aura, Pelopeia, and Taygete, who commit suicide.

[34] Cf. H. Lloyd-Jones, "Pindar," in *Academic Papers* (Oxford, 1990), 78.

[35] Cf. *Il.* 24.524–33; cf. C. W. Macleod, *Homer, Iliad 24* (Cambridge, 1982), 133.

[36] There are some problems with the text, but the general sense is clear; cf. M. Griffith, ed., *Aeschylus: Prometheus Bound* (Cambridge, 1983), ad loc.

I am terrified when I look at the male-hating maiden Io, tormented by Hera in cruel wanderings. (896–900)

Since these fears are expressed by immortal Oceanids, who by definition cannot die or grow old, they must be afraid not so much of male sexuality as of change: "I do not know who I shall turn into" (τίς ἂν γενοίμαν, 905).[37] Will they be persecuted by Hera and metamorphosed into cows? Will they marry and need to leave the familiar environment of their father's home for a strange and hostile place? It is displacement and separation from her mother that Persephone complains of when she is carried off by Hades on his chariot to his realm in the lower world.[38] Persephone went to pick a marvelous radiant narcissus, with a hundred blossoms and the sweetest scent (HHom 2.1–15), which Earth made to grow as a lure (δόλος) for her. Modern scholars have suggested in various ways that the scene represents a *rite de passage* from girlhood to womanhood, or even a cruel perversion of the usual marriage ceremony.[39] But what the poet of the hymn has depicted is a particularly appealing setting for a divine encounter: as in the case of Europa, there is a meadow with flowers; like Creusa, Persephone was picking flowers, away from her mother; the narcissus has a scent that makes heaven and earth laugh for joy—Persephone tells her mother that it was like a *krokos,* the saffron flower (428), whose scent attracted Europa to the bull.[40]

But the goddess, unlike Tyro or even Creusa, is unwilling and weeping (ἀέκουσαν . . . ὀλοφυρομένην, 19–20). She calls out first to her father; so long as she can see the earth and the sea and heaven—the familiar surroundings of this world—Persephone still hopes to see her mother and the other gods, and still cries out. When the narrative returns to her again some time later with her husband, in his house, Persephone is still "very reluctant, out of longing for her mother" (πόλλ' ἀεκαζομένηι μητρὸς πόθωι, 344). In

---

[37] Although Griffith, *Prometheus,* ad loc. thinks here τίς means virtually the same thing as τί, it is probable that the chorus has metamorphosis in mind; cf. M. R. Lefkowitz, *Heroines and Hysterics* (London, 1981), 97.

[38] In the case of most ordinary marriages, transfer to her husband's home would not require the bride to sever ties with her mother; cf. Sourvinou-Inwood, *Reading Greek Culture,* 73–74.

[39] Cf. most recently W. B. Tyrrell and F. S. Brown, *Athenian Myths and Institutions* (New York, 1991), 106–7.

[40] In vase painting, a flower held in a woman's hand represents this moment of erotic "ripeness"; cf. Sourvinou-Inwood, *Reading Greek Culture,* 65.

obedience to Zeus' command, Hades allows Persephone to return to her mother, but he gives her a seed of a pomegranate to eat, after consecrating it secretly (λάθρηι / ἀμφὶ ἓ νωμήσας), so that she will not stay with her mother permanently. The language suggests that what is involved here is an act of ritual magic rather than a euphemism for sexual intercourse. As in the case of love charms, or the apples that Hippomenes throws to Atalanta, the seed binds Persephone to Hades, since if one eats the food of the dead one must remain among them.[41] Persephone, in her account of the story to her mother, stresses that she was forced to eat it: "he secretly put the seed into my mouth, a sweet morsel, and forced me to eat it against my will" (ἄκουσαν . . . βίηι προσηνάγκασσε, 413). Whether the seed represents a sacrament, or should be regarded as a euphemism for sexual intercourse is not so important as its meaning for Persephone, that she was compelled by force to eat it, so that she cannot remain with her mother but must spend a third of the year with her husband "in the gloomy darkness," away from her mother and the rest of the gods (464).

If the reason Persephone gives for her reluctance to marry Hades is that she must leave her mother and her normal surroundings, it may not be (despite modern theory) the sexual act per se[42] but rather change of ambience and status that makes females complain of the transition from girlhood to womanhood. Mortal women married to mortal men complain instead of the transition from their childhood home to a new house and new family. In Euripides' drama Medea complains of the enslavement of marriage, "taking a master for your body" (δεσπότην τε σώματος λαβεῖν, 234), and of needing to be a prophetess when you arrive in a new environment with new customs, which you did not learn at home; unless you are in your own city near your family, you have no protector if your husband mistreats you (238–40, 252–58). Or as Procne describes it, in Sophocles' lost play Tereus:[43]

---

[41] Cf. C. A. Faraone, "Aphrodite's Κεστός and Apples for Atalanta," Phoenix 44 (1990), 236–37.

[42] Cf., e.g., W. Whallon, Problem and Spectacle: Studies in the Oresteia (Heidelberg, 1980), 57: "[Cassandra's] mood is not of post-coital tristesse, but of non-orgiastic inadequacy."

[43] Cf. Soph., Trach. 141–52, esp. 147–50: a young woman leads "an untroubled life in pleasure until she is called a woman instead of a girl (ἀντὶ παρθένου γυνή), and takes on her share of worries in the night, because she is afraid for her husband and children."

Our lives are of all mortals the sweetest when we are young in our
father's houses, for ignorance always keeps children safe and happy.
But when we come of age and can understand, we are thrust out and
sold away (ὠθούμεθ᾿ ἔξω καὶ διεμπολώμεθα) from our ancestral
gods and from our parents. Some go to strange men's homes, others
to foreigners', some to joyless houses, some to hostile. And all this
when one night has yoked us (ἐπειδὰν εὐφρόνη ζεύξηι μία), we are
forced to praise and say that all is well. (Sophocles, *TrGF* fr. 583)

Since both Medea and Procne had reason to complain of their husbands, they
cannot be taken to represent ordinary women who were happily married and
well treated. Procne, like most women in myth, was given in marriage to a
man picked by her father, in this case a close military ally—in her opinion,
she was "thrust out and sold."[44] But Medea, as the nurse says in the play's
prologue, fell passionately in love with Jason (7). Apparently even when the
woman consents she cannot guarantee that for that reason her marriage will
be happy. Whether the choice is deliberate or made on impulse, whether it is
herself or her father, whoever makes the choice for the woman must begin by
picking the right man.[45]

Perhaps it is because the Greeks believe that human beings do not always
(or usually) understand what they are doing that they enjoyed stories about
women who were seduced by the gods, where at least (like the victor in the
games) the woman will have her moment of glory to remember, and her honor
to enjoy throughout her life, and in addition her children to be proud of. In
recent years students of Greek mythology have tended to stress that the narrative pattern of myth suggests that marriage is (in effect) death for the individual female, either literally or figuratively.[46] But that, as we have seen, is
only the first half of the story; if the choice of consort is right, even if the
woman has not made it herself, even if she is only seduced or persuaded to
accede to it, she can in fact be recognized and remembered as an individual,
even apart from the accomplishments of her sons. That is also the message

---

[44] In his tirade against women, Hippolytus uses the dowry as evidence that
women are evil: "her father offers a dowry to settle her elsewhere, in order to be rid
of the evil" (Eur., *Hipp.* 627–29).

[45] As apparently the father seems to have done in a lost comedy, *PDidot* I. 17–
18, ed. Sandbach, p. 328: "he is all that I wished with regard to me, and my pleasure
is his pleasure, father."

[46] E.g. Lefkowitz, *Heroines*, 93; Zeitlin, "Configurations of Rape," 123.

of the influential myth of Persephone's abduction: however unwilling Persephone has been to be led off by Hades and to remain for some part of the year
in his home, through her marriage she gains a new importance and a kingdom
of her own.[47]

The positive side of the pattern can perhaps most easily be seen in the
many myths of abduction that serve as charters for new colonies. In an ode
for a victor from Cyrene, the fifth-century lyric poet Pindar tells how Apollo
admired the maiden Cyrene when he saw her in Thessaly wrestling with a
lion without her weapons, and asks the centaur Cheiron if it would be "permissible for me to lay my famous hand on her and to cull the sweet flowers
of her bed" (ἐκ λεχέων κεῖραι μελιαδέα ποίαν, *Pyth.* 9.36–37). Cheiron
tells Apollo that he will carry her beyond the sea to the fine garden of Zeus
in Libya, where she will be queen, and bear a son, Aristaeus. Pindar does
not say, and Apollo does not ask, whether Cyrene approved of his plan; but
not only does the god help her deal with the lion, he gives her a city of her
own to rule.

In another ode, Pindar describes how Zeus carried off Protogeneia, the
daughter of the king of the city Opous in Elis, had intercourse with her in the
mountains of Arcadia, and brought her to Italy to the king Locrus, so that
he would not die childless. Locrus was delighted that his wife was pregnant
with the god's son and named him for her father, Opous, and it is this second
Opous who is the eponymous hero of a new colony in Italy (*Ol.* 9.57–66).
Again, the poet says nothing about how Protogeneia felt about the matter.
But what are the alternatives to marriage for a woman? She cannot be truly
independent or self-sufficient, but must remain under the protection of a male
relative, a father or a brother, in households run by their wives. At least if
she has her own home she might have children who would be loyal to her,
defend her in case of trouble, and look after her in her old age. If she was
seduced by a god, she would not only have children, but strong and remarkable children, who could save her life, like Tyro's or Antiope's sons; she
would also have lasting fame and perhaps a city or colony named for her.

In many myths the women chosen by the gods get another advantage: a
special gift in return for consenting to the god's wishes. Amymone was rescued by Poseidon from the unwelcome attentions of a satyr; he also asked
what wish she would like him to grant, and since she had been searching for

---

[47] Cf. esp. Jenkins, "Life after Marriage," 142.

water, she asked for a fountain.[48] But when Poseidon asked Caenis what he might do for her, she asked to be turned into a man and be made invulnerable. The god complied, and she became the hero Caeneus. In that way she was able to avoid giving birth to the god's child, but in the end her fate as a man seems to have been even less happy than it might have been had she followed the same course as Creusa or Tyro. Caeneus became arrogant, and eventually Zeus arranged that since Caeneus, being invulnerable, could not be killed, he be driven into the ground by Centaurs pounding him with tree trunks.[49]

If these myths have any lesson to teach, it is simply what, in Aeschylus' *Choephoroe*, Pylades tells Orestes when Orestes asks him if he must obey Apollo's command to kill his mother: "count all men your enemies rather than the god" (902). Given that life is by nature difficult for mortals, the gods will do what is best in the end, as Orestes and Creusa discovered. Another example is Cassandra, who refused to have intercourse with Apollo, although at first she consented (ξυναινέσασα), when Apollo, while wrestling with her, "breathed grace" upon her. But then she "played him false" in regard to the "production of children" (τέκνων εἰς ἔργον, 1206–8).[50] As a result of her refusal, she lost both the prospect of famous children and her gift. The god had already given her what she asked for, the gift of prophetic power, and could not take it away again, but he fixed it so that she would not be believed.

It is significant that, despite the gods' undeniably greater power, they ask for the woman's consent and honor her right of refusal, even though that refusal may bring about her death, as it did for Cassandra and Caenis.[51] But the gods, at least as they are portrayed by the poets, wish to persuade mortals

---

[48] Apollodorus ii.i.4; [Hesiod], *Catalogue,* fr. 122–29 M-W.

[49] Cf. [Hes.], fr. 87–88; Acusilaus 2 *FGrHist* F 22; Lefkowitz, *Women in Greek Myth,* 37, 138.

[50] Cf. E. Fraenkel, *Aeschylus: Agamemnon* (Oxford, 1962), II 555: "but from the beginning it is not merely brute force which is here at work; with all her resisting Cassandra is susceptible to the power of the god's χάρις." But does she resist at first or only at the last moment, since it is not simply ἔργον ἀφροδίσιον (cf. Semonides, fr. 7.48 W), but ἔργον τέκνων that is involved? For wrestling as a metaphor for sexual activity, cf. M. B. Poliakoff, *Studies in the Terminology of Greek Combat Sports* (Königstein, 1982), 104–7.

[51] Or metamorphosis (to escape from the god), e.g., Daphne, Dryope, Taygete, Arethusa.

to carry out their will rather than to make them comply by force. At the beginning of the *Odyssey*, Zeus sends Hermes to advise Aegisthus not to murder Agamemnon and to warn him of the consequences of the action he intends. Opportunity for choice and human responsibility are distinctive (and often misunderstood) characteristics of Greek religion, and nowhere are they more evident than in these stories of seduction of women by gods.

Surprisingly, perhaps, the notion that these seductions are beneficial and honorific survives in Alexandrian literature after the status of women had become a subject of debate and women had gained greater rights under the law. Plato's dialogue about the nature of love, the *Phaedrus,* takes place not far from the very spot on the banks of the Ilissus river where the god Boreas was said to have carried off Oreithyia.[52] Poems written far from mainland Greece in space and time and that describe love, both requited and unrequited, like Theocritus' idylls, are set in attractive landscapes.

A short epyllion or "mini-epic," written in Alexandria in Egypt in the second century B.C. by a pupil of the famous Homeric scholar Aristarchus, tells the old story of Zeus' seduction of Europa in much greater detail than even the Hesiodic catalogue would have allowed, and with a different focus: Moschus' poem concentrates not on the god's predictions about the names and accomplishments of her progeny but on Europa's own feelings.[53] It begins with a dream sent to her by Aphrodite: Asia and Europe appear to her as two women. Asia, her homeland, appeals to her as her child; the other female, however, pulls her away with her strong arms and claims that she was Zeus' gift to her, *her* Europa, but she is "not unwilling" (14). She wakes up frightened and interested in the strange woman who claimed her as her own, but hopes for the best. She then goes out to pick flowers, carrying a basket her mother had given her with the story of Io depicted on it; as so often in Hellenistic poetry, the description of a work of art is closely tied to the main narrative, and the story of Io predicts Europa's fate.

We have seen how Procne in Sophocles' *Tereus,* like Euripides' Medea, described the anguish young women experience when they are forced to make

---

[52] Cf. the meadow where Phaedra hopes to find rest (and Hippolytus; cf. Bremer, "Meadow of Love," 278), and the beautiful setting on the banks of the Ilissus that is the site of Plato's dialogue on the nature of love, *Phaedrus* 229b; cf. A. M. Parry, *The Language of Achilles and Other Papers* (Oxford, 1989), 22.

[53] Cf. W. Bühler, *Die Europa des Moschos* (Wiesbaden, 1960).

the critical transition from girlhood to becoming a bride.[54] The same longing
for the innocence of childhood is expressed in a remarkable poem dating from
the fourth century, this time by a women poet, Erinna. Although only fragments of her epyllion, the *Distaff,* survive, it is clear that she described her
friendship with another girl, Baucis, and the games they played, and regrets
that Baucis forgot about her and their pastimes after she married:[55] "you forgot everything that you heard from your mother . . . forgetfulness . . .
Aphrodite" (29–30). Even though Baucis is now dead, Erinna seems not to
be permitted to leave her house, and "blood-red shame tears . . . me" (34–
35). But in Moschus' poem, Europa is curious and even eager to learn about
the world outside.

In the meadow Europa encounters a remarkably beautiful bull—it is of
course Zeus in disguise hoping both to avoid Hera's jealous anger and to fool
Europa. Like Nausicaa in the *Odyssey* when she meets Odysseus, Europa
does not run away. The bull is mild and gentle; there is a scent of ambrosia
and the sound of music; he kneels before her and she climbs on his back. As
the bull carries her off to the sea, she calls to her friends, who cannot come
to her (112); but even then she does not despair but speaks to the bull, asks
him if he is a god, and prays to Poseidon for help. Finally the god speaks to
her and tells her what will happen. The poem ends with the lines "and she
who had been a girl became the bride of Zeus, and bore his children, and
became a mother" (165–66). It is a transition as swift and painless as Zeus'
metamorphosis into animal form: "he hid the god and changed his shape and
became a bull" (79).

Whatever modern women might think of this ending, for her it is clearly
happy, and almost romantic, with the music, and the flowers, and the scent,
and the beautiful Nereids rising from the sea. Perhaps it is wishful thinking
on the part of a male poet; certainly it has none of the anguish expressed by
Erinna or by Procne about a past happiness that is forever lost after marriage
to a mortal man. Perhaps the critical difference between these female and
male descriptions of marriage may be accounted for by the nature of the
bridegrooms involved. Europa became the hesitant but willing bride (however
temporarily) of the greatest god, and for her, as the dream indicates, her
seduction marked the beginning of a new and autonomous life.

---

[54] *TrGF* 583; cf. above, note 43.
[55] Cf. J. M. Snyder, *The Woman and the Lyre* (Carbondale, Ill., 1989), 93–97.

To speak about the "rape" of Europa or Io or other females seduced or abducted by gods gives the wrong impression of what the experience was like for the women involved. In all the stories that have come down to us, the women give their consent before having intercourse with a god. The experience brings them lasting fame, and they do not complain that they were persuaded by the gods to have intercourse with them, but rather lament the consequences of that intercourse, a child born in disgrace or abandoned, and separation from their families and friends.

Although most Greek literature was written by male authors, there is no reason to think that women writers would have condemned these stories or complained more actively of the gods' behavior than the male writers whose works have come down to us. The Greeks did not expect their gods to show sustained concern for mortals, even toward those who were closest to them. Because gods live forever and know the future, they do not intervene as frequently or as forcefully in human life as humans would wish. But at the same time they are not wholly inhumane or careless of the mortals whose lives they have in some way affected directly, and this concern is nowhere more evident than in their attention (however brief and episodic) to their mortal children and the mortal women whom they chose to be their mothers.

Wellesley College

Livy's Lucretia and the Validity
of Coerced Consent in Roman Law

DIANA C. MOSES

Under vexed circumstances Lucretia has sex with her husband's cousin, son of the reigning king. She consequently kills herself, and the avenging of her death results in the deposition of Rome's kings and the inauguration of the Republic.

Why does the Lucretia in Livy's account of the story of Lucretia fear becoming a bad precedent by means of which some unchaste woman thereafter will escape punishment?[1] It is the suggestion of this paper that she is made to fear this scenario because during the period when Livy was writing and publishing his history of Rome the difficulty of deciding what significance coerced consent should have was being explored both in Roman law and in Roman society more generally. For while Roman law expresses no "unified theory" of coerced consent, nevertheless its tolerance of the use of force in some places and its strict reliance on objective criteria in much of its civil component (*ius*

An earlier version of this paper was presented as part of the Harvard Law School's Legal History Speaker Series in March 1990. I am grateful for the inspiration, patient help, and judicious suggestions of Gordon Williams and John E. Boswell, and to Angeliki Laiou and the participants in our seminar on "Free, Coerced and Circumscribed (Sexual) Consent in Byzantium and the Roman Empire" at Dumbarton Oaks during the fall of 1991 for the opportunity to refine my ideas and to learn from theirs. Thanks are also due Charles Donahue, Jr.

[1] Livy, *ab Urbe Condita* I.58.10.

civile) might raise the question of whether Lucretia could by Roman standards have been said to have in some way consented: after all, Tarquin had succeeded in accomplishing his goal of having sex with Lucretia, and he had done so by threatening Lucretia with an alternative that she wished to avoid more—arranging her corpse with that of a slave so that it would look as if she had committed adultery with the slave.[2] Could it be said of her, as was said of coerced parties in other contexts, "coacta voluit,"[3] although she was forced she willed it, or "maluisse hoc videtur,"[4] she is held to have preferred, and hence chosen, this course of action? And if the defense of force were allowed to exempt her from punishment, would this lead to the defense's subsequent widespread and less appropriate use, and thus hobble Augustus' attempts, in Horace's words,[5] "to curb unbridled licence" ("indomitam . . . refrenare licentiam") and render his laws "empty" ("vanae")?[6]

Investigation of how Roman law treats consent procured by force and other forms of coercion and of the historical context in which it came to do this shows that, for the Romans of the very end of the Republic and the very beginning of the Principate, the acceptability of the use of force was a vexed question of all too much renewed relevance and that these Romans' attempts to address this question led to their development of two middle grounds: a conceptual middle ground between the poles of objective accomplishment and failure (he did it, but because it was under extenuating circumstances we will relieve him of the consequences) and a temporal middle ground between the poles of permitting the use of force and forbidding it (he should not compel consent and we are forbidding him to do so, but if he does and he succeeds in accomplishing the act in this way the act stands). The evidence also suggests that this attention to subjective detail had, in turn, problematic implications for Augustus' vision of a morally reformed Rome.

---

[2] Livy, I.58.4.

[3] *Digesta Iustiniani*, ed. Th. Mommsen and P. Krueger (hereafter *D.*), *Corpus iuris civilis*, I, 16th ed. (Berlin, 1954), 4.2.21.5.

[4] *D.* 23.2.22.

[5] These seem to refer to (failed) attempts at legislation earlier than his *lex Julia de adulteriis coercendis* of 18 B.C. See Gordon Williams, "Poetry in the Moral Climate of Augustan Rome," *Journal of Roman Studies* 52 (1962), 28–46, 30. On dating the *lex Julia de adulteriis* to 17 B.C., see H. M. Last, *Cambridge Ancient History*, vol. X (Cambridge, 1934) (hereafter *CAH*), 441 ff, Leo Ferrero Raditsa, "Augustus' Legislation Concerning Marriage, Procreation, Love Affairs and Adultery," *Aufstieg und Niedergang der Römischen Welt*, II.13 (Berlin, 1980), 278–339, 296–97.

[6] Horace, *Odes* III.24.28–29, 35–36, trans. Williams in "Moral Climate," 30.

The Story of Lucretia

In Livy's account of the story of Lucretia, as a result of a bet among fellow, and kindred,[7] soldiers as to which of their wives is the most outstanding in womanly virtue, Sextus Tarquinius, son of the king of Rome, is smitten by the beauty and chastity of Lucretia, the wife of his second cousin.[8] The men make unannounced nocturnal visits to their wives to see how they are conducting themselves, and in contrast to the other wives who are engaging in dinner parties, Lucretia is found spinning with her maidservants.[9] Neither the bet nor the ensuing glimpse of Lucretia spinning is found in the accounts of the story by Livy's contemporaries Dionysius of Halicarnassus and Diodorus Siculus, who do not give Tarquin's lust such dramatic motivation.[10]

Tarquin is seized by "an evil lustful desire to have illicit sex through force with Lucretia": "Ibi Sex. Tarquinium mala libido Lucretiae per vim stuprandae capit."[11] He tries various means of getting her to comply with his wishes, starting with armed force, moving into words designed to persuade (but, significantly, not including promises of marriage, as are found in Dionysius' and Diodorus' accounts), and finally threatening her with a scenario that she will fear more.[12] "By means of the terror (of this threat)," says Livy, "lust, victorious as it were by force, conquered stubborn chastity; and proud

---

[7] Sextus was a son of Lucius Tarquinius Superbus, who was a son of Lucius Tarquinius Priscus, whose previous name had been Lucumo. Lucumo had a brother Arruns, who had a posthumous son Egerius, who had a son Lucius Tarquinius Collatinus, who married Lucretia. Lucius Junius Brutus was a cognatic first cousin of Sextus, being the son of Tarquinia, who was the daughter of Lucius Tarquinius Priscus. (Priscus also had a son Arruns in addition to his children Lucius Tarquinius Superbus and Tarquinia, and Superbus had sons Arruns and Titus and daughter Tarquinia in addition to his son Sextus.) Note in contrast that Sextus and Collatinus were agnatic second cousins. Livy, I.34, I.53.5, I.56.7, I.57.6, and Dionysius of Halicarnassus, *Roman Antiquities* (hereafter DH), IV.64.2–3, IV.67.1.

[8] Livy, I.57.6–11.

[9] Livy, I.57.8–9.

[10] In Dionysius' account, Tarquin's lust is said to be of long standing, the result of multiple routine visits to his cousin Collatinus' house, and simply awaiting opportunity (DH IV.64.4); in Diodorus' account, it is merely implied and seems to be a spur-of-the-moment thing that occurred at an opportune moment (Diodorus Siculus, *The Library of History* (hereafter DS), X.20.1).

[11] Livy, I.57.10.

[12] Livy, I.58.3–4; DH IV.65.2; DS X.20.2.

at having stormed a woman's virtue, Tarquin left": "Quo terrore cum vicisset obstinatam pudicitiam velut <vi> victrix libido, profectusque inde Tarquinius ferox expugnato decore muliebri esset."[13] Livy has managed to convey the gist of what happened in abstract terms, to compact the event itself that for-ever changes the life of Lucretia and the constitutional structure of Rome into three words in an ablative absolute, and to do all this in a subordinate tem-poral clause in the pluperfect tense, thus making it difficult to discern what "really" happened.

Lucretia sets in motion a family council[14] by sending for her father and her husband. In front of the council she makes the case that can be summed up as Augustine says someone once put it: " 'Two persons, but only one adulterer.' "[15] She tells her husband that the imprint of another man is in his bed but that for all that, while her body was violated, her *animus* remained innocent.[16] She asks that the adulterer not be allowed to get away with it, and terms Tarquin "an enemy instead of a guest [who came] by night and armed with force" ("qui hostis pro hospite priore nocte vi armatus").[17] Lucretia's menfolk swear their revenge and try to console her in her distress with the argument that one should shift the injurious behavior ("noxa") from the coerced party onto the author of the wrongdoing, that the mind ("mentem") is what commits the wrong, not the body, and that guilt ("culpa") is absent where purpose ("consilium") is missing: "Dant ordine omnes fidem; conso-lantur aegram animi avertendo noxam ab coacta in auctorem delicti: mentem peccare, non corpus, et unde consilium afuerit culpam abesse."[18] This last conclusion seems to involve a leap in logic from the menfolk's previous state-

---

[13] Livy, I.58.5.

[14] See Alan Watson, *Rome of the XII Tables* (Princeton, N.J., 1975), 34 ff, 167–68 (story not paradigmatic or etiological); cf. W. Kunkel, "Das Konsilium im Haus-gericht," *Zeitschrift der Savigny-Stiftung für Rechtsgeschichte* (Romanistische Abtei-lung) 83 (1966), 219–51.

[15] Augustine, *de Civitate Dei* I.19, trans. in Saint Augustine, *The City of God*, trans. Gerald G. Walsh, Demetrius B. Zema, Grace Monahan, and Daniel J. Honan, abridged ed. (New York, 1958), 53.

[16] " 'Quid enim salvi est mulieri amissa pudicitia? Vestigia viri alieni, Collatine, in lecto sunt tuo; ceterum corpus est tantum violatum, animus insons; mors testis erit.' " Livy, I.58.7.

[17] " 'Sed date dexteras fidemque haud impune adultero fore. Sex. est Tarquinius qui hostis pro hospite priore nocte vi armatus mihi sibique, si vos viri estis, pestiferum hinc abstulit gaudium.' " Livy, I.58.7–8.

[18] Livy, I.58.9.

ment about the intellect and not the body sinning, since it seems to assume that where there is no deliberate plan there is no mental involvement whatsoever, no preference for one course of action over another (no "maluisse hoc videtur"), no will despite coercion (no "coactus voluit"), no "weak intentionality"[19] (that one intends the direct consequences of one's physical muscular contractions even if one does not have any deliberate plan to accomplish something by them).

It appears that Livy is trying to raise the issue of Lucretia's consent by the way in which he tells the story, and to raise the question of whether Lucretia has the *voluntas* necessary to have committed an offense under Roman law,[20] perhaps a *voluntas* necessary to be culpable of (a contemporary notion of) *stuprum*. For although *voluntas* was not a necessary element for the archaic Roman law of *stuprum*, in which the focus was on result, not intent,[21] the Augustan law of *stuprum* in its pursuit of moral reform does seem to have brought into question the state of mind of the woman who has been involved in *stuprum*.[22] This debate between Lucretia and her menfolk, in which Livy explores the ambiguities of what happened to Lucretia and hence of the word, *stuprum*, that he uses in varying ways in the narrative surrounding the story to refer to the act, is, indeed, not presented by Dionysius of Halicarnassus in his account of Lucretia's story, in which it is merely related that Lucretia told her story and then killed herself.[23]

---

[19] Prof. Morton J. Horwitz, torts class, Harvard Law School, fall 1980.

[20] Jacques Heurgon, *Tite-Live, Histoires, Livre Premier* (Paris, 1963), 190, citing the tag "in maleficiis voluntas spectatur, non exitus" (*D.* 48.8.14). This tag turns out to be from a rescript of Hadrian, excerpted from Callistratus on *cognitiones,* and included in the *Digest* in the title on the *lex Cornelia de sicariis et veneficis.* Heurgon, *Tite-Live,* 190. See also Watson, *XII Tables,* 35.

[21] "Mais ses principes se mêlent ici au souvenir des tabous primitifs: ils poursuivaient dans l'adultère la souillure du sang, qui rendait impurs les enfants à venir, et exigeait l'élimination de la famille de l'élément souillé." Heurgon, *Tite-Live,* 190, citation omitted. Cf. R. M. Ogilvie, *A Commentary on Livy Books 1–5* (Oxford, 1965), 225, on Livy's use of legal terms in this sentence. See also Ian Donaldson, *The Rapes of Lucretia. A Myth and Its Transformations* (Oxford, 1962), 173–74, note 3.

[22] "'Let no one hereafter commit *stuprum* or adultery knowingly and with bad faith (*dolo malo*).'" (*D.* 48.5.13(12): "'ne quis posthac stuprum adulterium facito sciens dolo malo.'") See also "wartime force exception" to *stuprum,* discussed below.

[23] DH IV.67.1. Dionysius' debate, of course, would have to have had a slightly different focus since in his account of the story it is made more explicit that Lucretia

Finally, Lucretia resolves the debate between herself and her menfolk by maintaining that regardless of what is due Tarquin, she still must die: even if she is free from some sort of moral guilt (free from the guilt of disloyalty to her marriage, her freedom from which produced the comment "two persons, [but only] one adulterer" quoted by Augustine), that does not mean that she does not merit punishment, or more specifically, that she can afford to go unpunished. For Lucretia's final argument is that she cannot afford to live and thus be used as precedent for allowing women who are not innocent in the way that she is, to live: " 'Even if I acquit myself of fault, I do not exempt myself from punishment. For no unchaste woman hereafter will live because of Lucretia's precedent.' " (" 'Vos' inquit 'videritis quid illi debeatur: ego me etsi peccato absolvo, supplicio non libero; nec ulla deinde impudica Lucretiae exemplo vivet.' "[24]) And so she kills herself.

Even in death, Livy's Lucretia seems to evoke contemporary, Augustan moral concerns, for in his oration over the body in the marketplace, Brutus distills the episode into "the force and lust of Tarquin, the unspeakable *stuprum* and pitiful slaughter of Lucretia, the bereavement (*orbitate*) of Lucretia's father, who [is said to] regard his daughter's death as more undeserving and pitiable in its cause than in its fact." (". . . de vi ac libidine Sex. Tarquini, de stupro infando Lucretiae et miserabili caede, de orbitate Tricipitini cui

---

has suffered Tarquin to accomplish his ends, albeit out of fear. The culpability of one who has "looked the other way" ("περιϊδεῖν"; DH IV.65.4) would perhaps have been the focus here. Note that Diodorus Siculus or his Byzantine excerptor, in a commentary external to the account of the story itself, goes on at great length about the "nobility" of Lucretia's "choice"; the author's concern, however, is not about whether Lucretia consented (he seems to assume she did not but that her slanderers would have contended otherwise) but about her being able to maintain her reputation as a wife who meticulously followed the rules and hence to be a shining example for future women. And although the author worries about other, less innocent women's behavior and Lucretia's reputation, he does not combine these concerns, as will be seen Livy does, into a concern that if Lucretia lives she will provide a precedent for allowing women who are shameless to live; her usefulness as a precedent in the Diodorus commentary is to virtuous women and as a friendly, inspirational point for comparison. DS X.21.

[24] Livy, I.58.10. See Heurgon for the view that she is merely following the ancient law, against the arguments based on law contemporary to Livy made by her family counselors: "Ici les consolateurs parlent en contemporains de T.-L., Lucrèce agit selon la loi ancienne." Heurgon, *Tite-Live*, 190.

morte filiae causa mortis indignior ac miserabilior esset."[25]) Brutus' tricolon, rather than reaching a crescendo, falls off precipitously both emotionally and structurally, lacking a doublet for Lucretia's father's issues and leaving off (adjectival) description of an emotional content to his reaction. This makes Livy's use of the word *orbitas* stand out in all its cold Augustan legislative starkness, *orbitas* being, along with being unmarried (*caelebs*), the target of Augustus' penalties in his drive, conducted largely through legislation, to replenish Rome's esteemed population. In Dionysius' account, by contrast, Lucretia's father is allowed to express his heartache, first by his vain attempt to heal her from her (fatal) wound as she dies in his arms[26] and later, at the point in the story at which Brutus speaks, by his embraces of her dead body and his voluminous wails and lamentations.[27]

Stuprum

Livy uses the word *stuprum,* at first with the qualification *per vim,*[28] to refer to what happened between Tarquin and Lucretia. While this use surely has

---

[25] Livy, I.59.8. Livy as narrator also refers to the episode as "per stuprum caedemque Lucretiae" in his introduction to the story of Virginia: Livy, III.44.1.

[26] Cf. Livy's "Conclamat vir paterque." Livy, I.58.12.

[27] DH IV.67.2, IV.70.2–3. Note also that for Shakespeare, the issue for Lucretia's father was his claim on behalf of Lucretia for sorrow in comparison to her husband's claim. Shakespeare, *Lucrece* 1793–99. C. Kahn, "The Rape in Shakespeare's *Lucrece*," *Shakespeare Studies* 9 (1976), 45–72, 55–56. Cf. Ovid's use of the motif of loss of a child in his account of the story of Lucretia to communicate wrenching grief, where he uses it to color Lucretia's reaction to the incident; by comparing her disarray to that of a mother at her child's funeral pyre he characterizes her reaction as being less one of degradation and more one of grief for a tremendous loss. Ovid, *Fasti* 813–14. There is really no good reason in terms of the archaic story itself to worry about Lucretius' childlessness, for although Lucretius' "family line" will admittedly die out with his daughter's death, she could not have continued his line in a meaningful way within the agnatic system of the Roman (civil) law of succession. It is true that had she lived, Lucretia might have provided her father with grandsons to adopt. (I have demonstrated elsewhere, in an unpublished paper, that the Romans often adopted men already related to them cognatically.) Nevertheless, Lucretia's death would not have prevented her father from adopting other cognatic relatives or someone not previously related.

[28] As does Cicero in *de Legibus* 2.10 and *de Finibus* 2.66, 5.64. See also Cicero, *de Republica* II.46 ("eius filius Lucretiae . . . vim attulisset"). At the end of the episode (Livy, I.59.8), Livy has Brutus refer to what happened as *stuprum* qualified

something to do with keeping faith with Lucretia's position that she maintained mental marital loyalty, the way in which Livy tells the story also makes the term resonate with the difficulties in the development of public punishment for *stuprum,* a category that included both forcible and consensual sex, during the very late Republic and very early Principate.

During the historical period of Rome, *stuprum* seems to have referred at base to sex in which one person was used by the other to gratify his lust.[29] What circumstances constituted "using" or "lust" seem to have been dependent upon the absolute and relative status[30] of the persons involved; thus, one could not "use" a slave, probably because one could not *but* use a slave,[31] and married couples could not commit *stuprum* with each other.[32]

only by the word *infandum,* and perhaps this too is intentional, a bit of encouragement by Livy to the reader to feel that whether Lucretia consented is a detail too subtle and dangerous for posterity to take into account.

[29] This would seem to be the common denominator explaining its being coupled both with wartime acts of violence and with consensual adultery. See also its usage to encompass both incest and adultery in *D.* 48.5.39(38).1.

[30] John Boswell, *Christianity, Social Tolerance, and Homosexuality: Gay People in Western Europe from the Beginning of the Christian Era to the Fourteenth Century* (Chicago, 1980), 122, for the framing of the issue in this way.

[31] See Susan Treggiari, *Roman Marriage. Iusti Coniuges from the time of Cicero to the time of Ulpian* (Oxford, 1991), 301, on slaves' lack of moral responsibility for sex initiated by a free man. The *lex Julia de adulteriis* only applied to free persons; however, the owner of a slave could recover under the *lex Aquilia, iniuria,* or the praetorian action of "corruption of a slave." *D.* 48.5.6.pr., *D.* 47.10.25 (which I take to be solely about slaves, *pace* Jane F. Gardner, *Women in Roman Law and Society* (Bloomington, 1986), 125; the text seems to indicate how the delict may be compounded and aggravated by attendant circumstances), *D.* 48.19.38.3; see also *Codex Justinianus,* ed. P. Krueger (hereafter *CJ*), *Corpus iuris civilis,* II, 11th ed. (Berlin, 1954), 9.9.23 (slave wife cannot be accused of adultery), 9.9.25 (sex with female slaves rather than free women leads to loss of reputation rather than legal disability). (The action for *iniuria* could also be brought for *stuprum* committed against a free woman, one infers, but the texts conspicuously never state this, although they do state that *iniuria* may be brought for "soliciting" [*appellare*] her. *D.* 47.10.15.15, 20, 22–26; *Institutiones,* ed. P. Krueger, *Corpus iuris civilis,* I, 16th ed. [Berlin, 1954], 4.4.1; see Sarah B. Pomeroy, *Goddesses, Whores, Wives, and Slaves: Women in Classical Antiquity* [New York, 1975], 160, for the inference; *pace* Treggiari, 309–10, who seems to conflate this with an action under the *lex Aquilia.* The extent to which *stuprum* was commonly redressed through the courts before Augustus' legislation and the extent to which actions under this legislation superseded, for the purposes of the

Stuprum did not itself mean forcible sex.[33] While the meaning of *stuprum* was not antithetical to the use of force to procure the sex, it did not include it either;[34] rather, the idea of force had to be supplied through other

---

jurists' discussions, whatever actions were technically available under more general law are relevant considerations here.) Somewhat similarly, in the sense that one could do so with impunity, one could not commit *stuprum* with a prostitute. *D.* 48.5.14(13).2; see also *CJ* 9.9.22 (no adultery with a prostitute). See Boswell, *Social Tolerance,* 74, 122. There were other permitted categories of women—women with whom one could have such sex with impunity, that is. In fact, the limitations on circumstances constituting *stuprum* seem to have reduced it to sex in which a freeborn woman or boy was used by a male to gratify his lust. (An interesting legal point is whether sex with a *libertina* by someone other than her patron constituted *stuprum*. Aline Rousselle, in *Porneia: On Desire and the Body in Antiquity,* trans. Felicia Pheasant [Oxford, 1988], 82, seems to imply that with some *libertinae* it would, since some would be categorized as *matres familiarum*. See *D.* 23.2.24, 25.7.1.1, 25.7.3.pr.–1, 48.5.35[34].pr. on question of whether relations with a concubine constitute *stuprum*.) Note also that there were some women with whom sex would be adultery if the women were married but would not be *stuprum* if they were not. *D.* 48.5.14(13).2. How broadly the *lex Julia de adulteriis* extended seems to be discussed in *D.* 48.5.14(13), although it is not clear when these various peripheral categories were accepted as included within the law's ambit (there is a reference to Sextus Caecilius for its extension to *matrimonia non iusta,* and he lived during the mid-second century A.D.) and to what extent their inclusion was primarily a matter of extending procedural advantages or uxorious liability to the husband without changing a basic concept underlying Augustus' law, that *adulterium* was to be eradicated in order to facilitate the proper production of Roman upper-class citizens. See *D.* 48.5.12(11).1 (hypothetical of soldier "married" to sister's daughter), 48.5.14(13).pr. (different procedure but substantive charge applies), 48.5.14(13).7 (woman in enemy hands, marriage therefore suspended, technically, but procedure in right of husband allowed).

[32] *D.* 48.6.35(34) defining *stuprum* as keeping a free woman "consuetudinis causa, non matrimonii," unless the woman is a concubine.

[33] An early example is Plautus' Alcmena's use of *stuprum* to refer to her husband's accusations of what he thinks is her infidelity and what is actually her unforced but contrived union with Jupiter disguised as her husband. Plautus, *Amphitryo* 898. In this case, Alcmena was "used" by Jupiter but not forced (although it is arguable whether she really consented to the union that actually took place).

[34] See the *Oxford Latin Dictionary*'s second definition for *stuprum:* "Illicit sexual intercourse in any form (whether forced or not) or an instance of it." P. G. W. Glare, *Oxford Latin Dictionary* (Oxford, 1982). Actually, whether the sex was forced or not was irrelevant, not sometimes included within and sometimes absent from the concept denoted by the word "stuprum." See below.

words and phrases,[35] such as the phrase "per vim,"[36] some form or derivative of "violo,"[37] or some form of "rapio,"[38] when such a meaning was intended. On the other hand, the term *stuprum* did not *exclude* the possibility that force was involved, either—the word was neutral[39] as to the details of the circumstances under which the sex occurred, probably because the aspect of the act that imparted shame to the victim was his or her having been used; whether

[35] See also "constupro," in which the intensifying prefix may have brought in the idea of violence, but the use of the verb and its noun derivative does not clearly indicate this since in some cases other words of violence are also present and in other cases it is unclear whether violence is actually necessarily meant to be indicated. Cicero, *Epistulae ad Atticum* I.18.3; [Q. Cicero,] *Commentariolum Petitionis* 10; *Rhetorica ad Herennium* 4.12; Livy, 29.17.15, 39.15.9.

[36] Cicero, *de Legibus* 2.10, *de Finibus* 2.66, 5.64; Livy, I.57.10, 38.24.3, 39.10.7; Valerius Maximus, *Facta et Dicta Memorabilia* 6.1.1 ("per vim stuprum pati coacta"); Tacitus, *Historiae* 2.56; Ulpian in *D*.48.5.30(29).9; Servius, *In Vergilii Carmina Commentarii, A.* 8.635 ("raptas, stupratas, id est per vim"). See Gardner, *Women in Roman Law and Society,* 118.

[37] Tacitus, *Annales* 14.31; see also Cicero, *in Verrem* 2.4.102, *de Haruspicum Responso* 8.13, Livy, 39.18.4, Phaedrus, *Appendix Perottina* 6.14.

[38] Sallust, *Historiae* frag. III.98: "Ac statim fugitivi co⟨n⟩|tra praeceptum ducis | rapere ad stuprum virg⟨i⟩nes matr⟨ona⟩sque et alii"; Livy, 3.50.6, 26.13.15 (nec dirui incendio patriam videbo, nec rapi ad stuprum matres Campanas virginesque et ingenuos pueros); see also Livy, 29.17.15. Seneca, *Controversiae* II.3 and VIII.6 are consistent with this interpretation, but VII.8 seems to equate *stuprum* without any qualifiers with the result of *rapui* and *vitiavi*. However, Seneca's *Controversiae* on *raptus* all revolve around the "law" that the female victim may choose between marrying her "assailant" or having him executed. Perhaps Seneca's unqualified use of *stuprum* in *Controversia* VII.8 reflects the other ambiguity of *raptus* once it came to encompass elopement as well as abduction and (abduction for the purpose of) forced sex. Judith Evans-Grubbs seems to group the categories used in the *Controversiae* with those in post-classical law such as Constantine's *Codex Theodosianus,* ed. Th. Mommsen, I.2 (Hildesheim, 1990), 9.24.1, that is, elopement and abduction. Judith Evans-Grubbs, "Abduction Marriage in Antiquity: A Law of Constantine (*CTh* IX.24.1) and Its Social Context," *Journal of Roman Studies* 79 (1989), 59–83, 70. On the use of literary sources to inform our understanding of legal texts and vice versa, see Boswell, *Social Tolerance,* 122 note 7.

[39] Cf. *Oxford Latin Dictionary* definition given above; J. N. Adams, *The Latin Sexual Vocabulary* (Baltimore, 1982), 201 (who also seems to think the notion of force could be comprised by the term); Pierre Grimal, *Love in Ancient Rome,* trans. Arthur Train, Jr. (Norman, Okla., 1986), 103 ("The *stuprum* was essentially the defilement, affected by illegitimate sexual relations, which was considered to taint the blood of the 'passive' partner, willing or unwilling, in intercourse.").

the victim had consented to being thus used was irrelevant. A consequence of this focus, however, was that an appellation of *stuprum* by itself was ambiguous as to the complicity or resistance of the person who was being used.

Within this general framework, the concept of *stuprum* did, it seems, change over time, at least with respect to the consequential social opprobrium attached to the victim. The archaic notion of *stuprum* seems to have been one of pollution, so that the victim, however innocent of causing the act, was nevertheless irreparably tainted.[40] On the other hand, in Augustan times the notion seems to have come to include a moralistic condemnation of the "victim," the person being used. This is in keeping with the general tenor of Augustus' program of moral reform (for the upper classes) and is supported by the usage of the term by the jurists in the *Digest*. An accusation of *stuprum* under the *lex Julia de adulteriis*, for example, is considered there an accusation against the woman's *mores*,[41] and Papinian felt that the *lex Julia de adulteriis* "calls it *stuprum* and adultery indiscriminately and rather misappliedly";[42] this suggests that *stuprum* was seen, at least by this time, as consensual and incriminating as adultery.[43]

Punishing *Stuprum*: The Need to Distinguish Forcible from Consensual *Stuprum*

During the very end of the Republic and the very beginning of the Principate, *stuprum* came to be penalized under public law.[44] The process by which *stu-*

---

[40] Indeed, originally the meaning of *stuprum* probably was not even restricted to sex at all. Adams, *Sexual Vocabulary*, 200–201; see entries in Charlton T. Lewis and Charles Short, *A Latin Dictionary* (Oxford, 1879) and *Oxford Latin Dictionary* giving the first definition as "defilement, dishonor, disgrace" and "dishonour, shame," respectively. See also Grimal, *Love in Ancient Rome*, 103.

[41] *D*.48.5.14(13).10.

[42] "Lex stuprum et adulterium promiscue et καταχρηστικώτερον appellat." *D*. 48.5.6.1.

[43] *D*. 48.5.6.1 (Papinian, libro primo de adulteris). See also Modestinus from his *Differentiae* in *D*. 50.16.101.pr. It was so taught in Justinian's *Institutes* 4.18.4.

[44] As noted above, it has been inferred that the action for *iniuria* could have been brought on behalf of the victim privately, by "the man under whose authority the wronged woman fell." Pomeroy, *Goddesses, Whores, Wives, and Slaves*, 160. Note also the questionable comment, attributed to the jurist Paul, in the post-classical *Collatio*, that the first chapter of the *lex Julia de adulteriis* (the statute that we shall see culminated this effort) replaced many previous legal enactments on the subject: "prior-

prum became criminalized involved an explicit articulation of a distinction between an act accomplished by force and that same act accomplished consensually; this articulation itself did not always fit easily into Roman legal thinking and categories.

Laws for prosecuting violence (*leges de vi*), which seem to begin in the late Republic as a response to the extraordinary violence of the social and civil wars, eventually included the category *raptus*.[45] *Raptus* did not itself actually denote, at least strictly speaking, a sexual act, although it may have come regularly to include one by the classical period. Its primary meaning was forcible abduction.[46]

At some point, it seems, *per vim stuprum* became included within the category *raptus* at least in the interpretation of the *leges de vi*, perhaps by

---

ibus legibus pluribus obrogat." *Mosaicarum et Romanarum Legum Collatio*, ed. J. Baviera, *Fontes Iuris Romani Antejustiniani*, S. Riccobono et al., eds., 2d ed., II.543 ff (Florence, 1940), 4.2.2. See Gardner, *Women in Roman Law and Society*, 123; Treggiari, *Roman Marriage*, 274 and 277 note 79, for differing reactions.

[45] *D*. 48.6.5.2, 48.6.6 (title 48.6 is "ad Legem Iuliam de Vi Publica"); *CJ* 5.1.1, 9.12.3. The *lex Julia de vi publica* is probably from the dictatorship of Caesar (see Th. Mommsen, *Römisches Strafrecht* [Berlin, 1899], 655; Gardner, *Women in Roman Law and Society*, 118), although some have argued it is Augustan (see A. W. Lintott, *Violence in Republican Rome* [Oxford, 1968], 108, for example). Even if it was Augustan, there were previous incarnations of the *lex de vi*, which in all likelihood also included the crime of *raptus*. See Lintott, *Violence*, 107 ff, and R. G. Austin, *M. Tulli Ciceronis, Pro M. Caelio Oratio*, 3rd ed. (Oxford, 1960), 42–43.

[46] See Adams' entry for *rapio*: "The basic sense of *rapio* was 'to drag off into captivity (sc. *coeundi causa*)': ([footnote:] See Nisbet and Hubbard II on Hor. *Carm.* 2.4.8) see, e.g., Livy 1.9.10[–11—the story of the rape of the Sabine women], Ovid *Met.* 12.225; cf. *rapto* at *Met.* 12.223. It is possible that it tended to be weakened into a synonym of *vim afferre, vitiare*, etc., expressing an act of sexual aggression without a concomitant 'capture' . . . *Rapio* is a similar type of euphemism to *duco*: both express the taking off of someone for unspecified purposes. But *rapio* had a strong implication that the act was carried out against the will of the victim." Adams, *Sexual Vocabulary*, 175. Cf. "(vi) bona rapta" for aggravated robbery. A passage by Ulpian in the *Digest* shows that even as late as the 3rd century *raptus* focused on the violence and physical control over the victim, not on sexual violation. In the instructions to the person holding the hearing in a case in which it was alleged that the accused "puerum ingenuum rapuit," the boy is said to have been "raptum atque conclusum, mox verberibus ac tormentis usque ad summum periculum adflictum." *D*. 48.6.6. Cf. focus of *raptus* under Constantine and his successors.

means of the familiar combination *raptus ad stuprum*.[47] The evidence that this was happening during the very late Republic comes from Cicero, whose works also suggest that attempts were being made to extend the category even further and include sexual immorality per se, that is, *stuprum sine vi*.[48]

In 56 B.C. in his defense of Caelius,[49] Cicero transforms the technical charges against his client *de vi*[50] into an investigation of his moral character and behavior.[51] Toward the end of his speech Cicero responds to the prosecution's apparent attempt to argue that *leges de vi* apply to immoral behavior per se. In his peroration, he alludes to the *causa Camurti et Caeserni*, a case in which two men were apparently convicted of *vis* for an act related in some

---

[47] Given the violence of the late Republic and the use of *vis* legislation to root out unsavory behavior, however private (e.g., Cicero, *pro S. Roscio Amerino* 93), in the name of preserving the *Res Publica* (see Lintott, *Violence*), this would not be surprising. The *Digest* indicates that *raptus* and *per vim stuprum* were used synonymously by the late classical jurists. (Texts about the statute of limitations for "*raptus*" in the title on the *lex de vi publica* and for "*per vim stuprum*" in the title on the *lex de adulteriis* demonstrate this. In *D.*48.6.5.2 it is said that the statute of limitations for the crime of *raptus* exceeds five years. In *D.* 48.5.30(29).9 it is said that an act of *per vim stuprum* can be prosecuted at any time, that there is no statute of limitations.) See also Servius' comment from the 4th or 5th century, " '*raptas*' stupratas, id est per vim." Servius, *A.* 8.635.

[48] The language of *D.* 48.6.5.2 and *D.* 48.5.30(29).9 also seems to reflect the notion that *stuprum* is a subset of *per vim stuprum,* itself a subset of *raptus:* "cum raptus crimen legis Iuliae de adulteris potestatem excedit" and "Eum autem, qui per vim stuprum intulit vel mari vel feminae, sine praefitione huius temporis accusari posse dubium non est, cum eum publicam vim committere nulla dubitatio est," respectively.

[49] Cicero was defending Caelius, who was Cicero's protégé of sorts and a young up-and-coming figure in the highest political and fastest social circles at Rome. The prosecution against Caelius had been strategically launched and supported by relatives of his enemies, both political and social. These relatives included those of his former mistress. See Austin, Introduction, vii.

[50] How the particular charges actually came under the statute *de vi* to begin with is itself a vexed question. Austin, Appendix V, 153. Lintott, *Violence,* esp. 122 ff, 133 ff.

[51] See Austin, Appendix V, 153–54. Perhaps this was connected to the agenda to avenge Caelius' former mistress that is thought to underlie the prosecution in part. See Austin, Introduction, vi–viii.

way to an act of *stuprum*.[52] This case was apparently cited by Cicero's opponents (the prosecution against Caelius) as a precedent, that is, evidence, for expansively interpreting existing legislation against violence to include instances of simply immoral behavior.[53] It is not clear from Cicero's disposal of the prosecution's argument or from Caelius' acquittal[54] whether the case of Camurtius and Caesernius was aberrant or merely distinguishable from Caelius', or whether Cicero was successful in arresting a larger jurisprudential trend to extend the reach of *leges de vi* to cover immorality as a subset of violence.[55] Although Cicero refers to the men's conviction,[56] he goes on to question whether the law actually applied to their act, suggesting instead that

---

[52] It is not clear whether the act of Camurtius and Caesernius was the act of *stuprum* alluded to itself, the "Vettiano nefario stupro," or whether their act was a subsequent disgraceful act (*flagitium*) taken to avenge it. "Nempe quod eiusdem mulieris dolorem et iniuriam Vettiano nefario sunt stupro persecuti." Cicero, *pro Caelio* 71. Nevertheless, the context in which the reference comes up indicates that in any case the precedent of their case was being used as one for using *vis* legislation to cover charges involving immorality. See Austin's Commentary, 133–34 and Michael Grant's translation and footnote in Michael Grant, *Selected Political Speeches of Cicero* (New York, 1985), 209. Cf. Lintott, *Violence,* 119, 217. It is clear that the episode had something to do with Caelius' former mistress ("that woman" in Cicero, *pro Caelio* 71), the infamous Clodia. See Austin, 133. Cf. Lintott's rather flat interpretation that Vettius' *stuprum* was his informing on Clodius of his association with Catiline. Lintott, *Violence,* 119, 217.

[53] Austin, 133.

[54] Austin, Introduction, viii. It is difficult to know whether this implies that Cicero's argument against using a statute *de vi* to cover *stuprum* actually worked, or whether Caelius was acquitted for some other reason (for example, because the particular technical charges against him could not be proved, or because of some "political" reason), and the issue was of particular moment only for Cicero, because of his trial strategy of focusing on Caelius' morality (indeed, actually, on Clodia's immorality).

[55] Austin sees an "undoubted tendency of the time to widen the official scope of the [*vis*] law." Austin, Appendix V, 153. Indeed, it appears that this tendency was not so much to include issues of private morality under the heading *vis publica,* but to use the statute to root out politically motivated, "subversive" activity dangerous to the Republic by somehow characterizing it as "violence." See Austin, Commentary on sec. 1, sentence 2, on p. 42. We know that the late Republic saw the passage of a number of laws concerning *vis,* apparently in response to the threat of gangs, and that various incarnations of these laws were successfully used against seditious conspiracies such as Catiline's and gangsters such as Milo. Cicero, *pro Caelio* 70, sentence 4; Lintott, *Violence,* esp. chap. 8; Austin's commentary on 1.7 and citations therein.

[56] "M. Camurti et C. Caeserni damnatio." Cicero, *pro Caelio* 70.

they were so deeply into illegal activity that any law would have seemed to apply—that they seemed to have broken all laws[57]—and is at pains to point out that their "disgraceful act" (*flagitium*) was far more serious than anything having to do with his client.[58] Thus, Cicero's rhetorical and adversarial smokescreen makes it difficult to know for certain the extent to which the use of the *vis* law to cover their case was part of a trend, and Cicero's syntax makes it difficult to know whether the act for which Camurtius and Caesernius were convicted was technically one of *stuprum*.[59] Nevertheless, it remains true, regardless of what lies behind these obfuscations, that the way in which the case of Camurtius and Caesernius was apparently used by Caelius' prosecutors, if not the way in which that case actually used the *vis* legislation, and the way in which this use was rebutted by Cicero reflects that it was a conceptually plausible thing to try to use *vis* legislation to cover immoral sexual behavior: *vis* and immorality could be connected through the ambiguous concept of *stuprum*.

It is tempting to think that the attempt to use *vis* legislation to prosecute Camurtius and Caesernius succeeded because their (sexual) crime involved actual force, whereas Caelius' alleged offense, as Cicero argued, was merely one of (sexual) immorality (and, of course, untrue at that). Cicero may have been arguing that while *raptus* might have come to be interpreted as including *per vim stuprum*, it did not nevertheless include (consensual) *stuprum*. And without a positive law to subsume customary notions of morally correct behavior, Cicero and his fellow Romans could continue to maintain a distinction between illegality and immorality.[60]

---

[57] "Qui quamquam lege de vi certe non tenebantur, eo maleficio tamen erant implicati ut ex nullius legis laqueis eximendi viderentur." Cicero, *pro Caelio* 71. Perhaps the chief offense of the condemned was meant, by Caelius' defense, to be seen as having acted on Clodia's behalf; this would carry further the apparent subtext of the social feud between Caelius and Clodia in the case, which seems to have involved successive rounds of accusations of immorality.

[58] Cicero, *pro Caelio* 71.

[59] And not something else (*flagitium*), which of course might equally plausibly have involved sexual misconduct.

[60] Cicero links but distinguishes the offense of *stuprum* from the crime of *vis* in a passage in the *de Legibus* in which he, perhaps not coincidentally, uses the example of Tarquin to contrast Tarquin's offense against positive legislation concerning *stuprum* with his crime against natural law by his use of *vis:* "Even if while Lucius Tarquin reigned there was no written law on *stuprum* at Rome, we cannot say on that

Attempts to extend the category *raptus* to include sexual immorality per se, that is, *stuprum* without force, by means of expansive interpretation and application of existing laws in the courts were thus apparently unsuccessful. So also it seems that an attempt in 28 B.C. to expand the law's involvement in regulating the morality of behavior[61] failed. Augustus apparently attempted unsuccessfully to introduce legislation to implement his program of moral reform in 28 B.C.[62] Propertius seems to allude to Augustus' attempt in 28 B.C., with relief at its failure,[63] and Livy himself seems to comment indirectly, and morosely, on this controversial failure of Augustus' in his preface to his history of Rome.[64] Livy writes:

---

account that Sextus Tarquin's using force against Lucretia was not against that Everlasting Law . . ." ("Nec, si regnante L. Tarquinio nulla erat Romae scripta lex de stupris, idcirco non contra illam legem sempiternam Sex. Tarquinius vim Lucretiae, Tricipitini filiae, attulit."). Cicero, *de Legibus* II.4.10.

[61] This attempt may have tried to bring *stuprum* within the ambit of recent public law by means of legislation. Even if the legislation only encompassed marriage rules, perhaps it was the first step in a planned, general program. See Gordon Williams, *Tradition and Originality in Roman Poetry* (Oxford, 1968, 1985) (hereafter *TORP*), 532 and Williams, "Moral Climate." Williams seems to see the attempt in 28 B.C. as broader than mere marriage legislation. On previous use of public law in such matters, cf. prosecution by aedile for charge of *stuprum:* Livy, VIII.22.2 (*crimine stupratae matris familiae*), 25.2.9; Plutarch, *Marcellus* 2; Valerius Maximus VI.1.7; maybe Livy, X.31.9, discussed in Lintott, *Violence,* 97 ff; note also *Collatio* 4.2.2 and Gardner, *Women in Roman Law and Society,* 121–23 and Treggiari, *Roman Marriage,* 277.

[62] Note that even Syme, who would downplay the possibility of references in Livy's preface to early Augustan moral legislation, sees Augustus' moral policy as predating his actual "programme." Ronald Syme, "Livy and Augustus," *Harvard Studies in Classical Philology* 64 (1959), 27–87, 54. See Williams, "Moral Climate," and *TORP,* 532. Cf. Ernst Badian, "A Phantom Marriage Law," *Philologus* 129 (1985), 82–98. For broader discussion of sources see P. Jörs, "Die Ehegesetze des Augustus," in *Festschrift Theodor Mommsen zum fünfzigjährigen Doctorjubiläum* (Marburg, 1893), 1–65; *CAH* X, 441 ff; Raditsa, "Augustus' Legislation," 295 ff.

[63] Propertius, *Elegiae* II.7. See, e.g., Williams, "Moral Climate," 28, *TORP,* 531 ff. Cf. Badian, "Phantom Marriage Law," for rejection of this interpretation of Propertius (and of other supporting evidence as well). However, note that even Syme concedes that the Propertius poem indicates that a law had at least been "proposed." Syme, "Livy and Augustus," 42.

[64] See Williams for the persuasive argument that these comments in Livy's preface refer to Augustus' failed moral legislation of 28 B.C. and not to "'order and concord.'" Williams, "Moral Climate," 33–34, quoting Syme, "Livy and Augustus,"

Next let him track how *mores,* with *disciplina* slipping little by little, first, as it were, were crumbling, next that they had slipped more and more, then that they had begun to fall headlong, until to these times, in which we are able to stand neither our vices nor remedies, to these points, he, and we, have come.[65]

A few sentences later, Livy comments more directly and specifically on contemporary *vitia,* including *libido:*

For the less material wealth there was, the less greed; lately wealth has brought in avarice, and overflowing pleasures have brought in longing, by means of excessive behavior and lustful appetite (*libidinem*), for self-annihilation and destruction of everything.[66]

Indeed, such a program was also apparently in the air even before Octavian came to power; Caesar is known to have given incentives to encourage the birthrate and Cicero is known to have advocated (to Caesar) reform, including the restraint of (dissolute) sexual appetites.[67]

---

42 ff. See Hermann Dessau, "Die Vorrede des Livius," in *Festschrift zu Otto Hirschfelds sechzigstem Geburtstage* (1903), 461 ff, for the origin of this interpretation. See also Karl Galinsky, "Augustus' Legislation on Morals and Marriage," *Philologus* 125 (1981), 126–44, 129 and 132, concurring with Williams. Cf. Syme, "Livy and Augustus," 42 ff, 49–50 (whose explication of Livy's preface as referring to political stability is what is being refuted by Williams in "Moral Climate," 33–34, and, in any case, makes Livy's allusion seem awfully wooden and crude) and Badian, "Phantom Marriage Law," 92 ff (who finds it "difficult to see" "[w]hy this very general—and very Roman—epigrammatic complaint should be thus defined in what might well seem excessively limited terms."). See also Ogilvie, *Commentary,* 28, endorsing the view that Livy is reacting to failed moral legislation by Augustus.

[65] ". . . labente deinde paulatim disciplina velut desidentes primo mores sequatur animo, deinde ut magis magisque lapsi sint, tum ire coeperint praecipites, donec ad haec tempora quibus nec vitia nostra nec remedia pati possumus perventum est." Livy, *praefatio* 9.

[66] "Adeo quanto rerum minus, tanto minus cupiditas erat: nuper divitiae avaritiam et abundantes voluptates desiderium per luxum atque libidinem pereundi perdendique omnia invexere." Livy, *praef.* 12. These passages not only give evidence of failed attempts to correct Rome's moral ills, but also evidence that Livy was himself concerned with the perceived moral problems of his day and (Augustus') attempts to remedy them. See below.

[67] Cicero, *pro Marcello* 23. See William's discussion, "Moral Climate," 29 and sources cited therein. See also Williams' analysis of the similarity of the pessimistic moralizing by Republican historians to the basis underlying the Augustan moral legislation. Williams, *TORP,* 632–33.

It took Augustus' *lex Julia de adulteriis coercendis* of 18 B.C., which explicitly criminalized consensual *stuprum*, to penalize sexual misconduct, and this legislation did so on moral rather than public safety grounds, although like the earlier *vis* legislation, the ultimate justification for its intervention was the welfare of the common weal.[68] And like Livy's comments on earlier failed attempts at reform, Horace voiced doubts about the effectiveness of such external methods for producing moral behavior.[69]

Even within Augustus' "successful" legislation and its application there is evidence of continued difficulty in separating forcible from consensual *stuprum* and treating them differently. This was so, despite the simple hornbook statement in Justinian's *Institutes* that the law punished "the disgraceful act of *stuprum*, when someone has committed *stuprum* without force against a maiden or a widow living honestly."[70] There is, on the one hand, a quotation from the statute itself in the *Digest* stating that it was *stuprum* and *adulterium* committed *sciens dolo malo* that was being proscribed: " 'Let no one hereafter commit *stuprum* or adultery knowingly and with bad faith (*dolo malo*).' "[71] On the other hand, there is in the *Digest* also evidence of an apparent "wartime force exception" (and here one might recall Lucretia's characterization of Tarquin as an enemy) to prosecution of women for *stuprum* under Augustus' law: an exception[72] was made for women who had engaged in what would have otherwise been *stuprum* or *adulterium*, but who were, at the time, in the hands of the enemy and had been subjected to force by the enemy in the event.[73] The contours of this "wartime force exception" are difficult to

---

[68] See Lintott, *Violence*, 121.

[69] See below.

[70] Justinian's *Institutes* 4.18.4: "sed eadem lege Iulia etiam stupri flagitium punitur, cum quis sine vi vel virginem vel viduam honeste viventem stupraverit." See also *CJ* 9.9.20.

[71] *D.* 48.5.13(12): "Haec verba legis 'ne quis posthac stuprum adulterium facito sciens dolo malo' et ad eum, qui suasit, et ad eum, qui stuprum vel adulterium intulit, pertinent."

[72] The issue of force would be raised by the woman as a defense, somewhat analogous to the *exceptio* of *metus* (and *vis*) in private law actions before the praetor. See discussion below.

[73] This recognition of force in the event was perhaps inferred from the overall circumstances, from the woman's general loss of freedom and free will while in enemy hands. N.b., for example, the rules of *postliminium*, on which see *D.* 49.15. See also *rapio* as a taking into captivity, discussed above. Perhaps the resultant rule relieving women who have been forced to have sex during wartime captivity is similar to the

discern from the meager evidence, but what has survived does suggest that a vexed attempt was being made to overcome the presumption that sexual relations outside of war were consensual.

A text by Ulpian, making a procedural point concerning the circumstances under which the mechanism of the husband's right of prosecution under the *lex Julia de adulteriis* may be used, testifies to the "wartime force exception":

> If someone should prove clearly that his wife, while she was in enemy hands, committed adultery, we hold with the kinder rule that he be able to accuse her by a husband's right; but the husband will only be able to exact punishment for adultery in this way if she did not suffer force from the enemy; otherwise, she who suffers force is not covered by this, so that she is not condemned for adultery or *stuprum*.[74]

The context of being in enemy hands in the passage is interesting because there, while the exception seems to be based conceptually on the notion of will, the wartime context seems to imply that willingness will be presumed outside of war. That *stuprum* was not normally thought of as forcible sex outside of a wartime context and had to be qualified in other cases in order to be so thought seems to lie behind another Ulpian passage, *D.* 3.1.1.6. This text gives two contexts, robbery and war, for "*vi. . .stupratus*," and it could well be that the former had been an extension of the latter, the underlying principle being that a previous global deprivation of freedom will be taken to prove a lack of consent in a particular transaction. Such a principle would also explain the development of a category of *per vim stuprum* within the category *raptus*.[75]

---

concept that slaves lacked moral responsibility for sex initiated by a free man. Treggiari, *Roman Marriage*, 301.

[74] "Si quis plane uxorem suam, cum apud hostes esset, adulterium commisisse arguat, benignius dicetur posse eum accusare iure viri: sed ita demum adulterium maritus vindicabit, si vim hostium passa non est: ceterum quae vim patitur, non est in ea causa, ut adulterii vel stupri damnetur." *D.* 48.5.14(13).7 (Ulpian, Book 2 *de adulteriis*).

[75] There are admittedly two passages that do not, at least as we have them, mention context, war or otherwise. One of these, *D.* 48.5.30(29).9, is about relative lengths of statutes of limitation for prosecutions under the *lex Julia de adulteriis* and prosecutions under the *lex Julia de vi publica*, so it is not surprising that details concerning the substance of the charge are not mentioned. *D.* 48.8.1.4, an excerpt from Marcian, lists defending oneself or a family member against someone "*stuprum . . .*

It is not clear why an explicit "wartime force exception" should have been necessary to avoid conviction under the *lex Julia de adulteriis* if a necessary element of the crime was some sort of wrongful intent (*sciens dolo*

---

per vim inferentem" as a defense to a charge of murder by virtue of a rescript by Hadrian and does not mention context. That this should have required, even for Marcian and the compilers of the *Digest,* the authority of an imperial rescript from the 2d century A.D. is not inconsistent with peacetime *per vim stuprum* being treated as an extension of wartime *stuprum:* in war, especially one with a foreign enemy, a charge of murder for killing the enemy would not arise.

There is one other passage in the *Digest,* a passage which technically only applies to married women, that seems to indicate that the wartime context was not crucial to this "wartime force exception." The passage relates Papinian's *responsum* that a woman against whom *vis* had, according to the judgment of a provincial governor, been committed had not violated the *lex Julia de adulteriis* although she had forbidden her *iniuria* be told to her husband. ("Vim passam mulierem sententia praesidis provinciae continebatur: in lege*m* Julia*m* de adulteriis non commisisse respondi, licet injuriam suam protegendae pudicitiae causa confestim marito renuntiari prohibuit.") *D.* 48.5.40(39).pr. (Papinian, Book 15, *responsa*). That the *vis* is of a sexual nature is indicated by the fact that the issue is whether the woman has violated the *lex Julia de adulteriis,* but perhaps it is significant that the episode is referred to as "vis" itself: there was no ambiguity about it and any presumption of consent had been already rebutted.

Literary texts provide some confirmation of this apparent "wartime force exception" of the legal texts. It is striking that the uses of the phrase *per vim stuprum,* or some variation of it, by authors other than Livy (when they are not referring to Lucretia: Cicero, *de Legibus* 2.10, *de Finibus* 2.66, 5.64) and even by Livy himself in episodes other than the story of Lucretia and the story of Virginia, occur in war contexts (Livy, 38.24.3, Tacitus, *Historiae* 2.56), or refer to another context in which free will has been removed by the general circumstances (Livy, 39.10.7—Bacchic rites as corrupt cult). Moreover, even in the stories of Lucretia and Virginia, the war motif creeps in. In the story of Virginia, Virginia's father likens what Appius intends to do to Virginia as that which is done in war: "What's the use if even while the city is safe, things which are feared as the most extreme when a city has been captured must be suffered by their children?" ("Quid prodesse si, incolumi urbe, quae capta ultima timeantur liberis suis sint patienda.") Livy, III.47.2. In the story of Lucretia, the comparison is more subtle, and is done by means of a metaphor. The narrator uses the verb *expugno* to allude to the act of forcible sex against Lucretia, and then uses the same verb to describe what Brutus vows to do as an act of revenge. Livy, I.58.5, I.59.2. For the Romans, then, it seems, forcible sex happened in a war context (or a context that had the attributes of war) and was significant for the power and violence of the perpetrator. Sex outside of marriage in peacetime, within the proverbial safety

malo).[76] However, regardless of what the particular prosecutorial scheme under the statute was, it seems beyond doubt that the detail of subjective states of mind of the participants to the transaction were brought into issue, that the objective fact of accomplishment was not the only or sufficient criterion, and that this detail did not fit easily into legal thinking and categories.

Middle Grounds in Coerced Consent in Other Areas of Roman Law

Even the notion that *dolus malus* was a legally significant factor in assessing a situation was an innovation in many ways parallel to and as recent (if not more so) as the view in Roman legal thinking that *vis* was a legally relevant factor.[77] The notion had in fact been developed as part of the praetor's *ius honorarium* to modify, in effect, the strict operation of the objectively oriented civil law (*ius civile*).[78] Cicero tells us that his friend and colleague the distinguished jurist and praetor Gaius Aquilius Gallus had introduced *formulae de dolo malo*.[79] The categories of the strict Roman civil law (*ius civile*)

---

of the woman's (husband's) home, was presumed to be consensual and was significant for the shame it caused the woman and her family.

[76] Treggiari's treatment of this inconsistency attempts to see the "wartime force exception" as an example of the need for wrongful intent. Treggiari, *Roman Marriage*, 279. However, this approach does not explain why judicial interpretation should have been necessary (and uncertain enough to be submitted by a provincial governor to an eminent jurist) to create the exception if the actual words of the statute provided a basis for relieving women who had been forced to have sex while in enemy hands; this would be especially so since such circumstances would seem to constitute one of the easiest cases for finding force and hence a lack of wrongful intent.

[77] See Cicero, *Epistulae ad Quintum Fratrem* I.1.21 from the end of 60 B.C., dating some form of remedy for dispossession *per vim et metum* to the situation created by the actions of the *Sullani homines,* the "'men of Sulla.'" The evidence concerns official recognition of the legal relevance of such factors, but it is also entirely possible that such factors, involving subjective detail, were already being considered "behind the scenes" by *iudices* in their determinations of fact and their application of the praetor's instruction to those facts.

[78] "Iam illis promissis standum non esse quis non videt, quae coactus quis metu, quae deceptus dolo promiserit? Quae quidem pleraque iure praetorio liberantur, non nulla legibus." ("Moreover, who does not see that those promises which were made by someone coerced by fear or deceived by a trick are not to stand? In fact most of these are released by praetorian law or some legislation.") Cicero, *de Officiis* I.10.32.

[79] "Nondum enim C. Aquilius, collega et familiaris meus, protulerat de dolo malo formulas." Cicero, *de Officiis* III.14.60.

did not admit of such fine distinctions, and it required the judicial intervention of the praetor or legislative modification by the assemblies (*comitia*) to bring such considerations as the subjective state of mind of a party into the evaluation of the legal sufficiency of his or her act.[80]

Like the chancellor's equity in Anglo-American law, the praetor's remedy operated on the individuals, not on the rules, although of course in effect it modified if not annulled the rules: the praetor would simply give a defense to the victim of the coercion if sued by the coercer, or give a penal action to the victim in order to recover from the coercer if the coercer did not restore the situation voluntarily, or treat the victim as if the victim had not made the coerced transaction, or provide for *restitutio in integrum,* restoration to one's previous intact state.[81] Thus, the praetor's selective enforcement of legal rights in effect modified them, and his announcement was, "I will not hold valid what has been accomplished as a result of force or duress,"[82] although what he would do in fact was to provide an overlay of remedial adjustments on top of the technically legally sufficiently accomplished transaction.

A nice text included in the *Digest* demonstrates how the praetor could intervene in transactions involving coerced consent. Its source also contains a glimpse of the Roman legal thinking that apparently lay behind this praetorian attitude of "the transaction stands but we gut its consequences." The area of law is inheritance, the issue the validity of a compelled acceptance or repudiation of an inheritance. The text is from Paulus, commenting on the praetor's edict:

> If coerced by duress I have entered upon an inheritance, I think that I am made (become) heir because although if it had been a free choice I would not have willed it (and refused), nevertheless, *coactus volui*— while being compelled, I willed it. But I am to be restored to my original position through the praetor, so that the power of refraining (from entering upon the inheritance) is granted to me. If I am compelled to refuse to enter upon an inheritance, the praetor helps me in two ways, either by giving me a praetorian action as if I were heir or

[80] Cicero, *de Officiis* I.10.32, above.

[81] See *Gai Institutionum, The Institutes of Gaius,* ed. Francis De Zulueta, Part I (Oxford, 1946), IV.116a, 117; *D.* 4.2.14.1, *D.* 4.2.21.6, *D.* 4.2 generally.

[82] "Ait praetor: 'Quod vi metusve causa gestum erit, ratum non habebo.'" From *D.* 4.2.1.

by providing me with an action on account of duress, so that whichever way I pick is open to me.[83]

From this it seems that Roman legal thinking[84] could construe coercion as in fact directing the victim's will where otherwise it would not have run, as opposed to thwarting what others might call the victim's "real," subjective intent. Similar thinking is made even more explicit in a text in the *Digest* involving formation of marriage.[85] Here, attributed to Celsus, is the articulation of the principle *maluisse hoc videtur,* reasoned as follows:

> If with his father coercing him he marries someone whom he would not have married if it had been for him to decide, nevertheless he has made marriage, because marriage is not made between unwilling par-

[83] "Si metu coactus adii hereditatem, puto me heredem effici, quia quamvis si liberum esset noluissem, tamen coactus volui: sed per praetorem restituendus sum, ut abstinendi mihi potestas tribuatur. Si coactus hereditatem repudiem, duplici via praetor mihi succurrit aut utiles actiones quasi heredi dando aut actionem metus causa praestando, ut quam viam ego elegerim, haec mihi pateat." *D.* 4.2.21.5–6.

[84] The notion that although compelled one still willed the action was apparently of great antiquity and occurs in literary as well as legal texts—Terence seems to quote a maxim based on it. See below. See also Charles Appleton, "Trois épisodes de l'histoire ancienne de Rome: Les Sabines, Lucrèce, Virginie," *Revue historique de droit français et étranger,* 4e sér. (1924), 193–271 and 592–670, 264.

[85] The situation there is much more legally complex since it involves coercion of a son by his father. If the son involved was a *filiusfamilias* (as is the son in the directly preceding text, *D.* 23.2.21), this case would have implicated a whole nexus of legal factors arising out of the system of relative rights, duties, privileges, and responsibilities between people already joined in a relationship recognized at the level of legal status, in which one person had power (*imperium* or *potestas*) over the other even before the actual coercive order at issue. If the son was not in power, the case would have at least implicated a complex nexus of ethical and social licenses and obligations. Something like this is expressed in *D.* 43.30.1.5: concerning a father who wishes to dissolve the harmonious marriage of his daughter, "et certo iure utimur, ne bene concordantia matrimonia iure patriae potestatis turbentur. Quod tamen sic erit adhibendum, ut patri persuadeatur, ne acerbe patriam potestatem exerceat." ("Yes we make use of the fixed authority [*ius*] that nicely harmonious marriages should not be disturbed by the authority [*ius*] of *patria potestas*. This, however, is to be put into practice in this way by persuading the father not to exercise his *patria potestas* harshly.") Note also that, in the case of marriage, divorce rather than praetorian restitution would have been the "remedy." W. W. Buckland, *A Text-book of Roman Law from Augustus to Justinian,* 3rd ed., ed. Peter Stein (Cambridge, 1963), 720.

ties: he is held to have preferred this course of action (*maluisse hoc videtur*).[86]

In the case of coerced marriage formation, the analysis may be developed further, since Celsus'[87] position can be juxtaposed against the superficially contradictory text directly previous to it (attributed to Terentius Clemens), which says that "a *filiusfamilias* is not compelled to marry." ("Non cogitur filius familias uxorem ducere.")[88]

There are a number of ways of resolving the apparent contradiction of the adjacent coerced marriage formation texts. If *cogitur* is translated as the simple passive "is not compelled," rather than as "cannot be compelled," as it has often been translated,[89] then the passage is not necessarily at all at odds

---

[86] "Si patre cogente ducit uxorem, quam non duceret, si sui arbitrii esset, contraxit tamen matrimonium, quod inter invitos non contrahitur: maluisse hoc videtur." *D.* 23.2.22. It is worth noting that the inclusion in the praetor's edict *Qui ne dent cognitorem* of the case in which the son has married at the *iussum* of his father (see Alan Watson, *The Law of Persons in the Later Roman Republic* [Oxford, 1967], 41 ff) indicates that it was recognized that filial consent did not always originate with the son himself, and perhaps that (therefore) such consent was not always genuine.

[87] But n.b. *D.* 29.2.6.7, in which Celsus is apparently alleged by Ulpian to take a position at odds with the position taken in *D.* 23.2.22, that if a freeman is coerced into entering upon an inheritance it is held (*placet*) that he does not become heir. This text is apparently contradictory to the coerced heir text from Paulus but is of little help in this discussion because it adds nothing to the understanding of the concepts being accepted or rejected but in any case used by Roman legal thinkers. Furthermore, the text is thought to be corrupt in a number of places (see Mommsen's apparatus criticus, Ernest Levy and Ernst Rabel, *Index Interpolationum quae in Iustiniani Digestis inesse dicuntur,* II [Weimar, 1931], col. 210, Buckland, 315 note 8): "Celsus libro quinto decimo digestorum scripsit eum, qui metu uerborum uel aliquo timore coactus fallens adierit hereditatem, siue liber sit, heredem non fieri placet, siue seruus sit, dominum heredem non facere." ("Celsus has written in the fifteenth book of his *Digest* that it is agreed that he who, coerced by fear of words [lashes?] or some terror, mistakenly entered upon the inheritance, if he be free, does not become heir, if he be a slave, does not make his master heir.") *D.* 29.2.6.7.

[88] *D.* 23.2.21 (*Terentius Clemens libro tertio ad legem Iuliam et Papiam*).

[89] See translation in *The Digest of Justinian,* ed. Alan Watson (Philadelphia, 1985) and Charles Donahue, Jr., "The Case of the Man Who Fell into the Tiber: The Roman Law of Marriage at the Time of the Glossators," *American Journal of Legal History* 22 (1978), 1–53, 10. See also Susan Treggiari, "Consent to Roman Marriage: Some Aspects of Law and Reality," *Échos du monde classique / Classical Views* 26, n.s. 1 (1982), 34–44, 43. Compare the use of "cogitur" in *D.* 23.2.21 with the construction "cogi potest" in *CJ* 5.4.14, which communicates a normative proscription

with the Celsus passage. However, the Terentius Clemens passage may merely be saying that a son is not compelled to marry, and the situation that gave rise to this pronouncement may simply not have been included, but have been nothing more than the observation that the "*lex Julia et Papia*" (the "law" on which the passage is apparently a comment) did not absolutely require such a marriage although it would reward one and penalize its absence. If this is the case, then it is possible that the Celsus passage following it was seen by the compilers of the *Digest* as perfectly compatible with it; it would explain the next type of case, that in which the *paterfamilias* and not the law was the coercive force at issue. *CJ* 5.4.12 makes a similar point:

> Not even an unwilling *filiusfamilias* does the teaching of the laws allow to be forced to marry. Therefore, as you desire, with the precepts of law having been complied with, you are not impeded from marrying the woman you wish so long as your father's consent accedes to the marriage to be contracted.[90]

In the case considered in *D*. 23.2.22, in which the son did do something that looked like entering into a marriage (as opposed to the previous case in which the son did nothing and could not be punished for having done so), the law would infer the son's consent despite the father's coercive role.[91]

---

against coercing consent in the formation of marriage more explicitly. The context here is to provide a basis for the more difficult case of whether it is proper for the power to form or dissolve a marriage to be foisted upon (perhaps inferred from) necessity. "Neque ab initio matrimonium contrahere neque dissociatum reconciliare quisquam cogi potest. unde intellegis liberam facultatem contrahendi atque distrahendi matrimonii transferri ad necessitatem non oportere." *CJ* 5.4.14. This text is consistent with the interpretation of the Roman chronologically contingent "doctrine" of coerced marriage laid out below.

[90] "Ne filium quidem familias invitum ad ducendam uxorem cogi legum disciplina permittit. igitur, sicut desideras, observatis iuris praeceptis sociare coniugio tuo quam volueris non impediris, ita tamen, ut in contrahendis nuptiis patris tui consensus accedat."

[91] Although it is true that *D*. 23.2.21 refers explicitly to the son as being in the *patria potestas* of his father while *D*. 23.2.22 does not, it does not seem very helpful to distinguish the texts on that basis since it would mean concluding that fathers could compel their emancipated sons but not their sons under their *potestas* to marry. One could also focus on the difference in the texts that in *D*. 23.2.21 there is no particular bride in mind, just a general order to marry, while in *D*. 23.2.22 the father has a particular bride in mind for his son, but this distinction is better viewed as a particular case of the more fundamental distinction made by the texts about the point in time at

The best way to resolve the apparent contradiction between the adjacent coerced marriage formation texts *D*. 23.2.22 and 21 is to distinguish them by noting that they refer to different points in time at which the validity of the marriage is brought into question. This line of distinction is in fact supported by other texts in the *Digest* in which it is indicated that different remedies will be available depending upon the point in the history of the transaction that the dispute is raised.[92] The argument goes like this: practical consideration is given to whether people have already relied on the (coerced) consent's being effective and the transaction's having been accomplished, so that in effect, while coercing consent is forbidden, if "consent" is successfully obtained through coercion, the marriage stands despite the prohibition against

---

which the issue of the validity of the compelled consent is raised. Donahue tries gamely to reconcile the two *Digest* passages on the grounds that in the Celsus passage *cogere* means to urge while in the Terentius Clemens passage it means to compel. Donahue, "Tiber," 10, including note 42 and citation therein. Treggiari seems to accept the contradiction in the passages, seeing it as a reflection of "the old tension" between a father's power over his son's marriage choice through his *patria potestas* and the role of the son's consent in establishing the marriage. Treggiari, "Consent to Marriage," 43. There is also evidence that the concept of valid coerced consent to marriage embodied in *D*. 23.2.22 would have been familiar to Romans from literature, whatever its perhaps foreign (Greek) origins in this context. The playwright Terence seems to quote a well-known but probably translated tag that supports the notion that a man could be compelled by law to take a wife: " 'Coactus legibus / eam uxorem ducet.' " Terence, *Andria* 780–81. He invokes a similar idea in the *Adelphoe*, although here the coerced party is the bride and seems to refer to the certainly Greek rules regulating the marriage of an ἐπίκληρος (heiress): "Haec virgo orbast patre; / hic meus amicus illi genere est proximus: / huic leges cogunt nubere hanc." Terence, *Adelphoe* 650–52. In a third play Terence seems to allude to a maxim endorsing the opposite point of view, that coercion does not imply willingness: "*GE.:* vi coactum te esse invitum. *PH.:* lege, iudicio." Terence, *Phormio* 214.

[92] *D*. 4.2.9.2–3 (whether one gets a defense or one can also bring an action seems to depend on whether the matter has been completed or not—but the emperor's rescript seems to say that one can get both, says Ulpian; the time frame may also dictate substantive relief—i.e., whether the transaction stands or not—indirectly, by dictating the type of penalty, injunctive relief or damages; thus, substantive rights may be defined by the workings of procedure); *D*. 44.4.1.pr. ("intra quae tempora competit exceptio," with respect to when one may bring a defense of *dolus malus, metus* [query whether this time frame referred to is in regard to a statute of limitations or to the point in time in the transaction]).

coercing consent. Thus, if this way of thinking is applied to the apparent contradiction in the coerced marriage formation texts *D.* 23.2.21 and 22, the two passages, rather than contradict each other or refer to different types of sons or coercion, are both true and complementary, referring to different points in time in relation to a marriage in which the groom's consent is coerced: in the one, the groom's consent is never obtained, and in the other it is, there is some objective manifestation that a marriage has taken place, and this is not challenged until later.[93]

This attitude that a deed may be proscribed but yet if accomplished is valid is analogous to that of a *lex imperfecta* in Roman law, which forbids something from being done but does not rescind or penalize the activity if the law is contravened and the activity is done, or a *lex minus quam perfecta* in which the activity is not rescinded but the successful but wrongdoing accomplisher is in fact penalized. This schema is attested in a reconstructed text from the post-classical "Ulpian's *Regulae.*" According to this:

> '<*Leges* are either *perfectae, imperfectae* or *minus quam perfectae*. A *lex perfecta* (perfect statute) is one which forbids something to be done and if it be done rescinds it. . . . A *lex imperfecta* (imperfect statute) is one which forbids something to be done, and if it be done neither rescinds it nor imposes a penalty on him who has acted contrary to the law . . . . > (2) A *lex minus quam perfecta* (statute less than perfect) is one which forbids something to be done, and if it be

---

[93] See also Josef Huber, *Der Ehekonsens im Römischen Recht* (Rome, 1977), 110 note 29, for the idea that the distinction between the two texts lies in whether the father succeeded by coercion in getting his son to "consent," and O. Robleda, *El matrimonio en derecho romano* (Rome, 1970), 105–6. *CJ* 5.4.14 is consistent with a chronologically contingent doctrine of coerced marriage since it espouses a general prescriptive norm that the formation (and dissolution) of marriages cannot be coerced and does not address what the consequences are if it has. Note also that a successful *raptus* made at least some Romans wonder whether the *rapta* had indeed consented or even colluded in entering into a marriage not arranged and sanctioned by parents. E.g., Seneca, *Controversiae* II.3.17 (although here it is the consent and possible collusion of her father that seem mainly to be at issue), VII.8.6, and VIII.6 and *Codex Theodosianus,* ed. Th. Mommsen, I.2 (hereafter *CTh*) (Berlin, 1905; repr. Hildesheim, 1990), 9.24.1 (suggesting that she could have prevented her *raptus*—e.g., had she screamed sufficiently, help would have arrived). One also wonders whether the "law" in Seneca allowing the *rapta* the choice of marrying her *raptor* and Justinian's pains to forbid this apparent "custom" in *CJ* 9.13 reflect a similar inference that the woman may have consented.

done does not rescind it but imposes a penalty on him who has acted contrary to the statute.'[94]

Thus, in the case of marriage formed under coercion, the rule underlying the marriage text *D.* 23.2.22 would be classified as analogous to a *lex imperfecta,* while the case of the heir coerced into entering upon the inheritance in *D.* 4.2.21.5 would be analogous to a *lex minus quam perfecta.*

The rationale for proceeding along these lines and upholding the coerced transaction in these cases is interesting and leads back to the discussion of how the law approached its role in limiting *vis* and *stuprum.* Defective transactions upon which others have subsequently relied are upheld when voiding the transaction would cause more trouble for more people than having it stand.[95] For the context of defective consent to marriage, there is a passage from "Paul's *Sententiae*" about defective parental consent that displays this attitude explicitly:

> Marriages of those who are in their father's *patria potestas* are not legally contracted without the willingness of their father, but having been contracted they are not undone: for consideration of *publica utilitas* is preferred to the *commoda* of private individuals.[96]

---

[94] "1. . . . . prohibet, exceptis quibusdam cognatis, et si plus donatum sit, non rescind*i*t. 2. Minus quam perfecta lex est quae vetat aliquid fieri, et si factum sit, non rescind*i*t, sed poenam iniungit et qui contra legem fecit: qualis est lex Furia testamentaria, quae plus quam mille as*s*ium legatum mortisve causa prohibet capere, praeter exceptas personas, et adversus eum qui plus ceperit quadrupli poena*m* constituit." Ulpian, *Liber singularis regularum,* pr., 1–2, text from *Fontes Iuris Romani Anteiustiniani,* II, *Auctores* (hereafter *FIRA*), ed. J. Baviera (Florence, 1940), 262, reconstructed by Cujas, translated in A. Arthur Schiller, *Roman Law: Mechanisms of Development* (The Hague, 1978), 247.

[95] This attitude pervades, for example, the rules governing contractual liability and benefit, and acquisition and alienation of property in business transactions (especially where slaves are parties) in Roman law, situations in which Anglo-American law would infer "agency."

[96] "Eorum qui in potestate patris sunt sine voluntate ejus matrimonia jure non contrahuntur, sed contracta non solvuntur: contemplatio enim publicae utilitatis privatorum commodis praefertur." *Pauli Sententiae* 2.19.2 from *FIRA,* 345. *Pace* Scott's translation in S. P. Scott, *The Civil Law,* I (Cincinnati, 1932), 276 and the attempt by Corbett to limit the passage's meaning by hedging it with qualifications as to the circumstances under which it applies: Percy Ellwood Corbett, *The Roman Law of Marriage* (Oxford, 1930), 62.

Public convenience, expedience, the common good, is more important than individuals' interests and advantages. For the area of the praetor's *restitutio in integrum* (for example, for transactions accomplished through force or duress), there is a text expressing a similar sentiment, *D.* 4.1.4, which, while about the practical application of the "rules" and not their underlying theory, discloses openly what competing interests the praetor probably took into account in developing the rules for relief originally:

> I know that it has been the practice of some magistrates not to hear a person who asks for *restitutio in integrum* in respect of a very trivial matter or sum, if this would prejudice a claim in respect of a more substantial matter or sum.[97]

Here the calculus is not only in terms of expediency, but this expediency is even reduced to mercenary, rather than social, values.

The preservation of the common good, the welfare of the *Res Publica*, was the benchmark for deciding whether a prosecution for *vis*[98] was appropriate, according to Cicero in the *pro Milone*,[99] and according to the biographical and autobiographical accounts for Augustus, Augustus' ostensible rationale for his package of moral legislation, of which the *lex de adulteriis* which criminalized consensual *stuprum* was a part, was the strengthening of Roman society by returning to traditional values and customs for the sake of Rome and her future.[100] There was thus in all cases an exploration of the "middle ground" between complete approval and total rejection of the act, and, in all cases, a decision that how to proceed in this exploration and what consequences to give the act should be guided by public policy in terms of the common good. That this procedure was considered the height of justice is suggested by one of Suetonius' anecdotes illustrating the lengths to which Augustus would go in "carefulness" (*diligentia*) and "leniency" (*lenitas*) in his personal administration of justice. In a trial concerning a forged will, Augustus gave the "jurors" not just "guilty" and "not guilty" tablets, but also a third tablet so that they might find that the defendants had indeed signed

---

[97] "Scio illud a quibusdam observatum, ne propter satis minimam rem vel summam, si maiori rei vel summae praeiudicetur, audiatur is qui in integrum restitui postulat." Trans. from "Watson," ed. *Digest.*

[98] Including *per vim stuprum,* one infers. See above.

[99] Cicero, *pro Milone* 13–14. See Lintott, *Violence,* 116.

[100] Suetonius, *Augustus* 34; *Res Gestae Divi Augusti* 8.

the instrument but that they had been induced to do so by "deceit" (*fraus*) or "mistake" (*error*).[101] Thus, the innovation in the administration of justice that had developed in the more violent and complex world of the late Republic and early Principate was not only approved but even adulated. No longer were the administrators of justice merely to observe whether the technical formalities of the transaction had been objectively achieved or not, but they were to look to the complexity of the case and sort out the subjective intent of the parties, which might lead to a point somewhere in between.

Did Lucretia Consent? Was Her "Consent" "Valid"?

Against this background, the rather delicate question of whether by Roman standards and ways of thinking Livy's Lucretia could be said to have "consented," and if so, whether that "consent" would be judged "valid," assumes greater historical significance. It is true that Tarquin succeeds in accomplishing his ends and that his success is ultimately the result of the last of his threats ("*quo terrore*") to frame a dead Lucretia as having committed adultery with one of her slaves. In this way, in fact, Lucretia's conduct changes in the face of the dire threat and, one might say, Tarquin's use of force actually shapes Lucretia's conduct and induces her to physical acquiescence.[102] Indeed, in Dionysius of Halicarnassus' account of the story of Lucretia, it is made explicit that Lucretia, forced (out of fear) to yield to Tarquin, actually allowed, in the sense of "looking the other way," of "suffering" ("περιϊδεῖν") him to commit the act, to accomplish his goal,[103] although Dionysius does not make much of this aspect of Lucretia's conduct, which was troubling to Livy.[104]

What stands out in Livy's account of the story of Lucretia is the prominence given to the question of whether Lucretia consented. This occurs most obviously in the debate between Lucretia and her menfolk during the family council. The menfolk advocate the use of a subjective standard for assessing whether Lucretia consented. According to this standard, Lucretia would be

---

[101]   Suetonius, *Augustus* 33.

[102]   See Appleton, "Trois épisodes," 264.

[103]   DH IV.65.4.

[104]   In the account of the story by Diodorus Siculus, the possibility of her consent is raised by the fact that she had not cried out at the time. DS X.20.3. Note the similar position of *CTh* 9.24.1.

acquitted of blame because she lacked purpose, because she did not affirmatively desire to participate in the act.[105] They opine that her body's act by itself does not imply *consilium;* their logic is not clear, however, for as has been mentioned above they seem to assume that *consilium* is the only type of mental participation possible and is a necessary element to culpability.[106] This, in some ways, glosses over the point of contention, namely, whether physical participation by itself implies some (lesser) kind of mental participation, according to an objective standard.[107]

During the period when Livy was writing and publishing, the issue of what significance coerced consent should have was being explored in court cases and in legislation. Legislation against violence was passed, attempts to have this legislation cover acts of *per vim stuprum* were made, a judicial attempt to extend its coverage further to include consensual *stuprum* failed, the praetor provided restitutive remedies to those whose consent was coerced, Augustus eventually succeeded in criminalizing consensual *stuprum* by means of legislation, and the question of what standard this legislation was to use in assessing culpability continued to vex. Thus, this period during which the effects of the violence from the civil wars were being sorted out, during which Livy was writing and publishing, and during which Augustus was trying to legislate morality was a period when the issue of the significance of coerced consent was being explored. Women who had been forced to commit *stuprum* were being distinguished, at least in a legal context, from women who had engaged in consensual *stuprum*. Augustus' successful leg-

---

[105] Note that force and consent are not logically polar opposites, and that consent does not necessarily imply affirmative enjoyment of participation in the deed: force and internal motivation, rather than force and consent, are more exactly antithetical, with consent being the antithesis of protestation. And where there has been a conflict between consent and protestation, it will not be clear from this alone whether the act will actually occur—that protest has been demonstrated does not rule out the subsequent demonstration of consent. In addition, "consent" can refer to two very different things, the subjective desire of the participant to be involved in the first place, or the objective fact of the participant's actual involvement. No distinction between affirmatively desired actions and muscular contractions constituting passive acquiescence is made within a system using an objective standard. It is such a distinction that Lucretia herself rejects as having legal effect but her menfolk endorse.

[106] Livy, I.58.9.

[107] A finer point is whether some degree of mental participation gives rise to valid consent, and if so, what degree is sufficient.

islation made women who had consented to *stuprum* liable to public punishment (and this scheme may also have been mooted well before this). With the concern to criminalize consensual *stuprum,* a new problem was introduced: the two differently treated acts of *per vim stuprum* and *stuprum* had now become distinguished by whether the passive partner consented, and whether she had or not may have been ambiguous. It would not be surprising, therefore, to find that the point of interest in discussing *stuprum* shifted from the irreparable consequences of the act to the woman's consent:[108] and this is achieved in Livy's telling of the story of Lucretia.

The Shift in Focus to Contemporary Times

In Livy's account of the story of Lucretia, the apparently earlier focus of the story on Lucretia's pollution has been shifted to that of Lucretia's consent. In particular, Livy seems to have shifted his focus to contemporary issues regarding consent. It is probable that originally, in the archaic versions of the story, Lucretia had to die regardless of her innocence or complicity in order to eradicate the physical taint to her husband's family line and the social taint to her husband's (and her father's) honor.[109] Now, in Livy's version, Lucretia has to die in order to ensure that the *remedia* to the *vitia* of his times are foolproof. Livy lays the groundwork for conveying this message subtly, through his selection of detail in his telling of the story.

When Livy's account of the story of Lucretia is contrasted with the accounts of Dionysius and Diodorus, differences in the details of the story become apparent. Dionysius and Diodorus do not include in their motivation of the episode a contest over wifely virtue or the image of Lucretia spinning among her slaves, and Livy does not have Tarquin promise marriage to Lucretia as part of his verbal attempts to procure Lucretia's consent. The sorrow

---

[108] Note, however, that Lucretia's menfolk avenge her death, not the adultery or *stuprum* or whatever it was that happened between her and Tarquin, despite what Lucretia asks; it is often observed that Lucretia's being killed was necessary in order to supply the men with an act that would unequivocally require vengeance and support a blood feud. In other words, what happened in the story could well have been not clear even to the participants. See also DS X.21.5.

[109] This was so in a world in which women were at least structurally conceptualized in abstract thought as proprietary pawns and conduits for transmitting property and making alliances.

and pain of Lucretia's father are given full expression in Dionysius' account, and while Diodorus' Lucretia proclaims that she must die, perhaps to preserve her good name, Livy's Lucretia argues the point at length and then insists on the necessity of her death in terms of how her fate will be used by others as camouflage for their own dirty deeds in the future.[110]

These details, including the ones that direct attention to the issue of Lucretia's consent, seem to have been selected by Livy, since his contemporaries' accounts do not contain them. Their cumulative effect seems to be to evoke the concerns, especially moral, of early Augustan Rome, directing attention as they do to the issues of marriage, chastity, and procreation, all hallmarks of Augustus' attempts at moral reform. However, two points must be disposed of before discussing the significance of Livy's selection of detail and his concern with early Augustan Rome: first, whether each detail selected in Livy's account can be explained otherwise, and second, whether the selection in Livy's account is really his own.

The contest of wives has been explained as generically "hellenistic,"[111] Tarquin's promises of marriage in Dionysius' and Diodorus' accounts as part of the seducer's regular arsenal, not to be taken at face value,[112] and Lucretia's insistence upon the necessity of her death as reflecting an archaic notion of

---

[110] Note how Lucretia is viewed as setting a different sort of example in Dionysius of Halicarnassus' account, where her suicide is an example of "ἀρετή" to politically and militarily active men. DH IV.82.3.

[111] Ogilvie, *Commentary*, 221.

[112] Appleton, "Trois épisodes," 259. In dismissing those commentators who would take the proposals seriously, he opines that even a Roman of later times would have been outraged by the notion of a subsequent marriage [to the "seducer" and presumably upon divorce from her current husband, in the case of the married Lucretia], "expiant le viol et réparant l'adultère." Appleton, "Trois épisodes," 260. Although one wonders how Appleton would explain the apparent later Roman custom of subsequent marriage as a possible legal resolution for a *raptus* that seems to be reflected in *CJ* 9.13 and Seneca's *Controversiae* I.5, II.3, III.5, IV.3, VII.8, and VIII.6, Appleton may be saying here simply that the notion was not (originally) Roman. If the detail did, however, exist in the Roman tradition of the telling of the story of Lucretia (even if it was meant to indicate the deceitfulness of the seducer and the lengths to which he would go in order to trick his presumably credulous victim into consenting, and not meant to be a promise which a sober Roman reader would find believable or acceptable), Livy's omission of it may have a more specific point than general Roman outrage at the concept of subsequent marriage to a seducer. Note also the concept in Antiquity that seduction was worse than violation because it involved

adultery as pollution, pollution that would taint even offspring from subsequent unions of Lucretia with her husband, and hence the entire ensuing family line.[113] However, the contest among the young princes at war is about whose wife is the most virtuous, and it leads to the discovery of Lucretia doing just what Augustus wished his womenfolk to be known for: spinning.[114] Indeed, these two details are embroidered on by Ovid in a way that seems to confirm that Livy was, or at least was seen as, trying to evoke contemporary motifs. For Ovid's contest is explicitly about uxorial fidelity and Ovid's Lucretia is found spinning cloth for her husband's cloak.[115] Livy's omission of Tarquin's promises of marriage seems to relate to similar concerns about the sanctity of marriage, for such a base use of marriage as an inducement to engage in sex outside of marriage would have disparaged it. The concern of Livy's Lucretia, that if she does not die she will be used as an unwilling precedent by shameless women who have committed consensual *stuprum* and are trying to escape rightful punishment, fits nicely with the scheme of prosecution for *stuprum* under the *lex Julia de adulteriis*. Brutus' summation of the episode that reduces it to Tarquin's violence and lust, Lucretia's unspeakable *stuprum* and wretched slaughter, and Lucretia's father's *orbitas,* recalls

---

alienation of affection. Lysias, *Oratio* 1 *On the Murder of Eratosthenes* 32–33; Treggiari, *Roman Marriage,* 309. This concept may have been more rhetorical than real or, at any rate, legal. See Raphael Sealey, *Women and Law in Classical Greece* (Chapel Hill, N.C., 1990), 28.

[113] E.g., Ogilvie, *Commentary,* 225; Appleton, "Trois épisodes," 265; Kahn, "Shakespeare's *Lucrece,*" 49 and 60. In this context, her refusal to be a precedent for allowing *impudicae* to live might be merely an extension of her convictions about preventing taint of the family line. It might also merely be meant to make the point Diodorus or his excerptor makes explicitly, namely, that Lucretia killed herself in order to save her reputation and prevent others from concluding that she was herself a guileful *impudica*. DS X.20.2 ff. However, again Livy's choice of detail might have a more pointed purpose.

[114] See Suetonius, *Augustus* 64.2 and 73.1. Ogilvie also hears echoes of contemporary concerns in Lucretia's spinning, but denies any purpose on Livy's part. He warns that "[c]ertainly L. [Livy] is not making deliberate propaganda for Augustus' moral reforms which were in any case later than this book. Both are reacting to the same ethos." Ogilvie, *Commentary,* 222. See also T. J. Luce, "The Dating of Livy's First Decade," *Transactions and Proceedings of the American Philological Association* 96 (1965), 209–40, 239.

[115] Ovid, *Fasti* 729–30 and 740–46, respectively.

motifs current in contemporary vocabulary.[116] Thus, while there are competing explanations for the inclusion of individual details in Livy's account of the story, the overall effect of these details is to lead the reader to think of the story in Augustan terms, in terms of marriage, chastity, and procreation.

The very fact that the details of Livy's account of the story of Lucretia contrast with those in the other accounts of the story suggests that these details were intentionally selected by Livy, since it points up that there existed at least another tradition for the story and that Livy therefore was exercising some sort of authorial discretion in his selection, or indeed creation, of the details included in his account.[117] However, we still need to consider briefly whether these details, seemingly peculiar to Livy, may reflect the concerns, and even the didactic point, not of Livy and his period, but of an earlier historian used by Livy and the period from which that source dates, and whether their selection predates Livy's working of the story.[118]

The annals of Fabius Pictor and Calpurnius Piso, both possible sources for Livy either directly or through their use by the intermediate annalist Valerius Antias,[119] are known to have been concerned with Roman morals, their previous strength and regrettable contemporary decline.[120] Dionysius of Halicarnassus certainly used Pictor, or some source citing him, for his account of the story of Lucretia, since he cites Pictor explicitly for some of his

---

[116] Ogilvie cautions that Brutus the Liberator (in Livy, I.59.8) is not reflecting the speeches of Brutus the assassin over Caesar's body, but rather the opposite, conceding, however, that "his [Brutus the Liberator's] language (*de vi ac libidine, de stupro infando, de miserabili caede*) is the political vocabulary of the late Republic." Ogilvie, *Commentary,* 227. Nevertheless, for Ogilvie, Livy's allusions are without point when contemporary. See also, for example, his comment on Livy's description of Tarquin as *vi armatus:* Ogilvie, *Commentary,* 225.

[117] Gabba sees the difference between accounts of episodes in Livy and Dionysius in many cases as being "intentional," and Dionysius' accounts as being the "closer" of the two to the "accepted models of the later annalists," the "more faithful to his sources." Emilio Gabba, *Dionysius and the History of Archaic Rome* (Berkeley, Calif., 1991), 95–96, 10.

[118] Syme, "Livy and Augustus," 28 and 48.

[119] "[M]ore probably, however, Livy made the acquaintance of . . . [Piso and Pictor] at second hand in the work of Valerius Antias and Licinius Macer." P. G. Walsh, *Livy* (Oxford, 1974), 14.

[120] See Frier's Prospectus of Pictor's fragments and his discussions of Pictor's and Piso's moralizing in Bruce Woodward Frier, *Libri Annales Pontificum Maximorum: The Origins of the Annalistic Tradition* (Rome, 1979), 322, 240, 211.

prosopographical details.[121] Livy has been thought by some to be following Antias in his account of Lucretia's story.[122] Antias is known to have relied heavily on Calpurnius Piso.[123] Thus, it is possible that the moral concerns adumbrated in Livy's account of the story of Lucretia belong to an earlier period.[124]

However, there is direct evidence in Livy's preface that he himself was concerned with the moral condition of his times and the difficulty of improving it, and that he was of a mind to express this concern in his work. Having alluded to Rome's moral ills and the failure of the society to accept the necessary antidotes, Livy links the moral degeneracy of his times to a sequence of newfound riches, greed, and self-destruction,[125] but then breaks off abruptly, saying he will comment no further on such unpleasant things than that, at least now: "But complaints, not pleasing even when they will perhaps be necessary, let them be absent from at least the beginning of so great a thing beginning its course."[126]

---

[121] DH IV.64.3.

[122] Ogilvie, *Commentary,* 219–20. The argument is indirect: Antias is Livy's source for a very similar story in Book XXXVIII.24.3. See also Ogilvie, *Commentary,* 224. Cf. Pais, seeing Licinius Macer as Livy's main source for his accounts of myths associated with Ardea. Ettore Pais, *Ancient Legends of Roman History,* trans. Mario E. Cosenza (London, 1906), 190. Walsh lists Livy's main authorities generally for Books I–V as Valerius Antias, Licinius Macer, and Aelius Tubero. Walsh, *Livy,* 14. Briscoe names Macer and Antias as "the two chief sources" for the first decade, citing Ogilvie. J. Briscoe, "The First Decade," in *Livy,* ed. T. A. Dorey (London, 1971), 1–20, 9–10. Watson suggests tentatively Q. Aelius Tubero as a possible source for Livy's early stories that have "some private legal content," but notes immediately that these stories had probably already been fixed by 70 B.C. and thus before the time Tubero was writing. Watson, *XII Tables,* 171. (Tubero has also been identified as Lucius Aelius Tubero, the friend of Cicero. See Ernst Badian, "The Early Historians," in *Latin Historians,* ed. T. A. Dorey [New York, 1966], 1–38, 22.)

[123] Frier, *Libri Annales,* 215 and Ogilvie, *Commentary,* 9, 14.

[124] Certainly the connection of some form of the phrase *per vim stupr—* to the story of Lucretia predates Livy since it is used by Cicero so consistently: Cicero, *de Legibus* 2.10.8, *de Finibus* 2.66, 5.64. See also Cicero, *de Republica* II.46 ("eius filius Lucretiae . . . vim attulisset").

[125] Livy, *praef.* 9 and 12. See discussion of Augustus' failed moral legislation in 28 B.C., above.

[126] "Sed querellae, ne tum quidem gratae futurae cum forsitan necessariae erunt, ab initio certe tantae ordiendae rei absint." Livy, *praef.* 12.

His qualification that the discussion of these issues should be dropped at least at *this* point in his work, "ab initio certe," leaves open the possibility that perhaps Livy will return to them later. Indeed, this qualification can be read as a flag, a warning by a sort of "praeteritio paraleipsis" that Livy will, in fact, be using his narrative to voice such *querellae*. Reading his account of the story of Lucretia as a moral parable for his times fits nicely into this framework.[127] It also fits nicely with what is known of the dates and method of its composition and publication.

Livy certainly worked on the first five books of his history between 27 and 25 B.C.,[128] perhaps revising parts of them at that time[129] or perhaps still engaged in initial composition then.[130] It is more easily inferred that they were published during this interval with a general preface written after the main body was composed.[131] At least some kind of work on Livy's first book (in which the story of Lucretia appears) is datable to this narrow period of 27 to 25 B.C. with certainty, because it is that book that contains the conspicuous reference to the (only) one occasion of closing the Temple of Janus due to "Augustus"; this passage points clearly to this specific period because it must have been written between the Senate's bestowal of the title on Octavian and the second closing of the Temple by Augustus.[132] Whether this sentence is the

---

[127] *Pace* Frier, *Libri Annales,* 203 note 5 ("Livv's [sic] depiction of Roman morals sliding to ruin (*praef* 7) is not carried through in the history . . ."). See also Williams on how historians and poets use moralizing statements to organize their facts and visions, respectively. Williams, *TORP,* 609.

[128] The work includes a reference to two closings of the Temple of Janus after the reign of Numa Pompilius, one after the first Punic War and the other after the Battle of Actium. Livy, I.19.3. In connection with the latter, the honorific "Augustus" conferred on Octavian in 27 B.C. is used. No mention is made of the second closing of the Temple of Janus during Augustus' rule, in 25 B.C. See, e.g., Syme, "Livy and Augustus," 42.

[129] Luce, "Dating," esp. 209, 210, 232, 238 (revisions in three places made then); Ogilvie, *Commentary,* 784.

[130] "The common assumption" criticized by Syme in his "Livy and Augustus," 43, and sources cited therefore, 42–49. See also Ogilvie, *Commentary,* 564 (and 784); Luce, "Dating," 214 ff, 229 ff.

[131] Syme, "Livy and Augustus," 42–49 and 37. Preface written between 30 and 23 B.C., Williams, "Moral Climate," 34; before 26 B.C., Galinsky, "Augustus' Legislation on Morals and Marriage," 126–44, 129 note 18.

[132] Syme, "Livy and Augustus," 42. See note above.

product of original composition, revision for a second edition, revision for *addenda et corrigenda,* or revision for an as yet unpublished but already privately circulated or orally delivered work is not critical here,[133] for as long as Livy was still at work on Book I in some way at this time,[134] the events of this time may have influenced its presentation of material. That is, if Livy was still at least tinkering with Book I between 27 and 25 B.C., what is contained in his account of the story of Lucretia, and in his preface, would have had the benefit of the experience of Augustus' (failed) attempt at moral reform of 28 B.C., and may reflect a (failed) attempt to prosecute women for adultery and (consensual) *stuprum*—women who could be characterized as *impudicae*—within this program.[135]

There is more direct evidence that Livy was aware of the possibility that he could use his writing of Rome's history to comment on contemporary times, including Augustan programs, and of doing so in particular episodes recounted in the body of his work. Indeed, Livy's explicitness about the way in which his account of another episode in his first pentad was shaped gives an idea of how the author may have factored such concerns into his accounts of other episodes and what therefore he may have meant by his expression of these concerns.

In Book IV of his history, Livy relates the story of Aulus Cornelius Cossus' dedication of the *spolia opima* in the fifth century B.C.[136] Having recounted the episode, Livy then digresses in order to take into account, without really adopting it, an emendation of a detail of the story which was promoted, indeed apparently insisted upon, by Augustus. For the story went that Cossus had dedicated the spoils while a military tribune, and so Livy had related it. Nevertheless, it appears that for current political reasons, Augustus needed the story to show that Cossus had dedicated his *spolia opima* as consul.[137] Augustus apparently wanted to keep M. Licinius Crassus from being able to dedicate *spolia opima,* which he was claiming the right to do, and this

---

[133] Nor does it matter when the bulk of Book I or the account of the story of Lucretia was originally composed.

[134] It is tempting to think that Livy sprinkled his work with morally didactic points about his times when he wrote his preface, after the initial composition of the body of the work but before its publication. See below.

[135] See below.

[136] Livy, IV.20.

[137] Syme, "Livy and Augustus," 44.

honor had not been repeated for centuries and hence there was very little in the way of other precedent for determining eligibility for this right.[138] Crassus would be disqualified if being consul could be shown to be necessary.[139] Thus Livy writes of his firsthand report from Augustus of *his* firsthand inspection of direct evidence that Cossus had been consul at the time.[140] Livy's doubts are not suppressed, however, as his ultimate disposition of the matter shows: he writes, "What is the error in this matter . . . is something for everybody on the street to make up his or her mind about,"[141] does not change his account to reflect this information[142] despite his pronouncement that it would be almost a sacrilege ("*prope sacrilegium*") to deprive Cossus of Augustus' witness,[143] and concludes his digression with another markedly unaggressive attempt to persuade the reader of Augustus' sudden new insight (namely, the argument that the evidence that Augustus gathered was likely not to have been forged by its author).[144] Livy is clearly not convinced but nevertheless scrupulously, perhaps a little bit too scrupulously, respectful. His digression regarding Cossus' *spolia opima* and Augustus' evi-

---

[138] Ibid.

[139] That some such debate was going on is indicated by Cassius Dio's account (Cassius Dio, *Roman History* 44.4.2); see Syme's discussion, "Livy and Augustus," 44.

[140] Livy, IV.20.7. Note also that Livy was on intimate enough terms with Augustus for Augustus to chide him about his Republican sympathies, calling him Pompeianus. Tacitus, *Annales* 4.34.

[141] In which the ellipsis comprises material underscoring the weightiness of the tradition following the other, standard version, that is, that Cossus was not a consul at the time. "Quis ea in re sit error quod tam veteres annales quodque magistratuum libri, quos linteos in aede repositos Monetae Macer Licinius citat identidem auctores, septimo post demum anno cum T. Quinctio Poeno A. Cornelium Cossum consulem habeant, existimatio communis omnibus est." Livy, IV.20.8.

[142] See (also) Livy, IV.32.4.

[143] Livy, IV.20.7. N.b. that Livy does not deprive Cossus of Augustus' witness, but merely declines to endorse it, to be his oath-helper. One also wonders at the tone of this sentence, as does Syme about the next sentence discussed, Livy, IV.20.11. Syme, "Livy and Augustus," 44.

[144] "Ea libera coniectura est sed, ut ego arbitror, vana versare in omnes opiniones licet, cum auctor pugnae, recentibus spoliis in sacra sede positis, Iovem prope ipsum, cui vota erant, Romulumque intuens, haud spernendos falsi tituli testes, se A. Cornelium Cossum consulem scripserit." Livy, IV.20.11. On punctuation, see Ogilvie, *Commentary* 567.

dence is generally regarded as a later insertion,[145] indeed, it has even been seen as an insertion at Augustus' admonition.[146] Thus, there is evidence that Livy's work does actually reflect concerns of Augustus,[147] albeit not necessarily Augustus' attitude.

If Livy's account of the story of Lucretia does indeed direct attention to contemporary times, to Augustan Rome, as the evidence about his selection of details that evoke those times suggests,[148] what is the significance of that direction? With the explanation of why Lucretia must die that Livy has put into Lucretia's mouth, Livy has shifted attention not only from Lucretia's physical defilement to her consent, but also from her personal reputation to how her story will be used in the future. Lucretia is made to fear that an *impudica* will in the future use Lucretia as an example of a woman who successfully avoided punishment for *stuprum* by pleading force. This *impudica* must be a woman who has committed *stuprum* consensually, for otherwise Lucretia's lack of sympathy for her and characterization of her as unchaste would make no sense. The need of this putative woman for an

---

[145] Syme, "Livy and Augustus," 44 and note 82 and scholarship cited therein (including the opinion that Book IV contains other insertions); Luce, "Dating," 211 ff, esp. 212; R. M. Ogilvie, "Livy, Licinius Macer and the *Libri Lintei*," *Journal of Roman Studies* 48 (1958), 40–46, 41; Ogilvie, *Commentary* 564 and 784.

[146] Syme, "Livy and Augustus," 47. Given the scheme for the composition and publication of Livy's first pentad laid out by Syme ("Livy and Augustus," 42–49), it would be logical that Livy would have made the insertion at some point around the time of its publication (that is, after its original composition and before its final publication). See above.

[147] And that at least some of those concerns were probably edited into the work after it had been originally composed, perhaps even at the time Livy was adding the preface that foreshadowed their inclusion. See above.

[148] One technique that Livy uses in his telling of the story that contributes to this is the inclusion of details reminiscent of contemporary concerns at the beginning of the account (the wife contest, Lucretia found spinning) that, while not irrelevant to the story being presented, may stick in the reader's mind (especially if the reader is familiar with the story from other accounts), because they seem to lay the groundwork for something to happen or for some point to be made. However, although such details highlight Lucretia's chastity and thus generally make the contrast with her subsequent status after her catastrophe all the sharper, they are never actually developed later in the story. And at the dramatic point in the story where Lucretia kills herself, an even more puzzling detail occurs; why, as Appleton asks, is Lucretia worrying about how others will use her story at a time like this? Appleton, "Trois épisodes," 263.

exemplum of a woman who under colorably similar circumstances was allowed to live, to go unpunished, suggests further that this future *impudica* is being in some way "prosecuted" for having committed *stuprum* and is in response pleading force as an exception to her prosecution. [149]

In converting what was probably the archaic resolution of the story of Lucretia into a contemporary commentary, Livy seems to be trying to express concern about the danger and hence the appropriate treatment of women who have committed contemporary (consensual) *stuprum*. [150] In Livy's hands the story of Lucretia becomes the story of the necessary consequences of having been the object of *stuprum* in a world in which *stuprum* has come to be viewed as an immoral, consensual sexual act that must be eradicated by public law. In such a world, exceptions to punishment for *stuprum* are dangerous, for the immoral people, including *impudicae*, targeted by the reform program would not be above hiding behind such exceptions. [151] As a paragon of Augustan Roman matronal chastity and morals, Lucretia voices the extreme opinion that society cannot afford to tolerate exceptions to punishment for the commission of *stuprum*, whatever the circumstances. Lucretia must die so that she cannot be made an accomplice to this avoidance of the law. Livy gives further recognition to the difficulty of distinguishing forcible from consensual *stuprum* and allowing participants in the former to be exculpated by

---

[149] The fact that force at least came to be a defense to prosecution for *stuprum* (the evidence is from third-century jurists) under the successful moral legislation suggests that Lucretia's distrust reflects a predictable, and hence very possibly predicted, problem with enforcing the legislation; if it was known that the moral legislation was targeting the commission of (consensual) *stuprum* for its immorality and if it had been similarly understood even earlier that *per vim stuprum* was a different sort of crime, a crime of violence with a victim (who should not be penalized), then it would not be surprising to hear voiced concern that the targeted consensual offenders would pretend to fall into the protected group of victims of force. Thus, the *impudicae* Lucretia distrusts must be the same women targeted by Augustus' moral legislation, and her suspicions about the ruses to which they will resort must be those already detected as loopholes in the mooted legislative scheme and those to which they probably actually did resort, given the evidence about exceptions to prosecution under the law, which in turn seem to be based on older notions of suspending the application of law during war. That Livy was able to foresee this should not, therefore, be discounted.

[150] See Heurgon, *Tite-Live,* 190, noted above.

[151] Note also the opinion by some Romans that women enjoy sexual violence: Ovid, *Ars* 1.673. See Adams, *Sexual Vocabulary,* 198.

having Brutus afterwards refer to what happened to Lucretia, which had been introduced by Livy at the outset of the story as *per vim stuprum,* simply as *stuprum.*

Perhaps such strong measures as Lucretia advocates *were* seen as necessary for the times, for, as mentioned before, Livy laments in his preface "these times in which we are unable to endure either our vices or their cure";[152] that the remedies, as well as the vices, were not being tolerated suggests that drastic measures were indeed being entertained.

A complementary[153] sentiment is expressed in the twenty-fourth poem of the third book of Horace's *Odes,* where Horace writes, "What good are statutes hollow without *mores?*"[154] Here Horace comments on the impossibility of legislating morality given the contemporary moral bankruptcy. In his account of Lucretia's position regarding the validity of her coerced consent, Livy seems to be going a step further than Horace (or, indeed, than his own preface) in commenting on this state of affairs and exploring the problem of the relation between morality and law: Lucretia's insistence that she must die indicates that subjective standards invalidating the validity of coerced consent are all well and good in the moral sphere but will lead to chaos and injustice if adopted in the legal sphere; the law must be stricter than the moral code, the cure for vices must be very strong and not be dependent upon morals if it is to be effective against the state of affairs inherited by Augustus. This message of Livy's Lucretia is a more stinging and trenchant indictment of Livy's times and a more pessimistic prognosis for their improvement than is to be found earlier in his work or in Horace's *Ode* III.24, for it not only seems to lament society's lack of response to a call to reform but to question the wisdom of the caller's strategy.

Livy put the problem of the validity of coerced consent (in sexual relations) before his readers and suggested that the solution would not come from legal innovation that relies on subjective detail implicating moral rectitude.

---

[152] "[H]aec tempora quibus nec vitia nostra nec remedia pati possumus." Livy, *praef.* 9. See discussion of this as allusion to failed moral legislation in 28 B.C., above.

[153] "Livy and Horace, using similar language, are surely talking about the same thing." Williams, "Moral Climate," 34; *TORP,* 607 ff. Cf. Badian, "Phantom Marriage Law," 93.

[154] "[Q]uid leges sine moribus / vanae proficiunt?" Horace, *Odes* III.24, 35–36. On its referring to the failed moral legislation of 28 B.C., see Williams, "Moral Climate," 30. *Pace* Badian, "Phantom Marriage Law," 93.

In the event, public prosecution of women for consensual *stuprum* remained a troublesome issue not only for Augustus, but for his successors, Roman and beyond,[155] while official attention to subjective detail in legal adjudication of disputed transactions helped Roman jurisprudence (and subsequent systems based on it) to grow and flourish.

Arlington, Mass.

---

[155] Besides the "wartime force exception" and element of intent, on which see above, see *CTh* 9.24, *CJ* 9.13, and other essays in this volume.

The Social Dynamics of Consent
to Marriage and Sexual Relations:
The Evidence of Roman Comedy

RICHARD P. SALLER

Since the fact of marriage (or more precisely, of *iustum matrimonium*) had significant legal consequences in Roman society for both persons and property, jurists took an interest in defining its legal requirements. Consent to marriage, one of the requirements, was in principle straightforward in classical law: "A marriage cannot be made unless all consent—that is, those who are coming together and those in whose *potestas* they are" (*Digest* 23.2.2, Paulus). In other words, the husband- and the wife-to-be must consent, and also the *paterfamilias* of each. This stark legal formulation makes the matter look simple. Perhaps in most instances it was, either because the bride or groom had no living *paterfamilias* or because *paterfamilias* and child were in agreement over the match. Had consent regularly been problematic, we might expect there to have been some explicit means specified for clearly signifying it. There was not, and participation in the arrangements and ceremony could be assumed to imply tacit consent.[1]

In this paper I want to explore the dynamics in cases of disagreement between *paterfamilias* and child where difficulties could arise from the fact

[1] Susan Treggiari, *Roman Marriage:* Iusti Coniuges *from the Time of Cicero to the Time of Ulpian* (Oxford, 1991), 170–80.

that consent was not just an outcome of four autonomous individuals, each with a veto, independently coming to a decision, but was the result of personal interactions and conflicting pressures. The jurists indicate the possibility of conflicts and problems related to consent. Celsus addressed the issue of the validity of consent given under compulsion: "if a man, under pressure from his father, takes a wife, whom he would not have married had the choice been his, he has nevertheless contracted a marriage, despite the fact that a marriage is not contracted between unwilling parties: he seems to have preferred this choice."[2] The reader is left to wonder what form the paternal compulsion (*cogere*) could take and at what point the compulsion would imply that a party to the marriage was "unwilling" (*invitus*), thus precluding marriage. These questions are not answered in the juristic texts: Celsus dismissed the problem by taking a narrow view of *invitus*, saying that once the *filius* agreed, whatever his own personal wishes, the requirement of consent was satisfied.

For the social historian the personal interactions leading to the consent— interactions which Celsus considered irrelevant from a legal point of view— are of central interest, yet poorly documented because they took place within the household. The arrangement of marriage between Cicero's daughter, Tullia, and Dolabella is unusually well known precisely because it was negotiated during Cicero's governorship of Cilicia in 51–50 B.C., when his participation and agreement had to be committed to writing in letters later published. Susan Treggiari has sensitively analyzed the roles of the women and men involved, which the law of consent does not adequately capture. She concludes that even in this best-attested example much remains unknown, in particular the part played by Tullia.[3] Consequently, even this example does not provide much insight into the negotiation between father and child leading to mutual consent.

The search for evidence to illuminate the negotiations within the family

---

[2] *Digest* 23.2.22: "Si patre cogente ducit uxorem, quam non educeret, si sui arbitrii esset, contraxit tamen matrimonium, quod inter invitos non contrahitur: maluisse hoc videtur." The final clause is taken by some to have been interpolated; see E. Volterra, "Quelques observations sur le mariage des *filiifamilias*," *Revue internationale des droits de l'Antiquité* 1 (1948), 230, who also points out that it is not certain that the son is *in potestate* or that the father's compulsion is based on *patria potestas*.

[3] Susan Treggiari, "*Digna condicio:* Betrothals in the Roman Upper Class," *Échos du monde classique/Classical Views,* n.s. 3 (1984), 450.

takes us to the fictional scenarios of Roman comedy.[4] More than any other genre of Latin literature, the comedies of Plautus and Terence portray conflicts of will and desire within the family over marriage arrangements and show how those conflicts might play out. Of course, the use of Roman comedy to illuminate social relations in historical Rome is fraught with serious methodological difficulties: what is the relation of comic representation to social practice outside the theater—mirror, caricature, or Saturnalian inversion? If some contact between theatrical roles and social behavior existed, do the plays of Plautus and Terence illuminate the Roman world or the Hellenistic Greek world, in which New Comedy originated, or both? These questions have provoked lengthy debate without decisive answers, in part because no single, general answer can be given to either question. I would like to bracket these questions for the moment and return to them after a discussion of the content of the plays.

Daughters and Fathers

Any analysis of consent to marriage and to sexual relations must start from the basic Greco-Roman distinctions of gender, and consider the matter in terms of the ancient classification of women. For men and women the codes of honor and paternal control over sexual relations and marriage were applied in different ways. The plots of many of the plays revolve around a conflict between a son wishing to pursue his youthful passion for a woman not of his status and his father who presses his son to enter a respectable and prosperous marriage. The essential difference of status between the youth and the woman rests on a classification of women fundamental to the ancient city-state: the division between free women with honor and slave women without honor or protection; among free women, the division between citizens eligible for *iustum matrimonium* and foreigners ineligible for a marriage producing legitimate citizen children; and among citizen women, the division between those from a propertied family with the means to provide a substantial dowry and

---

[4] Susan Treggiari, "Consent to Roman Marriage: Some Aspects of Law and Reality," *Échos du monde classique/Classical Views*, n.s. 1 (1982), 20, noted briefly in the final footnote that "Terence gives some idea of the possible influence of family affection in winning over hostile fathers."

those poor women without.[5] Slave women were excluded from the privileged group for whom personal and paternal consent to sexual relations and marriage was relevant: they lacked personal honor and a father or other family member to protect them; their bodies were at the disposal of their masters. This boundary between respectable women and slave women, essential to the plots of many of the comedies, is a matter of explicit concern in Plautus' *Persa,* where the characters manipulate it. As a part of a scam to defraud a slave-dealing pimp, Saturio prepares to pretend to sell his daughter as a slave to the pimp so that the pimp can be deprived of money and accused of enslaving a citizen. The daughter is torn between the obligation of filial obedience to participate in her father's scam and her worries about her own honor. She fears that even the transient appearance of having crossed the line between citizen and slave could taint her with *infamia* and so make her unattractive for an honorable marriage (343–84), because for a short time she would have lost the prerogative of consent that would protect her chastity.[6] The violation of that prerogative of a free woman through forcible rape provides the starting point of several comedies (e.g., Plautus' *Aulularia* and *Cistellaria,* Terence's *Hecyra* and *Adelphoe*). These plots have been discussed elsewhere;[7] here it is worth noting that without consent the sexual violation of a free woman is represented as a wrong to her father and to her an *iniuria,* an insult to honor (as in Plautus, *Aulularia* 794).

For the respectable Roman woman, chastity entailed confining sexual relations to marriage: since legitimate marriage was regarded as having the purpose of producing children, consent to marriage was tantamount to consent to sexual relations. Although there is some disagreement among historians of Roman law, it seems probable that in the age of Plautus and Terence both the woman and her *paterfamilias* had to give consent to form a valid marriage.[8] The comedies give little evidence about this or about how the mutual consent of father and daughter might have been reached, in contrast

---

[5] On the ideological bases of these plays and these distinctions, see E. Fantham, "Sex, Status, and Survival in Hellenistic Athens: A Study of Women in New Comedy," *Phoenix* 29 (1975), 45–74; D. Konstan, *Roman Comedy* (Ithaca, N.Y., 1983), 16–25.

[6] Her father tries to reassure her that money can fix any problem and that with a dowry she will find a respectable husband (387).

[7] Fantham, "Women in New Comedy," 53–57.

[8] Volterra, "Quelques observations," 213–42; Treggiari, *Roman Marriage,* 171.

to the attention given to the consent of fathers and sons. The contrast may be explained by dramatic conventions, rooted in expectations of gender: unmarried citizen girls are generally not allowed to speak in New Comedy, the product of cultures where males valued the quiet obedience of daughters to their father's wishes.[9] Quiet obedience is not likely to have been far from the reality for those many daughters whose first marriages were arranged when they were in their early teens or even younger.[10] Therefore, even though in law the daughter's consent to a marriage may have been required, her father could in practice be assumed to take the initiative and to bestow her (*collocare*) on a husband.[11]

Once married, the female character could be endowed by the playwright with a voice to express her own wishes against that of her father in regard to the dissolution of her marriage. Plautus' *Stichus* and Terence's *Hecyra* portray situations in which fathers and daughters have to negotiate their differences to reach agreement about divorce. In the *Stichus*, two sisters are married to two brothers, who have lost their fortunes and gone to sea for several years to trade. The father of the two sisters presses them to divorce their absent husbands so that they can remarry. The women resist out of devotion and affection (*pietas*) for their husbands. Panegyris says to her sister: "We must endure what [father] does; his *potestas* is greater. I believe that our enterprise ought to be undertaken by pleading, not by opposing: if we ask in a charming way [to remain married], I hope that we will obtain it from him. We cannot oppose him without dishonor and wickedness."[12] Panegyris is successful: against his daughters' kisses, the father gives up his plan, unwilling to engage

---

[9] D. Konstan, "Between Courtesan and Wife: Menander's *Perikeiromene*," *Phoenix* 41 (1987), 134.

[10] K. Hopkins, "The Age of Roman Girls at Marriage," *Population Studies* 20 (1964–65), 309–27; modified by B. Shaw, "The Age of Roman Girls at Marriage: Some Reconsiderations," *Journal of Roman Studies* 77 (1987), 30–46. It must be remembered that many women remarried later in life and would have had much greater control over the arrangements at that time on account of their greater maturity and the likelihood that their fathers had died. Once the woman became *sui iuris* upon the death of her *paterfamilias*, no other male relative had any formal legal power over her choice of a husband.

[11] Volterra, "Quelques observations," 228.

[12] *Stichus* 68–72: "pati / nos oportet quod ille faciat, quoius potestas plus potest. / exorando, haud advorsando sumendam operam censeo: / gratiam per si petimus, spero ab eo impetrassere; / advorsari sine dedecore et scelere summo hau pos-

in "war with my family" (*bellum cum meis,* 81–82). This play illustrates the resolution of tension between father and married daughters, between *potestas* and *amor.* If it were not for the fact that early Republican families continue to be portrayed in starkly legalistic terms as ruled by the severe, affectionless *paterfamilias,*[13] it would not be necessary to insist that *patria potestas* was wielded within a field of multifaceted relationships. The underpinning of *potestas* in this episode is not legal—recourse to a law court is not contemplated. Rather, the child's sense of duty is represented as the motive for obedience: to disobey a father would be, in Panegyris' words, *dedecus* and *scelus.* Moreover, the moral imperative of obedience does not make the child a passive subject of the father's will, because the father's power is susceptible to reason and to manipulation by his daughters—in this instance, successful blandishments. Furthermore, Panegyris points out to her father the folly of forcing her to remarry, saying "the wife who has been given in marriage to a husband against her will is an enemy" ("hostis est uxor, invita quae viro nuptum datur," 140). This line suggests the practical difficulties a father could expect, if he tried to compel his daughter's consent: presumably few husbands would want to bring an enemy into the house; in the longer term, the prospects of success of a compelled marriage must have been limited after 200 B.C. by the option of divorce open to the woman as soon as the father's compulsion ceased upon his death.[14]

In Terence's *Hecyra,* the father also gives in to his daughter's wishes, this time in the opposite direction. The pregnant Philumena wants her father, Phidippus, to take her home after her divorce from Pamphilus. Because the marriage is an honorable one, Phidippus would prefer that Philumena stay with her husband. Yet he tells her: "Although I know, Philumena, that it is my right (*ius*) to compel you to do what I order, nevertheless overcome by a paternal spirit I will act in a way to yield to you, nor will I oppose your

---

sumus." (All texts of Plautus and Terence are taken from the Oxford Classical Text editions; all translations are mine.)

[13] The stereotype is often repeated; for a recent example, see J. K. Evans, *War, Women, and Children in Ancient Rome* (London-New York, 1991).

[14] In general, it is reasonable to suppose that the effects of paternal compulsion were less grave in the classical era, when divorce was available, than in the Christian era, when marriage was meant to be a lifetime arrangement.

desire."[15] Here Phidippus claims the *ius* to have his way, but that is not the end of the story, because it is in a father's nature (*patrius animus*) to protect his daughter's welfare.[16] In yielding, Phidippus has to suffer criticism from Pamphilus' father Laches for being "in his women's power" (*in illarum potestate*), an embarrassing reversal of gender roles. These plays show the senior generation of males defining *ius* and *potestas,* which gives them the power to arrange and to break off marriages of daughters, and putting social pressure on each other to maintain their collective dominance. But the legal rights are not enforced in court; rather they are manipulable in the context of personal relationships based on duty and love.

Sons and Fathers

With youthful sons (*adulescentes*) as stock characters, Roman comedies present far more dialogue about the conflicts and negotiations over their sexual relations and marriage. The terms and values of the discussion (*pietas, pudor, potestas, officium*) are similar to those associated with marriage of daughters, but deployed in different ways on account of the basic gender distinctions regulating sexuality. In order to understand the negotiation of consent to marriage between son and father, it must be situated within the broader context of paternal attitudes toward the son's sexual attachments through his life course. In Rome, as in Athens, the appropriate time for young men to enter legitimate marriage was relatively late in life, ten years or so later than young women.[17] As a result, during the long interval between puberty and marriage, young men were expected to seek sexual gratification from those women who were unprotected by honor and family in the city-state ideology (*concubina, meretrix,* or *scortum*).[18] The conflict driving the plots of many comedies

[15] *Hecyra* 243–45: "Etsi scio ego, Philumena, meum ius esse ut te cogam / quae ego imperem facere, ego tamen patrio animo victu' faciam / ut tibi concedam neque tuae lubidini advorsabor."

[16] On fathers' relations with daughters more generally, see J. Hallett, *Fathers and Daughters in Roman Society* (Princeton, 1984).

[17] R. Saller, "Men's Age at Marriage and Its Consequences in the Roman Family," *Classical Philology* 82 (1987), 21–34; Shaw, "The Age of Roman Girls"; for Greece, M. Golden, "Demography and the Exposure of Girls at Athens," *Phoenix* 35 (1981), 316–31.

[18] R. Saller, "Slavery and the Roman Family," in *Classical Slavery,* ed. M. I. Finley (London, 1987), 71–76.

arises at the time of transition to legitimate marriage from the youthful attachment to prostitute or concubine.[19] How could fathers attempt to control their sons' passions and guide them into socially appropriate unions at the proper time?

The comedies point not to a single answer to this question but to a debate about how a parent could strike the right balance between indulgence and social propriety. In the plays the debate recurs in the form of an opposition between the *lenis pater* and the *durus pater,* with both extremes caricatured and held up for ridicule. The *lenis pater* is characterized as favoring a permissive attitude toward his son's premarital loves, on the grounds that: (1) young men need an opportunity to sow their wild oats, just as their fathers had done in youth;[20] (2) fathers ought to be willing to overlook and forgive peccadilloes of sons, so that the sons will confide in them and not lie or deceive out of fear.

In Plautus' *Asinaria,* the father Demaenetus gives both reasons for his indulgent attitude: "All parents, Libanus, who will listen to me, will be compliant toward their children so that they will more enjoy a friendly and good-willed child. And I am anxious to do this myself, I wish to be loved by mine; I wish to be like my father, who for my sake in a sea captain's outfit led away from a pimp under false pretenses the girl whom I loved. Nor was he ashamed at his age to manufacture deceits and to buy me, his son, for himself with favors."[21] Imitating his own father, then, Demaenetus plots with his son to secure the son's *amica* Philaenium. Although Demaenetus here represents the

---

[19] That this was a long-enduring life-course problem is suggested by its appearance more than five centuries later in Augustine's *Confessions.*

[20] Through the comedies there is a familiar, recurrent discussion about whether father-son relations had been different or similar in the past: it is sometimes claimed that youths of the fathers' generation had been more disciplined and more respectful (Plautus, *Bacchides* 437–47, *Mercator* 62–64); at other points it is said that fathers in their youth had acted with the same adolescent wildness as their sons (Plautus, *Asinaria* 64–83, *Bacchides* 410, *Epidicus* 382–91, *Pseudolus* 437; Terence, *Heautontimorumenos* 213).

[21] *Asinaria,* 64–72: "omnes parentes, Libane, liberis suis, / qui mi auscultabunt, facient †obsequellam† / quipp' qui mage amico utantur gnato et benevolo. / atque ego me id facere studeo, volo amari a meis; / volo me patris mei similem, qui caussa mea / nauclerico ipse ornatu per fallaciam / quam amabam abduxit ab leone mulierem; / neque puduit eum id aetatis sycophantias / struere et beneficiis me emere gnatum suom sibi."

extreme *lenis pater* ridiculed through caricature, his basic rationale for parental indulgence—to secure the goodwill of one's child—is not intrinsically ridiculous. The desire of the father to enjoy his children's affection, not just their obedience, is repeated in other plays and in other forms of Latin literature. Demaenetus becomes silly in going to the extreme of trying to buy (*emere*) his son's attachment.

Terence's *Adelphoe* most clearly articulates the debate between the *lenis* and *durus pater* in the contrast between the brothers Micio and Demea. The indulgent Micio has adopted one of the severe Demea's two sons and raised him in an easygoing way. When Micio's son Aeschinus gets into trouble by raping a poor freeborn girl, Micio explains his approach to child-rearing, based on his intense love for his son: "I try hard so that in return he may feel the same [love] toward me. I give, I overlook, I do not think it necessary to do everything to the extent of my right (*ius*); finally, adolescent pranks which other sons engage in without their fathers knowing it, I have accustomed my son not to hide from me. For a son who starts out upon lying to and deceiving his father or will dare do so, all the more he will dare treat others in the same way. I believe it better to restrain children by *pudor* and *liberalitas* than by fear."[22] Here again is the familiar wisdom: a father wants love as well as obedience; he should cultivate trust rather than fear; he should raise his son to internalize a sense of right and wrong, articulated as *pudor*. *Pudor* or modesty, encompassing sexual restraint, is a recognized moral standard, which an indulgent father might not insist on, knowing that he would do so in vain and alienate his son. While the plot of the *Adelphoe* partially vindicates the *lenitas* of Micio insofar as Demea's severity turns out to be conspicuously impotent, Demea shows by the end of the play that unadulterated *lenitas* can lead to disastrous dissipation of the family's estate.

The *durus pater* in the plays tries to enforce the standard of *pudor,* albeit always in vain. What are the reasons given for trying to control or restrict the sexual liaisons of a son? Most often it is the expense of keeping an *amica,* resulting in the dissipation of the patrimony. The motif of the expensive *mer-*

---

[22] *Adelphoe* 50–58: "ille ut item contra me habeat facio sedulo: / do praetermitto, non necesse habeo omnia / pro meo iure agere; postremo, alii clanculum / patres quae faciunt, quae fert adulescentia, / ea ne me celet consuefeci filium. / nam qui mentiri aut fallere instituerit patrem aut / audebit, tanto magis audebit ceteros. / pudore et liberalitate liberos / retinere satius esse credo quam metu."

etrix, of *amor* versus *res* (love versus property), recurs in numerous plays of Plautus and Terence.[23] In an agrarian society with limited land as the source of family income, the cost of courting a *meretrix* threatened to cut into the patrimony and is therefore very much a family matter.

Yet property is not the sole concern: proper child-rearing includes instilling a sense of *pudor* in boys, and one aspect of that modesty is sexual restraint. In the *Bacchides,* Plautus portrays Lydus, the pedagogue of young Pistoclerus, as the advocate of old-fashioned morals. Lydus takes it to be the duty of parent and pedagogue to make sure that boys grow up with a sense of sexual shame. His reaction to finding his pupil in an amorous embrace with a *meretrix* is comically exaggerated: "To recall other things which I saw him do is very shameful: when he put his hand under her dress to touch Bacchis' body in my presence and wasn't shamed. What's the point of words? For me a student has perished, for you a companion, for his father a son; for I say that man has perished in whom *pudor* has perished."[24] Lydus complains that Pistoclerus' father has failed to discipline his son, and so has undercut the pedagogue's authority; the father gives the standard reason for indulgence that, like his son, he had been involved in love affairs as a youth. Although there is certainly a double standard for the sexual mores of sons and daughters, the language of shame and honor is not wholly irrelevant to unmarried young men.[25] However, chastity is not a strong restraint on youths in these plays.

What could the *durus pater* do in an attempt to enforce *pudor* on a son and to limit his sexual liaisons? Fathers most often verbally chastise their

---

[23] Plautus, *Asinaria* 126–204, *Epidicus* 220, *Mercator* 42, 52, 1015, *Mostellaria* 229, *Pseudolus* 288, 415–22, *Trinummus* 244, *Truculentus* 59, 572; Terence, *Heautontimorumenos* 203, 1040, *Adelphoe* 148. E. Fantham, "Stuprum: Public Attitudes and Penalties for Sexual Offences in Republican Rome," *Échos du monde classique/Classical Views* 35 (1991), 289.

[24] *Bacchides* 481–85: "nam alia memorare quae illum facere vidi dispudet: / quom manum sub vestimenta ad corpus tetulit Bacchidi / me praesente, neque pudere quicquam. quid verbis opust? / mihi discipulus, tibi sodalis periit, huic filius; / nam ego illum periisse dico quoi quidem periit pudor."

[25] I stress this point because readers of some recent work on ancient sexuality (e.g., P. Veyne, *A History of Private Life,* trans. A. Goldhammer [Cambridge, Mass., 1987], 23–25) might conclude that chastity came to be regarded as a virtue for young men only in the imperial era. Fantham, "Stuprum," offers a more balanced discussion.

sons.[26] A more determined father could try to cut off loans to sons to stop the patrimonial waste, as in Plautus' *Mercator* (52), or could even exile the son from the house. Another paternal strategy is to push the son into marriage, a possibility suggested in Plautus' *Epidicus*. The youth in love, Stratippocles, has purchased his slave *amica*. The family slave Epidicus tells the youth's father Periphanes that the *adulescens* is madly in love in a way that will cost both son and father *fidemque remque* (220). Epidicus advises the father to stop the affair by arranging his son's marriage. Possession of an *amica* costs the reputation and property of the family as a whole, not just the son's. But, upon self-reflection, Periphanes decides not to force his son's marriage: his own *malefacta* in youth were *plurima,* and his son does not wrong him personally with this *amica.* Just as with daughters, so with sons, a father's moral self-awareness might limit his exercise of power in forcing a marriage.

If the fathers in the *Bacchides* and the *Epidicus* decline to force their sons toward *pudor,* Terence's *Andria* suggests why at a certain point in his son's life course an indulgent father might become more demanding. The youth Pamphilus has impregnated young Glycerium, a girl initially of slave status on account of mistaken identity. Pamphilus' father, Simo, is willing to overlook his son's love affairs, until he arrives at an age for a proper marriage, as Simo explains to his slave Davus: "For me to investigate these matters [my son's earlier affairs with an *amica*] is to be an unfair father; for what he did before has nothing to do with me. As long as the time was conducive to it, I permitted him to fulfill his own passion; now this day brings a different way of life and demands different habits: from this point I demand, or if it is more proper, I ask you, Davus, to lead him back onto this path. What's this? All who are in love accept a wife given to them with great difficulty."[27] Simo's words suggest that the standards of propriety in sexual unions change through a man's life and that the transition from youthful extramarital loves to legitimate marriage may be a difficult one, sometimes in need of a push by a father.

---

[26] Plautus, *Mercator* 42, *Mostellaria* 750; Terence, *Heautontimorumenos* 356, *Phormio* 219–20.

[27] *Andria* 186–91: "sed nunc ea me exquirere / iniqui patris est; nam quod ant(e)hac fecit nil ad me attinet. / dum tempus ad eam rem tulit, sivi animum ut expleret suom; / nunc hic dies aliam vitam defert, alios mores postulat: / de(h)inc postulo sive aequomst te oro, Dave, ut redeat iam in viam. / hoc quid sit? omnes qui amant graviter sibi dari uxorem ferunt."

Since in law the consent of both father and son was required for legitimate marriage, the son had grounds to resist paternal pressure. The conflict between son and father over the decision to marry and the choice of a wife is represented in many comedies as one between love on the son's side and considerations of property and status on the father's. In Plautus' *Trinummus,* this latent conflict of interests does not develop into a confrontation because of a departure from the usual stereotype of the rebellious son. Lysiteles has generally been a good son, obedient to his father's orders (*imperia,* 301). Father Philto gives his son practical advice on the importance of maintaining their patrimony, but to Lysiteles' request for money, Philto replies: "I can't deny you anything you wish." [28] It comes as no surprise when a few lines later Philto gives up his resistance to his son's wish to marry a certain woman "without a dowry" (*sine dote*), a financial sacrifice, saying "have your way, marry her." [29] The interaction between Lysiteles and Philto suggests that being an obedient son does not necessarily entail complete acquiescence to a father's will; indeed, past obedience can be used as justification for special concessions from a father. [30] It has been said that the reciprocal of *patria potestas* in Roman culture is filial *pietas,* interpreted as obedience; here the reciprocal of filial *pietas* is a father's acquiescence to his son's request. Later in the play reference is made to how submissive (*obnoxiosus,* 1037) parents generally are to their children.

Fathers in other plays are portrayed as more insistent on their powers in arranging sons' marriages. In Plautus' *Cistellaria,* young Alcesimarchus has promised to marry Selenium, thought to be a prostitute on account of mistaken identity. His father is intent on forcing him into a more honorable marriage, as Selenium describes: "But he swore a formal vow before my mother that he would take me as his wife; now he must marry another woman, his Lemnian relative, who is living next door. For his father has forced (*subegit*) him. Now my mother is angry at me, since I did not return home to her, after I learned of the arrangement for him to take another woman as his wife." [31]

---

[28] Line 357: "non edepol tibi pernegare possum quicquam quod velis."

[29] Lines 383–84: "etsi adversatus tibi fui, istac iudico: tibi permitto; posce, duce."

[30] At line 310 Lysiteles pleads with his father on the grounds that he has served his father's *imperia* and endured *servitus.*

[31] *Cistellaria* 98–103: "at ille conceptis iuravit verbis apud matrem meam / me uxorem ducturum esse: ei nunc alia ducendast domum, / sua cognata Lemniensis, quae

The father is represented as forcing his son to consent.[32] The god Auxilium's description of the father's intent is that "the father wishes to give a wife to his son";[33] the father is motivated by property, his desire for a rich dowry from the bride's family. The father here takes the initiative in making a marriage arrangement and then puts pressure on his son to consent; the son is able to resist until the conflict is happily resolved upon discovery of Selenium's true citizen identity.

The nature of paternal pressure on a son to accept a marriage is described in Terence's *Hecyra*. At his father's insistence, young Pamphilus married, despite his passion for the *meretrix* Bacchis. The slave Parmeno narrates the background: "Pamphilus was in love with this Bacchis as much as ever when his father began to implore (*orare*) him to take a wife and said the usual things that all fathers say, that he is an old man, yet has only his one son: that he wants protection for his old age. The son at first refused, but after his father insisted more sharply (*acrius*), he made him unsure whether he should give more heed to *pudor* or to *amor*. Finally the old man had his way by keeping at him and by unpleasantness (*tundendo atque odio*): he engaged to him the daughter of his next-door neighbor."[34] The father can take the initiative in arranging the marriage, but cannot immediately force his son to consent; the son is faced with a decision between *amor* and *pudor*, here meaning obedience to his father. The slave describes the escalating pressure: first pleading on the basis of his needs, then pushing pointedly, and finally haranguing. As in other plays, paternal coercion takes a verbal form throughout but becomes progressively more aggressive.

----

habitat hic in proxumo. / nam eum pater eius subegit. nunc mea mater iratast mihi, / quia non redierim domum ad se, postquam hanc rem resciverim, / eum uxorem ducturum esse aliam."

[32] Since Greek fathers are often thought to have been less authoritarian than their Roman counterparts, it is worth noting here that this passage has the earmarks of its Greek original insofar as the marriage is to *sua cognata*. Close-kin marriage was more a Greek than a Roman practice.

[33] Line 195: "pater adulescenti dare volt uxorem."

[34] *Hecyra* 114–24: "hanc Bacchidem / amabat ut quom maxume tum Pamphilus / quom pater uxorem ut ducat orare occipit / et haec communia omnium quae sunt patrum, / sese senem esse dicere, illum autem unicum: / praesidium velle se senectuti suae. / ill' primo se negare; sed postquam acrius / pater instat, fecit animi ut incertus foret / pudorin anne amori obsequeretur magis. / tundendo atque odio denique effecit senex: / despondit ei gnatum hui(u)s vicini proxumi."

In Terence's *Andria*, the father, Simo, tries to detach his son, also named Pamphilus, from his *amica* Mysis, treated virtually as a wife, in order to marry him to the daughter of Chremes "with the greatest dowry" (*cum dote summa*, 101)—again the familiar theme of *amor* and *res* coming into collision in the arrangement of a son's marriage. In this plot Simo forces the issue by committing his son to the lucrative marriage without his agreement, prompting Pamphilus to challenge his father's unilateral action by appealing to "a father's duty" (*officium patris*). Another youth, Charinus, is eager to marry Chremes' daughter, despite the fact that she has already been promised. The slave Davus urges Charinus to seek Chremes' approval by going and pleading his cause with the old man's *amici* (373)—an indication that a father's consent might be arrived at with the advice of friends. For Chremes' part, when he learns that Pamphilus has had a baby by his *amica*, he considers withdrawing his consent to the marriage, because it is his duty as a father to protect his daughter from a troubled marriage (*incertae nuptiae*, 831). The reaction of Pamphilus' father, Simo, to the arrangement's falling apart is to lament Pietas. When Pamphilus then addresses him as "my father" (*mi pater*), his response is: "Why call me 'my father'? As if you were in need of this father. Home, wife, children have been found against your father's will. Men have been brought forward to say that she is a citizen: you have won."[35] Old Simo is finally reconciled to Pamphilus' marriage to his *amica*, when her true citizen identity is accepted and she is given a huge dowry worth ten talents. This play neatly illustrates how *pietas* may influence the negotiation of consent to marriage in different ways: *pietas* is a moral value that could be invoked to constrain sons to follow their fathers' wishes in consenting to marriage; *pietas* and *officium* also are supposed to constrain fathers to act in consultation with their children and in their best interest by not arranging a troubling marriage for them.

In the *Trinummus*, the *Cistellaria*, the *Hecyra*, and the *Andria*, father and son come to an agreement over the son's marriage and resolve the conflict between *amor* and *res* through negotiation and argument, together with some unbelievably good luck in the discovery of true identities. In Terence's *Phormio*, the intensely angry father Demipho threatens to take the conflict beyond words by exiling his son from his house: "I will prohibit him along with this

---

[35] *Andria* 890–92: "quid 'mi pater'? quasi tu huius indigeas pater. / domus uxor liberi inventi invito patre; / adducti qui illam hinc civem dicant: viceris."

wife from the house."[36] This is the most severe punishment threatened against a disobedient son in the comedies, and in this play it is not carried out. As Phormio points out to Demipho, a father who casts his son out of his house will be punishing himself as well by ruining his family.[37]

The suffering of a father who has driven his son away on account of an unapproved union is voiced by Menedemus in Terence's *Heautontimorumenos:* "When I learned of [my son's] affair, I did not react kindly nor handle the love-sick spirit of the youth as is proper, but in anger and the usual way of fathers. I was accusing him daily: 'hey, do you hope, while I your father am alive, to be allowed to do this any longer, to have an *amica* virtually in place of a wife? You are wrong if you think so, and you don't know me, Clinia. I want you to be called my son only as long as you do what is worthy of you; but if you do not, I will find what is worthy of me to do to you.' "[38] In response to this hectoring, Clinia left home, to his father's anguish. The suggestion here is that fathers commonly grow angry at the disobedience of their sons, and the lesson is that lack of restraint can lead to consequences as painful for father as for son. Menedemus' grief prompts his old friend Chremes to offer some conventional wisdom to Menedemus on the need to cultivate trust in child-rearing: "I think that you have an indulgent attitude toward children and that he is an obeying sort if treated properly or kindly. But you did not know him well enough, nor he you. Where does this occur? Where people don't live candidly. You have never shown him how much you valued him, and he did not dare trust in you as is right

---

[36] Line 425: "cum uxore hac ipsum prohibebo domo."

[37] Line 426: "tu te idem melius feceris." Physical punishment is not threatened against sons by their fathers in the comedies, and for that reason their situation is contrasted with that of recalcitrant slaves; see Plautus, *Mostellaria* 743–50; Terence, *Heautontimorumenos* 356, *Phormio* 219–20. On sanctions against disobedient sons in comedy, see J. C. Dumont, "L'imperium du paterfamilias," in *Parenté et stratégies familiales dans l'antiquité romaine,* ed. J. Andreau and H. Bruhns, Colloques de l'École Française de Rome 129 (Rome, 1990), 489.

[38] Lines 99–108: "ubi rem rescivi, coepi non humanitus / neque ut animum decuit aegrotum adulescentuli / tractare, sed vi et via pervolgata patrum. / cotidie accusabam: 'hem tibine haec diutius / licere speras facere me vivo patre, / amicam ut habeas prope iam in uxoris loco? / erras, si id credis, et me ignoras, Clinia. / ego te meum esse dici tantisper volo / dum quod te dignumst facies; sed si id non facis, ego quod me in te sit facere dignum invenero."

in a father. If this had been done, these things would never have happened to you."[39]

Such thoughtful advice is easier to give than to follow in difficult situations, as Chremes discovers when he tries to force his own son Clitipho to give up his *amica* and enter a respectable marriage. In dialogue with his father and his mother, Sostrata, at the end of the play, Clitipho finally agrees to take a legitimate wife.

Clit. I will do it father.
Sos. My child, I will give you a charming wife, whom you will easily love—the daughter of our Phanocrates.
Clit. That red-headed, blue-eyed girl, with a freckled face and a hooked nose? I cannot, father.
Chr. Ah, how discriminating he is! You would think his mind is in this.
Sos. I will give another.
Clit. No, since a wife must be found, I have one whom I more or less want.
Chr. Now I praise you, son.
Clit. The daughter of this Archonides.
Sos. Good enough.[40]

Several aspects of the negotiation of consent are worth noting: the mother participates in the choice of a bride though she has no legal role;[41] the father pushes the son toward legitimate marriage but does not have a strong view about the choice of a wife; conversely, the son agrees to marry as long as it is to a woman of his choosing. Compromise in coming to consent to marriage

---

[39] Lines 151–57: "ingenio te esse in liberos leni puto, / et illum obsequentem siqui' recte aut commode / tractaret. verum nec tu illumsati' noveras / nec te ille; hoc qui fit? ubi non vere vivitur. tu illum numquam ostendisti quanti penderes / nec tibi illest credere ausu' quae aequom patri. / quod si esset factum, haec numquam evenissent tibi."

[40] Lines 1059–66: "CL. faciam, pater. / SO. gnate mi, ego pol tibi dabo illam lepidam, quam tu facile ames, / filiam Phanocratae nostri. CL. rufamne illam virginem, / caesiam, sparso ore, adunco naso? non possum, pater. / CH. heia ut elegans est! credas animum ibi esse. SO. aliam dabo. / CL. immo, quandoquidem ducendast, egomet habeo propemodum / quam volo. CH. nunc laudo, gnate. CL. Archonidi huiu' filiam. / SO. perplacet."

[41] For a discussion of the non-fictional evidence for the participation of female relatives, see Treggiari, "*Digna condicio.*"

is possible in this scenario because the family members are able to satisfy their different concerns.

To generalize, the plots of Roman comedies repeatedly illustrate conflict between father and child over decisions about the child's marriage, choice of spouse, and divorce. In this context, the issue of consent to marriage and sexual relations arises. The disagreement between father and child is most often represented as one between the child's *amor* and the father's concern for property and respectability. Conflict between father and son over consent to marriage is situated at the point of transition from informal attachment to lower-class women to legitimate marriage to a citizen woman. Though mutual consent of bride, groom, and the *paterfamilias* of each was a legal requirement for a valid marriage, differences between father and child are not settled in the plays by recourse to legal procedure or threat of it. Rather, the negotiation leading to consensus is a matter of give and take, mainly within the household and based on appeals to duty and love. The *paterfamilias* possesses *ius* and *potestas,* but does not have the latitude of unrestrained, arbitrary actions.[42] Indeed, several plays present a debate about how fathers can find the golden mean between severity and indulgence in the exercise of their power. Sons and daughters are shown manipulating paternal authority by appeal to paternal love and *officium* toward children. Ultimately, fathers have the power to exile sons from home, and sons can threaten to run away from home—extreme actions shown to result in grief for all concerned. The plots are happily resolved, often through the discovery of mistaken identity, so that the son can marry his beloved, who in the end meets the father's criteria of social and civic propriety.

New Comedy and Roman Culture

What can a social historian glean from this genre about the nature of consent to marriage and sexual relations in early second-century Rome? The skeptic would answer "little or nothing," on the grounds that the plays are imaginative literature and Greek in origin. Although the die-hard skeptic may not be convinced, several responses may be suggested in order to salvage the plays as historical evidence for a period otherwise thinly documented.

---

[42] Dumont, "L'*imperium,*" 493–94, makes the important point that paternal *imperium* has force only as long as it is exercised on behalf of traditional *mores.* Therefore, it is not an arbitrary or unrestrained power, as sometimes portrayed.

First, despite the Ciceronian description of comedy as the "mirror of social custom" (*speculum consuetudinis*),[43] it is obvious that the plays are not a direct reflection of social realities or of typical family behavior. The typical Roman father is not likely to have attempted a fraudulent sale of his daughter to a pimp or to have dressed as a sea captain to secure an *amica* for a son. This admission, however, is not good reason for dismissal of the plays as historical evidence. After all, it would be naive to think that texts of laws or anecdotes reported by the historians are a sure guide to typical social behavior, and yet they are taken as evidence for social history—ancient historians cannot afford to be overly selective in the evidence they consider.

Though not a direct reflection, the comedies were a part of the cultural and social reality of early second-century Rome in at least two ways. First, the plays were part of a public discourse giving expression to debates over moral issues like the nature of *pudor,* the virtues of the severe as against the indulgent approach to raising children, the obligations of *pietas* in the arrangement of marriages, and so on. As Elizabeth Rawson observed in her assessment of the influence of Greek culture on Republican Rome: "Plautus keeps much of the sententiousness that marked Greek New Comedy, even expands on it; we know that later at least Roman audiences greatly enjoyed the moralizing they heard on both the comic and the tragic stage. . . . This, for Plautus, is 'philosophizing,' and seen as learned and Greek. In the absence of many other sources of moral advice, it may be that ordinary Romans articulated many of their moral perceptions by what they experienced in the theater."[44] Although the size of audiences for the plays in Rome should not be overestimated, the performances no doubt were meant for a wider and more varied group than written texts.[45] Within the moral discourse of the plays, certain views and characters are clearly set up for ridicule, playing off of reality as inversions of social expectations. So the extremes of the *lenis* and *durus pater* are patently caricatures and laughable. But it would be very hard to dismiss as inversions the many other father characters pursuing the middle

---

[43] Quoted by Fantham in "Sex, Status, and Survival," 44; I find the interpretive approaches of Fantham and Konstan convincing.

[44] *Cambridge Ancient History* (Cambridge, 1989), vol. VIII, 2d ed., 439.

[45] On the nature of the audience, see now R. MacMullen, "Hellenizing the Romans (2nd Century B.C.)," *Historia* 40 (1991), 420–29, who concludes his article by stressing how unrealistic it would be to claim that the issues voiced in the comedies were completely foreign to Romans of the 2d century.

ground in child-rearing and offering what would pass for conventional wisdom about love and trust in other eras including today. While we may not know the audience reaction to this discourse on stage, at the very least the plays demonstrate (against some recent claims) that the sentimental conception of the family bound by love as well as duty was not beyond the purview of a Roman audience.[46]

Second, the plots are based on the fundamental ideological assumptions that in reality did organize Roman society.[47] The world of comedy, the basic situations, are not utopian but include slave households, classification of characters in accordance with citizenship and wealth, and a consequent concern for family status based on wealth. In other words, the plays assume "the rules and values of ancient city-state society [which] constitute a cultural system. The system may be said to define, by the operation of inclusion and exclusion, the several groups or statuses of the society."[48] Despite some differences, that fundamental cultural system was as much a basis of life in Republican Rome as in classical Athens. That point is the beginning of an

---

[46] S. Dixon, "The Sentimental Ideal of the Roman Family," in *Marriage, Divorce and Children in Ancient Rome,* ed. B. Rawson (Oxford, 1991), 99–113, following M. Manson, "The Emergence of the Small Child in Rome (Third Century BC–First Century AD)," *History of Education* 12 (1983), 149–59. Manson argues for the absence of a sentimental ideal in the plays on the basis of the absence of adjectives like *dulcis* and *suavis* for children. That argument is much too narrow to be convincing. By dramatic convention, young children rarely have any place in plays, so the full range of vocabulary is unlikely to appear. Though *dulcis* and *suavis* are not used to describe children, other terms of endearment, such as diminutives, are used: e.g., *delectatio* (Terence, *Heautontimorumenos* 987); *mea voluptas* and *pullus tuus* (Plautus, *Poenulus* 1292); *parvola* (Plautus, *Poenulus* 26, 1105); *filiola parvola* (Plautus, *Rudens* 39); and a *parvolus* who provides *oblectatio* (Terence, *Adelphoe* 49). Finally, part of the background to Plautus' *Menaechmi* is the death of a father by heartbreak over the presumed death of one of his two seven-year-old sons— it is difficult to imagine a more poignant expression of sentimental attachment and it cannot be explained as selfish concern over loss of an heir since another son survived.

[47] P. B. Harvey, Jr., "Historical Topicality in Plautus," *Classical World* 79 (1986), 303, surveys scholarly efforts to find historical allusions in Plautus' comedies. He draws a useful distinction between attempts to discover allusions to general aspects of Roman affairs and those to a specific person, place, or institution. My concern is with "the general Roman atmosphere," to use Harvey's phrase.

[48] Konstan, *Roman Comedy,* 18.

answer to the second cause for skepticism—the Greek origin of New Comedy.

The fact that Plautus and Terence started from Greek models in writing their plays has been the subject of much discussion among literary scholars, but is of only limited relevance to the issues under examination in this paper. The originality of the comedies is of direct consequence to the assessment of their literary achievement. The central question here, however, is whether the plays resonated with Roman experience outside the theater in a way to reveal something of that experience. Several reasons suggest such resonance.[49] Above all, some of the most common themes of the comedies clearly do correspond to the moral discourse of second-century Rome known from other sources, thin though the evidence may be.

Much of our evidence for the debate about traditional morality in the early second century centers on the elder Cato, who as censor of 184 B.C. tried to enforce it. Plutarch's biography and fragments of Cato's speeches preserved by Aulus Gellius show that Cato was interested in many of the same moral issues on display in the comedies.[50] Like Plautus and Terence, Cato joked about the inversion of the proper relationship of authority in marriage. Plutarch reports Cato's saying that "men usually command women, but we command all men, and the women command us," and notes that Cato borrowed the line from Themistocles. The similarity of cultural assumptions about gender that made the quip transferable from Athens to Rome also made comedies about hen-pecked husbands translatable. More specifically, Cato, like Plautus and Terence, attributed this inversion of household authority to the wealth of wives that made their husbands dependent on them. The carping *uxor dotata* is a figure familiar both from Cato's oratory and from the come-

---

[49] E. Gruen, *Studies in Greek Culture and Roman Policy* (Leiden, 1990), chap. 4, has recently discussed various resonances in Plautine allusions to public issues, suggesting that "generations of scholars have found it devilishly difficult to disentangle the Greek and Roman elements [in Plautine comedy]. The reason is simple enough: they were not meant to be disentangled." Given the similarities of household economy and distinctions of status in Rome and Athens, Gruen's comment would be all the more true of representations of family and household.

[50] O. Jurewicz, "Plautus, Cato der Ältere und die römische Gesellschaft," in *Aus der altertumswissenschaftlichen Arbeit Volkspolens,* ed. J. Irmscher und K. Kumaniecki (Berlin, 1959), 52–72, discusses some of these points of contact from a general interest in ideological conflict in Rome.

dies.[51] In addition, in Cato's oratory, as in the comedies, the double standard regarding adultery for husband and wife is noted or questioned.[52]

Of more direct interest to this paper, Cato was very much concerned with the proper approach to child-rearing. Plutarch describes him as a "good father" who took a hand in tending his son from infancy and devoted considerable energy to his proper education (20.2–3). While advocating strictness, Cato eschewed corporal punishment of children (in contrast to slaves), saying that a man who beat (*tuptonta*) his wife or child was laying hands on what was most sacred. Of special concern to Cato was the development of a sense of *pudor* in his son. Plutarch reports that he avoided obscene language and nude bathing in the presence of his son (20.2–3). His interest in the *pudor* of youth did not stop with his son; he is supposed to have commented favorably on young men who blushed (9.4), and he expelled from the senate a man who kissed his wife in front of his daughter in the light of day (17.7). Perhaps more interesting is Cato's famous comment about Socrates (20.2) that there was nothing to admire in the philosopher of old except that he treated his difficult wife and stupid sons "tolerantly" (*epieikos*) and "gently" (*praos*). The remark is revealing because it suggests a continuity in basic Greek and Roman attitudes toward child-rearing: Cato condemned various Greek influences on Roman *mores*, but did not attribute to the Greeks some softening of *patria potestas* in Rome—on the virtue of gentleness toward family members, Cato saw eye to eye with Socrates. The common moral themes of Cato and the playwrights make it impossible to believe that a Cato in the audience would have laughed off the debate about the *pudor* of youth or the dilemmas of child-rearing as foreign, exotic, and of no relevance to Romans.

Scipio Aemilianus, one of the most prominent youths of the early second century, would not have made a good character in comedy, to judge by Polybius' description (31.25), because he was too virtuous to be entertaining. Endowed with *sophrosyne*, Aemilianus cultivated a reputation for chastity; through his restraint he was able to preserve his fortune and thereby have the means to be generous to his family. The young men with whom he is con-

---

[51] E. Schuhmann, "Der Typ der *uxor dotata* in den Komödien des Plautus," *Philologus* 121 (1977), 45–65; A. Gellius, *Noctes Atticae* 17.6 for Cato's comment on a wife with *magna dos* and her own property.

[52] A. Gellius, *Noctes Atticae* 10.23.5; Plautus, *Menaechmi* passim, *Mercator* 823; Terence, *Hecyra* 538–50.

trasted are characterized as dissolute, "some wasting their energies on favorite youths, others on mistresses, and a great many on banquets enlivened with poetry and wine, and all the extravagant expenditure which they entailed." These youths resemble the stock characters of comedy in their dissipation of *res* in pursuit of *amor*. That Polybius chose to differentiate Aemilianus from his peers on the basis of these particular traits demonstrates that the stock situations of comedy were perceived to be commonplace in Roman elite society. It may be no accident that Plautus and Terence so often chose Greek plays involving father-son conflict over money and women as models to entertain their Roman audiences.[53]

Finally, because the basic situations represented in the comedies were familiar (though not necessarily typical), the personal interactions of characters could be translated into terms embodying the most traditional Roman values. The negotiation leading to consent to marriage could be presented in terms of the father's *potestas* being obeyed out of *pietas,* or resisted and manipulated by his children's appeals to paternal *officium* and affection. The value of the plays lies in illustrating how these traditional values could have been appropriately invoked in situations of opposing family interests. In a sense, the plays have a heuristic value to the historian, just as they had to the audience: they do not tell us what really happened within real families, but they indicated to the audience and indicate to us possible Roman scenarios starting from stock situations and negotiated on the basis of traditional values. The scenarios encourage us to think of legal consent to marriage as an outcome of a dynamic process rather than the imposition of an arbitrary paternal will.[54]

University of Chicago

[53] A point made to me by David Konstan in correspondence.

[54] I am grateful to the participants in the colloquium held at Dumbarton Oaks in February 1992 for their comments, and especially to Robert Kaster, Peter White, and David Konstan, who offered many helpful suggestions.

Part Two

Byzantium

A Varangian soldier raped a woman "in the wilderness"; she then killed him, a scene illustrated on the left; on the right, we see his companions giving the woman "all of his possessions," symbolized by his clothes. The man was left unburied. The legend of the miniature reads: "the woman who was raped by the barbarian and killed him"; "the Varangians give to the raped woman all of the property of the violator." From the Madrid manuscript of the *Synopsis Historiarum* of John Skylitzes, fol. 208; after A. Grabar and M. Manoussacas, *L'illustration du manuscrit de Skylitzès de la Bibliothèque nationale de Madrid* (Venice, 1979), pl. 37. *(Courtesy of the Istituto Ellenico di Studi Bizantini e Postbizantini di Venezia)*

Sex, Consent, and Coercion in Byzantium

ANGELIKI E. LAIOU

Preface

In Byzantium of the late twelfth century, a lively debate took place, primarily among canonists, on the question of the validity of coerced consent to monastic life. The question arose out of specific and actual situations, in which force, violence, or duress were used to persuade individuals to enter the monastic life, a decision whose validity by definition depended on the free consent of the individual. The occasions were many and varied: a bishop was forced, by imperial officials, and for reasons which remain unclear, to become a monk; many members of the aristocracy, male and female, were coerced into monastic life by emperors who wanted to reduce their political power; women in particular were tonsured unwillingly, so that their marriages would be dissolved; the wives of men elevated to the episcopate were forced to become nuns, as opposed to simply living in a monastery, immediately after their husband's ordination.[1] The last two issues were the ones which were most hotly debated. The forced tonsure and divorce of women was of particular importance to aristocratic society, since it was a way for emperors, and occasionally others, including members of the families of the spouses, to break up marriages and therefore political alliances. Used since at least the early eleventh century specifically for this purpose, forced tonsure became, during the brief reign of Andronikos I (1183–85), a relatively frequent means of dissolving the marriages of the aristocracy. After his deposition and death, both the civil courts and the canonists were faced with political questions as

[1] For a discussion of a number of these cases, see A. Laiou, *Mariage, amour et parenté à Byzance, XIème–XIIIème siècles* (Paris, 1992), chap. 4.

109

well as with the theoretical question of what constitutes and what establishes free and coerced consent, and in what circumstances the validity of monastic vows was undermined by coercion. It was, I think, because of these very real problems that the debate then took place among canonists on the second issue, that is, on the coerced tonsure of the wives of bishops, a question which in the end produced imperial legislation, namely, a Novel of Emperor Isaac II Angelos.[2] The debate was real, and quite sophisticated.

In the course of investigating these twelfth-century developments, I became interested in the general question of free and coerced consent, and the ways in which Byzantine society dealt with it. As far as the twelfth century is concerned, the issue clearly came to the fore as a result of the increasing effort of Comnenian emperors to control society, especially aristocratic society, and therefore the matrimonial alliances of its members. The other side of this coin is the desire of members of the aristocracy to control and further their own interests; the combination led both to political clashes and to the debate of more general issues. However, the posture of the aristocracy did not in itself mean a greater respect for the free will of the individual, but rather an insistence on control by the family rather than by the state. It was the canonists, and perhaps the civil judges, faced with specific issues in court, who generalized and brought the question of free and coerced individual consent to the forefront of the discussion. Although the debate centered around the question of free consent to monastic life, the interplay of individual free will and the limiting factors of state, church, family, and custom governed and governs many other aspects of life, including the transfer of property and intervention in religious and political life.

In this effort to approach the issue insofar as Byzantium is concerned, I have concentrated on the question of consent to sexual and matrimonial relations. In some ways, this aspect of the larger question is the easiest to treat, since free consent, at least to marriage, was an element society explicitly recognized as necessary, and equally explicitly circumscribed by the just as necessary consent of the parents of the spouses. It is also an issue to whose subtleties we have become sensitive because of current debates concerning sexual harassment and rape, debates now taking place in both western Europe and North America. While one must be cautious not to superimpose current concerns on past societies, nevertheless it would be absurd not to recognize

---

[2] J. and P. Zepos, *Jus Graecoromanum* (hereafter *JGR*), I (Athens, 1931), 435–36.

the fact that historians are moved and informed by the debates of their own day.

In Byzantium, as in Rome and much more than in Rome, sexual activity was to be confined within institutional limits defined by law. In the Roman Empire, these institutions consisted of marriage and concubinage. In Byzantium, monogamous marriage was the ideal promulgated by the church, and to some extent adopted by the state. In the eighth century, the Isaurian emperors promoted productive and stable unions to the extent of assimilating long-term cohabitation with marriage, while early in the tenth century Emperor Leo VI finally forbade concubinage.[3] Concubinage was far from abolished by these measures, and the woman who had a long-term cohabitation with a man outside the confines of marriage even enjoyed some protection which seems to have been customary rather than legal.[4] Nevertheless, sexual activity outside of marriage, as well as adultery, was considered illicit in various degrees. The purpose of this study is to examine the role of consent in establishing legal categories, and, further, the role of consent in the determination of culpability and punishment, not only in the law but, more importantly, in social thought and practice. Was consent the main factor distinguishing various aspects of illicit sexual activity, or were other factors, such as social position or marital status, more important? Was society conscious of and interested in how free one's consent was, and in the elements which constitute or prove coercion? Was coerced consent considered valid?

The illicit sexual activities to which the question is pertinent are several. In Roman law, and in Byzantium, the categories included adultery, that is, intercourse with a married woman; *stuprum,* or φθορά, which involves a man with a woman unmarried or no longer married; and *per vim stuprum,* which is *stuprum* with the addition of coercion or force. Incest, whatever its specific definition, was certainly an illicit sexual relationship, but the question of consent does not enter as a defining factor, and incest therefore will not be treated here. On the other hand, abduction, which was, strictly speaking, the forcible removal of a woman (or, indeed, a man) came very quickly to acquire sexual connotations, since it was thought either to be attended by

---

[3] *Ecloga,* L. Burgmann, ed., *Ecloga: Das Gesetzbuch Leons III. und Konstantinos' V.* (Frankfurt, 1983), 2.6; P. Noailles and A. Dain, *Les Novelles de Léon VI le Sage* (Paris, 1944), p. 91, and *Procheiros Nomos* 4.25–26.

[4] A. Laiou, "Contribution à l'étude de l'institution familiale en Épire au XIIIème siècle," *Fontes Minores* 6 (1984), 284 ff.

intercourse or to be occasioned by a desire to marry. Since force or the presumption of force is by definition inherent in at least some stages of abduction, the issue of consent does arise here, and will be discussed.

Many strains of thought, past elaborations, and inherited and new attitudes informed the Byzantine approach to these issues. From the Roman past, the Byzantines inherited legal categories as well as the important idea that consent was a differentiating factor in the categorization of actions. But the further elaboration of the problem depended on non-Roman antecedents. Shame and honor, so important in Greek Antiquity, played an important role.[5] So did ideas of sexual pollution, which were very old, but which were given new form by Christianity. The church, with its own ideas regarding sin, its expiation, and personal responsibility, played a fundamental role. The result of the combination and sometimes the opposition of ideas stemming from these different traditions was the creation of a new system, medieval in aspect and specific to Byzantium.

The subject could be treated in a number of ways. My own interests do not lie in the philosophical concepts that may underlie definitions of consent, but rather in social history. The present study is an effort to elucidate how the various issues connected with free or coerced consent were dealt with in Byzantine society, both formally and informally. Thus legal definitions, legal practice, and social attitudes and practice will all be considered, as will the literary treatment of these issues. While this is not a study in legal history, it does address legal issues. I am grateful to many people who, over the years, have helped me to understand the intricacies involved in such matters.

I am also grateful to the participants in the seminar for the lively discussion which helped me to clarify my thoughts, and for the insights which they contributed on a number of points, as well as for the occasional contribution of source references. I would like to thank particularly Hélène Ahrweiler, Robert Browning, Alexander Kazhdan, Jelisaveta Allen, Alice-Mary Talbot, Alexander Alexakis, and Denis Sullivan for their contributions. Some of the research on which this work is based was carried out in 1988–89, when I was on leave from my regular duties. I am grateful to the American Council of Learned Societies and the National Endowment for the Humanities for a grant which made that year possible.

---

[5] Hugh Lloyd-Jones, "Ehre und Schande in der griechischen Kultur," *Antike und Abendland* 33 (1987), 1–28.

I. The Legal Categories

Is law the proper place to start such an investigation? It can easily be argued that if the purpose is to understand social attitudes, formal legal pronouncements are not very useful and can, in fact, be misleading. Such an argument has a certain force. To some extent, undoubtedly, law reflects social attitudes; it also, surely, seeks to shape them. But legal systems can and do incorporate many laws which are capricious, or outdated, or unenforced because unenforceable. Furthermore, legal pronouncements have a subtext which is essential for understanding both their letter and their spirit and which one ignores at one's peril. It may be argued that less formal sources, literary and other, can be more useful than legal texts in providing information about the complexities, subtleties, and ambiguities which render this subject interesting. On the other hand, one of the first questions to be addressed is whether consent served to create legal categories insofar as sexual and matrimonial relations were concerned, and for an answer to such a question one must surely turn to the legal texts. Furthermore, the vocabulary of consent and coercion is a legal vocabulary, even though the elaboration of the concepts may be undertaken in the course of non-legal debates, primarily theological or philosophical, and even though the vocabulary itself is shaped by attitudes which originate from people other than the legislator or the legal commentator. It has, therefore, seemed best to start with the formal legal texts, and then bring other sources to bear upon the issue in order to help illuminate and interpret both the legal vocabulary and the utility and import of the legal system.

The Roman Background

In Roman law, there were certain sexual unions that were accepted and encouraged, and others that were tolerated. Marriage, the union of free Roman citizens, into which the partners entered with their free consent and that of their parents or those who had them in their authority, was the one fully accepted and recognized form of cohabitation. The regulations surrounding marriage had in view primarily the marriage of the upper class, which Augustus is known to have wished to safeguard and encourage. Concubinage was an accepted form of sexual union between social unequals. Categories of sexual behavior which were known to law, and which were condemned with varying degrees of severity, include *stuprum*, that is, sexual relations with those categories of women with whom *stuprum* could be committed. These categories consisted of women of good repute and social class, whether unmarried or *matres familiae* who were no longer married, that is, who were widowed or divorced.[1] Adultery, strongly condemned by the *lex Julia de adulteriis coercendis*, could, properly speaking, be committed only with and by a married woman. The category *per vim stuprum* would seem, at first glance, to consist of forced sexual intercourse, that is, rape. But it was somewhat ill-defined, and left many questions unanswered, such as the degree of force necessary to qualify an action as *per vim stuprum*, as well as the type of woman against whom this action could be committed.[2] Finally, abduction, whatever its origins, acquired an implication of sexual coercion, certainly by the time of Constantine I and possibly already at the time of Augustus. Seen as a crime against public order, it was punished by the *lex Julia de vi publica*.[3] Its characteristics were forcible removal to another place and the use of arms.

The intricacies and ambiguities of the Roman legal categorizations have been treated elsewhere in this volume. Here, a few observations will suffice. First, although the sources permit one to make the above statements, they themselves recognized the ambiguities. In particular, the difference between *stuprum* and adultery was blurred in people's minds. The difference should be clear: "Adultery is committed with a married woman; *stuprum* is committed with a widow, a virgin, or a boy."[4] But it was not quite clear, as Papinian acknowledged.[5] The confusion perhaps reflects the fact that the major concern

---

[1] Susan Treggiari, *Roman Marriage: Iusti Coniuges from the Time of Cicero to the Time of Ulpian* (Oxford, 1991); Diana Moses, "Livy's Lucretia and the Validity of Coerced Consent in Roman Law," in Part I of this volume. For the Roman background I am indebted to Diana Moses, who brought up a number of important issues in our seminar, and also collected and made available to me various relevant texts.

[2] For *per vim stuprum*, see Moses,"Livy's Lucretia." See also Aline Rousselle, *Porneia: On Desire and the Body in Antiquity* (Oxford, 1988), 78 ff. Cf. *D.* 48.5.30 (29).9, *D.* 48.6.3.4.

[3] *D.* 48.6.5.2.

[4] *D.* 48.5.35 (Modestinus) = *Bas.* 60.37.34: "Adulterium in nupta admittitur; stuprum in vidua vel virgine vel puero committitur."

[5] *D.* 48.5.6: "Lex stuprum et adulterium promiscue et καταχρηστικώτερον appellat. sed proprie adulterium in nupta committitur . . . stuprum uero in uirginem

was with adultery, which endangered the institution the legislation most aimed to protect, that is, marriage. This concern then led people to subsume the lesser crime of *stuprum* under the greater one of adultery, which thus became a generalized category. The confusion, however, seems to have affected common attitudes, and perhaps the attitudes of some lawyers, rather than the legal pronouncements themselves. Even so, there are other instances where qualifications refine the original statement. Thus, for example, while adultery involves primarily married women, a concubine, too, could be accused of adultery, even though her union was not considered a valid marriage.[6]

Second, for Roman law, social status, especially of the woman, was an important factor in defining the legal categories. It is clear that a slave, for example, could not be accused of adultery, since slaves could not contract marriages. At another level, social class also governed the categorization of *stuprum:* one could have sexual relations with a woman either of ill repute or of a low social class (e.g., a prostitute, a procuress, an innkeeper, or an actress) without committing *stuprum; stuprum* with a slave was considered to constitute property damage to her owner.[7] Social status is intimately connected to mores or perceived mores, since the legislation is explicitly made for the virgin and the *mater familias,* the latter being defined as one who lives honorably (*quae non inhoneste vixit,* the σεμνὴ γυνή of the Greek sources).[8] On the other hand, *stuprum* could be committed against another man's concubine. For, if Roman law made of social class a defining factor in its categorizations, so it also dealt with the marital status of a woman. In the all-important category of adultery, it was the marital status of the woman, not of the man, that defined the category. It can thus be argued that the legal categories of sexual crimes in Roman legislation were established according to

---

uiduamue committitur, quod Graeci φθοϱὰν appellant. In the *Basilics* 60.37.8 this is rendered as: Λέγεται μὲν μοιχεία καὶ ἡ πϱὸς παϱθένον ἢ χήϱαν φθοϱά, κυϱίως δὲ μοιχεία μὲν ἐστὶν ἡ τῆς ὑπάνδϱου, φθοϱὰ δὲ ἡ τῆς παϱθένου καὶ χήϱας. Roman law states that a "widow" signifies either a widowed or a divorced woman.

[6] *D.* 48.5.14 (13). The *Basilics* (60.37.14) state this differently: "there can be accusation of adultery in an *improperly constituted marriage,*" perhaps because by then Leo VI had forbidden concubinage.

[7] Rousselle, *Porneia,* 85; cf. *D.* 47.10.25. About the *stuprum* of slaves, see Diana Moses, "Livy's Lucretia," note 31.

[8] See Ulpian in *D.* 50.16.46, no. 1.

relationships between men: the perpetrator and the woman's husband, or lover, or father.[9] Punishment was relative to the social position of the culprit and the victim. The age of the woman involved (i.e., the question of whether she is under the age of consent or not) did not loom large.

As for consent, the only consent or absence of it that is envisaged is that of the woman. In Roman legislation, it serves to differentiate principally between the categories of *stuprum* and *per vim stuprum*. It is the only place where it makes a difference, that difference being in the severity of the punishment of the man (and possibly in the punishment of the woman). But if this differentiation is connected only with *stuprum,* it probably applies only to widows and virgins; it is nowhere specifically stated, for example, that a married woman may have withheld her consent from an adulterous act of sexual intercourse. Furthermore, none of the subtleties of establishing consent or defining force is evident in the various laws connected with sexual crimes, although some do appear in other connections.

It should be noted here that although Roman law does have different categories of illicit sexual behavior, these are somewhat fuzzy and punishments are sometimes not spelled out, often being implicit rather than explicit.[10] This being the case, one is left with the impression that the consent of the woman plays a role that is secondary to that of her marital and social status (and to the social status of the man) in the definition of legal categories. The point is made with crystal clarity in a late Roman text, the Novel of Constantine I on abduction (326), where the consent of the woman is explicitly said not to affect the categorization of the crime although, exceptionally, it does affect the punishment of the woman.[11]

It will be evident to the naked eye that Roman law has been discussed here in an entirely superficial way. Indeed, this short summary cannot accommodate the complexities and ambiguities, let alone the development, of Roman law. My purpose has been simply to provide a telescoped background to

---

[9] See also the remarks of Joëlle Beaucamp, "La prostitution féminine," in *Die Reaktion der Normalen,* Max-Planck-Institut für europäische Rechtsgeschichte (Frankfurt, 1988), 80 ff.

[10] See, for example, C. 9.9.20 on the (unspecified) punishment of women guilty of *stuprum.*

[11] *Codex Theodosianus,* ed. Th. Mommsen (hereafter *CTh*) (Berlin, 1905; repr. Hildesheim, 1990), 8.24.1.

the discussion of Byzantine law and practice. Perhaps one final comment is in order. The late Antique period, especially but not only under the Christian emperors, saw an increase of concern and therefore legislation about matters pertaining both to marriage and to sexual relations outside marriage. Studied in the last instance by Joëlle Beaucamp, the legislation is, according to this author, both a sign of repression where women are concerned and a measure of protection.[12] This is a period of legislative strictness on moral and sexual matters. Instead of detailing one more time the moral concerns of the emperors and the pertinent legislation, one could perhaps refer to an epigram of Agathias Scholastikos, who complains about the constraints thus imposed upon a man who also, it must be admitted, had claims to unusual fastidiousness in sexual matters. What is a man to do, he laments, to find love? In the streets, one meets with the prostitute's inordinate love of gold. The bed of a virgin is approachable only through marriage, else one is subject to the law on *stuprum* (ποινὰς τὰς περὶ τῶν φθορέων). At the same time, it is no fun to sleep with one's legitimate wife, for she claims it as her due. The couch of adultery is evil, and strange to love, as is that of a boy. A widow is too easy; a prude is too difficult, and prone to remorse. If one turns to his own slave, he feels degraded; if to the slave of another, he is guilty of a crime against the master's property. The conclusion? Πάντ' ἄρα Διογένης ἔφυγεν τάδε, τὸν δ' ὑμέναιον/ ἤειδεν παλάμῃ, Λαΐδος οὐ χατέων.[13]

The *Ecloga*

Although late Roman and early Byzantine emperors (Constantine I, Constans II, Theodosios II, and Justinian I) legislated on specific sexual crimes, such as adultery and, primarily, abduction, the categorization of illicit sexual activity is not renewed until the time of the *Ecloga*. The Isaurian law code, promulgated by Leo III and Constantine V in 741, introduced into the topic of illicit sexual relations innovations that were to last for a long time, since they were repeated with only a few changes in the ninth-century legal compilations, the *Procheiros Nomos* and the *Eisagoge,* and from there passed into the official codification, the *Basilics* (tenth century) and eventually into the

---

[12] Joëlle Beaucamp, *Le statut de la femme à Byzance (4e–7e siècle)*, I, *Le droit impérial* (Paris, 1990), 17 ff, 92 ff, 170 ff, 195 ff, 246 ff.

[13] *Anthologia Palatina,* V, ed. P. Waltz (Paris, 1928), 133. I owe this reference to Hélène Ahrweiler.

late Byzantine compilations of Harmenopoulos and Vlastares. The first and most obvious innovation is that the different categories of illicit sexual behavior seem much clearer in the *Ecloga* than they do in the Justinianic codification of Roman law. This is due to the fact that virtually all these categories are grouped together in the section on punishments. They no longer appear under the rubric of the *lex Julia de adulteriis coercendis* or the *lex Julia de vi publica,* nor must they be culled from individual laws and legal opinions, but form a coherent part of the penal code of the compilation. The one exception is adultery, which appears in both section 17 (on punishments) and section 2 (on marriage), since it is also, when the woman is guilty of adultery, one of the few recognized grounds for divorce.[14] The new grouping, which is repeated in the *Procheiros Nomos* and the *Eisagoge,* is perhaps occasioned by the purpose of the compilation, meant to serve as a practical guide to judges, especially those of the provinces, who could no longer understand or deal with the complex Justinianic corpus.[15] In the *Basilics,* the provisions of the *Ecloga,* as modified by the *Procheiros Nomos,* appear as an appendage to the rubric Νόμος Ἰουλίου περὶ τῶν ἐν μοιχείᾳ ἐνεχομένων καὶ περὶ φθορᾶς παρθένων καὶ χηρῶν.[16] Abduction is treated both under this rubric and in a special section (*Bas.* 60.58). Nevertheless, the grouping and definition of the categories as they appear in the *Ecloga* remain intact in the *Basilics.* This technical regrouping serves to point out one important fact and has one important effect. It makes clear that the differentiation of the categories had as a practical result, and perhaps as a purpose, the establishment of criteria for the punishment of the (male) culprit. Furthermore, marriage is even more important than in the Augustan legislation; it is not by chance that the very first chapter of the *Ecloga* is on betrothal and the second on marriage. With marriage assuming such an importance, all sexual activities outside it are seen as illicit, in various degrees, and so are grouped together. The effect is that, once the various categories of illicit sexual activity are grouped together, they come into sharper focus, as does the differentiation between them; and, whether for this reason or for other ones, so does the issue of consent as a differentiating factor.

---

[14] *Ecloga* 2.9.1, 2.9.2, 17.27. For the date, see Burgmann, *Ecloga,* pp. 10–12. All references will be to this edition.
[15] *Ecloga,* Prooimion, p. 162. The emperors mention specifically their desire to make plain in a detailed fashion the punishments appropriate to each crime.
[16] *Bas.* 60.27.

A first matter to notice concerns vocabulary. The term *stuprum*, as the Romans themselves said, rendered the classical Greek term φθορά.[17] The word φθορά reappears in the *Basilics* as the proper translation of *stuprum*.[18] In the *Ecloga*, derivatives of φθορά (e.g., ὁ φθείρων, ὁ φθορεύς, ἡ φθαρεῖσα) do indeed appear where we would expect them if *stuprum* is meant; but there is also the appearance of a new term, and possibly a new category. That is the term πορνεία, which means fornication generally, and seems to include sins of the flesh without further specification. It appears as a legal category for the first time in the *Ecloga*, and the punishments associated with it are in the first instance differentiated by the marital condition of the man, a new phenomenon. A married man who fornicates is punished by twelve lashes; the unmarried fornicator suffers half of this punishment.[19] Special provisions regarding fornication with a slave woman, whether one's own or that of another, add financial penalties to the corporal punishment, since the man either loses his own slave or remits to her master the sum of 36 nomismata (half a pound of gold), if he has slept with the slave of another man.[20] The same term, πορνεία, is used to describe fornication with a consecrated nun; this crime is then equated with adultery, at least as far as the punishment is concerned, and, exceptionally, the woman is punished as well as the man.[21] The importance and meaning of the category of πορνεία will be discussed later.[22] For the moment, suffice it to say that, although differentiation of the punishment according to the social condition of the woman is close to the spirit of Roman law, the use of the marital condition of the man

---

[17] Papinian in *D.* 48.5.6: "stuprum uero in uirginem uiduamue committitur, quod Graeci φθορὰν appellant."

[18] See, for example, *Bas.* 60.37.34 = *D.* 48.5.35 and *Bas.* 60.37.8 = *D.* 48.5.6.

[19] *Ecloga* 17.19, 17.20.

[20] *Ecloga* 17.21 and 17.22. The *Procheiros Nomos* adds corporal punishment in the case of the man who sleeps with his slave (39.60; cf. *Eisagoge* 40.58). The *Ecloga*, the *Procheiros Nomos*, and the *Eisagoge* all specify that if a man is poor, he should be beaten and remit as much as he can of the sum of 36 nomismata. The *Procheiros Nomos* and the *Eisagoge*, which also incorporate parts of the Justinianic corpus, have provisions, originating in Roman law, which punish a woman who sleeps with her slave: *Procheiros Nomos* 39.43 and 44; *Eisagoge* 40.49–50, and cf. *Bas.* 60.37.72 and 73. The penalties are different from those stated in a law of Constantine I: *C.* 9.11.

[21] *Ecloga* 17.23. Both are punished by the slitting of the nose.

[22] Below, pp. 128–32.

as a means of differentiating punishment, which appears in this section, is novel.

Let us now turn to the various categories of illicit sexual behavior as they appear in the *Ecloga*. *Adultery*, that is, intercourse with a married woman, is a relatively straightforward category; both the man and the woman involved are punished by the slitting of the nose and the woman is divorced, being allowed to take back "the things which she brought in to her husband and nothing more." The adulterer is not divorced from his wife.[23] As with the case of Roman law, the issue of consent to the adultery is not raised.[24]

The most important innovations of the *Ecloga* have to do with φθορά, which is dealt with in chapters 17.29, 17.31, and 17.32. The term φθορά is difficult to render into English; its original meaning is corruption, and sometimes this is retained.[25] At other times it has connotations which can be rendered variously as seduction, deflowering, or sexual intercourse even with a woman who is not a virgin. All of the relevant chapters of the *Ecloga* deal exclusively with the seduction of a virgin. That of a married woman comes under the rubric of adultery, but that of a widow is not envisaged at all, unless it is subsumed in the general statement about fornication in 17.19–20. It will be seen below that the consent or otherwise of the seduced girl looms large, since it establishes the level of punishment of the man.

The first case the *Ecloga* treats is that of *consensual stuprum*, where the girl is willing but her parents are not.[26] While the text literally speaks of "lack of knowledge" rather than lack of consent of the parents, I take the meaning to be that the parents were unwilling to give their consent not, certainly, to

---

[23] *Ecloga* 17.28; cf. 2.9.1, 2.9.2 on divorce. The translation is that of E. H. Freshfield, *A Manual of Roman Law: The Ecloga* (Cambridge, 1926). On adultery in Roman society, see Treggiari, *Roman Marriage*, 262 ff.

[24] Roman and Byzantine law hint at the fact that consent was important. Both state that the five-year proscription for accusation of adultery lapses if there is rape. In such a case, the crime can be prosecuted without limit of time: *D.* 48.5.29; *Eisagoge* 40.44; *Procheiros Nomos* 39.26; *Bas.* 60.67.29 and scholia. The Byzantine sources stress the difference between consensual adultery and rape. See, for example, *Eisagoge* 40.44: ἀλλὰ τοῦτο λέγομεν περὶ τῶν εἰς ἑκοῦσαν ἡμαρτηκότων. Ἐὰν δέ τις βιασάμενος . . . ἁμάρτῃ . . . ἀπροσδιορίστως δύναται κατηγορεῖσθαι.

[25] As such, it is strongly connected with ideas of pollution, on which cf. below, IV.

[26] *Ecloga* 17.29: προαιρέσει μὲν τῆς κόρης, ἀγνοίᾳ δὲ τῶν αὐτῆς γονέων.

the girl's deflowering, but rather to a marriage between her and the man who seduces her. If, after the fact, the man wishes to marry the girl, and her parents assent, the marriage is permitted. It is important to note that the girl's consent to the seduction is assumed to signify also consent to the marriage: it is nowhere stated that this consent must be sought, and since it was essential for a valid marriage, it must have been assumed. If the man is unwilling to marry the girl, or if her parents do not agree, he is subject to a fine or to what we would call civil damages: a well-off man will give the girl (not the fisc or her parents) one pound of gold; a poorer man will give half his property, and a man who has no property (πένης καὶ ἀνεύπορος) will be beaten, shorn, and exiled. The financial penalties are, *mutatis mutandis,* similar to those envisaged for the *stuprum* of a virgin or widow in *Institutes* 4.18.4, that is, the *lex Julia de adulteriis*. This punished the man guilty of *stuprum* without force (*sine vi*) with a fine of half his property if he were well-off or corporal punishment and exile if he were of a humble status. The important difference lies in the remedy envisaged in the first instance, that is, marriage, which is not presented as a remedy in the *Institutes*. Influenced perhaps by Christianity and canon law, the legislation seeks first to remedy the seduction of a virgin by having recourse to the institution of marriage, and only secondarily to punish the action by giving the girl a compensation which could, presumably, serve to increase her dowry for an eventual marriage. This, too, is an innovation, since in Roman legislation any compensation went to the fisc. The ecclesiastical influence on this legislation is highlighted by the scholia to *Basilics* 60.37.78, which add canon 67 of the Apostles and canons 25 and 26 of St. Basil, encouraging or permitting the marriage of a seducer with the girl he had seduced.

These provisions regarding consensual *stuprum* were slightly revised by the *Procheiros Nomos,* which made the marriage contingent on the consent of the parents of the man as well, and in this form it passed into the *Basilics*.[27] The emendation of the *Procheiros Nomos* was, in legal terms, a reasonable one, since once the possibility of marriage is broached, the consent of all the important parties, that is, the future spouses and their parents, becomes nec-

---

[27] *Procheiros Nomos* 39.65; cf. *Bas.* 60.37.78. On the change introduced by the *Procheiros Nomos,* as well as on the Isaurian legislation regarding φθορά, see the very good comments of M. A. Tourtoglou, Παρθενοφθορία καὶ εὕρεσις θησαυ-ροῦ (Athens, 1963), 20 ff.

essary. In real terms, of course, it adds to the number of people who could put an end to the marriage plans. It was a law that remained well known and was quoted in judicial decisions including the *Peira* and the decisions of Chomatianos. It seems, from the text of the *Ecloga*, that the provisions for the corporal punishment of fornicators (17.19 and 17.20) were not cumulative, that is, they were not added to the punishment of those guilty of seducing virgins; those provisions, therefore, must apply to *stuprum* with widows, divorced women, and generally with those who were neither currently married nor marriageable virgins.[28]

There is one exception to the provisions concerning consensual *stuprum,* and it has to do with the case of a man who sleeps with the fiancée of another. In such a case, the man is punished by having his nose slit, *even if the girl had consented.* The punishment of the man here is the same as for adultery, which must still be due to ecclesiastical influence, especially after the Council in Trullo, where betrothal was almost equated with marriage, although the civil legislation did not adopt such a measure until the time of Leo VI.[29] It is to be noted, however, that the girl is not punished, as a married woman would have been (*Ecloga* 17.32). The *Procheiros Nomos* (39.68) adds that if the seducer acted without the consent of the girl, his punishment will be increased by a monetary penalty and the girl will receive one-third of his property. The penalty is thus equal to the penalty for rape of an unmarried girl (*Procheiros Nomos* 39.66).

In the *Ecloga,* it is the girl's consent and her age that serve to differentiate the punishment of the seducer. Thus rape of an unmarried girl is punished by the slitting of the nose,[30] a penalty which in the *Procheiros Nomos* is increased since the man is to give the girl one-third of his property (39.66). The commentary to the *Basilics* insists on the matter of consent by repeating ἄκουσαν (*Bas.* 60.37.79 = *Procheiros Nomos* 39.66). The heaviest penalty is reserved for the seduction of a girl under the age of thirteen, that is, under the age at which she was allowed to contract a marriage. The man is punished by the slitting of the nose and by giving the girl one-half of his property; he

---

[28] Cf. below, II.

[29] Council in Trullo, canon 98, states that a man who marries the fiancée of another while the first man is still alive is guilty of adultery. For this purpose, therefore, betrothal is equivalent to marriage.

[30] *Ecloga* 17.30: ὁ βιαζόμενος κόρην καὶ φθείρων αὐτὴν ῥινοκοπείσθω.

is thus subject to both exemplary punishment and civil damages (*Ecloga* 17.31 and *Procheiros Nomos* 39.67). The scholion to the pertinent passage of the *Basilics* (60.80, repeating *Procheiros Nomos* 39.67) makes this punishment also dependent on the consent of the girl; it states that if the girl had been unwilling, the man should be punished according to the provisions of *Basilics* 60.51.35, no. 3, which legislate exile for a man of the upper class, while a lower-class man is sent to the mines.[31] It is my view, however, that the commentator misunderstood the spirit of this law, carried away perhaps by an overzealous attempt to reconcile the Isaurian legislation with those parts of the Justinianic corpus which were still preserved in the *Basilics*. Given the stricter provisions of Roman legislation, he thought that they should apply to the seduction of a girl before puberty, and thus he used the issue of consent to indicate the most severe form of that crime. My view is that, as far as the *Ecloga* and the *Procheiros Nomos* are concerned, the girl's absence of consent is inherent in the fact of her impuberty, in other words, consent is immaterial. A girl under the age of thirteen was incapable of contracting a marriage, and a marriage thus contracted could be dissolved, because the consent of the girl did not legally exist. By extension, this would apply also to sexual intercourse, because, as we have seen in *Ecloga* 17.29, the woman's consent to sexual intercourse was assumed to include her consent to marriage. Thus I would argue that for the Isaurians the impuberty of the girl makes the question of her consent moot, since she is legally incapable of giving it. If this is so, we have here a clear concept of what modern law recognizes as statutory rape, where age is the only relevant factor, impuberty creating a "conclusive presumption of force," and consent is immaterial.[32]

In the late Antique world, abduction (*raptus*) had been a subject of much imperial concern, and had occasioned extremely severe legislation on the part of Constantine I and slightly less severe pronouncements by Justinian I. The church fathers had also been much exercised about it.[33] By contrast, the

---

[31] *D.* 48.19.38, no. 3, which is the source for *Bas.* 60.51.35, no. 3, states these punishments for those who "nondum viripotentes virgines corrumpunt," *without* reference to the girl's consent. There is no mention of consent either in the *Digest* or in the *Basilics*.

[32] *Corpus Juris Secundum, A Complete Restatement of the Entire American Law,* vol. 75 (New York, 1952), "Rape," § 13.

[33] See below, II.

Ecloga barely deals with abduction. The term appears only once, in 17.24, a chapter which deals with a rather specific case, namely, with the abduction "from any place" of a nun or a παρθένον βιωτικήν, whom I take to be simply an unmarried girl. There is no stated punishment for abduction itself; but if the woman is seduced, that is, if there is sexual intercourse, the man is punished by having his nose slit. The punishment is the same one as for the rape of a virgin (*Ecloga* 17.30). Thus the legislator is much more interested in illicit sexual intercourse, a crime against persons, than in the violent crime of abduction; and he seems to assume that intercourse that follows abduction is equivalent to rape. Both of these elements concerning abduction will be seen in cases judged by Eustathios Romaios in the eleventh century.[34]

Interest in abduction revived under the Macedonian dynasty. The *Eisagoge* incorporates a summary of a law of Justinian I, while Leo VI legislated further on the issue.[35] The *Basilics,* too, has a section on abduction. This legislation, especially the Novel of Leo VI, was known to jurists in the eleventh century. It was summarized by Psellos, and commented upon by Eustathios Romaios. Whether it was applied or not is another question, which will be discussed below.

It is evident, then, that the *Ecloga* innovates in a number of ways in the matters of concern to us. Unlike Roman law, the legislation of the Isaurians seems to affect equally persons of any social status, with the exception of slaves (on whom see *Ecloga* 17.21 and 17.22). There is, thus, a blurring of social distinctions in such matters. Just as a valid marriage may be contracted by anyone (except slaves), so relations outside marriage are treated in the same manner, whether the persons involved are members of the aristocracy or not. The one case where punishment is differentiated according to economic, not social status, is the case of consensual *stuprum,* where the penalty imposed on the man differs according to his ability to pay it. As for the social position of the woman, that too does not loom large; nuns are treated differently from other women, but that is a matter not of the woman's social status but of her condition: she is a bride of Christ. Again unlike Roman legislation, the emphasis is very clearly on *stuprum,* seduction and rape; even abduction

---

[34] See below, III. On abduction, see P. Karlin-Hayter, "Further Notes on Byzantine Marriage: Raptus—ἁρπαγή or μνηστεῖαι?" *Dumbarton Oaks Papers* 46 (1992), 133–54.

[35] *Eisagoge* 40.45.

is seen as secondary to the seduction of the abducted girl. Once *stuprum* has been established, the consent or otherwise of the woman plays a much greater and clearer role than in Roman law. It serves to establish the legal category of rape, which is illicit carnal knowledge without consent, and statutory rape; and it is the telling factor that differentiates the punishment of the man. The consent of the woman, however, does not have legal consequences for her. Consensual sex with an unmarried woman carries penalties for the man, but not for the consenting woman. Only the adulteress, and, by extension, the nun who engages in sexual intercourse, is punished. That is not to say that the consenting woman was not punished at all; she was, by the church and by society, in ways which are not included in the law. The church established a concept of personal responsibility in the matter of sins, which was to affect what happened to a woman who consented to illicit sexual activity. But we will return to this.

As far as rape is concerned, it may be pointed out that the *Ecloga* envisages it only in certain cases: an unmarried girl or a nun who is abducted. It does not arise in the case of the adulterous woman or of a widow, which, of course, is different from our own concept and legislation. It is only in the Macedonian legislation that the rape of a married woman is envisaged, in a somewhat more precise form than it had been in the *Digest*.[36] James Brundage has shown the evolution of a medieval definition of rape that approximates the modern one. He traces this in the writings of the great canonists, starting with Gratian. Rape becomes a crime against persons, and in its medieval definition involves both abduction and sexual intercourse. By the end of the Middle Ages, coitus with a child is equated with rape, because of the absence of the possibility of consent.[37] The law of the *Ecloga* has many of these elements and in some ways comes closer to the modern definition of rape as unlawful "carnal knowledge of a female by force or forcibly" and against her will. Rape is a legal category here, and abduction is not a necessary element in its definition. On the contrary, the use of force, which is common in abduction, is presumed to make non-consensual (as far as the woman is concerned) any intercourse subsequent to it. Statutory rape, although there is no term for it, is also a legal category in the Isaurian law code. Finally, while

[36] *Eisagoge* 40.44, and see above, note 24.
[37] J. A. Brundage, "Rape and Marriage," *Revue de droit canonique* 28 (1978), 62 ff.

the possibility of marriage between a raped woman and the man who raped her is not envisaged in the Isaurian legislation, as it apparently is in the medieval West, marriage is indeed encouraged as a remedy for seduction.

Thus both the issue of the consent of the woman and the encouragement of marriage play an important role in both the *Ecloga* and, many centuries later, in medieval canon law. One of the sources of these changes is common to both situations: it is the influence of Christianity and the church, which will be discussed below. The other is specific to the Isaurian emperors: they were very much interested in encouraging marriage. This may be seen in a number of their measures: the prerequisites for marriage were greatly simplified, and the impediments on marriage between unequal partners were lifted; divorce was made very difficult; Constantine V, in his struggle against the monasteries, apparently attacked the celibacy of monks and nuns, possibly as a symbolic gesture.[38] The innovations in the *Ecloga* are due to both social policy and the influence of the church.

I have concentrated on the *Ecloga* because its provisions form the basis of the medieval Byzantine definition of categories of illicit sexual behavior. Through the thirteenth century, most discussions of such matters quoted the law of the *Ecloga,* as incorporated in the *Basilics* with the slight emendations brought about by the Macedonians. The one exception to this statement is the legislation on abduction, so briefly treated in the *Ecloga,* and the subject of concern to the Macedonian emperors. As for the *Basilics,* they did, of course, include many elements of the Justinianic compilation, changing in the process both the vocabulary and, to some degree, the substance. The commentaries on the *Basilics* also refer to canonical legislation on these issues. A study of the pertinent passages of the *Basilics,* to test the coherence of a legislation that incorporated such disparate elements, would be a highly meritorious and rewarding exercise. It is not undertaken here, because the primary concern of this study is neither antiquarian nor is it with internal legal history,[39] but rather with those aspects of the law which were invoked in court or in other ways influenced perceptions and behavior; and that is the law of the *Ecloga.* It is, however, to be noted that the *Ecloga* gives a fairly schematic definition of what constitutes the crimes. It provides us with no rules of procedure or evidence, no guidance for seeking proof. That was left to the courts, and we will examine some court decisions in due course.

---

[38] See *Ecloga* 2.9.1–4; Theophanes, *Chronographia,* I (Bonn, 1839), 675–81.
[39] Besides, I have no competence to do such a study.

The Name of Seduction

The terminology of seduction, deflowering, in short, of φθορά, presents a certain interest, for it changes and develops over time. The Romans had explained the term *stuprum* by reference to the ancient Greek word φθορά.[40] When the Byzantines then created their own legal texts that were based on Roman law, they normally translated *stuprum* by two terms: στοῦπρον (στροῦπτον, στροῦπτρον) or φθορά. Thus *Basilics* 60.37.34 (rendering *D.* 48.5.35) uses the term φθορά in the text, but στροῦπτον in the commentary; at one point the commentator uses both terms: Σημείωσαι, τί ἐστὶ μοιχεία καὶ τί ἐστι στροῦπτον ἤτοι φθορά.[41] The two terms do not have a distinguishable difference in meaning.

On the other hand, there are also very broad definitions of *stuprum*, and some of the Greek equivalents given to the term are surprising. This is evident in the legal dictionaries, compilations which have several different strata and which therefore are difficult to place with chronological accuracy. The broadest definitions appear in the Lexicon αὐσηθ, a compilation whose archetype apparently dates from before the tenth century. In this lexicon, *stuprum* is translated as στοῦπτρον, ἀθεμιτογαμία, and further defined as follows: μοιχεία λέγεται ἐπὶ ὑπάνδρου, στροῦπτρον δὲ ἐπὶ παρθένου καὶ χήρας ἀθεμίτως συνευναζομένων. Finally, the broadest meaning for *stuprum* is ἁμάρτημα.[42]

The Lexicon Μαγκίπιουν, whose original, according to the editor, dates to the eleventh century, and which sometimes draws on material as far back as the sixth century, also has interesting translations and definitions: Σ 44: στούπρουμ: πορνεία; Σ 55: στούπρουμ: φθορὰ χήρας. λέγεται καὶ

---

[40] *D.* 48.5.6.

[41] Cf. *Bas.* 60.37.8 = *D.* 48.5.6. Although the text distinguishes between adultery and φθορά, the commentator, at another point, having said that στροῦπτον is committed with a widow or an unmarried girl, proceeds to add, strangely, τὸ δὲ στροῦπτον οἱ Ἕλληνες καλοῦσι μοιχείαν. In general, the commentaries on the *Basilics* and the Byzantine sources try to distinguish more clearly between *stuprum* and adultery, and the commentary on the *Basilics* (888) clarifies the issue of consent.

[42] L. Burgmann, "Lexicon αὐσηθ," *Fontes Minores* 8 (1990), 283, 284, 285. The word ἁμαρτία is also used in the *Eisagoge* (40.57), to describe the fornication of an unmarried man: ὁ ἔχων γυναῖκα καὶ πορνεύων, διὰ ιβ′ ἀλλακτῶν σωφρονιζέσθω· καὶ ὁ μὴ ἔχων δὲ καὶ τῇ αὐτῇ περιπίπτων ἁμαρτία, διὰ στ′ ἀλλακτῶν σωφρονιζέσθω.

ἀσέλγεια, φθορὰ παρθενίου, which must be translated as: "*Stuprum:* the corruption (seduction) of a widow; the corruption of a young man and of a virgin girl is also called *stuprum*," a good Roman definition.[43]

With the exception of the last entry mentioned above, the others are very broad definitions, the broadest being "sin" (ἁμάρτημα). The second broadest is ἀθεμιτογαμία, which generally has the meaning "illicit (or, eventually, incestuous) marriage," but which here must rather mean illicit sexual intercourse. Thus the Byzantine concept of *stuprum* includes both a narrow sense, of illicit intercourse with a woman who is not married, or with a man, and a much wider sense of sins of the flesh. The second perhaps begins with the use of the word πορνεία to refer to *stuprum;* the first such use of the word in a text of civil law appears in the *Ecloga.*

Committing Fornication

As has already been mentioned, *Ecloga* 17.19 and 17.20 punish with beating the man who commits fornication (ὁ πορνεύων), doubling the punishment when the man is married. There are two points to be noted here: the use of the term itself and the fact that it is the marital status of the man that determines the level of the punishment, along with the condition of the woman, that is, whether she is a slave or a nun (17.22, 17.23).

Porneia is a term which can mean either fornication generally or, more specifically, prostitution or having commerce with a prostitute. In the language of the Justinianic corpus it carries both meanings, retaining for the most part that which is connected with prostitution.[44] Interestingly, a passage of the *Basilics* obscures the connection with prostitution which is clear in the Latin text, by using the term πορνεύω in a way that suggests the generalized meaning, by then current, of fornication. Thus, where the Latin text has: "Si ea quae tibi stupro cognita est passim venalem formam exhibuit ac prostituta meretricio more vulgo se praebuit, adulterii crimen in ea cessat" (*CJ* 9.9.22), the Greek text has: Ἐάν τις μοιχείαν ἁμαρτήσῃ πρὸς ἐκείνην πρὸς ἥν ἤδη πολλοὶ ἐπόρνευσαν, οὐκ ἐγκαλεῖται περὶ μοιχείας (*Bas.* 60.37.61). Thus incapacities which in the Roman text befell prostitutes now touch all women who have fornicated with many men.

In the *Ecloga,* the term is used a number of times. In 17.36, the topic is

---

[43] B. H. Stolte, "Lexicon Μαγκίπιουν," *Fontes Minores* 8 (1990), 355, 373, 374.

[44] Justinian, Novels, 18.5.41; 14 Praef. 1.31; 22.37; 18.5.41; 89.12.5.4.

abortion. Whereas the Justinianic Novel which is the basis of this text simply discusses the abortion and the punishment of the woman, with no reference to the sexual activity that resulted in pregnancy, the *Ecloga* says ἐὰν πορνεύσῃ, and if she then becomes pregnant and attempts to kill her fetus, she is to be beaten and exiled. The meaning of the term here is the general one of illicit sexual activity, since it seems to apply to all women, whether they are married (in which case the term adultery would have been more appropriate) or not. Similarly, chapter 2.9.2 states that a marriage is dissolved if the wife πορνεύσῃ. Here too the term has a general meaning, since the legally accurate word would have been μοιχεύσῃ. The inaccuracy, or, more correctly, the generalized meaning, does not come from the late Antique past: Justinian had used the correct term "adultery" when speaking of this type of divorce.[45]

The generalized meaning of the word πορνεία owes much to the Scriptures and to the church fathers. This is abundantly clear in the text concerning divorce for adultery, which is directly connected to the pertinent passages in the New Testament, namely, Matt. 5:32 (πᾶς ὁ ἀπολύων τὴν γυναῖκα αὐτοῦ παρεκτὸς λόγου πορνείας ποιεῖ αὐτὴν μοιχευθῆναι) and Matt. 19:9.[46] Besides, the word, as used in the New Testament and by the church fathers, frequently carries the general meaning of fornication.[47] Ecclesiastical literature uses the term the same way: the demon of fornication (ὁ δαίμων τῆς πορνείας) is responsible for feelings of lust, whether the object is a married woman, an unmarried woman, or indeed a man.[48] Thus in the *Pratum Spirituale* of John Moschos, compiled in the 630s, the verb πορνεύω is used to denote illicit sexual activity, as in the case of the man who fornicated with the wife of the tavern-keeper (ἐπόρνευσεν εἰς τὴν γυναῖκα τοῦ καπήλου), and in a sense that is connected with the older meaning of going to a whorehouse or having commerce with a prostitute.[49] No differentiation is made between fornication and adultery. Thus fornication is a sin of the flesh rather

---

[45] Novels 22.15.1 and 117.8.2.

[46] See *Ecloga* 2.9.1, 1.276.

[47] See 1 Cor. 7:2: διὰ τὰς πορνείας (to avoid fornication) ἕκαστος τὴν ἑαυτοῦ γυναῖκα ἐχέτω, and 1 Cor. 6:18: φεύγετε τὴν πορνείαν. Πᾶν ἁμάρτημα ὃ ἐὰν ποιήσῃ ἄνθρωπος ἐκτὸς τοῦ σώματός ἐστιν, ὁ δὲ πορνεύων εἰς τὸ ἴδιον σῶμα ἁμαρτάνει. Cf. also St. John Chrysostom, *De Virginitate*, passim.

[48] See Laiou, *Mariage, amour et parenté*, chap. 2.

[49] *Pratum Spirituale*, ed. J.-P. Migne, Patrologia Graeca (hereafter PG), 87.3, nos. 14, 45, 97, 136, 188. See also PG 99, col. 1728 and G. A. Ralles and M. Potles,

than a legal category in the ecclesiastical sources (for the canonical ones, see below), and this sense eventually passed into legal texts as well, for example, in the passages of the *Ecloga* (17.36 and 2.9.2) mentioned above.[50]

Since both men and women are prone to sin, the question arises whether the appearance of a category of sins of the flesh has an influence on the development of the concept of individual consent and responsibility, especially in the case of women. We have seen that civil legislation of the Roman and late Antique periods for the most part considers the man as the actor in and initiator of sexual crimes, with one exception, connected with abduction, which will be discussed in the next chapter; and that the consent of the woman is invoked primarily in order to determine the level of punishment of the man. In the *Ecloga,* the situation is somewhat different. In the two passages already mentioned (17.36 and 2.9.2), the verb πορνεύω is used in the active voice, and its subject is the woman, who is thus responsible for her actions and punished for them. In *Ecloga* 17.29, the consent of the girl (circumscribed, however, by that of her parents) can erase the crime. Is this a real rather than an illusory phenomenon, and do we have a new concept of the responsibility of the woman in sexual activity?

The last set of sources to which we must turn are the canonical sources, which may provide at least partial answers to these questions. The canons of the fourth-century Fathers are, indeed, instructive. Canon 21 of St. Basil does differentiate between πορνεία and μοιχεία, in terms which are consistent with the principles of Roman law, if *porneia* is taken as equivalent to *stuprum*. The married man who has intercourse with an unmarried woman is guilty of πορνεία, not μοιχεία. St. Basil does not agree with this principle, but, he says, it has been established by custom, and so he is forced to accept it.[51] Canon 38 of St. Basil establishes the principle that girls who follow (their lovers), even though their parents are unwilling to have them marry, commit fornication. If subsequently the parents agree, it is permitted for them to

---

Σύνταγμα τῶν θείων καὶ ἱερῶν κανόνων (hereafter Ralles-Potles), 6 vols. (Athens, 1852–59; repr. 1966), IV, 438.

[50] On a similar difference between Roman *stuprum* and Christian fornication, see Treggiari, *Roman Marriage,* p. 11 and chap. 9.

[51] P.-P. Joannou, *Discipline générale antique (IVe–IXe s.),* II, *Les canons des pères grecs* (Rome, 1963), canon 21. Cf. Ralles-Potles, IV, 149–51, with the 12th-century commentaries.

marry; but the girl is subject to three years' penance. This must be the direct antecedent of the provision in *Ecloga* 17.29 on consensual *stuprum* and the remedy of marriage. Canon 9 is a commentary on Matt. 5:32 and Matt. 19:9, which forbid divorce except for reason of fornication (παρεκτὸς λόγου πορνείας). Once again, St. Basil insists, as in canon 21, that the spirit of the Gospel would argue that a marriage should be dissolved whether the man or the woman is guilty of fornication, but custom has decreed otherwise, so that women are expected to retain their husbands, whether these are guilty of fornication or adultery (καὶ μοιχεύοντας ἄνδρας καὶ ἐν πορνείᾳ ὄντας). It then proceeds to discuss the circumstances in which a woman may be labeled an adulteress, circumstances that include the case of a woman who left her husband because he beat her or was a fornicator, if she subsequently lived with another man. Finally, when it comes to establishing the ecclesiastical penalties for various sexual crimes, the canons distinguish clearly between fornication and adultery, adultery carrying the heavier penalty, and the penalty for fornication being dependent on the marital status of the man. Canon 21 of St. Basil says that a married man who is guilty of fornication should be subjected to longer punishment than the (unmarried) man. The twelfth-century canonists elaborate on the rationale, saying that the unmarried man has some extenuating circumstances "because of the natural need" (Zonaras), and that the exact determination of the length of penance for a married man is left to the discretion of the confessor (Balsamon). The ecclesiastical punishment for fornication and adultery differ from one church father to another. St. Basil punishes fornication with the penance of a seven-year exclusion from communion, and adultery with fifteen years (canons 58, 59). This is exactly the spirit adopted by the *Ecloga* (17.19, 17.20). For St. Gregory of Nyssa, fornication is punishable with penance for five years, while other sins that also do injustice to others should receive double the punishment.

The contribution of the church to the development of the concept of sexual crime and that of individual responsibility is very important. *Porneia*, fornication, is almost a legal category in the canonical writings; but it also becomes a sin, and an all-embracing one: it is the complex of sins of the flesh, and so it appears in non-canonical writings.[52] St. Gregory of Nyssa, speaking of the various sins of the flesh, makes the point clearly: "whatever

---

[52] St. John Chrysostom, *In illud, propter fornicationes uxorem*, PG 51, cols. 213–17.

is not legitimate is fully illegitimate" (πᾶν τὸ μὴ νόμιμον παράνομον πάντως), which Balsamon glossed by saying that there is only one form of legitimate sexual relationship between man and woman; everything outside that is illegitimate.[53] At the same time, the general sin is subdivided into particular and different ones. As Balsamon put it in his commentary to canon 21 of St. Basil, fornication is not of a single type, nor is it always punished in the same manner. The level of punishment is a function of a number of things: the marital status of both partners, age, the sincerity of contrition, and so on.[54] The sanctity of marriage is safeguarded, as is made quite clear by the fact that the married fornicator is punished more severely than the unmarried one. And the woman is almost as responsible for her actions as the man is. Her consent to a course of action not only helps establish the level of punishment for the man, but also determines her own punishment.

Let us now return to the *Ecloga*. The Isaurians introduce several differentiations into the old category of *stuprum:* sexual relations between men are called ἀσέλγεια (17.38); sex with an unmarried girl is a category to which much attention is given, and where the consent and the age of the girl play a primary role. The term *porneia* embraces other categories of sexual activity, either implicitly or explicitly: explicitly for intercourse with a slave woman (17.21 and 17.22) and a nun (17.3); implicitly with widows or divorced women and possibly with prostitutes (17.19 and 17.20). The use of the term and the increased punishment for the married man are similar to what we find in ecclesiastical sources and probably derive from them; but "porneia" as a legal category in civil law first appears in the *Ecloga*. The increased importance of the woman's consent as a differentiating factor may also be due to ecclesiastical influence. In the *Ecloga*, the woman's consent does not bring direct punishment upon her, except in the case of adultery. The question must now be asked whether the consenting woman was truly not punished by Byzantine society.

---

[53] Ralles-Potles, IV, 312; commentary on canon 4 of St. Gregory of Nyssa.
[54] Cf. Laiou, *Mariage, amour et parenté,* chap. 2.

II. With Her Consent

We have seen that the consent or absence of consent of the woman to illicit sexual activity plays quite an important role both in canonical statements and in the *Ecloga*. The question of consent is, of course, a vexed one. It is important to determine how consent is established, what constitutes free consent, what the role of coerced consent is, and what level, if any, of coercion is deemed acceptable. These questions will be treated in subsequent chapters. For the moment, our investigation will focus on the consequences of consent for the woman. It is, after all, possible for consent to be a primary factor in establishing the nature of a crime and the penalties for the man, but without immediate and overt consequences for the woman. What was the situation in the Byzantine Empire? Was the woman who consented to unlawful sexual acts punished, and if so, how and in what circumstances? Since our focus here is on consent, the categories of illicit sexual activity will not be treated separately, as they would be if one were simply trying to list the penalties involved for each one. Adultery will be kept out of the investigation, since consent was not of capital importance in the legal approach to it. The topics that best lend themselves to our investigation are consensual sex outside marriage and abduction. These were two situations in which unlawful sexual activity could take place, and in which a woman might give her consent to it, or might be thought to give her consent to it. The issues involving consent are (a) whether there is punishment of the woman who consents to elopement, or abduction, or sex with the man with whom she runs away or who abducts her and (b) whether the woman's consent to marry the man is acceptable, and thus whether a marriage may result from elopement or abduction.[1]

Let us start with ecclesiastical legislation. Canon 38 of St. Basil, already mentioned,[2] bears closer investigation, and must be studied together with

---

[1] For a discussion of abduction and betrothal, see Karlin-Hayter, "Further Notes on Byzantine Marriage." My concern here is less with abduction itself and more with the effects of consent on the woman.

[2] See above, pp. 130–31.

the canons concerning abduction.[3] The situation envisaged by canon 38 is the following: a girl follows a man without the consent of her parents. If the parents then change their views, a marriage can take place. Nevertheless, the girl, who is considered guilty of fornication, is punished by not being able to take communion for three years. This seems to refer to what we would call elopement; the canon itself does not state explicitly that the elopement was attended by intercourse, although the word "fornication" suggests it. The twelfth-century commentators do not mention elopement in such a case, concentrating rather on consensual sexual intercourse, in the absence of agreement of the girl's parents, that is, a situation similar to that envisaged by *Ecloga* 17.29. The canons on abduction try to differentiate between abduction by force, without the consent of the girl, abduction with her consent, and feigned abduction, properly speaking elopement.

When the canonical legislation of the fourth century was being enacted, civil law punished abduction extremely harshly, especially after the law of Constantine I of 326, which punished with death the abductor and the consenting woman as well as all accomplices. The ecclesiastical legislation, while keeping the civil legislation in mind, was much less harsh. Indeed, canon 30 of St. Basil is exceedingly lenient, punishing the abductor and his accomplices with a three-year abstention from communion; compare this to the same Father's provision for punishment of the fornicator, who is to be excluded from communion for seven years (canon 59). Canon 30 then proceeds to differentiate between willing and unwilling abduction: if the abduction does not involve force, if the woman is a widow under her own authority (αὐτεξουσία), and if there is no *stuprum* beforehand, then there is no punishment for the man or the woman. Thus there are three factors which allow abduction to go unpunished: that there be no injury to the rights of others (those who might have the woman in their authority and who thus had the power to arrange her marriage), that the woman be willing, and that there be no intercourse attendant on the abduction. This is abduction with intent to marry. What must be stressed is that for ecclesiastical legislation the crime of abduction, so heinous to civil law, was not a crime of grave consequence. It could easily be remedied by marriage, unless the abducted girl was someone else's fiancée (canon 22 of St. Basil). Much more serious, for the canonical

---

[3] The canons on abduction are canons 22, 30, 53 of St. Basil; canon 27 of Chalcedon; canon 92 of the Council in Trullo; canon 11 of the Council of Ankyra.

legislation of the fourth century, was illicit sexual intercourse or fornication, even though it might be a marriage strategy, and a way of forcing unwilling parents to give their consent to marriage. St. Basil admitted that this situation too could be remedied by marriage; but it was punishable by *epitimia* of four years, whether the woman had consented to intercourse or not (canons 22 and 25). The combination of canons 22, 25, and 38 suggests that in the case of fornication, even if marriage was intended, both the man and the woman suffered ecclesiastical punishment. The marriage itself was somewhat tainted, since its origins were improper, involving unlawful sex (canon 26 of St. Basil). The relative leniency toward abduction and the condemnation of sexual intercourse before marriage runs through canonical legislation, particularly that of St. Basil, and the decisions of Byzantine judges throughout the history of the empire. Perhaps it reflects a more general social attitude that places a very great value on the girl's virginity at marriage, an attitude characteristic of Mediterranean societies.[4]

The canonical legislation of the early centuries, however, is not consistent, especially with regard to the effects of abduction, that is, whether the consent of the woman to abduction permits marriage or not. While St. Basil allows the marriage, other canons, such as canon 27 of the Council of Chalcedon and canon 92 of the Council in Trullo forbid it, being consonant with the civil legislation. Clearly, the church had difficulty reconciling a number of imperatives: that of consistency with civil law, the need to discourage the violence inherent in abduction, the need on the other hand to correct an existing illegal situation through the institution of marriage. The matter became particularly complex when the woman consented either to elopement, abduction, or illicit intercourse. In turn, twelfth-century canonists tried to make sense of the set of situations that the canons had envisaged. In the process, of course, the canonists also brought to bear the experience and the concerns of contemporary society. The principal differentiation in the commentaries is between abduction without sexual intercourse on the one hand, and fornication before marriage on the other; a strenuous but barely successful effort is further made to differentiate between elopement and abduction with the consent of the woman.

The twelfth-century canonists also had to take into account the civil

---

[4] See Jack Goody, *The Development of the Family and Marriage in Europe* (Cambridge, 1983), 29–30.

legislation which had developed in the meantime. That legislation made no mention of elopement, which could, however, be subsumed under the provisions governing φθορά with a consenting woman. As for abduction, the laws were relatively clear. If a man abducts a woman forcibly, with the use of arms, and sleeps with her, he is to be killed. His property and that of his accomplices will be confiscated and given to the woman. If arms are not used, the punishment is less harsh. The consent of the woman to the abduction is immaterial in fixing the man's punishment; indeed the punishment is the same even if a man abducts his own fiancée. Marriage between a woman and her abductor is strictly forbidden, even if the woman, her parents, and the man wish it.[5] Clearly, a problem arises because these provisions do not permit the regularization of irregular situations. The twelfth-century commentators tried to deal with some of the problems.

Zonaras is perhaps the most coherent. In his commentary on canon 30 of St. Basil, he explains the circumstances in which a voluntary abduction will go unpunished: a woman is *sui juris,* she surrenders herself voluntarily, no coercion is involved, and there has been no previous seduction (φθορά) or secret copulation. In such a case, there is no punishment of the man, and, it is implied but not stated, a marriage may be contracted.[6] The words of the canon, "let us not concern ourselves with appearances," allow Zonaras to give an example of what situation is being envisaged. The canon refers explicitly to a widow *sui juris,* in words that are ambiguous, and Zonaras explains that some commentators have taken this to mean that widows wore a distinctive dress.[7] However, he says, the better explanation is that a woman, ashamed to give herself to her lover perhaps because he is lowborn, pretends to be abducted but in truth follows him voluntarily. In such a case, the provisions on abduction do not apply, since the abduction is only a pretext. He then refers the reader to canon 53 of St. Basil, which speaks of the feigned abduction of

---

[5] These provisions, as outlined here, are a combination of *Bas.* 60.58.1 and Novel 35 of Leo VI. The *Basilics* does not refer to sexual intercourse but only to the abduction itself. Michael Psellos, in his versification of the laws, also conflates the provisions of the *Basilics* and the Novel of Leo VI: G. Weiss, "Die juristische Bibliothek des Michael Psellos," *Jahrbuch der Österreichischen Byzantinistik* 26 (1977), 91.

[6] If the woman is not *sui juris,* those who have her under their authority may dissolve the marriage; Ralles-Potles, IV, 169–71.

[7] The word σχῆμα may mean either "appearance" or "pretense."

a slave woman (a freed slave?) and allows the marriage because there is no real abduction. On the other hand, the unmarried girl who sleeps with her lover is guilty of fornication; her consent earns her an *epitimion* of three years, but she may marry her lover if the parents give their assent (commentary on canon 38 of St. Basil). Thus marriage is the remedy for both voluntary abduction and consensual fornication. Indeed, both actions seem to be paths leading to marriage; the rights of the parents or persons who have authority over the woman are safeguarded, since their consent is essential for the marriage. Zonaras does not much exercise himself about the differences between voluntary abduction and elopement. For him, the important point is the woman's consent.

Balsamon, on the other hand, who has a much stricter attitude toward illicit sexual activity and who also has a stronger concern for harmonizing civil and ecclesiastical law, is forced to do somersaults that have a certain elegance, but are hard to duplicate in reality. He, too, recognizes the reality that voluntary abduction is in truth a way for people to force their parents' hand and get married. In a *responsum* to Patriarch Mark of Alexandria, he deals with an example from real life either presented by the patriarch or made up by Balsamon himself: a woman was being forced by her father to marry someone she did not want; her father actually betrothed her, not in a church, but by written contracts (δι᾽ ἐγγράφων δεσμωτικῶν). She then sent word to her lover who came, one night, with some low-class (ἀπαιδεύτων) companions of his, abducted her with her consent (ἥρπασε θέλουσαν), and took her to his house in another village. The question is whether they may marry, since the parents are now willing to have the marriage take place. Balsamon's answer is uncompromising: they may not marry, according to the provisions of *Bas.* 60.58.1, which also states that the parents, if they agree to the marriage, are to be exiled. Furthermore, the abductor and his accomplices will be anathematized, according to the provisions of canon 27 of the Council of Chalcedon.[8] Thus the consent of the woman does not at all alleviate the penalty, as indeed it does not in formal civil law, but she herself is not punished. And yet this case has all the elements of elopement: the girl wishes to marry a man and the abduction is only a feint, presumably to protect her reputation; the parents' hand is forced, as it often is in such cases; in the end, all the relevant parties want the marriage. It might be thought that Balsamon ob-

---

[8] Ralles-Potles, IV, 495–96.

jected to the marriage because the girl was already engaged, but he does not at all mention this in his argumentation and, since the engagement was a civil one, not an ecclesiastical one, he perhaps did not find it binding in this respect.[9] His objections, therefore, are on the formalistic grounds that this was abduction, and the civil laws absolutely forbade marriages resulting from abduction.

This position is evident in his other commentaries as well. His commentary on canon 30 of St. Basil deals with the punishment of a man who abducts a woman (*epitimia* for three years). The canon also says that if the abduction was voluntary, and there has been no sexual intercourse, the man shall go blameless. Unlike Zonaras, Balsamon differentiates between civil and ecclesiastical punishment. The girl's consent frees the man only of ecclesiastical punishment; he remains subject to the severe penalties of *Bas.* 60.58.1. For Balsamon, consent of the woman is irrelevant, as it was in civil law. He further adds that a case which came before the imperial tribunal, concerning the abduction of the daughter of Neophotistos by a man named Seth, was adjudicated according to the provisions of civil law.[10]

A problem arises when Balsamon then tries to deal with the part of the canon that refers to the voluntary abduction of a woman *sui juris,* which Zonaras considered to be equivalent to elopement. Balsamon, in an embarrassed statement, says that, "if you should wish to say that there was no true abduction of the woman but a pretence . . . , then neither the *epitimia* will apply, nor the laws that punish the abductors." This is formally acceptable, but it gives no handle on how to treat real situations, for it does not state the conditions that would differentiate an elopement from a voluntary abduction: presumably, the difference would be whatever the various parties and the confessor stated them to be. The matter reappears in the commentary on canon

---

[9] Canon 22 of St. Basil, among others, states that a betrothed girl who has been abducted must be returned to her first fiancé. He is then free to marry her or not. Betrothal was a civil contract until the time of Leo VI; nevertheless, the church increasingly assimilated it to marriage, as may be seen in canon 98 of the Council in Trullo. When the early church legislation on abduction was being elaborated, the (civil) betrothal was considered binding for these purposes. But by the time of Balsamon, one could argue that only a betrothal with ecclesiastical blessing was binding.

[10] Cf. Balsamon's commentary on canons 67 of the Apostles, 27 of Chalcedon, and 92 of Trullo, where he insists on the provisions of civil law, the punishment of the man, and the prohibition of marriage. The woman's consent remains irrelevant.

38 of St. Basil, concerning the penalties imposed on a woman who "follows her lover" without the consent of her parents. Both Zonaras and Balsamon specify that this means that the girl had sexual intercourse with the man. Balsamon, but not Zonaras, then specifically explains that this does not refer to abduction, and therefore the remedies pertinent to it are not pertinent to abduction. In this case of consensual sex, when there is no abduction involved, the consent of the parents, obtained after the fact, can validate the marriage that had taken place, and that was considered fornication in the absence of parental consent.[11] But, says Balsamon, the situation is now different from what it was in the fourth century. Then, marriages were contracted by consent alone; this meant that the couple could marry and the girl could suffer the ecclesiastical punishment (three years without communion) subsequently. In his own day, where no marriage could take place without the benediction of the church, he submitted that a valid marriage could be contracted only after the three years (or, the saving statement, whatever length of punishment the bishop had ordered) had elapsed.

This embarrassment, and Balsamon's very strict interpretation of the canons regarding abduction, resulted from the development of marriage strategies among the aristocracy of the twelfth century, some of which very clearly had Balsamon's approval. Abduction and elopement were not unknown in the eleventh century. Then, as in the fourth century, and as in parts of Greece until recently, this kind of action could be taken in order to force the hand of unwilling parents. The fact, noted by anthropologists and historians of Antiquity, does not really need elaboration, beyond the mere notice that it evidently existed in Byzantine times as well, although I do not think it was widespread.[12] But the twelfth century was eminently the century in which the marriages of the aristocracy were very tightly controlled by the families, the

[11] It may be noted again that this is the situation, and the solution, envisaged by *Ecloga* 17.29. The canonists never refer to this law code, promulgated by Iconoclastic emperors and abrogated by the Macedonians.

[12] See, among others, Judith Evans-Grubb, "Abduction Marriage in Antiquity: A Law of Constantine (*CTh* IX.24.1) and Its Social Context," *Journal of Roman Studies* 79 (1989), 59–83; Michael Angold, "The Wedding of Digenes Akrites: Love and Marriage in the Eleventh and Twelfth Centuries," Πρακτικά του Α´ Διεθνούς Συμποσίου, η Καθημερινή Ζωή στο Βυζάντιο (Athens, 1989), 201–15; Michael Herzfeld, "Gender Pragmatics: Agency, Speech and Bride-Theft in a Cretan Mountain Village," *Anthropology* 9 (1985), 25–44; and Karlin-Hayter, "Further Notes on Byz-

state, and the church, each trying to establish its preeminent right. This was, furthermore, a period when mésalliance was abhorred and severely punished by none other than Emperor Manuel I, with whose measures, extending to the mutilation of the guilty men, Balsamon apparently agreed.[13] Abduction for the purpose of, at worst, mésalliance or, at best, marriage to someone of whom the parents disapproved was not in the interest of aristocratic society. Balsamon's own statements make his concern clear: in his commentary on canon 92 of the Council in Trullo, he specifically connects abduction with mésalliance: "some say that he who abducts a woman for the purpose of marriage, perhaps because she was unworthy of his family, . . . does no wrong." He insists that marriage cannot be allowed in such cases, because it destroys social order (τὴν εὐταξίαν τῶν πόλεων). As for sexual intercourse before marriage, it is, as we have seen, the major concern of all ecclesiastical law. Balsamon allows marriage to correct this act, because he cannot do otherwise, but he makes it very difficult.

Let us now recapitulate the canonical regulations insofar as the consent of the woman is concerned. The canons of St. Basil give the consent of the woman the greatest role: it is what differentiates between abduction and elopement; the woman's consent to marriage, always subject to the consent of the parents, can correct the crimes of abduction and fornication. The church's effort is to strengthen marriage, and by that token the role of the consent of the woman is strengthened, although a different position is taken by the Council of Chalcedon and the Council in Trullo. This importance of the consent of the woman is preserved in the commentary of Zonaras, but weakened by the statements of Balsamon, which reflect the twelfth-century concerns of aristocratic society with tightly controlled marriages. Churchmen did not speak with a single voice any more than laymen did. The consent of the woman to illicit intercourse also carries punishment for her, both in the canons of St. Basil and in the twelfth-century commentaries. Thus consent, in this case, establishes legal categories, differentiates the penalties involved, and recognizes the responsibility of the woman by punishing her. It is true that these illicit activities could lead to love matches, otherwise not provided for either by the law or by custom, which revolved around arranged mar-

---

antine Marriage." I argue below against the notion that abduction was a common phenomenon in Byzantium, especially in the 11th–12th centuries.

[13] See Laiou, *Mariage, amour et parenté*, chap. 1.

riages. However, it was not, as has been argued for Western medieval societies, "rape" that permitted this relative freedom of choice to women (and men), but rather elopement, however nebulously defined, which forced the parents to give their consent because of the fear of social stigma attached to a woman who had lost her virginity.[14]

Where civil law is concerned, there appear to be two strains of thought with regard to the effects of consensual sexual intercourse on the consenting (unmarried) woman. One strain, which proved not to be a prevalent one, is represented by the enactment of Constantine I on abduction (326).[15] This law, the harshest ever passed, provides for the execution in a degrading and horrible manner (by crucifixion, burning, or being thrown to the beasts) of the man who seizes a girl ("invitam . . . vel volentem abduxerit").[16] The consent or otherwise of the woman plays no role in the punishment of the man, nor, indeed, does her consent make it possible to correct the crime by marriage. Constantine invokes the foolishness and inconstancy of the female mind, which caused ancient lawgivers to deny women the right to testify. However, the same disadvantages do not protect her if she consented to her abduction. If the consent was overt, she is to suffer the same punishment as the man. If she claimed that she had been forced, this too will avail her only a little. Constantine does not admit the possibility of non-complicity of the girl in abduction for, as he puts it, girls should stay indoors or scream for help if they are attacked outside the house; if they did not do so, then they consented to the abduction even if they claimed they did not. The punishment, however, is lighter, the girl merely losing the right to inherit from her parents.

There are several points of interest in this piece of legislation, whose gruesome provisions (including, among other things, the execution of the girl's nurse by pouring molten lead down her throat) have excited the interest and even passion of a number of scholars.[17] First, the consent of the girl is

[14] For the idea that rape created greater freedom of action, see Brundage, "Rape and Marriage," 74–75.

[15] *CTh* 9.24.

[16] This is the interpretation of Evans-Grubb, "Abduction Marriage," 66, with which I agree. This part of the law was made somewhat less harsh in 349, when simple capital punishment (execution by the sword) was substituted: ibid., 66, with reference to *CTh* 24.2.

[17] Apart from Evans-Grubb, see Denise Grodzynski, "Ravies et coupables," *Mélanges de l'École française de Rome* 96 (1984), 697–726, who believes that Constantine wanted primarily to punish the consenting girl, and for that reason assumed her

indeed important, not for the abductor but for her. Second, there are two levels of consent that are envisaged here: active (and admitted?) consent and the absence of evident opposition, which is taken to imply consent. No woman is presumed innocent here. Third, the statements about the girl essentially inviting abduction by her behavior (not staying indoors) or not proving her opposition (by crying out to alert the neighbors) smacks of folk wisdom rather than jurisprudence. Judith Evans-Grubb suggests, undoubtedly correctly, that the assumptions of the Constantinian legislation about the girl's overt or covert consent are no different from those of Mediterranean societies generally, which consider that all abducted girls have agreed to the abduction.[18] In that sense, the edict is revealing, although its unrelieved harshness suggests that it was promulgated for a particular reason and provoked by a particular case, perhaps close to the emperor's family.[19] It is revealing precisely because it brings to the fore a certain concept of the woman's guilt and a concept of consent which we will find elsewhere, though rarely in official documents.[20]

The attitude toward the consenting woman which is expressed in Constantine's law was short-lived. The tenor of his legislation was progressively weakened, and his law was finally replaced by an edict of Justinian I on abduction (533).[21] In this piece of legislation, the consent of the woman plays no role at all: the man and his accomplices are punished by death, whether the woman had been willing or not. Furthermore, a woman who appears to have consented did not truly consent, for "unless a man solicited her and deceived her by his detestable arts, he would not have been able to induce her to submit to such dishonor: "nisi etiam eam sollicitaverit, nisi odiosis artibus circumvenerit, non facit eam velle in tantum dedecus sese prodere." Thus the woman's (or the girl's) consent to abduction is considered from the

---

to be responsible before the law; and Beaucamp, *Le statut de la femme à Byzance,* 111 ff.

[18] Evans-Grubb, "Abduction Marriage," 64–65.

[19] A. H. M. Jones, *Constantine and the Conversion of Europe* (London, 1948), 243 ff, suggests a connection with the fate of Constantine's son Crispus, without, however, any evidence.

[20] See below, especially V.

[21] See *CTh* 9.24.2 and 9.24.3, and *CJ* 9.13.1, *D.* 1.3.53; cf. Evans-Grubb, "Abduction Marriage," 76 ff.

beginning uninformed and therefore valueless. This provides protection for the woman; but since marriage is not allowed, there is certainly dishonor involved. As far as consent is concerned, it is not at all taken into consideration. It reappears with the *Ecloga,* not in the case of abduction but in the case of consensual sex, and it does play a role there, although it carries no punishment. Macedonian legislation on abduction admits that the woman may have consented, but gives no legal weight to her consent.

The only time, after 326, that the woman who consents to sex outside of marriage is held responsible to the extent of being punished is in the fourteenth century, in a Novel of Andronikos II (1306). The Novel is short, and may thus be quoted in full.[22]

> Let it be declared and obeyed, that a woman, and especially a virgin, should not throw her honor at the feet of the first comer, but if anyone should force her in the wilderness, let her be avenged according to the laws; if, however, she should give herself willingly, let her be chastened by having her hair shorn and by a dishonorable parade. Nor should the seducer be allowed to go unpunished in either case,[23] but he will certainly pay to the Fisc the legal fine. And if he cannot, still he will be held responsible according to the law.

The legal aspects of this text have already been discussed by Tourtoglou. Some points, however, should be brought out here. On the issue of consent, we note a reference to the ancient distinction, enunciated in Deut. 22:23–24, between seducing a woman in the city (where she is assumed to have consented) and in the country (where the absence of consent is assumed). In case of rape, the man would suffer the legal punishment, presumably the one in *Basilics* 60.37.79, by which the man gives the girl one-third of his property and is further punished by having his nose slit. If the girl was willing, he is punished by a fine, to be paid to the fisc: we notice that the remedy of marriage is not accepted here. The fine is the well-known fine for *parthenophthoria,* which appears in the documentary sources soon afterwards. What

---

[22] I am using the edition in *JGR,* I, 535; this is Novel 26 of Andronikos II, para. 3.

[23] Tourtoglou, Παρθενοφθορία, 75–76, quite rightly says that the law as published in this edition makes no sense, since in the first case the seducer's punishment has already been mentioned ("according to the laws"). He prefers another reading, namely, τῷ δέ γε φθορεῖ μὴ τὸ ἀζήμιον ᾖ, which would be translated "nor should the seducer go unpunished," and I have adopted this reading here.

is of particular interest for us here is the punishment of the woman, who is publicly shamed. If imposed, the parade and public shearing of the hair could be a very harsh punishment indeed.[24] It is evident that this law is an anomaly, both in its language and in the penalties it imposes. Indeed, in the form in which it is published, it is, in the first instance, a decision of the synod, which Patriarch Athanasios I proposed to Andronikos II, who then promulgated it as law. Its ecclesiastical provenance, and especially its attribution to a patriarch of strict morals whose purpose was the moral purification of society, explains its tone and the culpability attributed to the woman. The spirit of it, however, was probably very close to the informal punishment that women who had engaged in consensual sex outside marriage could suffer: if marriage did not take place, the girl was most probably shamed and dishonored, even if there were no public parading involved. This would have been a deterrent more powerful than the law was for men, and it may be the reason why the law does not, usually, mention a specific punishment for the woman; the woman's punishment would have taken place outside the realm of law, the man's inside it.[25] This statement, of course, refers to the majority of women, not to members of the aristocracy, whose mores varied with the times. In the twelfth century, aristocratic mores were nothing to boast about, but people were not punished for them, either formally or informally. By contrast, Zoe Zaoutzaina, who had been Leo VI's mistress and later became his second wife, did suffer public shame after her death, for her tombstone read "the poor woman was a daughter of Babylon."[26]

There are thus two strains of thought in civil legislation with regard to the woman who consents to illicit sexual activity. One (Justinian I's) is that a woman is not fully responsible for her actions in this respect and must be protected. The other strain (Constantine I's) is that she is fully responsible for what takes place, even if her consent is not overt and admitted, and must be punished. I have suggested here that in reality there are forms of punishment,

[24] On this, see Ph. Koukoules, *Βυζαντινῶν βίος καὶ πολιτισμός*, 6 vols. (Athens, 1948–57), III, 187 ff.

[25] For an inkling of such a social attitude, see canon 34 of St. Basil, which specifies that the ecclesiastical punishment of a repentant adulteress should not be made public, so as to spare her life.

[26] George the Monk, "De Leone Basilii Filii," *Theophanes Continuatus*, ed. I. Bekker (Bonn, 1938), 857. On all this, see Laiou, *Mariage, amour et parenté*, chap. 2.

mostly shame and dishonor, which the law does not enunciate, with the exception of Novel 26 of Andronikos II, which codifies them.

The Evidence of the Courts

A certain amount of evidence, both on how the law actually functioned and on the treatment of the consenting woman, may be found in court records. How much a reflection these are of reality is a vexed question, the answer to which must depend on the kind of reality one has in mind. It can certainly be argued that court cases do not reflect a statistical reality, since the majority of cases, especially those regarding sexual matters, would have been resolved informally and without recourse to the courts. I do indeed assume that any case that appeared in court was, in some way, extraordinary and thus not reflective of everyday reality. A second possible objection is more difficult to evaluate. The compilations we have—essentially the eleventh-century *Peira* and the thirteenth-century dossier of Demetrios Chomatianos—were undoubtedly made selectively, and the exact purpose of the compiler remains obscure. Thus it is theoretically possible that only those solutions which held a particular interest or curiosity for the compiler were included. If this is the case, it introduces a second remove from reality, since the compiler may have excluded from the collection those solutions which were exactly according to the law, and left us only the more complex solutions, which would be of interest to lawyers but would not be nearly so instructive in terms of social history.[27] To this argument I have no general answer. Each case must be taken as it stands, and the conclusions drawn from it can be instructive only to the degree that they show a gamut of legal possibilities, or to the degree that they encapsulate thoughts and concepts that are also present elsewhere, either in jurisprudential, ideological, or literary statements. The final caveat is connected with chronology: the legal cases that have survived, namely, the *Peira,* and the decisions of Chomatianos and Apokaukos, are concentrated in the eleventh through early thirteenth centuries, while the register of the acts of

---

[27] For a study of the possible purpose of the *Peira,* see N. Oikonomides, "The 'Peira' of Eustathius Rhomaios: An Abortive Attempt to Innovate in Byzantine Law," *Fontes Minores* 7 (1984), 169–92. The register of the acts of the Patriarchate of Constantinople is not, I believe, selective in the same way. As for the acts of John Apokaukos, they have survived in a haphazard fashion, and I do not believe that they form a compilation with any particular purpose in mind.

the Patriarchate of Constantinople is richest for the eleventh through four-teenth centuries, with only a few extant cases from earlier periods. This must be kept in mind, but there is nothing much to be done about it.

Three cases will be examined below, all referring to illicit sexual activity to which the woman had consented. The first case took place in Epiros in the thirteenth century.[28] A man named John, son of Rados, from the theme of Devol, presented to Demetrios Chomatianos a question about the following case. A married man had deflowered (φθείρας) Rados' sister, Stanna, who was unmarried and a virgin, with her consent but without the knowledge of her brother (προαιρέσει μὲν αὐτῆς, ἀγνοοῦντος δὲ τοῦ αὐταδέλφου αὐτῆς). The brother requested a written opinion as to whether the man was punishable. Chomatianos' court functioned both as a civil and as an ecclesi-astical tribunal, and he himself was deeply learned in the civil law. His *res-ponsum* to this query took into account both civil and ecclesiastical legisla-tion. First he turned to the civil law, and explained that it punishes differently the rape of a betrothed girl, that of a single girl, and that of an underage girl; it also differentiates between the abduction of a single and a betrothed girl, and the seduction of a consenting unmarried girl. Having listed these cate-gories, and having heard from John what the circumstances of the seduction were, Chomatianos then turns to the case: the girl, he says, was seduced willingly and, the man being already married, there is no question of a mar-riage between the two. The man must be punished according to the laws which are *Bas.* 60.37.78 (the seducer must give to the girl a pound of gold or, if he is not wealthy, half his property; if he is poor, he is beaten, shorn, and deported) and *Bas.* 60.37.82, which says that a married man who forni-cates is subject to beating. As for ecclesiastical legislation, Chomatianos quotes canon 21 of St. Basil, and finds that canon 59 is applicable, which provides for a seven-year abstention from communion.

His final response is that the man should pay to the girl, if he is wealthy, "as many nomismata of local currency as the law requires" (τῶν κατὰ χώραν ἐμπολιτευομένων καὶ πραττομένων νομισμάτων ὅσον ὁ νόμος δηλοῖ), and if he is not wealthy, half his property. The local prelate must subject him to the ecclesiastical punishment mentioned above.

---

[28] See the edition of J. B. Pitra, *Analecta sacra* . . . , 7 vols. (Paris, 1876–82), no. 74. The faults of this edition are well known; some necessary corrections will be incorporated in the discussion of the case.

A number of points of interest arise from this *responsum*. First, the question of the brother, which is not quoted but summarized, sets out clearly the factors that legally define the case: the seducer was married; the girl was a virgin; she was not betrothed; she was willing, but her brother was not aware of the affair. While this clarity may be due to the archbishop's secretary rather than to the brother, it is interesting that someone elicited sufficient facts to establish the legal category. The mention of the brother's ignorance seems to have been included precisely in order to establish the legal category; for, since the seducer was already married, even if the brother had known (and consented), there could not in any case have been a marriage of the girl and her seducer. Second, the brother is handling the affair, presumably because the girl is an orphan. Third, Chomatianos treats *Bas.* 60.37.82 (= *Ecloga* 17.19–22) as cumulative punishment, to be added to the compensation that is due to the girl. This is an interpretation which is not self-evident, and which was probably not the intent of the lawgiver. Chomatianos' interpretation makes fornication into a general category, affecting all sins of the flesh, and independent of the other subdivisions of sexual crimes. But it must be noted that the corporal punishment established by *Bas.* 60.37.82 is not to be applied. Interestingly, in his response Chomatianos also ignores the possibility that the man was poor, which would have led to his being punished by beating. Perhaps the corporal punishments originally legislated by the *Ecloga* for sexual crimes were no longer being applied. Finally, the consenting woman is not punished; on the contrary, she is to receive some property.

A second case, also from Chomatianos' court, takes a different attitude toward the woman. A potter named Chrysos had left Kastoria and his lawfully wedded wife and gone to Ochrid. There he lived with a Vlach woman named Tzola who, according to the description of the facts, was a seductive and tempting woman; she is called his concubine. Chrysos' wife learned of the matter, went to Ochrid, and managed to extract him from Tzola's "whorish embrace, helped by the law and by the might of the government according to Christ" (τῶν πορνικῶν ἐκείνης ἀπέσπασεν ἀγκαλῶν καὶ δεσμῶν, τῷ τε νόμῳ βοηθουμένη καὶ τῇ ἰσχύι τοῦ κατὰ Χριστὸν πολιτεύματος). Eventually, Tzola presented demands, presumably to Chomatianos' court: she argued that all of Chrysos' property in Ochrid had been acquired by their common labor, something that Chrysos admitted and against which his wife had nothing to say. A compromise was reached, whereby Tzola received a share of this common property, pronouncing herself satisfied. It was written that if

Tzola should ever again, by open or occult means (a reference to magic?), persuade Chrysos to sleep with her, or if she raised further property demands, she would lose the things she had received from him, and she would be punished by the civil authorities, "so as to be chastened" (εἰς σωφρονισμὸν αὐτῆς).[29]

Although the title of this case, "On those men who are married and fornicate" (περὶ τῶν ἐχόντων γυναῖκας καὶ πορνευόντων), is a direct reference to *Bas.* 60.37.82, it will be noticed that the man is not at all punished for his transgression. It is, on the contrary, the consenting woman who is threatened with punishment, even though the law nowhere provides for such punishment. Evidently, the case was resolved not by legal criteria but by social ones: the woman is identified as a Vlach, she is described by the pejorative term γυναικάριον, and she was obviously not a virgin, since she is described as a temptress of men; thus the crime of *parthenophthoria* is not relevant, although clearly the man should have been punished by beating, according to *Bas.* 60.37.82. It appears that he was threatened by the law and thus broke up his affair. The not so covert reference to Tzola's use of occult machinations may have been made in order to justify further this legally unorthodox but socially acceptable disposition of the case. The woman here appears as the seductress, the initiator of the illicit sexual activity, and is held responsible for it.

Such attitudes were, I think, more widespread than a single case suggests; they underlie much of the literature of monastic provenance that deals with sex and temptation. As an example, one may mention almost at random a striking little tale. It is a story told in the *Pratum Spirituale,* a seventh-century compilation of cautionary tales written for and by monks. It concerns a woman who lived the life of a nun in her own house, spending her days fasting, praying, and giving alms. The devil instilled a demonic desire in the heart of a young man, who kept vigil outside her house, and importuned her every time she left to go to church. As a result, *she was forced to stay inside.* Finally, she sent her maidservant to invite him into the house, where he went eagerly, thinking he had achieved his purpose. The woman, sitting at her loom, asked him what it was about her that made him so enamored. He replied that it was her eyes which had tempted him, at which point she took

---

[29] Pitra, no. 136. On this case, see also Laiou, "Contribution à l'étude de l'institution familiale en Épire," 286.

her shuttle and pierced her eyeballs.[30] The moral of the story is that this action cured him of his passion, and he became a monk.

The story is, of course, full of commonplaces, including the commonplace about passion being inspired by the devil, and that about the woman sitting at her loom, which is a shorthand statement denoting a good woman engaged in a proper female pursuit.[31] Precisely because it is so full of clichés, it provides a useful insight into the assumptions of that kind of milieu. The most powerful assumption is that, although the active role in the incident is played by the man, the cause of the man's passion and of the potential crime is the woman. Connected to this is the first solution adopted by the woman in question, namely, her staying indoors. The point made here is similar to the one that Constantine I makes explicitly in his Novel on abduction: if the woman really did not want to be bothered, she would have stayed home. Finally, it is to be noted that the only person punished here is the woman, although she had not committed any crime. She punishes herself, ostensibly to remove the temptation; but is it not also the case that she is punished privately for an unofficial crime, namely, for having brought the man into temptation? While this is a morality that is specifically monastic, it is likely that an attenuated form of it was pervasive in society, and must be taken into account when one discusses the treatment of the woman who consents to, or initiates, illicit sexual activity.

The next case we will examine is much more complex, has many interesting aspects, and for that reason has been frequently commented upon.[32] However, the story bears repeating here for the purpose at hand. We are in Constantinople, in the years 1025–28, probably closer to the later date, and the people involved are all members of the upper class, the civil aristocracy.[33]

---

[30] John Moschos, *Pratum Spirituale*, PG 87.3, no. LX, cols. 2912–13. The text says that she pierced her eyes and took them out: ἔδακεν καὶ ἐξέβαλεν τοὺς δύο ὀφθαλμοὺς αὐτῆς.

[31] See A. Laiou, "The Role of Women in Byzantine Society," in eadem, *Gender, Society and Economic Life in Byzantium* (London, 1992), pt. V, 243–44.

[32] See J. Beaucamp, "La situation juridique de la femme à Byzance," *Cahiers de civilisation médiévale* 20 (1977), 169; Laiou, *Mariage, amour et parenté*, chap. 3; D. Simon, Ἡ εὕρεση τοῦ δικαίου στὸ ἀνώτατο Βυζαντινό δικαστήριο (Athens, 1982), 15.

[33] The case is in the *Peira* 49.4. The text says that it was first judged by "the late Argyropoulos, who not much later came to the throne." This is Romanos Argyros,

The *protospatharios* Imerios, son of Solomon, fell in love with the daughter of a *protospatharios* and *teichiotes* (officer guarding the palace walls). He deflowered her (διεπαρθένευσεν αὐτὴν λάθρα), without her father's knowledge and consent. The girl became pregnant, and thus her father found out about the affair. The two young people went to church and declared their intention to marry; however, Imerios was still in his father's authority, and thus he delayed the marriage, presumably because Solomon was opposed (διὰ τὴν ὑπεξουσιότητα τὸν γάμον ὑπερετίθετο). But after Solomon died, Imerios refused to marry the girl, and proposed to make another marriage.

At this point, someone, presumably the girl's father, brought action against Imerios, before the court of the Hippodrome. The case was judged, in the first instance, by Romanos Argyros, Tornikios, and other judges. Eustathios Romaios was not present. There was much dispute, the judges found the case very complex, and they could not resolve it. At this point, the emperor (presumably Constantine VIII) intervened with two letters. One ordered Imerios to marry the daughter of the *protospatharios* Gregory Solomon (a relative of his?), and the other ordered the court to judge the case of the *teichiotes'* daughter. Once again, there was much dispute among the judges, and various points of view were expressed regarding the punishment of Imerios. Argyros took the strictest position, proposing that Imerios be punished by both the corporal punishment to which seducers are subject and a monetary fine, while the others proposed that he pay a fine of one pound of gold, according to the law governing the seduction of a consenting girl (*Bas.* 60.37.78). The solution, described by the compiler as an admirable one, was eventually found by Eustathios Romaios, who read the record of the first trial and also heard the case as presented at that moment. He considered corporal punishment to be too harsh, especially since the emperor himself had ordered Imerios to marry the other girl; as for the fine of one pound of gold, that seemed to him too picayune. He judged the case as a case of insult (ὕβρις) against the girl's father, and decided that the *teichiotes* should receive 150

---

later emperor. At the time he was, perhaps, prefect of the city, an office he reached in the late years of Constantine VIII; for his *cursus honorum,* see Laiou, *Mariage, amour et parenté,* chap. 4. Eustathios Romaios is mentioned as *patrikios,* a title with which he appears after 1025: Oikonomides, "Peira," 171–72. The case was written up after 1034, since Argyros was already dead.

nomismata, "according to the law."[34] As for the girl, who was seduced and deflowered (ἐφθάρη καὶ διεπαρθενεύθη), Eustathios produced a law which said that compensation for destruction (of property? τὰς φθορὰς καὶ τὰς ὑποφθοράς) should be estimated by the judge, and he decided that the girl should receive a compensation of 210 nomismata, so that the total fine, due to the girl and her father, came to five pounds of gold. The decision was then presented to the emperor, who confirmed it.[35]

There follows a description of Eustathios' opinion and argumentation. He explained, first of all, why he turned to the law on *injuria* (ὕβρις) and used it to compensate the father for the seduction and deflowering of the daughter. He then proceeded to argue by showing that Imerios' infraction was greater than the one to which the law applied. The law said that even entering a house without the master's consent in order to bring someone to court constitutes *injuria* (*Bas.* 60.21.23 = *D.* 47.10.23); how much greater an *injuria* it is, then, for a man to enter someone's house in order to destroy the entire household (ἐπὶ διαφθορᾷ οἰκίας ὅλης) and deflower a virgin. Having shown the greatness of the crime, he then invoked the law that says that punishments should be milder rather than harsher; the same case may be judged on several different grounds, according to the discretion of the judges; he chose to apply the law on *injuria*. He also explained why he did not apply the law on seduction and impose the penalty of one pound of gold. That law, he said, is an abstract law, which does not take account of specific circumstances; its application depends on the desire of two parties to marry, and it does not exclude even actors, or poor or unfree men, all of whom are expected by this legislation either to marry the girl or pay a fine, even though the actor or the unfree man may not marry the daughter of a senator, even if he should desire to do so. In the present case, the girl is the daughter of a senator, and the case could have been judged according to several different

---

[34] For the law on *injuria*, see *Bas.* 60.21.

[35] The summary of the case in the commentary on *Bas.* 60.37.78 says that the emperor was Romanos Argyros. However, the longer and more circumstantial description in the *Peira* does not name the emperor, and I see no reason to suppose that it was anyone other than Constantine VIII. Perhaps the commentator was carried away by the statement in the *Peira* that the first time around the case was judged by, among others, Romanos Argyros who "not much later came to the throne." The point does not in any way affect those parts of the case which are pertinent to our topic, but it might be of interest for an eventual biography of either of these two rulers.

laws, including seduction and *injuria;* if the lesser law (on seduction) had been invoked, the stricter one would have been ignored. Finally, he said that Imerios could, while his father was alive, have many times invoked the father's authority in order to avoid marriage and punishment, and this would have set a bad example. Hence, it is implied, the punishment should be more severe than that imposed by the law on seduction. Eustathios' brief was, says the compiler, greatly admired by all.

This fascinating case was, it would seem, a cause célèbre in Constantinople, widely discussed among legal circles; but the legal circles were no different from the circle of the two principal parties, so that it must have been a matter of heated discussion among the aristocracy of the city. And how could it have been otherwise? The people involved were all members of the aristocracy; Imerios must have been a dashing fellow, who had managed to seduce one girl in her father's house and perhaps had also seduced Gregory Solomon's daughter, whom the emperor finally ordered him to marry. Undoubtedly, although the record does not mention this, the interests of different members of the aristocracy were engaged, and the dissension among the judges may well have been due to political reasons, not only to legal disagreements. The very fact that the girl's father chose to bring the case to court, with all the attendant publicity, suggests that there was more to this than meets the eye, and in any case it must have constituted a fairly unusual course of action. Finally, the intervention of the emperor not once but three times shows the importance attached to the case.

As far as our topic is concerned, the following points of interest arise. First of all, the affair between Imerios and the daughter of the *teichiotes* is a clear case of seduction of a consenting girl. After the girl's father gave his consent (the words "the father became aware" must be interpreted to mean that he gave his consent to the match), an effort was made to resolve the matter in the most convenient way allowed by law, that is, by marriage. The formal declaration of intent, made in church, must have been undertaken in an effort to bypass the objections of Imerios' father, but it was unsuccessful: the consent of the parents of both parties was still a necessary precondition of a valid marriage. Second, it is probable that Imerios was also guilty of the seduction of the daughter of Gregory Solomon, since the emperor intervened and ordered him to marry her. This undoubtedly introduced a further complication into the affair, since there were competing claims of two girls and their families. Then one must note that Romanos Argyros, who demanded the harshest punishment of the seducer, seems to have treated *Bas.* 60.37.82 (*Ecloga* 17.19–20 = *Procheiros Nomos* 39.59), which decreed the beating of the fornicator, as a cumulative punishment, which would be added to the punishment for the seduction of a virgin. Eustathios Romaios did not dispute the idea, but he found the corporal punishment too harsh. It must be deduced that in the eleventh century the corporal punishment for fornication was not applied, at least where the members of the aristocracy were concerned, although the relevant law was known and could be invoked. Of great interest is Eustathios' judgment on the applicability of the law on the seduction of a consenting virgin: he thought this law inoperable because it was "abstract." His further explanation suggests that the inapplicability lay in the fact that a law passed in the eighth century was no longer appropriate to eleventh-century society, where the aristocracy was strong and was claiming for itself privileges for which it could find support in those parts of the *Basilics* which had their origins in Roman law. The fact that the girl and the man were both members of the aristocracy played an explicit role in Eustathios Romaios' eventual decision. Thus the incoherence of the *Basilics,* which incorporated both late Roman legislation and laws that originated under very different conditions in the eighth century, was recognized by Eustathios, who used his discretionary powers as judge to correct the incoherence. The fact that he found the penalty of one pound of gold too small also undoubtedly was due to the changed economic circumstances of the empire: the sum was negligible for members of the aristocracy in the eleventh century.

The freedom of the judge in choosing the law by which a case would be prosecuted is discussed with charming candor by Eustathios Romaios. The implications of this for the legal system are explored in a pathbreaking article by Dieter Simon.[36] For our purposes, it is only a certain part of this discretionary power that needs commentary. Specifically, when Eustathios Romaios decided to award the *teichiotes* the sum of 150 nomismata as compensation for the insult he had suffered, he was not doing so "according to the law," as he claimed, for the law nowhere states the size of the penalty. It seems quite clear that the judge first decided that the compensation should be five pounds of gold and then proceeded to apportion the sum between the girl and her father, as he saw fit. The decision was probably predicated upon the social position of the injured family more than upon anything else. It is also because

---

[36] Simon, Ἡ εὕρεση, 25 ff.

of the fact that the *teichiotes* was a member of the aristocracy that the case was ultimately judged as a case of insult.[37] It must also be noted that the case must have been notorious enough and of sufficient legal interest that a summary of it appears as part of the commentary on *Bas.* 60.37.78 (on the seduction of a consenting virgin). The summary emphasizes the reasoning that led to the appeal to the law on insult, which seems to be the most interesting aspect of the case in legal terms.

Finally, it is of interest to us to find out what the effects of consent were on the woman, according to this case. Certainly, the woman was not punished. However, in the first round of the trial, some of the judges wanted to impose such a paltry penalty on the man (in strict application of the law, to be sure) that this would by itself be a form of punishment for her. Eustathios Romaios' description of the heinous aspect of the crime of deflowering, and his likening of the seducer of virgins to the insects who destroy crops is undoubtedly a flowery rhetorical phrase; but it serves to remind us that even in the relatively easygoing eleventh century virginity was a highly prized commodity, and the girl involved in a notorious case like this one was publicly shamed. Whether the daughter of the *teichiotes* was subsequently married, entered a monastery, or lived with her family we do not know; nor do we know whether any adjudication was made on the matter of the child. If any arrangements did exist, they must have been either included in a different (and not extant) decision or made privately. What remains is the fact that the girl was not formally punished for her consent to the seduction, but the social condemnation seeps through the description of the case.

Not surprisingly, it is in literature that one gets the full flavor of this informal condemnation of girls who agree to their own seduction. The twelfth-century poem of *Digenes Akrites* shows the hero engaging in a number of illicit sexual activities. Interestingly enough, the only case of seduction of a consenting virgin is also the only one where the woman is punished. It

---

[37] There is no connection between Eustathios' reasoning on this point and the invocation of the law on insult in a different set of circumstances by Balsamon, in his commentary on canon 30 of St. Basil. Referring to the case where there is a fake abduction, that is, an elopement, Balsamon says that in such a case neither the civil nor the ecclesiastical punishments on abduction apply; however, if the couple was married against the wishes of the parents, the marriage will be dissolved, and the parents of the girl, assuming that she is under their authority, can bring an action for insult against him: Ralles-Potles, IV, 172.

is the case of Maximo, and the punishment is certainly not one that owes anything to any law, but it is severe indeed: in a fit of remorse, Digenes kills her. There is a discussion of the treatment of sexual crimes in literary texts in the last part of this essay. For the moment, suffice it to say that the punishment inflicted on Maximo is an exaggerated version of attitudes that one finds primarily in ecclesiastical texts, in which seduction is at least as much the fault of the woman as it is of the man.

Conclusion

In this, as in all other aspects of the topic under discussion, it is important to remember that the sources speak in different voices and that even within the same type of source there are divergent views. While it is generally true to say that a woman's consent to illicit sex outside marriage (adultery has been excluded from this discussion) does not create legal consequences for her, there are, as we have seen, specific points in time when legal consequences did indeed exist. As far as the man is concerned, the cases we have examined have shown that there was considerable latitude in the application of the law. Social class, which was almost wholly absent as a consideration in the *Ecloga,* when the prevalent provisions for sexual crimes were established, reappears as an important factor, certainly by the eleventh century.

The formal, that is, canonical ecclesiastical sources treat the woman's consent differently. It does have consequences for the woman, who is thus treated as responsible for her actions. The informal ecclesiastical sources, stemming from a monastic milieu, ascribe even greater responsibility to the woman. In the end, the spirit which imbues the ecclesiastical sources must be considered as generally prevalent. For we have seen that shame was an informal but nevertheless telling punishment, which was formalized by Andronikos II, acting under the influence of the patriarch. And we have also seen that as learned a jurist as Chomatianos did not hesitate to consider punishing a woman, when the combination of her low social status and her bad name made it unnecessary to give her the full benefit of the law. This being so, it is now time to turn to another set of questions and try to find out what, in the mind of the Byzantines, constituted consent, free, coerced, or otherwise.

III. The Meaning of Force

The consent or absence of consent of the woman to illicit sexual activity has been seen to have legal consequences insofar as the categorization of the crime is concerned, and also with regard to the punishment of the man. The consenting woman was also subject to punishment, probably at all times in an unofficial and private way, and sometimes by law. The question then becomes how the consent of the woman or its absence was established and what was recognized as constituting force in a legal sense. Consent can be stated and conscious, or it can simply mean the absence of objection. Which of these was recognized as valid consent? Insofar as marriage was concerned, absence of opposition was considered tantamount to consent.[1] Was it the same in the case of consent to sexual intercourse? On the other side, what was the type and level of force necessary to prove coercion? What circumstances proved the presence of force, and how did people seek to establish that such circumstances existed? Was the absence of consent sufficient to prove coercion, or did one have to show resistance? Consent can be the result of physical or mental force, but the way coerced consent is treated is not self-evident. It is entirely possible that coercion, even if established, does not invalidate the consent that was given under duress; it is also possible for a society to accept that coerced consent is invalid, and the acts that are its consequence also have no legal validity. These are thorny problems, whose solution varies with time and place. In this chapter we will investigate what the Byzantines thought constituted force, violence, duress. In the next chapter we will address the problem of the validity of coerced consent.

In answer to the first question asked above, namely, whether the absence of opposition is tantamount to consent, one may invoke the law of Constantine I on abduction. His assumption appears to be that a woman who could not prove opposition had consented to the act. However, even in this harsh

---

[1] *Bas.* 28.1.10 (*D.* 23.1.12): δοκεῖ δὲ τῷ πατρὶ συναινεῖν ἡ μὴ ἀντιλέγουσα.

law, the circumstances had to be such that the woman's opposition or absence of it was capable of being established.

When one seeks to establish whether someone was coerced into an act or undertook it out of his/her own free will, there are several ways the question may be addressed. In Byzantium the simplest way was to seek objective criteria; to ask, in other words, whether the circumstances or the external evidence were such that they justified a presumption of force. To take an example from modern legal systems, rape is assumed if there was physical force whose signs are evident, bruises or torn clothing being considered as signs.[2] What one needs to do in systems where such objective criteria are used is to look for those criteria which are accepted as establishing the existence or presumption of force, and examine also the ways in which the presence of such circumstances was proved. A second concept embraces subjective criteria: there are no circumstances which prove by themselves the use of force, but nevertheless consent to the act was not given. The problem of date rape, in contemporary American society, falls into this category. Each society has particular attitudes with regard to these approaches, and in our own society both the objective criteria and the legal weight given to subjective factors are in the process of changing. As an example, one may turn to the question of sexual harassment, where rules recently adopted by a number of institutions, universities in the first instance, incorporate the assumption that there is no free consent between two people when an inequality of hierarchical status exists.

Arms and the Woman

When we try to approach these issues in Byzantium, the law gives us no guidance, for it does not deal explicitly with them. One must, instead, seek enlightenment from court cases, which, indeed, would be the most useful source even for a study of similar phenomena today. The first case we will examine is deceptively simple: it involves an abduction with the use of arms, which in itself is proof of force; it is more difficult to establish whether there was also sexual intercourse with the use of force.

The case was judged in Constantinople, in the first quarter of the elev-

---

[2] *Corpus Juris Secundum: A Complete Restatement of the Entire American Law,* "Rape," § 55, 72, 80.

enth century, by the famous jurist, Eustathios Romaios. A translation of it is provided in the Appendix to this chapter, but, since it is a rather subtle and complex legal document, its elements will be reconstructed below.

A man named Theoktistos had, at a certain point, abducted, with the force of arms (ἐνόπλῳ βίᾳ), Maria, the fiancée of his nephew John. Eventually he returned her to her own house, either before or after a court case was brought against him. By imperial command, that case had been judged by Petros, *protospatharios* and prefect of the city of Constantinople, as well as by Eustathios Romaios.[3] An investigation was made, a decision was taken, and the culprit was punished, both "according to the laws and by imperial decision" (νόμοις τε καὶ βασιλικῇ κρίσει). The court decision (not extant) had described in detail the crime, the legal examination of the case, and the decision. The case had been judged as a pure case of abduction.

After Maria had returned to her own house, her parents and her fiancé called in certain reputable women, who examined Maria for physical evidence of deflowering, and found none. They gave sworn testimony, registered in a document (ἐκμαρτύριον) that Maria was a virgin. As a result of this testimony, the marriage of Maria and John could and did take place.[4]

Subsequently a certain Niketas Gypsokopos, whose relationship to John and Maria is not known, brought a case against John, and this is the document we have. Gypsokopos was seeking the divorce or annulment of John's marriage to Maria, on two grounds, both of them connected with incest. First,

---

[3] The circumstances of the first case, brought against Gypsokopos, are briefly discussed in the record of a second court case, which is the only one extant today: A. Schminck, "Vier Eherechtliche Entscheidungen aus dem 11. Jh.," *Fontes Minores* 3 (1979), 224 ff, with a German translation. The date of this text is established by the editor as being after 1028. As for the first case, against Theoktistos, since it was judged while Petros was *eparchos* (prefect of Constantinople), it must have taken place between June 1023 and November 1028 or possibly between June 1023 and sometime in 1026: Laiou, *Mariage, amour et parenté,* chap. 4.

[4] It is not stated whether the examination took place before or after the court case against Theoktistos. Eustathios Romaios, however, insists that in that first court case there was no mention of deflowering, so that one must assume that the examination preceded the accusation against Theoktistos. The course of events thus must be: abduction, discussions between the abductor and the girl's family (this is my assumption: the text does not mention it), return of the girl to her home, examination of the girl by the women, case against Theoktistos, marriage of John and Maria either before or after the decision had been issued by the court.

he charged that Maria had slept with John's uncle, Theoktistos, and that therefore her marriage to John was invalid because incestuous: Theoktistos was first cousin of John's father, and thus the two were related to the fifth degree.[5] The second charge was that the marriage was incestuous anyway, because John's brother had married a girl who was the daughter of Maria's first cousin. This second part of the accusation is of no concern to us here. It must be assumed that Gypsokopos wanted the marriage dissolved because he had some interest of his own; he may, for example, have wanted Maria as a bride for himself or for one of his close relatives.

The point at issue here was whether Theoktistos had slept with Maria, as charged, or not. Eustathios Romaios argued that no intercourse had taken place, on the following grounds. First, he said, the original accusation had made no mention of deflowering but only of abduction. Nor did the original court decision mention deflowering. He argued further that if there had been sexual intercourse, the plaintiffs would have brought such an accusation, which would have greatly aggravated Theoktistos' crime and increased his punishment. Against a possible (or actual: we don't know) argument that

---

[5] *Bas.* 60.37.74 (= *Procheiros Nomos* 39.69, *Ecloga* 17.33) forbids the marriage of a nephew with his aunt; the *Tomos* of Patriarch Sisinnios had forbidden marriages between people variously related by affinity to the fifth or sixth degree. It did not cover the type of relationship charged by Gypsokopos, but in this period there were efforts to extend the prohibitions of the *Tomos* to cover a considerable number of different circumstances: Laiou, *Mariage, amour et parenté*, chap. 1. The question of whether illicit intercourse could establish sufficient kinship to create impediments was open. A *responsum* of Patriarch Alexios Stoudites, contemporary with the case judged by Eustathios Romaios, can enlighten us as to contemporary ecclesiastical thinking on this issue. The archbishop of Thessaloniki brought to the attention of the patriarch a case eerily resembling the one at hand. The daughter of Theodore Karmalikios had been engaged to the son of Basil Kalos Kairos. Before the marriage had taken place, a relative of Basil abducted the girl; the fiancé wished the marriage to proceed, and the opinion of the patriarch was sought, apparently because there were others who wanted to dissolve the marriage; the grounds, though unstated, would have been incest. The patriarch was of the opinion that if there was only abduction, the marriage could take place; if there was also sexual intercourse, it could not; V. Beneševich, in *Vizantijskij vremennik* (hereafter *VizVrem*) 12 (1906), 516–17. The date of the document is 1027. Finally, it should be noted that, according to Novel 93 of Leo VI, Maria's betrothal to John would have been dissolved anyway, if she had slept with anyone (other than John) while being engaged. The Novel is not invoked in the decision.

parents would shirk at making such an accusation because it would have brought shame on the girl, he concedes the disgrace, but says that any hesitation stemming from fear of disgrace would have been overridden by people's desire to bring the maximum punishment on their enemies.

The second argument (and the only solid one) concerns the testimony as to Maria's virginity. Apparently the testimony was disputed by Gypsokopos, because women are not allowed to bear witness, and because the women who had testified had died in the interim (and so their testimony could not be reconfirmed). Eustathios Romaios said, quite properly, that the testimony of women is, in fact, allowed by law in matters where men cannot testify (*Bas.* 21.1.17). Furthermore, he said, Gypsokopos had not brought into question the qualifications of these women; therefore, their testimony would remain valid, and it had established that the girl was indeed a virgin.

Eustathios then abandons himself to his usual rhetorical argumentation. He may, once again, be responding to an argument of Gypsokopos, to wit, that deflowering should be assumed, since it always follows an abduction; it is also possible that he may simply be preempting such an argument. Eustathios treats Gypsokopos' argument as conjecture, and argues, on the other side, that rape does not necessarily follow abduction. His own assumption, at least for the purposes of this argument, seems to be that there are two possible reasons for abduction: a man who is carried away by passion alone may indeed sleep with the woman. But if abduction is undertaken with the purpose of marriage (which apparently was the case here), then a man does not rape the girl, because he knows that women are more amenable to flattery than to force, and because he wishes to elicit the girl's consent (to marriage). What this argumentation leaves out of consideration, of course, is the possibility of consensual sex between a girl and her abductor: he is only arguing that rape need not follow abduction. This is a logical leap, since he uses the word φθορά.

Finally, he turns from logical arguments, which are inconclusive, back to the law, stating that evidence must almost always be preferred to conjecture. The evidence, in this case, is that there was no deflowering, and so the marriage was valid.

The case presents a multiple interest, both in terms of the functioning of Byzantine courts and of the topic that concerns us here. Clearly the affair continued for some years, since the "reputable women" who testified on Maria's virginity died between one court case and the next. Clearly, too, the disputes were between social equals, and in fact the original crime, the abduction, had been committed by a close relative of the bridegroom. The people involved must have been important in some way. Although the names give few clues, it is evident that Maria must have been an interesting bride, since her hand was disputed by her bridegroom, his uncle, and probably Gypsokopos; she must have been an heiress of some importance. The imperial interference also suggests that we are dealing with important people. The only useful name for determining the social status of the parties is that of Niketas Gypsokopos (chalk-maker, plasterer?); it is certainly not an aristocratic name, denoting rather someone associated with the crafts. So it must have been wealth rather than aristocratic lineage that defined the importance of the parties in question. The fact that Gypsokopos tried to use the evolving legislation on incest to dissolve a perfectly valid marriage is interesting but far from unique in this period.[6]

Insofar as our topic is concerned, the following observations may be made.

1. The use of arms by the abductor in itself establishes the fact that there was force involved; in such a case, the consent or otherwise of the girl is irrelevant. Indeed, both the *Basilics* (60.58.1) and Novel 35 of Leo VI state explicitly that the consent of the girl plays no role in determining the punishment of the man and his eventual accomplices, and no role in the treatment of the case. Whether, therefore, the woman was willing or unwilling, the use of arms creates a presumption of force.[7] The punishment, according to the law, of an abductor who used a sword was death by the sword. What this means for our purposes is that if it could be established that a man abducted

---

[6] See Laiou, *Mariage, amour et parenté,* chap. 1, passim. For Western European medieval evidence that abduction was a marriage strategy and that the parties involved tended to be social equals, see R. Benveniste, "Γαμήλιες στρατηγικές στό Μεσαίωνα: οἱ ἀπαγωγές," *Τά ἱστορικά* 5 (1988), 103–14. Among the Sarakatsanoi, studied by J. C. Campbell, abduction (with the use of arms) takes place when a man is offended by the refusal of a girl's family to accept his offer of marriage. The offensive presumption is that he is not equal to the girl's family: J. C. Campbell, *Honour, Family and Patronage* (Oxford, 1964), 129 ff.

[7] See also G. Weiss, "Die Synopsis legum des Michael Psellos," *Fontes Minores* 2 (1977), 193: ὁ κόρην βιασάμενος καὶ βιαίως ἀρπάσας μετὰ ξιφῶν βαρβαρικῶς ξίφει τιμωρητέος. Cf. *Corpus Juris Secundum,* "Rape," § 74: the "display of weapons" is a threat that "would cause the prosecutrix to yield."

a woman with the use of arms, this would incur the heaviest penalty of the law, the consent of the woman being irrelevant.

2. The question then arises, and was discussed in court, whether abduction and the use of force also necessarily implies rape. The law of the *Basilics*, which is essentially that of Justinian I, refers exclusively to abduction and makes no mention of sexual intercourse. On the other hand, the law of Leo VI, which was known in the eleventh century, specifically ties abduction with rape, and the punishment it envisages strikes the man who abducts and violates a virgin: τὸν δι' ἁρπαγῆς καὶ βίας φθορέα γεγονότα κόρης θανάτῳ ὑπάγεσθαι.[8] It is the assumptions of this law that Eustathios Romaios contests in his rhetorical argument, although he does not refer to the law itself. In the case at hand, Gypsokopos may have argued that, since Leo VI's Novel treats rape as part of abduction, rape must always follow upon it. Eustathios Romaios, on the other hand, argued that rape is not a necessary corollary of abduction: he distinguished between the two, whereas the Novel of Leo VI did not. The basis on which he made the distinction, however, must owe more to practice than it does to law. For he argued that sometimes men abducted women in order to marry them; and this was expressly forbidden by civil law, both that of the *Basilics* and that of Leo VI, as indeed it was by canon law.[9] Eustathios Romaios seems willing to assume that, unless there is evidence to the contrary, every abduction is a feigned abduction, which he himself said was no abduction at all.

3. The description of the case states that Theoktistos was punished, "according to the laws," for the crime of abduction, but that he was spared the heavier punishment to which he would have been subjected if he had also slept with the girl. The question arises, under which law Theoktistos was punished. Certainly, neither *Bas.* 60.58.1, on abduction, nor Novel 35 of Leo VI could have been applied, since both of these imposed the death penalty;

[8] Noailles and Dain, Novel 35, p. 141, lines 14–15. Cf. *Bas.* 60.58.1, p. 3110: οἱ ἁρπάσαντες γυναῖκα . . . ξίφει τιμωρείσθωσαν. The commentaries on the *Basilics*, perhaps because of Novel 35 of Leo VI, do speak of the abducted woman as if she had been raped: *Bas.* 60.58.1.1: ὁ ἁρπάζων. . . . τῇ βιασθείσῃ. The relevant part of the *Basilics* repeats *Procheiros Nomos* 39.40. Leo VI innovated when he explicitly tied abduction to rape; the law of Basil I, in the *Procheiros Nomos*, speaks only of abduction.

[9] See Balsamon, on canon 91 of the Council in Trullo: Ralles-Potles, II, 521 and Nomocanon 9.30 (Ralles-Potles, I, 214 ff).

and there is no other law punishing abduction without sexual intercourse. What must, therefore, have happened, is that there was a different form of punishment, outside the legal provisions, which may be why an imperial decision was necessary. There was clearly a mitigation of the law, perhaps because of an argument that Theoktistos' motive in abducting the girl was marriage, with which motive Eustathios Romaios seems sympathetic. The only thing we can say with certainty is that the law on abduction was not applied, and that, if the girl had been deflowered, the punishment would have been more severe.

4. We thus see once again[10] that, at least in this period, there was more concern with the seduction of a virgin than with abduction. At the same time, it remains a fact that seduction could still be corrected by marriage; and it is in this light that one must see Eustathios Romaios' differentiation between abduction and elopement. Elopement is punishable as seduction, to be sure, but by allowing certain cases of abduction to be treated as seduction, Eustathios makes it possible for marriage to correct the crime.

5. A question, important for our purposes, is not explicitly addressed by our text. If Maria had been found not to be a virgin, would it have been *assumed* that she had been raped, or would she have had to *prove* that she had been forced and not been a willing participant in the act? Eustathios' argumentation, as that of Leo VI, envisages only the possibility of rape, not of consensual sex. Thus it appears that once abduction had been proved, any sexual contact attendant upon it would have been considered forced. The external circumstance of abduction, with the violence which is a defining element of it, would also have been sufficient to establish the crime of rape. It would not have been admitted that the woman was capable of free consent in such circumstances.

The use of arms, then, is one circumstance which establishes *ipso facto* absence of consent, both to the abduction and to sexual intercourse.[11] The

---

[10] Cf. above, pp. 120–21. J. C. Campbell observes that, among the Sarakatsanoi, when a girl is abducted, she is held for three days and three nights, after which her abductor presents himself to the police. The girl is asked three times whether she wishes to marry him, and most often she does, for during those three days and nights she has been told, among other things, that no one will believe she is still a virgin after having been in the company of armed men for so long: Campbell, *Honour*, 130.

[11] Other sources show an age-old assumption that a woman, when in the company of armed men, must expect rape. See, for example, the case of St. Pelagia,

investigative aspect of all this is not stated; the testimony of witnesses is the only mechanism of establishing facts that is apparent in the case.

The Use of Accomplices

In the eleventh century the courts had elaborated another rule of thumb for determining that there was a crime of abduction, which by definition is a violent crime. Eustathios Romaios stated that the use of accomplices by itself establishes the crime of *raptus* (abduction) and renders irrelevant the consent of the woman. On the other hand, if a man takes a woman away without accomplices, but secretly and with her consent, that is not considered abduction, but rather seduction of a virgin, for which the punishment was more lenient, and marriage could be a remedy.[12] This, apparently, was the decision of a court case rendered by the old *censor* against a certain Protokaravos. Surprisingly, we find this judicial determination quoted as *the law* in a *Tomos* of Patriarch Kosmas (1081), which summarizes certain canonical provisions on aspects of marriage. Having brought forth several canons on *raptus*, he turns to "the civil law," and quotes, verbatim, *Peira* 63.5, omitting only the last sentence, which establishes that this was a judicial decision. I find this an extraordinary text, first because of the use of precedent as law, and second because it seems that the patriarch is using legal texts selectively to strengthen the possibility of marriage following elopement. The *Tomos* makes no mention either of *Bas.* 60.58 or of Novel 35 of Leo VI.[13] Accomplices thus create a presumption of force, while the lack of accomplices suggests that the woman consented to the abduction/elopement.

Crying in the Wilderness

Another objective factor which is taken into account in determining the presence or absence of consent is whether a woman's outcry could be heard. In

---

mentioned in the *Synaxarium Ecclesiae Constantinopolitanae* (hereafter *SynCP*), ed. H. Delehaye (Brussels, 1902), col. 120, and discussed at length by St. John Chrysostom, PG 50, cols. 579–84.

[12] *Peira* 63.5. This was incorporated into the *Scholia* to *Bas.* 58.60. Cf. Karlin Hayter, "Further Notes on Byzantine Marriage," 139, with a faulty citation to the *Peira*.

[13] A. Papadopoulos-Kerameus, *Varia Graeca Sacra* (St. Petersburg, 1909), xxxiv–xxxvi. On some problems with this document, see J. Darrouzès, *Les Regestes des Actes du Patriarcat de Constantinople,* I (Paris, 1989), no. 919.

Byzantium this is a function of the locality in which the crime was committed. We have already seen that Novel 26 of Andronikos II differentiates between a woman being forced "in the wilderness" and one who gives herself willingly. The distinction, as we have noted, is an ancient one, stemming from Deuteronomy. What it means, in effect, is that the benefit of the doubt goes to the woman who is seduced in a place where her outcry cannot be heard or noticed: that fact by itself establishes presumption of force. Thus, since the external circumstances in which consent might be established are absent, the woman is held not to have consented. She need not prove absence of consent; she need only prove that the circumstances existed which rendered it impossible for her objections to be registered.

This type of circumstantial proof appears in the civil legislation only with the Novel of Andronikos II, but it seems to have been used earlier either in ecclesiastical courts or possibly in provincial courts. This, at least, is suggested by a case discussed by John Apokaukos. The text is a *semeioma* of Apokaukos, written in the presence of witnesses.[14] It is not a court decision, but rather a description of an affair that was brought to his attention by chance.

The pertinent circumstances are as follows. One day, when Apokaukos was visiting the bishop of Vonitza, a man named Symeon Sgouropoulos came to them and complained of his troubles. He explained that in the previous year, his daughter, Vlasia, who was young and a virgin, had gone out to a spring, very near her house, to draw water. There she was found by a Vlach, Constantine Avrilionis, who took her to a crevice, "where he thought that no help could come to her from anywhere, nor would she be heard if she cried out," and deflowered her. After that, every time he found her he would rape her (ἐπάγων βίαν ἐμίγνυτο). Eventually, she became pregnant and bore a child. This, said Sgouropoulos, was the first offense of Avrilionis. A few days before the birth, Avrilionis and about thirty other Vlachs had met Sgouropoulos and his son-in-law (who had married another of his daughters), and beat them up severely, either because he was angry at Sgouropoulos' efforts on behalf of his daughter, or because he thought that Sgouropoulos was too poor and inconsequential, and thus an easy prey. The son-in-law was now at the point of death, while Sgouropoulos was suffering from terrible wounds. The

---

[14] N. A. Bees, "Unedierte Schriftstücke aus der Kanzlei des Johannes Apokaukos des Metropoliten von Naupaktos (in Aetolien)," *Byzantinisch-Neugriechische Jahrbücher* 21 (1971–74), no. 5, pp. 60–62.

metropolitan then launches into a graphic description of the wounds, which upset both him and the bishop. The bishop of Vonitza advised Sgouropoulos to turn to the civil authorities and bring his case to the *protovestiarios;* Apokaukos wrote up the circumstances, so that Sgouropoulos could bring the letter to the civil authorities.

One is here confronted with a situation where reality has the upper hand, and the law has very little chance of being heard. True, the circumstances are specific: this was in the country, in an area and at a time of uncertainty and troubles. It is, therefore, not surprising that private vengeance seems more in evidence than legal arrangements. Nor is it astonishing that the bishop of Vonitza and Apokaukos were much more concerned with the life-threatening attack on Sgouropoulos and his son-in-law than with the rape, which is treated almost as a prelude to the attack. It is, therefore, all the more interesting to discover what it was that the girl's father (or, more likely, Apokaukos) wanted to establish with regard to the sexual crime.

Indisputably, the main element that the girl's side wanted to establish was the use of force. It was thus stressed that the first encounter took place in a spot where she could not be heard if she cried out, and that the subsequent encounters took place by force. The explanation of the girl's presence in a lonely spot serves the same purpose: it is explained that she was out on a legitimate errand (the good biblical errand of drawing water), and that the spring where she went was the one closest to the house. No one could argue that she courted disaster.[15] It was further stated that the girl was young and had been a virgin. By law, Avrilionis should have been punished by having his nose slit and giving the girl one-third of his property. But no mention is made of that. What is of interest here is that the locality in which the crime occurred is the primary factor in establishing presumption of force. It is, for our purposes, irrelevant to ask why the crime was not reported the first time around, or under what circumstances it was repeated. It is relevant to note that no mention of marriage is made, which may be why the girl's father was eventually moved to take steps, as is implied in the description of the sequence of events.

In terms of our inquiry, two things are especially notable. First, that once it had been stated that the encounter took place in a lonely spot, the question of the girl's consent appeared moot: she would not have been heard if she had

---

[15] The point was made by Alice-Mary Talbot.

cried out, and therefore she got the benefit of the doubt. Second, it is reasonable to assume that private solutions, peaceful or otherwise, were sought before the parties had recourse to the authorities, and not only in the wilds of Epiros.

The chronicle of Skylitzes preserves the story of a woman who was raped by a Varangian soldier in the theme of Thrakesion, where the Varangians were spending the winter. The soldier found her in the "wilderness" and, unable to persuade her to sleep with him, raped her (βίαν . . . ἐπῆγεν). She grabbed his sword and killed him. The other Varangians, hearing of the story, gave her all of the dead soldier's property and left him unburied, "according to the law regarding suicides" (κατὰ τῶν βιοθανάτων τὸν νόμον).[16]

Here force is established by two circumstances, the location and the use of arms. The private justice exacted by the woman (and by the other soldiers) is more severe than the provisions of the law regarding rape, but is very close to the spirit of the law governing abduction and rape. That law, of Leo VI, it will be remembered, posits death for the man, and gives his property to the abducted and raped maiden.

As far as locality is concerned, it should be noted that "the wilderness" and the spring of water have a significance beyond that which stems from Deuteronomy. These are liminal areas, where extraordinary events can occur and danger lurks. It is, perhaps, this ambiance of liminality that lifts the woman's guilt. It will be remembered that brooks and streams were the seduction spot of choice in the case of the gods of ancient Greece.[17]

The Factor of Age

In Chapter I we saw that, according to the *Ecloga,* followed by the *Procheiros Nomos* and the *Basilics,* the seduction of a virgin before puberty is tantamount to rape in terms of the punishment involved.[18] There was, then, the

[16] John Skylitzes, *Ioannis Scylitzae Synopsis historiarum,* ed. I. Thurn (Berlin and New York, 1973), 394 (in 1034). The Madrid manuscript of Skylitzes has a miniature illustrating the incident.

[17] I thank Professor Stanley Tambiah for pointing out the importance of liminality. For ancient Greece, see Mary Lefkowitz, "Seduction and Rape in Greek Myth," in Part I of this volume.

[18] See above, I. The modern definition of statutory rape is the unlawful carnal knowledge of an underage girl.

concept of statutory rape, according to which age is an external, objective factor which by itself makes the question of consent immaterial, if the woman has not attained puberty. It will not escape notice that the age limitation is the same for marriage and for sexual intercourse: an underage girl is legally incapable of consent to marriage, as she is to consent to sexual intercourse.

Curiously enough, we are better informed about statutory rape than about any other sexual crime, with the exception of adultery. The matrimonial policies of the Byzantines, at least as they emerge with some clarity in the eleventh century, meant that marriage arrangements were made when the girls were very young.[19] Whereas both civil and ecclesiastical law forbade the marriage of a girl below the age of puberty, it was often a short step from negotiating an arrangement to actually performing the marriage ceremony before the statutory age of thirteen years for the girl. Even when no marriage had been contracted, sometimes the fiancé would live in the house of the bride-to-be; and although Alexios I tried to forbid the free and unsupervised congress of betrothed young people, specifically in order to reduce the risk of a sexual encounter, it is not at all certain that his legislation was followed.[20] The preconditions thus were often present for illicit sexual activity in a family setting. Sometimes the fiancé might sleep with his prospective mother-in-law, who might be closer to his age than was his betrothed.[21] And sometimes the girl was deflowered by her fiancé long before puberty. A well-known historical example is the case of Simonis, daughter of Andronikos II, who was married, at the age of five, to the Serbian kral Stefan Uroš II Milutin, then about forty years old. He apparently consummated the union while Simonis was still under age, and she became sterile as a result.[22] John Apokaukos in the thirteenth century, Patriarchs Athanasios I and Kallistos I in the fourteenth century, and the moralist Joseph Bryennios in the fifteenth, all

[19] Among the numerous reported cases, I mention almost at random *Peira* 49.34 (seven-year-old girl), 42.5; Ralles-Potles, V, 381 (a girl engaged at five and seven), and 32–36; Bees, "Apokaukos," nos. 9, 10. A longer list may be found in M.-T. Fögen, "Rechtsprechung mit Aristophanes," *Rechtshistorisches Journal* 1 (1982), 77 note 10.

[20] *JGR,* I, 309, 325.

[21] See the responsa of Niketas of Herakleia, *VizVrem* 2 (1895), 167–69.

[22] Angeliki E. Laiou, *Constantinople and the Latins: The Foreign Policy of Andronicus II, 1282–1328* (Cambridge, Mass., 1972), 95–96.

complained about the crime of παιδοφθορία, the deflowering of girls before puberty.[23]

As can be readily seen, this type of illicit sexual activity could create a number of serious problems, quite apart from the infraction of the laws of church and state. If the man subsequently decided not to marry the girl, she could well find herself unmarriageable. In any case, she might suffer physical damage, including sterility, as well as damage to her reputation. The situation became vexed if the parents of the girl had in some way contributed to the circumstances leading up to the crime. It is, perhaps, for these reasons that the courts tried such cases in ways that are intriguing. The two cases discussed below were chosen because they address, albeit indirectly, the question of the consent of the girl, which is our primary interest here.

In the *Peira* (49.22), we find the story of a girl who was betrothed at the age of seven, although her father lied and pretended that she was ten years old. It should be remembered that, according to the law, a simple engagement could be made when the girl (or the boy) was seven years old, but it could not be confirmed by a church ceremony until the age of thirteen for the girl and fourteen for the boy. In our case, there was a church ceremony one year later, presumably the ceremony of betrothal rather than marriage, since the man is still called the girl's fiancé. The man raped the girl (ἐβιάσατο τὴν κόρην); she resisted, so he held her down and covered her mouth so violently that blood rushed from her ears. The text says that the girl was damaged (ἐβλάβη), for she became afraid even to look at a man. The judge dissolved the marriage (the word γάμος is used), calling it a φθορά (seduction of a virgin), and invoking the law which punished the seduction of a virgin before puberty by the slitting of the nose and by the transfer to the girl of one-half of the man's property. The girl did, indeed, receive the monetary compensation, but the corporal punishment was not imposed. On the other hand, the judge ordered the man to be beaten and shorn, since he did not hold imperial office (διὰ τὸ μὴ τετιμῆσθαι βασιλικῷ ἀξιώματι).

The most important decision taken by the judge was the dissolution of the engagement/marriage, undoubtedly on the basis of the fact that it was invalid because the girl was below the statutory age at which a marriage could

[23] F. Miklosich and J. Müller, *Acta et diplomata graeca medii aevi*, 6 vols. (Vienna, 1860–90), I, 397–99; Bees, "Apokaukos," nos. 9, 10; Koukoules, *Βυζαντινῶν βίος καὶ πολιτισμός*, IV, 77 note 45.

be contracted. The subsequent seduction thus was not a case of a man forcing his wife. Therefore, the judge could treat it as φθορά, not because of the force involved but because there was no marriage. He could then apply, although only in part, the provisions of *Bas.* 60.37.80, coupled with a punishment not envisaged by the law, that is, ordering the man to be beaten and shorn. It should be noted that this corporal punishment could be imposed only on a man who was not an imperial official.

What about the role of violence and of the girl's absence of consent? In fact, the decision formally depended only on the girl's age, which was sufficient to invalidate the marriage. Furthermore, the legislation invoked assumes the absence of (legal) consent to sexual activity if the girl is under age. And yet the judge goes to some lengths to describe vividly the force involved, and its consequences. Is it possible that evidentiary proof of force was necessary to establish statutory rape, or can the matter be explained in other ways? To start with, there is a practical explanation. It is evident that the case was brought to court by the girl's parents or guardians, and that for it to reach the court private efforts at accommodation must have failed. It may have been the parents who justified their complaint by mentioning the fact that force was used, and it must have been an important part of their suit: they could not simply appeal to the law that forbids an engagement (with church ceremony) or a marriage before the age of thirteen, since the girl's father himself had allowed it to take place. Second, the judge may have used the issue of force in order to show that the crime was aggravated, and thus to impose the maximum penalty.[24] Possibly the argumentation may have been influenced by other cases of rape, where the girl was not under age and force played an important legal role. All of the above are possible and plausible.

What seems most important, however, is a factor which is quite outside formal law, but very important in real terms. The permanent injury to the girl was the fact that she became afraid of men; thus it was no longer possible to remedy the situation by an eventual marriage, either to her fiancé or to another man, or at least it could so be argued. That, in fact, was the factor that truly aggravated the crime of rape, and that was what was established by the insistence on the use of force.

To summarize, it is clear that in this particular case the factor of age,

---

[24] In modern American law, evidence of force in statutory rape, while immaterial to the crime, is admissible in order to determine civil damages.

which legally would have established absence of consent, and even circumstantial force,[25] was not considered adequate. The actual use of force, as proven by the physical violence involved, was considered important, primarily, it would seem, because of its effects: it had the socially undesirable consequence of making marriage impossible for the girl. This is further illuminated by a case which was judged by the patriarchal court of Constantinople in 1325.[26]

The affair engaged members of the clergy of the metropolis of Ainos, and was brought to court by John Manglavites. He reported that he had betrothed his eleven-year old daughter to the son of the *archon ton ekklesion* of Ainos, Argyros.[27] Since the girl was under age, the *dikaiophylax* of the church of Ainos did not allow her to live in the same house as the groom. Her father, Manglavites, on the other hand, did allow her to live in the bridegroom's house, but only, as he insisted, after having received guarantees from his father that no sexual intercourse would take place until she came of age. But then, Manglavites charged, the young man forced her, and slept with her,[28] causing her great harm (παντελοῦς βλάβης καὶ ἐρημώσεως ταύτῃ γενόμενος πρόξενος). The injury, in this case, was physical. So, since the girl was also present when the case was brought, the court ordered her examined by a midwife, who testified that she had indeed suffered physical injury, with the result that she could no longer sleep with a man.

After the examination, the court decided to dissolve the betrothal, and granted to Manglavites the return of the dowry which he had promised, plus the θεωρετροϋπόβολον, that is, the man's marriage gifts to her. The disso-

---

[25] Cf. *Peira* 42.5: Βία ἐστὶν οὐ μόνον τὸ στρεβλῶσαι καὶ ἐγκλεῖσαι, ἀλλὰ καὶ τὸ παρὰ γνώμην τινός, ὅτε μάλιστα κύριος θελήματος οὐκ ἐστὶ διὰ τὸ ἀνήλικον, πρὸς συνάλλαγμα συνωθεῖσθαι.

[26] H. Hunger and O. Kresten, *Das Register des Patriarchats von Konstantinopel,* I (Vienna, 1981), no. 89, pp. 510–13.

[27] The term used is ἠγάγετο γαμβρόν. Since Manglavites then proceeds to state that the girl was not of a legal age to contract a marriage, it would logically follow that the arrangement was a simple betrothal, without the church blessing. However, logic is not always the best guide, and by this period betrothal in church was a practice long established; so it is entirely possible that it is to such a betrothal that Manglavites refers.

[28] ἐμίγη παρὰ φύσιν αὐτῇ. The words "against nature" in all probability refer to the fact that she was too young for sexual intercourse, rather than to "unnatural" intercourse.

lution was granted on two grounds: the girl's age, which is the first ground mentioned in the decision, and the injury she had sustained and her inability to have sex, which was the ground to which the court gave the heavier weight. The court further took notice of the responsibility of the groom's father, who allowed the girl to come to harm, even though she had gone to his house under his protection and guarantee.

Once again, the basic decision is the dissolution of the matrimonial arrangement, and the financial penalty imposed upon the groom and his father—since presumably the man's marriage gifts were given by the father. The court which, it must be remembered, was an ecclesiastical court, gave two grounds for the dissolution. The first was the girl's impuberty; this would not invalidate a simple betrothal but it would invalidate one blessed by the church. Ecclesiastical courts had also established the principle that a church betrothal or marriage would be dissolved if there was sexual intercourse before the girl reached puberty.[29] The court's further decision, that the son of Argyros should not, in future, go near the girl, is interesting. In other circumstances, it would have been possible to keep the betrothal or to dissolve the current engagement but envisage the possibility of its being renewed once the girl had come of age. That, at least, would seem to be the tenor of canons 22 and 25 of St. Basil, which permits the marriage of a man with the girl he has deflowered, even where force was involved.[30] Indeed, canon 67 of the Apostles insists that a man who has violated a virgin must marry *her* and no other; admittedly, the reference is to a virgin who is not engaged, but it could easily be thought to cover the rape of one's own fiancée.[31] So the girl's impuberty by itself would not seem to justify the decision as it stands. In any case, according to the law, the decision was up to the parents.

At the same time, the civil law on rape was not applied, nor was the case fully treated as a case of rape. The court imposed a punishment ad hoc, and justified it primarily by reference to the injury sustained by the girl and

---

[29] See, for example, Ralles-Potles, V, 109.

[30] Ralles-Potles, IV, 150–54, 157–59. The Σύνταγμα κατὰ στοιχεῖον of Matthew Blastares states that if a man seduces (φθείρας) his fiancée before her thirteenth year, the resolution is up to the parents of the girl. They can allow the betrothal to stand; if they prefer to break it, because of the seduction (διὰ τὴν φθοράν), the fiancé has to give the girl one-third of his property (Ralles-Potles, VI, 374). The reference derives, in a remote way, from *Procheiros Nomos* 39.65. Cf. *Eclogadion* 17.28.

[31] See the commentary of Balsamon, in Ralles-Potles, II, 86.

her inability to contract a marriage in the future. Thus the girl's absence of consent per se was not treated as a legal issue in this case. The punishment was decided, rather, on the basis of the effect of the sexual intercourse on the future of the girl. Once again, it becomes clear that marriage was considered to be the remedy for a number of sexual crimes, and when marriage was impossible, the severity of the crime increased. At the same time, it is interesting that the patriarchal court did not apply the law on rape, nor did it insist on the issue of rape, as Eustathios Romaios had done.

It is also noteworthy that the court castigated the groom's father for his carelessness in allowing sexual intercourse to take place. This had been a matter of concern for a long time, and a Novel of Alexios I addressed the issue directly. In dealing with betrothal, he said that the engaged couple should not be allowed to meet unsupervised until they had reached puberty. The parents were charged with following this prescription diligently. In case of sexual intercourse before puberty, both the young man and his parents were to be considered guilty of *parthenophthoria*.[32] This Novel was not applied by the patriarchal court to the letter, but a memory of it may well have remained.

Conclusion

As far as sexual crimes are concerned, it seems that the Byzantines placed great importance on objective rather than subjective factors. There are a number of circumstances—the use of arms and accomplices, the locality—which are understood to make it impossible for free consent to be given, and equally impossible to establish whether consent was given or not. In these circumstances, consent is assumed to be absent. In such circumstances, too, it would seem that consent was considered to be the absence of objection: and when this could not be freely exercised or ascertained, the advantage was with the violated woman. On the other hand, sometimes an effort was made to prove the girl's absence of consent: this was so in *Peira* 49.22, where the physical evidence of a struggle was brought forth and accepted by the court, even though it was not necessary for the categorization of the crime. Here something more than absence of objection was sought and proven, not for legal reasons, but rather so as to justify the punishment imposed by the court. The

---

[32] See *JGR*, I, 324. Elsewhere the emperor says that the parents of both parties would be guilty of *porneia*, and should suffer the appropriate ecclesiastical punishment as well as pay a penalty to the fisc: ibid., p. 109.

claim of psychological injury to the girl strikes a modern note, even though it is tied to a thoroughly medieval and Byzantine concept: the importance of marriage and the evaporation of the girl's hopes for a future marriage. Both the *Peira* 49.22 and the decision of 1325 leave one with the impression that if the marriage had been found valid, the use of force would not have justified an accusation of rape. This question requires further examination, as does the question of coerced consent, that is, consent which was not freely given.

Appendix

Legal Opinion of Eustathios (Romaios) the Magistros (after 1028)
(ed. A. Schminck, *Fontes Minores* 3 [1979], 224–28)

In two ways[1] Niketas Gypsokopos tried to shake and destroy a properly constituted marriage, putting forward like siege engines and palisade stakes arguments which, he thought, were excellent. But he was shown under cover of piety and propriety to be insolently attacking John, who had taken in marriage Maria, to whom he had first been legally betrothed.

The accusation was as follows: Theoktistos, who had as his nephew[2] John, the son of his cousin, abducted by armed force John's fiancée, and he "knew" her, even though illegally and by force. And the unholy act had already been punished by law and imperial decision. And the girl is taken from her abductor, being returned to her own home and her mother. But John, on the pretext that he stood by the betrothal and remained faithful to the marriage agreement, took no umbrage at his uncle's congress with Maria, although he brought shame on himself, but for his own part also he stained with condemnation and horror the unlawful union.

So with this first action the accuser pounced on John, but he responded that the attack was false; that during the entire action for abduction the topic of carnal knowledge (φθορά) was never raised.

And indeed this was true; for the legal opinion, which was written by imperial order by the then *protospatharios* and eparch Petros and by us who judged the case, and which described from beginning to end the crime committed, the investigation of the case, and the decision, made no mention at all of deflowering, although such a grave offense would not have been overlooked by the plaintiffs if it actually happened, as it could make the accusation much more terrible and serious and harm the culprit, even if it would add disgrace to the dishonored woman. For nothing which harms an enemy seems shameful to those in the heat of passion.

Furthermore, evidence was also brought forward by well-reputed women who met and confirmed by physical examination and testimony that the girl was untouched.

---

[1] Only the account of the first attempt is translated here.

[2] Greek uses nephew and uncle to describe what in English would be "first cousins once removed" or, in popular usage, "second cousins."

And their evidence is not to be discarded; for what must be hidden from the eyes of men, in these (matters) it is not forbidden for women to be witnesses, and the law relates as follows: "a woman cannot be a witness to a will, but in other matters she may bear witness." In what other (matters)? Clearly "in matters in which men are not called." Thus, as their testimony was not invalidated according to legal regulation, there is no ground for complaint against the marriage.

For if someone following conjectures may be carried away to assume that it is likely that a girl separated from her family and staying with her abductor will suffer something undesirable, yet another who uses secure reasoning and knows that the possible is between what happens and what does not, will find that carnal knowledge (φθορά) does not of absolute necessity follow abduction. For the man who is smitten by the sight of physical beauty, embracing an insane desire and being love-sick with passion, such a man when he gains control of what he desires may be led down to a slip. But a man whom concern for marriage and for living together as a prelude (to marriage) drives to such an attack, this man does not think it necessary to use force at all, knowing well that a woman's nature is won more by flattery than by force, so as not to have the girl accusing him with the others, but by kindness he may draw her to consent.

Reasoning which considers opposites knows how to create these (possibilities), but the law, which leads matters which are indeterminate and initially hanging in the balance through evidence to clear knowledge, proceeds to the truth, which it respects and prefers to supposition except in some (few) instances.

As the women who were called to testify by the betrothed man and the family of the betrothed girl and who testified to the virginity of the girl were not discredited by the accuser, the marriage already constituted through this testimony will not be dissolved, but will have validity, the women, although they have since died, being believed to have given sworn testimony.

Translation by Denis Sullivan.

IV. Coerced Consent

Subjective criteria for establishing consent and its absence are notoriously more difficult to deal with than objective criteria. It is debatable whether, if the circumstances themselves do not prove absence of consent but the woman nevertheless claims that she did not give her consent, this internal absence of consent can be accepted. But the most difficult problem, both to define in theory and to deal with in practice, is connected with consent given under duress. There are a number of questions that modern scholars can raise. The one which seems of primary importance today is the validity of coerced consent: if one agrees to take a certain action under duress, physical or moral, is that action valid? If coercion is established, is the act and its consequences invalidated? Is someone responsible for actions taken under duress? At what point can one claim coercion and expect legal consequences to follow? What are the circumstances in which consent can be said to have been coerced, and do some of them have greater weight than others? And how is coercion proved? The problems are more complex than is apparent at first glance. To take a perfectly contemporary example, the problem is posed if a man persuades a woman over whom he holds some kind of power to sleep with him: an employer and his employee, or a teacher and his student. Can the consent of a woman in such a situation be considered free, or is it to be assumed that the relationship in and by itself is such that an element of force exists or may be feared, thus rendering suspect (and potentially invalid) the consent of the woman?[1] How much force has to be used or threatened for consent to be considered coerced? Does the woman's life have to be threatened, and in what way? Or is fear of much lesser consequences, such as loss of a job, or a threat (real or imagined) to one's career, sufficient to establish coercion? Legal thinking on such issues is evolving in our day, and has been posed differently in different societies. In some societies these problems are not considered to exist, and thus do not give rise to any debate. By extension, it must not be assumed that because such questions are evident in some modern societies

[1] The male and female roles can be reversed in our society.

they were also present in societies of the past; the evidence for each society under discussion must be examined.

The difficulty of dealing with coerced consent can, perhaps, be best understood by a look at some twentieth-century positions. American law, as of 1952, posited that, in cases of alleged rape and except when the woman was under age, instructions to the jury must state that "consent on the part of the female, however reluctantly given, prevents the act from being rape." However, the judge must also know that "where there is evidence not only of force, but of threat of serious bodily harm, an instruction that force may be exerted not only by physical violence but also by threats of serious bodily harm, so as to overpower the female and cause her to yield against her will, is not erroneous."[2] It cannot be said that such instructions are crystal clear.

Insofar as Byzantine society is concerned, the issue of coerced consent was indeed debated, and with some force, but not necessarily in connection with circumstances that are of particular relevance today. Coerced consent to marriage was certainly a matter which was considered grave and which would dissolve a marriage, whether the coercion was due to force, fraud, or fear. The consent extracted from a boy or a girl before puberty was considered *ipso facto* invalid, but this is somewhat different from coerced consent. A number of court cases indicate the types of coercion that were, at various times, thought to invalidate the act. In thirteenth-century Epiros, the lady Theodora tou Indanou, a woman who seems to have been a person of power in Malaina, forced a man and a woman, who were under her authority, to marry. The man was unwilling, resisted, and was imprisoned. His unwillingness was well known in the region, so that the local clerics refused to perform the marriage ceremony. Eventually a priest was called from outside the region, and the wedding took place; although the text does not say so, the young man must have given some sort of consent which the priest found acceptable. However, John Apokaukos, to whom the young man later presented his case, found that the groom had not consented to the marriage, which was dissolved for that reason.[3] In this case, both the authority of the lady Theodora over the young man and her use of physical force invalidated whatever consent he had given

---

[2] *Corpus Juris Secundum*, "Rape," § 82. For the difficulties posed by coerced consent in Roman society, see Moses, "Livy's Lucretia."

[3] Bees, "Unedierte Schriftstücke," no. 19, and cf. Laiou, "Institution familiale," 308–9.

under duress. A similar case was heard before the patriarchal court of Constantinople in 1401: the *chartophylax* of the church of Thessalonike was powerful enough to force a man named Glavas to marry one of his nieces, despite the fact that Glavas was unwilling to do so. The circumstances, as reported, are rather suspicious: Glavas, we are told, had already been engaged to another niece of the *chartophylax* and had slept with her, when the *chartophylax* accused him of having deflowered the second niece and forced him to marry her; at that point, Glavas slept with his wife once, to prove that she was a virgin, and then disappeared! The story, as related, does not make intuitive sense; nevertheless, what is of interest here is that Glavas' (assumed) consent was considered by the court to have been invalid because he was unwilling and acted under duress.[4]

Less clear is the validity ascribed to consent which was given because the person was fraudulently misinformed. Such was the case of Constantine Palates, who became betrothed to a woman with serious physical flaws of which he was unaware. When he recognized the "fraud" (τὴν ἀπάτην), he withdrew his consent and left the area. Eventually the betrothal was dissolved by the patriarchal court, not because Palates' consent was extracted from him fraudulently, but rather because his parents had not consented, and he himself had developed a violent hatred of his fiancée.[5]

Forced marriage, then, was one area in which the question of free consent was considered important by the Byzantines, and where consent given under duress would invalidate the marriage. The matter did not, as far as I know, give rise to much debate, perhaps because the law was quite unambiguous: no marriage could be valid that was not undertaken with the consent of the future spouses and those who had them under their authority. Whereas questions might arise as to the circumstances in which consent was obtained, and it was possible for the desires of parents and children to differ, the theoretical issues that could be raised did not engage the Byzantines. On the other hand, the eleventh and twelfth centuries saw quite a heated debate on the validity of coerced consent to monastic life and on two other issues connected

---

[4] Miklosich-Müller, *Acta*, II, 522–23.

[5] Hunger and Kresten, *Das Register des Patriarchats von Konstantinopel*, I, no. 11 (Sept.–Dec. 1315). The fiancée's extreme ugliness or unhealthiness are the only acceptable grounds for breaking an engagement among the modern Sarakatsanoi: Campbell, *Honour*, 128–29.

with it: the forced tonsure of women in order to dissolve their marriages, and the forced tonsure of the former wife of someone who was elected bishop.[6] In principle, monastic life could only be entered upon with the free will, freely exercised, of the person in question. In practice, however, some people were forced to enter a monastery, often by imperial command. Balsamon, a well-known advocate of imperial prerogative, argued that such tonsures were valid, precisely because they were mandated by imperial command.[7] Otherwise, coercion, in the form, for example, of force exercised by an official, invalidated the act. A subtler form of duress, namely, fear of death, which frequently caused men or women to take monastic vows when they were sick, was recognized as duress but was not thought to be a circumstance which invalidated the vow. The forced tonsure of women (or, more rarely, men) as a form of divorce was not easily accepted, although it was practiced. The debate on the validity of such acts centered on the question of whether the divorce that was achieved by the forced tonsure of one of the spouses was valid or not. Opinions were split on the issue, which sometimes had important political overtones. The implicit assumption of those who accepted that the divorce was valid must have been that tonsure, even when forced, was irreversible. In the late twelfth century, a new element was injected, which sought to investigate, even though in a cursory fashion, whether there might be consent after the fact: thus if a woman remained cloistered after the force had been removed, it could be argued that she was acting freely. The implicit assumption of those who did not accept such divorces as valid was that consent obtained by force invalidated the monastic vow and so also the divorce attendant upon it.

The debate on the forced tonsure of the wives of elected bishops had the most interesting theoretical overtones, partly because the canonists who carried out the debate were very eager to establish that these women were, in fact, acting freely. The most coherent argument was that if one freely consents to a course of action, one consents equally freely and fully to its consequences. Thus a woman who consented to divorcing her husband so that he could ascend to the episcopate was held to consent as well to the consequences, that is, to the monastic life.[8]

---

[6] Laiou, *Mariage, amour et parenté*, chap. 4.
[7] Ibid., and Ralles-Potles, IV, 203.
[8] For the documentation, see Laiou, *Mariage, amour et parenté*, chap. 4.

If there were theoretical debates by civil jurists on the validity of coerced consent to sexual intercourse, they have not survived. The issue of coerced consent, closely connected with internal, subjective criteria of force, was debated only in canonical sources, and raised in literature from a monastic milieu, as we shall see below.

Before discussing the pertinent texts, it will be useful to try to establish a distinction between rape and coerced consent to sexual intercourse, although the boundaries between the two are hazy. In a formal sense, it could be argued that rape in Byzantium was intercourse in conditions that clearly indicated the use of force, or where consent could not be exercised or could not be proved. There are, however, other circumstances, where the woman consented to the act, but her consent was not freely exercised because she acted under duress. The distinguishing line is fine, and sometimes the distinction depends on whether our sources decide to raise the question of consent or not: such is the case of the rape of a woman in captivity. In other cases, the distinction is clear, as, for example, when a woman assents to sexual intercourse although she does not want to, under the force of circumstances such as poverty.

The Legitimation of Coercion

The documents emanating from the court or the hand of John Apokaukos preserve a curious and unique case of coercion sanctioned by society. The people involved were a married couple, Constantine and Irene, peasants who lived in the village of Govlastou, which was, apparently, part of the landed property of the see of Naupaktos.[9] They were married, but a year later Irene had still not allowed the marriage to be consummated. This clearly offended the community, and the inhabitants of the village exercised pressure— through ridicule—on Irene, to no good effect. The administrators of the church tried to threaten her into submission, again without result. They then locked the couple in a hut, repeatedly, so that Constantine would sleep with Irene, *"even though she was unwilling"* (καὶ μὴ θελούσῃ). She fought him, and he bore the scars of her scratches and bites on his hands. Eventually, the dumbfounded Apokaukos pronounced the marriage dissolved, on the grounds of Irene's evident hatred of her husband.

[9] Bees, "Unedierte Schriftstücke," no. 7; cf. Laiou, *Mariage, amour et parenté,* chap. 3.

The affair is, of course, what we would today call marital rape, although the word is not mentioned, and, from the description, the concept could not be further from the mind of Apokaukos. Among the many interesting facts of the case, one may mention the evident interference of the community in the marital affairs of its members. We get a rare glimpse into that aspect of village society, which has been studied in some detail in Western Europe where the documentation is much richer.[10] Of greater interest to us here is the fact that the community, the church administrators, and Apokaukos all considered forced intercourse with equanimity and indeed tried to impose it on an unwilling married woman. What does this legitimation of force within the context of marital sexual activity imply?

The first question that must be asked is whether there is the concept of marital debt, and whether that duty is considered more important than the absence of consent of one of the partners to sexual intercourse. A related question is whether the woman and, indeed, the man, surrenders the free disposition of her/his body at marriage. The sum of these two questions is whether the concept of marital rape existed in Byzantine society. The formal legal statements about marriage do not specifically mention sexual intercourse as a duty, but every presumption of the legislator indicates that sexual intercourse was considered to be a constituent element of marriage. The fact that the legal age of marriage was directly tied to puberty, and the fact that impotence in a man was considered grounds for divorce even in the strict anti-divorce legislation of the *Ecloga* (2.9.3) make the point with some force. Furthermore, Christian theologians and moralists, from St. John Chrysostom on, and starting with St. Paul's grudging statement, "let every man have his own wife to avoid fornication,"[11] had attributed two purposes to marriage: procreation and a legal outlet to sexual urges, although the two carried a different weight at different times.[12]

Canonists had discussed not so much the positive argument that husband and wife had a duty to sleep with each other, but the negative argument that

---

[10] I am thinking of the Charivari, on which see, for example, Natalie Zemon Davis, *Society and Culture in Early Modern France* (Stanford, Calif., 1975), 97–123, esp. 104–9.

[11] 1 Cor. 7:1. On the marital debt in Western medieval Europe, see James A. Brundage, "Implied Consent to Intercourse," in Part III of this volume.

[12] Laiou, *Mariage, amour et parenté*, chap. 2.

spouses should abstain from intercourse only by common consent. The main text is canon 3 of St. Denys of Alexandria, and especially the twelfth-century commentaries. The canon refers to 1 Cor. 7:5 which says: "defraud ye not one the other, except it be with consent for a time, that ye may give yourselves to fasting and prayer," and adds that they must control this period of abstinence themselves. The twelfth-century commentators insist on the idea that the abstinence must be by mutual agreement. Otherwise, says Zonaras, the partner who does not desire intercourse is depriving the other partner of what Zonaras clearly considers to be his/her legitimate due. He also refers to the statement that "the wife hath not power of her body but the husband; and likewise also the husband hath no power of his own body, but the wife" (1 Cor. 7:4), to argue that the partner who does desire intercourse is the master of the body of his/her spouse. The argument further goes that if one is forced into abstinence, he/she may fall into sin by engaging in illicit sexual activity.[13] Indeed, there is good historical evidence that the clergy counseled wives against abstinence, even when undertaken in the cause of piety, precisely because it endangered the soul of the husband. Thus Patriarch Euthymios advised Theophano, the pious first wife of Leo VI, to rethink her desire to enter a monastery, since this would tempt her husband into adultery. The patriarch referred specifically to 1 Cor. 7:4.[14] Whereas neither the canon of St. Denys nor the commentaries take the further step of sanctioning the use of force, it would not be impossible to argue that this mode of thinking made the use of force acceptable, at least unofficially. Perhaps the issue would have been seen less as forcing the unwilling partner and more as ensuring the payment of the marital debt. In a permutation of this, a woman named Athanasia, who wanted to leave her husband, a man of lewd disposition, and enter a monastery, did her best to persuade him to let her go, even offering him large sums of money. She feared that, if she left him, she could be branded an adulteress, and he would go searching for her in the monastery.[15] A systematic review of hagiographic sources would perhaps yield some interesting information on the topic.

---

[13] Ralles-Potles, IV, 10. Balsamon repeats the same arguments. The further statement, that the period of abstinence refers only to major times of prayer, and not to every time one prays, is not relevant to our topic.

[14] P. Karlin-Hayter, *Vita Euthymii patriarchae CP* (Brussels, 1970), 37–39.

[15] The story of Athanasia may be found in the *vita* of the 5th-century St. Matrona, *Acta Sanctorum,* Nov. III, 810B.

The case reported by Apokaukos also raises the question of whether sexual intercourse was considered to be a necessary constituent element of a valid marriage. Byzantine law, following Roman law, was formal in stating that it was intent, not intercourse that made a marriage.[16] In the twelfth century, Emperor Manuel I insisted that this was the case. Nevertheless, such a position was hard to maintain in practice, and was undermined by the law itself which considered impotence after three years of marriage sufficient grounds for divorce. The problem became evident in the debate on marriage impediments deriving from consanguinity or affinity. The question was raised, for example, whether it was marriage or sexual intercourse which created relationships that could pose impediments, and the answers were far from consistent. In 1183, when Andronikos I wanted to wed his illegitimate daughter Irene to Manuel I's illegitimate son Alexios, the synod took a highly disputed decision which allowed the marriage on the basis of the argument that illegitimate unions do not create recognizable relationships.[17] The decision was rescinded after Andronikos' demise. On the contrary, Demetrios Chomatianos informed the kral of Serbia that a certain marriage arrangement was impossible because the parties were related, even though by a sexual relationship outside marriage: "for the law does not cast aside the relationships created by fornication."[18] The insistence of the community of Govlastou that Irene and her husband sleep together is undoubtedly an illustration of a general phenomenon: whatever the formal law might say, intercourse was the element which people considered to be the constituent element of a marriage.

In a previous chapter we have seen the concern of the Byzantine legislator with the seduction of unmarried girls and the considerable incentives offered to the man to marry the seduced girl. We have further seen that the law and the courts were primarily concerned with the crime of seduction (rather than abduction, for example) and with its remedy, marriage. We also saw that if a woman consented to the seduction the law seems to assume that she also consented, *ipso facto,* to marriage. Her formal consent to the marriage was undoubtedly essential, but her consent to sexual intercourse created a presumption of consent to marriage. The examination of the issues involved

[16] *D.* 50.17.30 and Justinian, Nov. 22.3.

[17] Niketas Choniates, *Historia,* ed. J. L. van Dieten (Berlin and New York, 1975), 260–62, 309–10; cf. Laiou, *Mariage, amour et parenté,* chap. 1.

[18] Pitra, no. 16.

in sexual intercourse between man and wife seems to establish that consent to marriage also implies necessary consent to sexual intercourse, except when the spouses agree to abstain; thus the very concept of marital rape seems to be absent.

"I will agree to it unwillingly" or, the Consent of the Virtuous Woman

The moralizing literature of the Byzantines contains quite a number of little tales of the following sort. A virtuous woman finds herself in straitened circumstances; her husband is in deep debt or in jail. A rich or powerful man approaches her and offers to rescue her, in return for sexual favors. She hesitates, and then consents with or without the permission of her husband; but before the act can take place, the rich man realizes the error of his ways, and rescues her anyway, for which he is compensated in one way or another.[19] These stories were, one supposes, interesting to their audience because of the inherent tension and drama of the situation, increased by the very mildly salacious sexual element. For us, the interest lies in the attitude of the sources toward coerced consent in such circumstances.

Perhaps the most telling story of this genre is one related by Paul of Monembasia. According to the editor, the story was elaborated between the sixth and the tenth centuries, probably closer to the later date.[20] An old monk describes his meeting with Sergios, *demotes* of Alexandria, whom he found in a tavern, disporting himself with prostitutes whose pimp he was. The monk persuaded Sergios to tell him of at least one good thing he had done in his life, and after demurring at first, Sergios obliged. He related how one day he had gone into a shop and seen a very beautiful woman seated at the loom. He wanted to sleep with her, but was told by the mistress of the shop that this was not possible: the woman was noble, albeit in reduced circumstances since her husband, who owed one hundred gold coins to the governor of Alexandria, was in jail and her two children reduced to slavery. She herself toiled

---

[19] See, for example, *Pratum Spirituale,* nos. 186, 189. Ibid., no. 39, has a variant case where a young woman feigns consent to her own rape, but argues the amorous monk out of his intention, by waving his responsibilities before him: he could not possibly afford to marry her, and if he insists on violating her he will be responsible for her death, for she will hang herself. The monk, of course, is dissuaded.

[20] John Wortley, *Les récits édifiants de Paul de Monembasie,* (Paris, 1987), 18, 23.

day and night to free them. The shopowner thought that the woman would never agree to sleep with Sergios, even though he offered to pay the hundred gold coins. However, when the woman was approached, she consented (συν-έθετο) fairly readily, after an initial outburst of tears. Her reasoning was that God would forgive her because of her *prior blameless life,* and because she would sleep with the man unwillingly. She would surrender her body *moved by necessity* (ἐξ ἀνάγκης), the necessity being the fact that she wanted to free her husband and children, but was unable to manage it. Sergios, having been apprised of her consent, paid her the agreed sum, and she came to his bedroom with tears and sighs, "but still, she came." He, however, seeing her distress, thought that it would be just as easy (and as sinful) for him to sleep with a prostitute; so he let her go but let her keep the cash.[21]

The narrator of this story sets out clearly the circumstances of coerced consent, and insists on both the consent and the coercion. It must be said that his use of language suggests the possibility of a certain tongue-in-cheek attitude toward the woman's protestations. The phrases Εἰ καὶ μετὰ στεναγμοῦ καὶ δακρύων, ὅμως συνέθετο ("even though she sighed and cried, still she agreed"), and ἦκε μετὰ στεναγμῶν καὶ δακρύων οὐ μετρίων, ἀλλ᾽ οὖν εἰσῆλθεν εἰς τὸν κοιτῶνα μου ("she came, with many sighs and tears, but still she entered my bedchamber") suggest that the tears and the sighs may have simply been to save appearances; so does the fact that the woman consented even though the shopkeeper had been sure that she would not. Be that as it may, the point is that the "necessity" or *force majeure* here invoked is economic and family necessity. The woman's consent, although given unwillingly, is valid, that is, there is no hint that the man forced her, although she was forced by circumstances; in other words, the act, had it taken place, would have been fornication rather than rape. Consent, therefore, was valid, even though it was unwilling, indeed forced. In the end, the day was saved by the change of heart of the man, so we never get to learn what the narrator's attitude would have been toward the woman if sexual intercourse had taken place: would she, for example, have suffered some sort of punishment?

In fact, this story, and the others similar to it, are not very useful for our inquiry. The main fact they establish is that economic necessity was seen as a kind of force that produced coerced consent. But, although the circumstances are presented as attenuating the sin, the point is never tested since the

---

[21] Wortley, *Récits édifiants,* 129–32.

act does not take place. Other evidence suggests that the kind of necessity presented here might not be accepted as sufficient to excuse the consent.

The Limits of Coercion

The Byzantine canonical sources do address the question of the coerced consent of a woman to sexual activity. The most prominent issues here are, first, the kind and degree of coercion that has to be established before it can be proven that consent was really forced; and second, assuming that the woman did not act freely, does this excuse her entirely, in part, or not at all? In other words, does consent, even if extracted by force, make the woman culpable, and does the act itself have consequences for the woman even if she acted under duress?

The issue arose in various contexts, for example, in the matter of sexual relations between a slave woman and her master (canon 49 of St. Basil). The most important context, however, was connected with the circumstances of the early church, which was concerned to establish the limits of punishment for those who had acted under duress in other circumstances: people who had, during the time of persecutions, been forced to sacrifice to the idols, or who had been captured by pagans in a war context and had been forced to eat forbidden food or perform sacrifices to the idols. The consent of women to sexual intercourse in similar circumstances is treated as part of this problem. Although early canonical legislation arose out of specific realities, the broad issue remained important in the twelfth-century commentaries. The advance of the Turks in Asia Minor created once again situations in which men became renegades, and the church had to define its position toward apostasy under duress.[22] Second, the arbitrary and authoritarian actions of twelfth-century emperors, who intervened with a heavy hand in matrimonial affairs and sometimes forced people to enter monastic life, also gave the canonists the occasion to comment on the validity of actions undertaken under duress.[23]

Roman law had also contended with the problem of married women who slept with their captors in the context of war. The relevant legislation is pro-

---

[22] On this, see N. Oikonomidès, "La brebis égarée et retrouvée: l'apostat et son retour," in D. Simon, ed., *Religiöse Devianz, Jus Commune,* no. 48 (Frankfurt, 1990), 143–57; on the 12th century, see esp. pp. 147–54. The reader will also find in this article the various canons that deal with apostasy.

[23] See above, pp. 139–40, and Laiou, *Mariage, amour et parenté* chap. 4.

cedural, that is, it has to do with what happens to the woman's marriage, and what action the husband can bring against her when she returns. The marriage is dissolved, since captivity deprives the woman of her free status, and it is renewed when she returns. The husband, then, may bring an action of adultery against her, though not by right of being her husband, since he was not married to her during the period of her captivity. However, if she was *forced* to commit adultery, no action may be taken against her.[24] It would thus seem that according to civil law captivity itself was not proof of coercion, but that if the woman could somehow prove that she was forced to sleep with her captor(s), she was restored to her former position and suffered no punishment. It is interesting that the commentary on the *Basilics* includes canon 1 of St. Gregory of Neocaesareia and canon 49 of St. Basil, which discuss how one should deal with women who had sexual intercourse with a man under duress. Thus the commentators saw that, although civil and canon law treat the matter very differently, they address the same general problem.

For our purposes, the first important text is canon 1 of St. Gregory of Neocaesareia, which is interesting in itself and is also a point of reference in the commentaries on other canons. The canon discusses two related topics: the treatment of people who ate forbidden foods when in captivity, and of the women who slept with their captors. The context is barbarian invasions. On the first issue, the resolution is that this act did not entail sin, especially since the barbarians in question did not sacrifice to idols, so that the forbidden foods were not sacrificial meats. On the second issue, involving women, the saint is not quite so sanguine. Here he wishes to examine whether the act really took place under duress, and the criterion is simple: it is the woman's prior life. If she was known to have led a virtuous life, and "now she has suffered an insult under violence and duress," the presumption will be that she is blameless. The presumption is justified by an appeal to Deut. 22:26, which speaks of rape that takes place in the wilderness. Thus the act is, for all intents and purposes, equated to rape, and the woman is not subject to

---

[24] *Bas.* 60.37.14 = *D.* 48.5.13.14: καὶ ἡ παρὰ τοῖς πολεμίοις μοιχευθεῖσα καὶ ὑποστρέψασα κατηγορεῖται παρὰ τοῦ ἀνδρὸς οὐ δικαίῳ ἀνδρός, εἰ μὴ βίᾳ τοῦτο πέπονθεν. The commentary says that there are two divergent readings, οὐ δικαίῳ ἀνδρὸς and δικαίῳ ἀνδρός, with the second reading being the most frequent, and proceeds to explain the meaning of both readings. Cf. Moses, "Livy's Lucretia."

punishment. On the other hand, a woman whose prior life was not virtuous must be suspected of a propensity to fornication in times of captivity as well, and such a woman should not be easily readmitted to communion.[25] Thus the woman's prior life is made the criterion on the basis of which one differentiates between (presumed) coerced consent and (presumed) free consent to the act. The focus of attention is not on whether the woman acquiesced or not to a particular act, but on whether she was of good character or not; an extension of this argument would be that a woman of suspect morals always consented to sexual intercourse, and could not be raped.

The commentaries on this canon are particularly interesting. Zonaras starts with a historical statement, setting the canon within the historical circumstances of the barbarian invasions. On the matter of those who ate forbidden foods, he proceeds to elaborate and make a distinction which the canon had not made, between eating out of gluttony and eating in order to sustain life; the prisoners who ate these foods, being enslaved (and therefore, it is presumed, not having freedom of action), if they did it to sustain life, will be excused. By the same token, he makes the even clearer distinction between women whose prior life was not virtuous, and who must suffer ecclesiastical punishment, and those who had led a virtuous prior life and who, "having been enslaved because of the captivity, suffered the barbarians' insult by force"; they did not sin and will not be punished. Zonaras introduces here the concept that a war captive is enslaved, and therefore by definition incapable of free will and subject to the consent of the master. The corollary of this position (which owes a good deal to Roman law) would be that *all* women captives who slept with their captors must be assumed to have been forced. Therefore, the exception concerning the woman whose prior morals were suspect is even more anomalous than it was in the canon. The explanation lies in Zonaras' gloss of the words "whorish habit" (πορνικὴ ἕξις). "Habit," he says, "is long-term behavior which has been solidified by time, so that it becomes second nature." Presumably, then, these women acted according to their nature, and their nature is to consent to sexual intercourse in all circumstances.

---

[25] Joannou, *Les canons des pères grecs,* 19–21; Ralles-Potles, IV, 45–46. On the connection between food pollution and sexual pollution, see Mary Douglas, *Purity and Danger: An Analysis of Concepts of Pollution and Taboo* (New York and Washington, D.C., 1966), 123 ff.

Balsamon's position was more subtle, and stricter, both in the case of those who ate forbidden food and in the case of the women who slept with their captors. After having repeated Zonaras' commentary, he goes on to establish distinctions of his own. His premise is that St. Gregory had said that the sin of those who eat sacrificial meats is not great, not that it should not be punished at all. For his part, Balsamon divides people among those who ate sacrificial meats willingly and with pleasure; those who ate because they were forced by the barbarians; those who ate because of natural need; and those who were forced by barbarians who did not sacrifice to the idols. All of them must be punished, but with different degrees of severity, depending on consent and duress, the heaviest punishment going to those who ate willingly, the lightest to those who were forced by the need to survive. The most important distinction he makes is between being forced by circumstances to take a certain action, and performing the action itself under clear force: thus, in the case at hand, someone who has food or drink pushed or poured down his throat by force is blameless. By contrast, those forced by general circumstances (captivity, the need to survive) to eat forbidden meats did so with a certain measure of consent (ὑποκύψαντες τῷ θελήματι τοῦ τυράννου) and thus must be punished to some extent. These distinctions, not mentioned in the canon under discussion, are nevertheless made by other canons. Balsamon is here glossing the relatively mild dispositions of St. Gregory by introducing the more severe attitude of other canons.[26]

Having discussed the matter of forbidden foods, Balsamon adds that, by the same token, the women who slept with the barbarians by force (τὸ ὑποστῆναι φθορὰν βαρβαρικὴν κατὰ βίαν) must suffer some ecclesiastical punishment, although a mild one. Here he departs quite clearly from the

---

[26] Ralles-Potles, IV, 47–49. The Council of Ankyra dealt extensively with the question of those who were forced to sacrifice or to eat forbidden meats, and the 12th-century commentators also discuss the distinction between various degrees of force: canons 3, 4–6, 8, 12. Balsamon takes the opportunity presented by canon 3 of the Council of Ankyra to discuss the case of the forced tonsure of a bishop and the forced tonsure of noble ladies by Emperor Andronikos I. None of these canons refer to women who might have been violated by pagans or while they were captive; nor do the other relevant canons, for example, canons 73 and 81 of St. Basil, canon 2 of Gregory of Nyssa, canons 1–14 of St. Peter of Alexandria, and canons 11 and 12 of the Council of Nicaea. Note that pollution is expiated by the ecclesiastical punishment, and cf. Douglas, *Purity*, 134.

canon, and seeks to support his position by simply reiterating that canon law, unlike civil law, will not suffer the polluted (μολυνθεῖσαν) woman to go unpunished. Unfortunately for the logic of his argument, the canon law he invokes is the one he is trying to establish. Of the civil laws he invokes, Novel 33 (not 103 as in the text) of Leo VI the Wise has nothing to do with the topic, and *Bas.* 60.37.14 does not support his position, as he himself recognizes.

Balsamon's commentary on this canon shows him to be much stricter than the canon itself and stricter than Zonaras in his attitude toward the woman who is violated while in captivity. Since he uses variants of the word "force" (βία, κατὰ βίαν, βιασθεῖσαι), it is quite clear that he is speaking of a situation in which the women acted under duress. But he also establishes that the woman nevertheless consented, even though under duress (she could, one supposes, have opted for death). So he is speaking of coerced consent, which he pronounces punishable. In the case of women whose prior behavior was immoral, he concurs with the canon and with Zonaras that this establishes the presumption of a consent freely given: prior behavior supersedes the duress of the woman's present situation. In the case of a woman of blameless prior morals, coercion does not entirely absolve her from punishment either, although the punishment would be milder. If he is arguing from analogy with the case of people who ate forbidden foods under duress, it would seem that the telling point is the degree of force the person suffered, the residual being a degree of consent: she would have had to prove lack of consent to the act itself, not to the circumstances. However, Balsamon does not explicitly develop the analogy; in the end, it would seem that for the woman it is the act itself which is punishable, as well as her intention.

A similar position may be discerned in the commentary on canon 49 of St. Basil. The canon itself is short and, it would seem, clear: "The seductions (fornications) which are carried out by force carry no guilt; thus the slave who is forced by her master is innocent."[27] Zonaras elaborates somewhat on the lack of consent, stressing that the slave woman who is forced, and who submits to her master's desires *unwillingly,* will not be subject to the ecclesiastical punishment given to fornicators. He then extends the provisions of the

[27] Ralles-Potles, IV, 202: αἱ πρὸς ἀνάγκην γενόμεναι φθοραί, ἀνεύθυνοι ἔστωσαν· ὥστε καὶ ἡ δούλη, εἰ ἐβιάσθη παρὰ τοῦ ἰδίου δεσπότου, ἀνεύθυνος ἐστίν. The commentaries are on pp. 202–3.

canon to those women who were abducted against their will and to "the others who were seduced (ἐφθάρησαν) in similar ways," with specific reference to the canon of St. Gregory of Neocaesareia which was discussed above. Thus he assimilates all sexual intercourse in which the woman was under duress, physical or formal, and finds the woman blameless, always, presumably, subject to the restriction of a virtuous prior life which was enunciated in the canon of St. Gregory.

Balsamon takes a different attitude. He, too, extends the canon to cover all involuntary seductions, including that of free women who are somehow under the authority of a governor or official (ἀρχοντικῶν προσώπων). He refers one to the first canon of St. Denys of Alexandria, which, however, has nothing to do with the topic; the reference may be to the first canon of St. Peter of Alexandria, concerning those who abjured the Christian faith after torture, and which does mandate a mild ecclesiastical punishment. The careful reader of Balsamon's text would, perhaps, have seen this discrepancy. The canonist then proceeds to add some refinements to the canon and, it seems to me, to change its intent. He says that the woman violated under the conditions mentioned above will not suffer the *epitimia* proper to fornicators; however, the woman who was taken by force, if she had been a deaconess, will not be allowed to continue in this office.

Balsamon's argument is based on both analogy and an appeal to the inscrutable ways of God. The argument from analogy states that a priest who has been forced to do something that prohibits him from exercising the priestly function (or has done so through ignorance) will be deposed.[28] By an analogy that is not at all evident to the modern reader, Balsamon extends this to the case of people who became monks because the emperor forced them to: they will remain monks, "even though they were shorn by force." Equally by analogy, more evident in this case, the deaconess who has been violated will not be able to exercise that office.

In fact, slave women were never able to become deaconesses, and the office itself did not exist in Balsamon's time. Therefore, unless his argument deals with an anachronistic situation, which would not be typical for this canonist, the message he wishes to convey is general and not specific. That message is, quite simply, that the woman who has been forced to sleep with

---

[28] Balsamon is referring, correctly, to canon 1 of the Council of Ankyra and canon 27 of St. Basil.

someone is tainted, polluted. It is the act itself which changes the status of the woman, not her consent or absence of consent. In this case, as in the case of women violated by their captors, as, by an analogy of our own, in the case of any woman who is forced into sexual intercourse, her consent is only one of the factors which govern the consequences for her: she is thought in any case to have given some sort of consent; coercion does not fully excuse her consent; and she remains tainted by the act. Whatever might seem to Balsamon's contemporaries problematic about punishing someone who has not consented freely to an act is resolved by the appeal to the inscrutable ways of God: "God allowed her to suffer an evil thing" (διὰ τὸ παρα-χωρήσει Θεοῦ ἐμπεσεῖν αὐτὴν εἰς κακόν).

Balsamon is, arguably, the most important Byzantine canonist. Although some of his opinions were later disputed by less eminent figures like John of Kitros, and although his own writings recognize the fact that certain issues were hotly debated by other canonists, he was not *sui generis,* and his statements are worthy of serious consideration. He was, furthermore, deeply interested in the question of coerced consent, and his position can be discerned through his various statements. He upheld, on the whole, the right of imperial authority to force people into taking certain actions which were predicated upon a semblance, at least, of free consent; and he upheld that position even for an emperor who was widely considered a tyrant, namely, Andronikos I. But his attitude was also dependent on the gender of the person who gave coerced consent. Thus, when specific cases came up, he was much more ready to accept coerced tonsure when it happened to a woman than to a man. On the issue at hand, his attitude is also incoherent. It has been argued that he was particularly lenient to repentant renegades who acted under pressure from the Turks.[29] That, I think, is true, and a credit to Balsamon's political

---

[29] Oikonomidès, "La brebis égarée," 148–50. I do not, however, agree with the author that Balsamon is shocked by the very strict provisions of canon 62 of the Apostles for clerics who abjure the Christian faith (Ralles-Potles, II, 80). On the contrary, I would take Balsamon's argument not as sarcastic but at face value. The fact that he adduces the civil law, much more lenient than the ecclesiastical law on this issue, does not mean that he was favoring civil law. The point he is making here is exactly the same as in his commentary on canon 1 of St. Gregory of Neocaesareia (see above, pp. 190–91), where he does adduce the civil law, but only to say that the ecclesiastical law is stricter, and to follow the latter—even though his argument is specious, as I have tried to indicate.

acumen.[30] The liberal attitude does not, however, extend to women who were forced into sexual intercourse; here he is much less benevolent than Zonaras, and attaches a measure of culpability to the woman, however great the coercion may have been. The culpability is, it seems, primarily moral rather than legal.

I would suggest that Balsamon's less than watertight argumentation indicates a certain dissonance between legal principles and social assumptions. The legal principle, well established in Roman and Byzantine civil law, and adopted by ecclesiastical law, was that one is not responsible for actions undertaken because of violence or under duress; the validity of such acts was highly questionable. On the other hand, there seems to be a deeply engrained persuasion that a woman is never really and truly forced, but that an element of consent is present.[31] That may be why the judges who tried cases of statutory rape were so insistent on registering the evidence of violence. And this would explain why Balsamon finds it possible to hold the woman raped by someone who holds power over her guiltless legally but guilty morally (in his commentary on canon 49 of St. Basil).

It is, once again, literature which may give us an insight into the underlying assumptions. The source used here is, undoubtedly, specific to a particular, monastic milieu. But we shall see in the next chapter that similar assumptions appear in the poem of *Digenes Akrites,* written for an aristocratic, even court, audience. Paul of Monembasia relates the story of three women who lived in the theme of Anatolikon during the reign of Constantine VII, in

---

[30] As Oikonomidès has argued, the Byzantine church exhibited the same liberal attitude toward renegades in the 13th century. An interesting case appears in the acts of the Patriarchate of Constantinople in the late 14th century. A certain Merxes (Mrkša Žarković), "cousin" of Emperor Manuel II, had sent, through an intermediary, a request for the recognition of his marriage or, possibly, only for a confirmation that he was held blameless for it. The marriage was within the prohibited degrees of relationship (fourth degree by affinity), and the patriarch found the matter to be a vexed one. However, he recognized the marriage, and sent Merxes his blessing, because the marriage had been undertaken by necessity and force, exercised by the Turks. The duress was that if the marriage had not taken place, a great number of Christians stood in peril of their lives, although we do not know why. Thus the synod accepted the evident necessity, and held Merxes not only blameless but praiseworthy: Miklosich-Müller, *Acta,* II, pp. 230–31; Darrouzès, *Regestes,* no. 2975.

[31] For similar attitudes in classical Greece, see Lefkowitz, "Seduction and Rape in Greek Myth."

conditions sufficient to arouse anyone's pity: they inhabited a ravine, went naked for lack of clothing, and ate only the fruits brought them by a raven. One of the women explained to a newly arrived tax collector that she was the widow of a *protospatharios* from Constantinople. She was widowed at a young age, and a powerful man became enamored of her, so he sent his servants to abduct her by force (ἁρπᾶσαι με βίᾳ). She, on the other hand, tried to persuade them not to use force, and told them that she would go happily with them, except that she suffered from an ugly illness from which, however, she would be cured within forty days. They agreed to return after forty days, and she immediately distributed all her belongings to the poor, freed her slaves, and fled, with the two faithful servants whom she had kept. The tax collector and the abbot of a neighboring monastery were duly impressed, gave the women food and holy communion, and remained to bury them as they died, one after another, within three days.[32]

The moral of this story, and of others like it, is quite clear. Women can avoid rape or abduction. There are alternatives, hard ones to be sure, such as death or a form of living death, but nevertheless they are there for the woman who really does not consent.[33] It is a harsh position, and an ecclesiastical one. We saw in the previous chapter that civil law gave the benefit of the doubt to the woman who was raped in circumstances where she was incapable of giving a valid consent; and we have seen that this premise was, indeed, followed in some court cases. However, no society has a single, consistent attitude to such issues, and the other set of assumptions, which does not give the woman the benefit of the doubt, is also present, visible in ecclesiastical sources but lurking elsewhere, and not only in the famous edict of Constantine I.

Conclusion

Byzantine law recognized, at least since the time of the *Ecloga*, the consent of the woman as a very important factor in the differentiation of sexual crimes and the differentiation of punishment for the man. If a woman could establish that she was forced to have sexual intercourse, not only was the man punished more severely, but she profited from the punitive damages the man had to pay

---

[32] Wortley, *Récits édifiants,* 28–32.

[33] For death as an alternative to which the woman did not ultimately have to resort, see *Pratum Spirituale,* chap. xxxix.

her. Thus, unless the situation was resolved informally and within the family setting, as most of the cases must have been, a woman and her family had every incentive to claim that she was forced; the law was not applied to the letter, but damages were, in fact, paid. Thus the courts had to address, in practice, the issue of what constitutes consent and what constitutes force. Civil law recognized a number of circumstances which established presumption of force, and thus the woman was, to some extent, protected.

The role of the church was rather complex. By insisting on the importance of the inner life, Christianity and the Christian church were an important force in developing the principle of individual responsibility and thus of consent. The church, at the same time, embraced older and widespread ideas about the importance of purity and the dangers of pollution. Anthropologists have taught us that pollution is independent of intentionality: "the distinctions of voluntary, involuntary, internal, external, are not relevant." What is relevant is simply whether a contact involving pollution has taken place.[34] Hence the ambivalent position of the church and the canonists. In some respects, the church was more sophisticated than civil law, for it was willing to go beyond appearances and face the issues of internal, subjective consent or absence of consent. On the other hand, it stated the fear of pollution which other sources may hint at, and at that level responsibility, intentionality, consent are less relevant. The end result is that in some ways women were less protected by ecclesiastical law than by civil law. For the church, the final proof of non-consent was always stark: the alternatives were recognized as death, living death, or some other extreme measure; furthermore, the criterion of a blameless prior life judges a woman's general behavior and not the particular act in question: finally, the church, which had recognized crying in the wilderness as a presumption of force, was unwilling to extend this to all similar circumstances. Balsamon undoubtedly was much stricter than others in this respect, but he was building upon an ideological substratum which recognized a subliminal responsibility of the woman who has been polluted. The role of the church in the development of the theory of consent thus has several different

---

[34] Douglas, *Purity,* 59 ff, 99 ff, 130 ff. I am grateful to Professor Tambiah for guiding me to the anthropological literature. The reader should note, however, Mary Douglas' statement that ideas of pollution form a part of society's general views and values. Since there is no analysis of Byzantine society in anthropological terms, one should be cautious about using the results of research that stem from other societies.

aspects to it. And when they have all been taken into account, it may be stated that canon law helped develop the idea of personal responsibility but that civil law, by recognizing intentionality as always pertinent, was often more beneficial to women.

V. The Evidence of Literature

What can literature contribute to an inquiry such as ours? If handled carefully, it can instruct us as to contemporary concerns and underlying attitudes. It can also be vastly misleading, for literature is not necessarily a reflection of reality, indeed it can be and often is a reversal of reality, and that too, if identified, is valuable information. But a straight reading of literary sources can lead us down a primrose path to lands that never were. Above all, one must remember that literature has its own rules and its own concerns: tension, conflict, taut situations are at a premium, as is their resolution. Abduction, rape, seduction, adultery, and temptation of all sorts make for a tense plot and good reading. Their presence in literary sources does not mean that they were rampant in society; it does mean that they provide a juicy plot, but what they reflect may be the very opposite of social practice.

In the Byzantine context, the pertinent sources are hagiography and tales of morality, to the extent that they can be considered literature, and, of course, the romances of the twelfth and fourteenth centuries, starting with the romance of *Digenes Akrites*. If one examines them internally, one would look primarily at the issues the authors choose to discuss and the terms in which the issues are presented. What is also of interest here are the attitudes that are projected and, since we are concerned with legal issues, the authors' knowledge and use of the laws. In what follows, I will concentrate on the romance of *Digenes Akrites* and the learned romances of the twelfth century.[1]

The story of *Digenes Akrites,* on which many studies have been written, is a romance set in a quasi-epic form, if only because the geographic setting of the story is the Arab-Byzantine frontier in Asia Minor, and we have been

---

[1] On the romances in general, see H.-G. Beck, *Byzantinisches Erotikon* (Munich, 1986); Roderick Beaton, *The Medieval Greek Romance* (Cambridge, 1989); L. Garland, "'Be Amorous but Be Chaste': Sexual Morality in Byzantine Learned and Vernacular Romance," *Byzantine and Modern Greek Studies* (hereafter *BMGS*) 14 (1990), 62–120. On *Digenes Akrites,* see H.-G. Beck, *Geschichte der byzantinischen Volksliteratur* (Munich, 1971), 62–97, and C. Galatariotou, "Structural Opposites in the Grottaferrata *Digenes Akrites,*" *BMGS* 11 (1987), 29–68.

taught to consider such frontiers as giving rise to epic songs. The story starts with the raid of an Arab emir into Byzantine territory and the capture of a Byzantine maiden whom he eventually marries. This part of the narrative is full of conflicts and reconciliations, memories of past wars between Byzantines and Arabs and the Byzantine armies and the Paulicians. It is the most martial part of the story, even if the wars are told at one or more removes and belong to a past recalled by the emir. The child of the emir and the Byzantine maiden, Digenes Akrites, the hero of the second part of the story, is a prodigy from a young age. A valiant young man, he falls in love with a girl, abducts her, marries her, and proceeds to have exciting adventures, both amorous and martial, all in single combat. He eventually builds a palace on the Euphrates and dies at the significant age of thirty-three, his loving wife dying of grief before him.[2] The original version of *Digenes Akrites* must have been written in the first half of the twelfth century, given the mention in the Ptochoprodromic poem.

[2] See Beaton, *Romance,* 29–32, for a fuller summary of the story. The romance is extant in a number of versions. The best edition is by Erich Trapp, *Digenes Akrites—synoptische Ausgabe der ältesten Versionen,* Wiener byzantinistische Studien 8 (Vienna, 1971). For an English translation, see J. Mavrogordato, *Digenes Akrites, Edited with an Introduction, Translation and Commentary* (Oxford, 1956). The vernacular Escorial version is now considered to be closest to the original, although the Grottaferrata version, in a more learned style, preserves parts of the story that are not extant in the Escorial version. For the primacy of the Escorial version, see St. Alexiou, *Vasileios Digenes Akrites kai to asma tou Armoure* (Athens, 1985), passim; on the matter, cf. Beaton, *Romance,* 40–41. It is not quite clear when the two extant versions (as opposed to the prototype) were written, although we do know that a version of the story was known in aristocratic circles in Constantinople during the reign of Manuel I Komnenos (1143–80): St. Kyriakides, "Forschungsbericht zum Akritas-Epos," *Berichte zum XI. Internationalen Byzantinisten-Kongress,* II (Munich, 1958), 22, quoting a poem of Ptochoprodromos which mentions Manuel I as τὸν νέον τὸν ᾿Ακρίτην. On the identity of the author of the Ptochoprodromic poems and Theodore Prodromos, and the dates of Theodore Prodromos, see A. Kazhdan and S. Franklin, *Studies on Byzantine Literature of the Eleventh and Twelfth Centuries* (Cambridge, 1984), 90–93. The manuscripts are not helpful for establishing the dates of the two versions, since the Escorial manuscript is of the 15th century and the Grottaferrata one of the 14th. Scholars have usually discussed both versions as if they were of the 12th century, and there is no reason to challenge that assumption. Fortunately, the two versions do not differ significantly in what concerns the most important part of the story for my purposes, that is, for the scene of the abduction of Digenes' bride. Those differences which may be significant will be noted below.

The Literature of Abduction

Scholars have noticed, usually in shocked tones, that this Byzantine story, which they variously classify as epic and romance, is replete with sexual misdeeds. The two most important couples (Digenes' father and mother as well as the hero and his bride) are created by abduction. There is a case of seduction and elopement, admittedly of an Arab girl, one rape and one adultery, both committed by the hero. Hans-Georg Beck, commenting on the evident disjunction between the laws of church and state on the one hand and the behavior of the hero on the other, takes the story at face value and gives it probative value for the statement that Byzantine legal norms were not followed in the provinces.[3] But the poem as we have it, whatever the origins of its kernel, was probably written in Constantinople,[4] and in any case Beck has not made a careful examination of the legal problems incorporated in the story. Michael Angold, in a relatively recent study, concentrates on abduction. He, too, gives the story a place in social history, considering it to be a quasi-realistic although exaggerated reflection of two alternative positions toward marriage: a private affair, which could embrace abduction, and a public matter, in which abduction was severely punished.[5] A close look, however, suggests quite a different reading.

Let us look at abduction first. Roderick Beaton has recognized the importance of abduction, as a literary ploy, in all the twelfth-century romances. He has made the point that the heroes of these stories take only one decisive action, abduction, which in ancient romances is contemplated but not carried out.[6] This, then, would seem to be a real innovation of the otherwise highly derivative twelfth-century romances. The story of *Digenes Akrites* is, of course, not derivative; and it is here that abduction plays the most important role and is described in loving and significant detail.

There are, as I have already indicated, two abduction scenes in the story.

---

[3] H.-G. Beck, "Orthodoxie und Alltag," in *Byzantium: Tribute to Andreas N. Stratos,* II (Athens, 1986), 342 ff.

[4] I find the arguments presented by N. Oikonomidès, "L''épopée' de Digénis et la frontière orientale de Byzance aux Xe et XIe siècles," *Travaux et mémoires* 7 (1979), 375–97, and especially 396–97, persuasive, even though they have not been taken into account sufficiently by Alexiou, *Vasileios Digenes.*

[5] Angold, "The Wedding of Digenes Akrites," 201–15.

[6] Beaton, *Romance,* 60–61.

The most interesting and detailed is the abduction by Digenes of the girl of whom he is enamored. She is young, rich, of excellent family, and jealously guarded by her father, the *strategos* (general). Many noble young men desired to carry her off because of her beauty, but were killed by her father. Digenes courts her, seizes her, and after being pursued by her father's army and her brothers, is reconciled with her family and marries her, with the consent of both families. It is this story which has been explained as reflecting a reality that admits abduction as an alternative path to a properly arranged marriage, and has been seen by scholars as an illegal, but nevertheless accepted, act.

The terminology used in the text is, indeed, unequivocally that of abduction. Both of the oldest texts, the Escorial and the Grottaferrata, use the words which, in law, describe the crime of abduction, that is, the verb ἁρπάζω in its various forms, and the noun ἁρπαγή.[7] For such a crime, we know, the civil law mandated very severe punishment. According to Novel 35 of Leo VI, which is meant to replace *Bas.* 60.58.1, if a girl is abducted and raped, and if she is noble-born, as this one certainly was, the culprit is punished by death and the confiscation of his property, assuming that the abduction has taken place with force of arms. If no weapons were employed, the man's hands are mutilated, and his property is confiscated. The girl's consent is immaterial: it does not change the man's punishment, nor does it make marriage possible; in such circumstances, marriage is absolutely forbidden.

But if the language in *Digenes Akrites* is that of abduction, the situation, as described, tells quite a different story. The abduction scene is preceded by a discussion of love and how it makes people behave. Digenes and the girl fall in love, and she wants to marry him. It is her father who keeps her locked up and has killed her other suitors—surely a ballad-like motif. When Digenes pleads with his father to ask for the girl's hand, he learns that his father, behaving absolutely properly within the Byzantine context, had tried to arrange a marriage between her and his son, even before Digenes expressed his love, but he had failed.[8] Everyone is behaving properly, except for the girl's father who is being unreasonable.

---

[7] References will be to the Trapp edition. G refers to the Grottaferrata text, and E to the Escorial. E 1013: ἁρπαγὴ τῆς κόρης; G IV, 954: πῶς τὴν κόρην ἥρπαξε; 1552, 1554: ἥρθη, ἡρπάγη; 1675; κλεψίγαμον, ἥρπασας.

[8] G IV, 1205 ff, 1235, 1252–60; cf. E 853–55.

Then the couple take things into their own hands. Digenes asks the girl to marry him, and we are treated to another disquisition on love. She gives him a ring, the symbol of betrothal. Marriage is the purpose from the very beginning, a fact which is reaffirmed several times and confirmed by the girl who says that she will marry him for love, even though it is illegal for her to give herself to him: εἰ καὶ λίαν πάρανομον ἑαυτὴν προδοῦναι. He wants to establish the fact of her consent to running away, and she gives it: πεί-θομαι νῦν καὶ βούλομαι μετὰ σοῦ πορευθῆναι. So the act will fall under the rubric of elopement rather than abduction.[9] Furthermore, the poet takes care to establish the fact that the hero is acting alone in the enterprise. The only accomplices he wishes to have are God and the night; otherwise he will act all by himself:

> [He] was imploring God from all his heart:
> Saying "O God and Master, hear my prayer,
> Sink me the sun and make the moon to rise,
> To be my complice in this business,
> For I shall have to go one and alone."[10]

The word used to show that the hero is acting alone is the superlative form of the adjective, the rare word μονώτατος. The Escorial version (786) also mentions that Digenes was on his own, although here the point that is stressed is his heroic valor, since, alone that he is, he will meet and fight an army to win her. In the Grottaferrata version, on the other hand, the effort made is to establish that Digenes is carrying out the *abduction* by himself, that is, without accomplices. Valiant acts performed earlier in the narrative, for example, his exploits against bears and lions, were carried out in the presence of, although not with the help of, his father and uncle. I insist on this point, because the absence of accomplices removes one of the presumptions of force, at least as the matter was perceived in the eleventh century. Therefore, we have the following elements: the young couple voice their desire to marry, and the girl gives not only her clear consent but also a ring; the girl's father is the only one to object; the couple recognize that going against his will is illegal, but nevertheless they decide to run away. The hero is acting alone, a fact stressed by the poet. Finally, and most importantly, they do not sleep

---

[9] On the above, see G IV, 889–92, 1268, 1315, 1325, 1357, 1422, 1463, 1515. E 840 ff.

[10] G IV, 1322–25: μονώτατος; cf. G IV, 1357, μόνος; Mavrogordato, p. 97.

together, so no seduction of an abducted virgin has taken place. Would this have been considered abduction by a Byzantine judge in the twelfth century?

In the story, the parents behave as though there has been a real abduction (G IV, 1550 ff; E 910 ff). The girl's father, the *strategos,* and her brothers send out an army to avenge the crime and kill the hero. They are acting correctly and legally, for the law punished the parents who agreed to abduction, before or after the fact.[11] After Digenes has proven his prowess (by killing some of the people sent against him), the *strategos* agrees that the young man will make a good son-in-law. But the *strategos* insists on proper marriage contracts, a dowry, a church blessing, and an open wedding, so that the propriety of the marriage will be unquestioned. Digenes at first shuns the dowry, but eventually he accepts it. There is a reconciliation of the parents and the two families, symbolized by the fact that the poet insists on the presence of the girl's brothers.[12] In the Escorial version, the reconciliation seems endangered by the insistence of the *strategos* that the wedding take place in his house, and Digenes' own desire that he take the girl home to marry her. The Grottaferrata version makes the best of this by having what seems to be two weddings, one in each venue. In both versions, the episode ends with a perfectly proper and glorious wedding and with the exchange of wedding gifts of great value.[13]

If, for the purposes of the story, the girl's parents treat the affair as abduction, I submit that in a court of law, and in the minds of informed contemporaries, it would not have counted as abduction, especially as the story is presented in the Grottaferrata version. The poet takes great care to establish,

---

[11] Leo VI, Novel 35.

[12] G IV, 1820, 1893. This does not appear in the E version.

[13] Much has been made of the fact that the description of the wedding does not include a church ceremony, and no priests are visible. Angold ("Wedding," 203–4, 213–14) thinks that this is a reflection of a reality in which the church had not yet established fully its claim that the only valid marriage was accomplished by a church wedding. On the contrary, I think that this was so well established that there was no need to insist on it, while the poet has to insist on those aspects that were disputed in the story, namely, parental consent and the exchange of marriage gifts. In fact, both versions have Digenes' father-in-law use terms which are proper to a church wedding: νὰ σᾶς εὐλογήσωμεν (E 991) and τὴν ἱερολογίαν (G IV, 1674). For a present-day parallel, see the description of marriage among the Sarakatsanoi by an eminent anthropologist. There is a long description of the customs and a bare mention of the (necessary) church wedding: Campbell, *Honour,* 60 ff.

first of all, that the hero has the girl's full consent and that the aim is marriage. Second, the hero has no accomplices; and, although when he has to defend himself he draws his sword, the abduction itself is carried out without the use of arms. According to Novel 35 of Leo VI, an abduction can take place with or without arms, and is punished differently depending precisely on whether or not they are used; the consent of the girl is immaterial; rape seems to be a constituent element of the crime. But we have also seen that the eleventh-century courts gave different interpretations to the law, making it much more lenient and establishing other criteria that differentiated between abduction and elopement.[14] According to Eustathios Romaios, in the absence of sexual intercourse, the man is punished more leniently than the law required, even when arms were used. Furthermore, still in the opinion of the same judge, the presence of accomplices is a real differentiating factor between elopement and abduction: "If a man comes to the house of another with a mob, and seizes a woman, whether with her consent or not, he is guilty of abduction and is punished; but if he comes alone, with no accomplices, and dares to take secretly a woman who has already offered herself to him, he is guilty not of abduction but of the seduction of a virgin; thus it was adjudicated by the old censor in the case of Protokaravos."[15] The seduction of a virgin, as we know, can easily be corrected by marriage, assuming that the parents consent, which they eventually do in the case of Digenes.

The problem that Eustathios Romaios and others before him tried to address was the distinction between real force and consensual elopement. This is not easy to do, since in such situations the various parties can subsequently claim different intent. The canons and the canonists, as we have seen, had also tried to differentiate between the two, with varying degrees of success. The canonical texts that most conform to the situation as described in the Grottaferrata version of *Digenes Akrites* are the commentaries on canon 30 of St. Basil, where the embarrassed twelfth-century canonists try to posit a difference between voluntary abduction and elopement. The courts had to find ways of proving one or the other, and *Peira* 63.5 makes the issue hinge on the question of consent of the woman and the absence of accomplices. The author of the Grottaferrata version of *Digenes* has presented a situation which gave a double thrill to his audience: on the one hand, we have the

[14] Above, III.
[15] *Peira* 63.5.

tension, danger, and adventure of abduction; on the other, there is no abduction in legal terms but rather a "pretended abduction," that is, elopement. The marriage that eventually takes place would have been considered legal at least since the eleventh century, or it could be so argued by a Byzantine judge. Is this pushing the text of the poem too much? I think not. I have tried to show how the poem, although using the word "abduction," is talking about something which both the civil courts of the eleventh century and the canonists of the twelfth would have considered to be elopement.[16] The question does remain whether the poet argued this deliberately or unconsciously. I would suggest that it is deliberate, and would point in this connection to the somewhat different presentation of the same abduction scene in the Escorial version.

In the Escorial version, the situation is the same, but the poet does not stress all of the points that would show that there was no true abduction as the legal minds of the time perceive it. There is, unfortunately, a lacuna in the text, which starts *in medias res*. Apparently, the hero and the girl had already met and exchanged vows not to be separated, although it is not clear that the poet explicitly said that the vow was to marry (E 840 ff). The young man sets out alone (εἶμαι μοναχὸς καὶ μόνος θέλω ὁδεύειν: E 786), but arms himself as he sets out to go "to a terrible necessity, an abduction."[17] This is to be contrasted to the Grottaferrata version which does not mention arms in the abduction itself. Digenes does try to make sure that he has the girl's full consent, and this, somehow, is considered to give them rights over each other: "they kissed sweetly, as they had the right."[18] The army that pursues them includes a Saracen, which surely puts the hero in the right, and gives him the opportunity to kill a representative of the father-in-law's forces, without doing damage to the girl's family, since he spares her brothers.[19] Interestingly, in terms of the substratum of common opinion that we have been trying

---

[16] It is important to insist that, according to the views of the 12th-century canonists, this affair, as presented here, would have been elopement, and perfectly capable of being corrected by marriage. There is nothing here that would justify the view of some scholars that Digenes was acting against or outside ecclesiastical pronouncements: see, for example, Beck, "Orthodoxie," 342 ff, and Angold, "Wedding."

[17] E 790 ff: εἰς ἀνάγκην φοβερὰν κ᾽ εἰς ἁρπαγὴν ὑπάγω; cf. E 820 ff.

[18] E 872 ff, 906; cf. G IV, 1539.

[19] The Saracen appears only in the Escorial version. On the matter, see the bibliography in Oikonomidès, "L' 'épopée' de Digénis," note 4.

to identify, the girl considers herself responsible for the threat to the hero's life from her father's army, and seeks her own punishment: "My sweet lord, let me die; I alone did this unfortunate thing, I alone should pay for it; you have a swift horse, save yourself" (E 945–47). As in the Grottaferrata version, the issue is resolved when all the parents consent to the marriage and the girl is given a great dowry by her family. Most of the elements that would make this an elopement are present here, but they are not stressed. Indeed, the description of Digenes' arming himself as he prepares for the feat gives a different flavor to this version and highlights the violence involved, although, as we have seen, the girl's consent is freely and fully given. The Escorial version is the more dramatic one, while the Grottaferrata poet sanitizes the story for his audience. We do not know who the author of the Grottaferrata version was; but whoever he may have been, he had a shrewd idea of the legal subtleties surrounding abduction and elopement, and took good care to show that this marriage had no legal problems. I, for my part, cannot believe that, whatever its origins, the story as we have it is an expression of frontier mores or practices, or that its author was anything like a retainer of a frontier aristocratic family. The entire treatment of abduction, marriage, social values is redolent of an aristocratic Constantinopolitan milieu.

What connection does this abduction story bear to reality? Does it indicate that abduction was commonplace or usual, does it have the elements of a formal and institutionalized bride-theft? It seems to me that it does not. The story takes place in a liminal environment, the eastern frontier, although the audience was the court of Constantinople. In that environment, things are supposed to happen which are, to some extent, a reversal of reality as it was known and practiced in high circles. True, there was, in the twelfth century, a documented case of elopement involving a member of the imperial aristocracy: this was the case of Andronikos Komnenos, eventually to become Emperor Andronikos I, who met in Acre Theodora, widow of Baldwin III, and persuaded her to flee with him and to roam for years all over the Near East. The story had an unhappy ending.[20] Yet this was a rare case, and he was a rare man, and besides, the event took place in another country. In the aristocratic society of the twelfth century, marriage was a highly regulated activity, and all that a romance such as *Digenes* provided was catharsis, and one de-

---

[20] Niketas Choniates, *Historia,* ed. van Dieten, 141–42, 226–27; Kinnamos, Bonn ed., 250; and cf. Laiou, *Mariage, amour et parenté,* chap. 1.

void of risk at that. For what looms large in the narrative is, above all, the eventual marriage of Digenes and the girl, attended by everyone's consent and all the proper festivities, as well as a large dowry. The consent of the girl's father was, indeed, forced, but nonetheless it was given. And the most stylized and formalized aspect of the poem lies in the description of the marriage arrangements.[21]

Indeed, the main straightforward (rather than reversed) connection the abduction story has with reality is the fear parents had of κλεψιγαμία: an improper marriage, tainted by the lack of consent of the parents, not confirmed by public ceremony, not grounded in good property relations symbolized by the dowry. As Balsamon suggests, this is what most elopements were about: inequality of social or economic status might cause people to elope, as it sometimes leads to abduction in Mediterranean societies studied by anthropologists. In such cases, the parents might know and secretly consent, for then the marriage can take place under a pretended *force majeure*, while preserving the social norms against mésalliance. This is the fear the girl's parents voice: that people might think Digenes had married someone beneath him, with all the attendant shame to the girl's family. Here is the girl's father speaking to Digenes after the hero had defeated the *strategos'* army:

> [I will] make your wedding famous in the world,
> The boys shall never cry you stole the match,
> And snatched a girl that had no share of goods,
> Which is disgrace to all are minded well.[22]

In fact, the poet has taken good care to establish the lineage and wealth of the girl at the very beginning of the incident; she, too, persuades herself that Digenes is fully worthy of her, in an exchange where she establishes the reassuring fact that the two are both from the eminent Doukas family and, therefore, kin (although, one hopes, distant kin). What is of importance here is that the parents are most afraid of the shame a marriage without a proper wedding and a dowry would bring on them and on the girl. That does seem to me to have the ring of reality, whereas the rest of the abduction story is a reversal of the truth regarding aristocratic marriages in the twelfth century.

---

[21] On aristocratic marriage, see Laiou, *Mariage, amour et parenté,* chaps. 1 and 3.

[22] G IV, 1675–78 (the translation is Mavrogordato's, 119). For the statement of the girl's mother, see E 1010–15.

This is not to argue that elopement and abduction did not occur. One supposes that they did, and the supposition is confirmed both by the twelfth-century commentaries on the canons and by occasional "true" stories, such as the by now well-known one of Alexios Kapandrites.[23] This has been interpreted several times in several languages, and there is no need to discuss it again here in detail. It is worth noting only one or two points. The affair took place in 1198 in Epiros, in a territory where all kinds of activities that were outside the law occurred, and concerns the second marriage of Kapandrites and Eudokia, both members of the local aristocracy. The woman's family disputed the marriage repeatedly, on two grounds, that of abduction and that of incest; only the first is of interest here. They charged that after the death of Eudokia's first husband, Kapandrites, already related to her by marriage, had abducted her, with armed accomplices, from the house of one of her relatives, had held her captive, and eventually married her, "by force and against the law." This charge was made twice, and the first time was dismissed by the emperor himself, on the testimony of Kapandrites' relatives and the bishop of Devol. Kapandrites himself charged that the woman's brother had abducted Eudokia from Kapandrites' home, by force, and married her "by force" to another. The issue went from court to court, with the question of incest playing a major role. The moral of the story is simple: force was not unknown, abductions took place, but subsequent interpretations of whether the woman had consented or not varied according to the interests of the parties, which in this case centered on the woman's property.[24]

What I am arguing is not that abduction and elopement did not exist; I am arguing that in the eleventh and twelfth centuries there is no evidence of institutionalized abduction as a recognized and therefore regulated alternative path to marriage. Certainly, the story of the abduction of Digenes' bride is no evidence of such an established and institutionalized social practice.

---

[23] See, for example, K. Pitsakis, Τὸ κώλυμα γάμου λόγῳ συγγενείας ἑβδό-μου βαθμοῦ ἐξ αἵματος στὸ Βυζαντινὸ δίκαιο (Athens, 1985), p. 321 and note 110, which is the best study of this case.

[24] Ralles-Potles, V, 103–5, 395–96. On the Kapandrites story, see in the last instance Karlin-Hayter, "Further Notes on Byzantine Marriage," 143–44, and Laiou, *Mariage, amour et parenté,* chap. 1, note 150, with the earlier bibliography. It may be that the importance of abduction marriages has been exaggerated in other societies as well: see Louis Dumont, *Homo hierarchicus: The Caste System and Its Implications,* complete revised English edition (Chicago and London, 1980), 115.

As we have seen, the abduction of Digenes' bride turns out not to be an abduction in legal terms, but only in terms of literature; the eventual marriage is blameless by both aristocratic and ecclesiastical norms. Such is not the case with the treatment of the abduction of Digenes' mother by his father, the Arab emir. The objective situation described here is different and so, perhaps, is the origin of this part of the story, which may go back to a much earlier prototype.[25] Briefly, the girl is seized as a result of an enemy raid by the Arabs, along with other women and other spoils; her brothers try to find her; the youngest one engages the emir in single combat (a folk motif); eventually the situation is resolved with the emir's conversion and marriage to the young woman.

The terminology used by both versions is that of abduction and captivity: ἠχμαλώτευσε . . . τυγχάνουσαν παρθένον; τὴν ἁρπαγὴν τῆς κόρης; κόρην τερπνὴν ἀφήρπαξας . . . πώλησον ταύτην πρὸς ἡμᾶς . . . κόρην τερπνὴν ἀφήρπαξεν εὐγενῆ τῶν Δουκάδων; ἠχμαλωτεύσατε; τὸ ἔρπαξες.[26] A simile of the abductor and the hawk, which occurs both here and in the Digenes episode, must be a literary commonplace.[27] This abduction, taking place in the context of an enemy raid, has all the elements of force and violence, including the slain corpses of the young women who would not submit to the lust of the captors. The poet is not at all interested in justifying the actions of the emir, who in any case, being a foreigner, is outside the strictures of civil and ecclesiastical law. On the other hand, the actions of the girl herself, her family, and the other captive women are of interest to the poet, and to us insofar as the poet wishes to project the image that they behaved properly. Several aspects are worthy of note.

Interestingly, there has been no sexual activity, although the poet seems to suggest that it would have been expected. When the girl's brothers think she was killed, they say, "Thank the Lord, you died a virgin."[28] The other girls were, in fact, killed, "because they did not want to do what we told them."[29] Surely no one would argue that this is a reflection of reality; women

---

[25] Oikonomidès, "L' 'épopée' de Digénis," passim.

[26] G I, 32, 38, 76, 191–92; IV, 994; E 124, 635.

[27] G II, 465 and IV, 1538. Cf. the eagle in R. Hercher, *Erotici Scriptores Graeci*, II (Leipzig, 1859), 219.

[28] E I, 116.

[29] E 70.

captives were undoubtedly raped, and there was probably no wholesale kill-ing of female captives. It is, however, a reflection of attitudes. Virginity is, as we have seen before, highly prized. And the passage may be the alternative (a stark one, to be sure) to coerced consent that Balsamon had in mind.[30] The girl's virginity is particularly useful, since it would remove some of the taint on her eventual marriage to the emir.

As for her family, the reaction is unimpeachable. The father being away at the time, the girl's mother sends her brothers to get her back. They give voice to the shame that has fallen on the family by saying that if they cannot recover her, they do not want to live any longer.[31] After they have offered the emir ransom money, and after the youngest brother's single combat with him, they eventually give in to his request and allow him to marry the girl.[32] So marriage sanitizes the abduction, although it was not originally intended; marriage is, in fact, the only honorable course that remains, after the brothers have failed to kill the captor.

The consent of the girl does not play a role, either in the original action or, explicitly, in the eventual resolution. It is only after her marriage that she is said to love the emir, and this, in a sense, is her consent after the fact. Surprisingly, the marriage is not as free of taint as one would expect in a piece of literature which seeks to give the hero a good pedigree. When the emir wants to go to Syria and his wife offers to accompany him, the brothers liken him to a hawk, which indicates that the original act had not been for-gotten.[33] This is the one place where the question of her consent is raised, as the emir bitterly berates his wife, telling her that it was her desire to go with him to Syria, and he did not force her:

Μὴ γάρ σε κατηνάγκασα, ἢ παρεβίασά σε·
Μᾶλλον σύ με ἠνάγκασας μετ' ἐμοῦ πορευθῆναι.[34]

[30] See above, Chap. IV. See, in this connection, the story reported in the Syn-axarion of Constantinople, regarding St. Pelagia. It purports to date to the 4th century and speaks of a Christian virgin arrested for her religion. She feared for her virginity, "lest she be raped by the soldiers," and prayed to God that she die pure. God heard her, and St. John Chrysostom wrote an encomium celebrating the fact that she pre-ferred to die rather than have her virginity sullied: *SynCP*, col. 120. For the encom-ium, see PG 50, cols. 579–84.

[31] G I, 192.

[32] G I, 275 ff, 299 ff.

[33] G II, 456 ff; cf. E 318 ff.

[34] G II, 490: "Did I constrain or do you violence?/ Rather you forced me you should go with me": Mavrogordato, p. 35. This does not appear in E.

The treatment of this abduction is much less sophisticated than that of the abduction of Digenes' bride, but then the situation is more clear-cut.[35] The civil and ecclesiastical laws on abduction would not apply in such a situation, and there is no response to their strictures on the part of the poet. What is particularly interesting for our purposes is that the only alternative to rape that the poet envisages is the death of the woman. We find similar positions in other pieces of literature, specifically in the tales of morality. In both the seventh-century *Pratum Spirituale* and the tenth-century tales of Paul of Monembasia, women escape rape or abduction (for the purpose of sexual contact) by death or by a form of living death.[36] Once again, the issue is not whether these stories reproduce reality or not; I doubt that they do in any statistically significant way. I further doubt that they represent any kind of morality that anyone could hope, or expect, would be followed. What they must represent is an extreme standard to set up against the woman who consents to sex under duress: ultimately, there are alternatives, and if the woman consented, under whatever duress, she bears a level of guilt. This is a contrived morality, contrived because the alternative it creates is hardly a viable one, as the stories themselves suggest by the very fact that some at least of the women (and the important ones to boot) do not take the alternative of death. It must therefore represent simply an underlying conviction that the woman sins by tempting the man, that she cannot be totally guilt-free, and that the fact of pollution remains. It is no accident that this attitude is most clearly expressed in texts of ecclesiastical provenance; but secular literature embraces it to some extent.

It is not irrelevant, in this connection, to say something about the problem as it appears in the other secular literature, the romances of the twelfth century. Written after *Digenes Akrites,* these are stories in the learned language, which owe a great deal to Hellenistic romances. It has already been observed that abduction plays a particular role here, being the one act in which the hero acts rather than being acted upon.[37] Compared with the sophisticated and lengthy discussion of abduction in *Digenes*, the treatment

---

[35] The lack of sophistication may also reflect a much earlier redaction of the original story which forms the first part of the extant narrative, a redaction before the elaborations of civil and canonical thought of the 11th and 12th centuries.

[36] *Pratum Spirituale*, chap. 39; Wortley, *Paul de Monembasie*, 32 ff; cf. above, IV.

[37] Beaton, *Romance*, 60–61, and above, p. 200.

here is trivial, which is useful because it points up the role of abduction as a literary device.[38] It is the action which starts the heroes on their adventures, and, unlike the story of *Digenes,* it creates the framework within which the misadventures can be justified. For every abduction is followed by disasters, captivity, threats to the girl's virginity (unsullied to the end, nevertheless),[39] and to the hero's own sexual purity, freedom, or life. Beaton has remarked that abduction is "only very cursorily motivated by the intelligence that the heroine has just been betrothed elsewhere."[40] That, indeed, is the excuse, but it is a perfunctory one. Nor is it possible to discern in these romances any elements which would justify the abduction, apart from the consent of the abducted girl. Thus in some cases the hero quite unabashedly has accomplices.[41] He also tries to persuade the girl to sleep with him without benefit of marriage, something which Digenes never did; the heroine, of course, resists virtuously, saying that she needs the consent of her father and mother.[42]

In the romance of *Ysmine and Ysminias,* abduction is treated at greater length, but not more elaborately. The abduction is preceded by omens, variously interpreted. According to the interpretation adopted by the lovers, it is Zeus himself who urged the abduction or elopement, which was certainly carried out with the full consent of the girl. The misadventures of the lovers are causally related to the abduction, both in Ysminias' view and in that of

---

[38] There are three complete romances which will be considered here: *Ysmine and Ysminias* by Eustathios Makrembolites, *Rodanthe and Dosikles* by Theodore Prodromos, and *Drosilla and Charikles* by Niketas Eugeneianos. They are all published in Hercher, *Erotici Scriptores Graeci,* II. The fourth romance survives only in fragments: O. Mazal, *Der Roman des Konstantinos Manasses: Überlieferung, Rekonstruktion, Textausgabe der Fragmente* (Vienna, 1967), and E. Tsolakis, Συμβολή στη μελέτη του ποιητικού έργου του Κωνσταντίνου Μανασσή και κριτική έκδοση του μυθιστορήματός του 'Τα κατ' Αρίστανδρον και Καλλιθέαν; Επιστημονική Επετηρίς της φιλοσοφικής Σχολής του Πανεπιστημίου Θεσσαλονίκης, Appendix X (Thessaloniki, 1967).

[39] In one of the romances, there is a quite extraordinary ceremonial ordeal by water to prove the heroine's virginity (and also, by the way, to fix the price of captive girls, since according to the story virgins were sold for a high price). When the heroine emerges unscathed, the people applaud and shout in loud and joyful tones, "the maiden is a virgin!" See *Ysmine and Ysminias,* Hercher, 241–42, 282–83.

[40] Beaton, *Romance,* 60–61.

[41] *Drosilla and Charikles,* 472–73 and 524; cf. *Ysmine and Ysminias,* 225.

[42] *Drosilla and Charikles,* 536–37.

the girl's parents. Ysmine's mother calls Ysminias a "wild beast" who seized the girl and carried her off. Her father, when he finally finds her, lays the blame squarely at her feet. He berates her for her false modesty and her reluctance to relate her adventures: "It is not a silent tongue that defines prudence, but, rather, orderly and seemly behavior. As for you, you had no shame when you behaved badly, but you are ashamed to speak about it."[43] Similarly, in the romance of Theodore Prodromos, Dosikles urges his beloved to tell her father that she had been abducted by force; and he himself admits that he abducted her (the verb "to steal" is used), that he was a wild beast, a robber, all in order to persuade the father to allow the marriage, which of course he does.[44]

In none of these romances is there any effort to present the (consensual) abduction as an elopement which would not be punishable. On the contrary, the young man essentially admits his fault, which is caused by love and by the fear of losing his beloved. The consent of the parents to the marriage is always sought and received, but the original act is unequivocally illegal, except perhaps in the realm of the laws of love. All of this simply points up the fictional character of the abduction scenes, and also serves to highlight the quite exceptional treatment of the subject in *Digenes Akrites*.

Of Rape, Adultery, and Punishment

Unlike the learned romances of the twelfth century, in which no sexual activity, apart from a kiss or coy caress, is seen to take place, the story of *Digenes Akrites* shows the hero engaging in feats of sexual valor, even though he professes to be deeply in love with his bride. There are two such episodes, both valuable in terms of the author's attitudes toward sex and the woman, consenting or not.

The story of the daughter of Aplorravdes, which appears in the Grottaferrata version but not in the Escorial manuscript, is almost a cautionary tale about what befalls girls who leave home to follow the wrong man. She was the daughter of an Arab emir who fell in love with a Greek captive of her father's and, with her mother's connivance, freed him and gave him presents and power. He eventually wanted to return to his homeland and persuaded

---

[43] *Ysmine and Ysminias*, 262, 268–70, 280.
[44] *Rodanthe and Dosikles*, 427–28.

her to follow him, promising her marriage. She took advantage of her mother's fatal illness and absconded with valuables from her home. While on the road, the couple made love "insatiably" for three nights, which is three times more than any other eloping couple did in the romances. Then the faithless lover left her, taking the money with him, and she dressed as a man and went on the road to find him. Digenes, who had already met the young man, then came upon the girl and expressed amazement at the depth of the girl's love and her sufferings. It was, indeed, her tale of love that aroused Digenes' own passion for her:

> This when I heard, friend, from the girl's mouth
> As it were a flame came up into my heart,
> Offered me love and lawless union.[45]

He proceeds to "lawless" actions (παράνομον μίξιν . . . ἁμαρτίαν . . . ἄθεσμος πρᾶξις . . . πράξεως παρανόμου . . . ἀπὸ τῆς ἀνομίας), even though the girl resists: "Although the woman much opposed the doing/ Calling on God and on her parents' souls." This rape is presented with a certain equanimity, which, however, is not difficult to understand. The girl was, after all, a foreigner, although she had converted to Christianity. Much more important, she was no longer a virgin and, moreover, she had already transgressed all sorts of boundaries for love: she had abandoned her parents' home and even her feminine dress. Would not all this, and her being alone on the road, be sufficient evidence of those depraved prior mores that the canonists thought justified the assumption that the woman had assented to the rape?[46] No rape at all, then, either in law, which spoke only of the rape of a virgin,[47] or insofar as the twelfth-century canonists were concerned. The act

---

[45] G V, 2275–78; Mavrogordato, 157. On this episode, cf. Galatariotou, "Structural Oppositions," 57–59.

[46] There is a hagiographic parallel to this in the *vita* of Lazaros Galeseiotes, as has already been noted by Kazhdan: A. P. Kazhdan, "Hagiographical Notes (Suite)," *Byzantion* 54 (1984), 182–84. The most striking parallel is that a girl who fled from her home with a man and found herself alone on the road would be assumed to be immoral and therefore fair game: *Acta Sanctorum,* Nov. III, sec. 7.

[47] Digenes' crime was, according to Byzantine law, fornication, punishable by beating according to the antiquated and no longer used provisions of *Ecloga* 17.19. Of course, if one were to consider that the girl was properly betrothed to her lover, Digenes was guilty of the much more serious crime of adultery, and indeed in one instance the poet says "[He has] fallen into the crime of adultery": G V, 2058. This,

remained, however, both illegal and a sin; although the Devil made him do it, the hero seeks to remedy the act. He forces the girl's lover to marry her, and goes through an internal process of repentance, which takes the external form of his abandoning his residence and moving elsewhere.

Insofar as the question of consent is concerned, the most important element of this story is the fact that the woman's avowed, illicit, and consummated love for a man takes her out of the protected world of virgins. Although she did not consent to sex with the hero, her prior life was such that sex was almost inevitable; interestingly, the attention of the poet is all concentrated on the remorse of Digenes, and not on the woman's reactions.

Digenes' encounter with the warrior Maximo has different and somewhat more complex elements.[48] She is a virgin, unvanquished in war, summoned by Digenes' adversaries to help them defeat him. The episode is replete with sexual overtones: the *apelatai*, Digenes' adversaries, want to defeat him and seize his wife (E 1399); Maximo, called a κούρβα, a whore, in the Escorial version, promises to cut off Digenes' head and bring the "girl" to the enemies who desire her; Digenes is reluctant to make war on a woman, but eventually is forced into it. In the single combat that follows, she is defeated, although Digenes refrains from killing her, saying that a man should not kill women, indeed should not even do battle with them.[49] This is, indeed, a battle of the sexes, for as soon as she is vanquished, Maximo declares that Digenes has won her. In a nice turn of phrase, the Escorial version equates the victory in battle to the winning of a woman: κ' ἐσὺ μόνος με κέρδισες κ' ἄλλος μὴ μὲ κερδίσῃ ("you alone have won over me, and let no one else win me over," a wordplay on the two meanings of the verb). In the Grottaferrata version, the connection is explicitly spelled out: "I am a virgin still by none seduced. / You alone have conquered, you shall win me all."[50] Digenes

---

however, must be simply a careless use of the term, for there is no way that her relationship with her lover could have been considered a proper betrothal in the 12th century.

[48] The episode is recounted in G VI, 3089 ff, and E 1546 ff. A leaf is missing from the G manuscript at the point where Digenes slept with Maximo (at G VI, 3118). Beck thinks it may have been taken by a reader who was offended by its (presumably) salacious contents: Beck, "Orthodoxie," 342.

[49] Only in the Grottaferrata version, G VI, 2920 ff.

[50] Mavrogordato, 208; G VI, 3101–2: ἔτι παρθένος γάρ εἰμι ὑπ' οὐδενὸς φθαρεῖσα· σὺ μόνος με ἐνίκησας, σύ με ἀποκερδίσεις.

tells her that he is married to a beautiful, rich girl from a powerful family, and so cannot marry her. In the Escorial version, he then makes an unequivocal proposition: "but if you want to fornicate, I'll do it to you" (εἰ δ' ἂν ὁρμῆς νὰ πορνευθῆς, ἐγὼ νὰ σοῦ τὸ ποίσω). The Grottaferrata version has, instead, the common motif that Digenes was seduced by her beauty and her sweet words; he sleeps with her, and dismisses her, asking her not to forget him. Again the Escorial version is brutally frank: "I dismounted, laid aside my arms, and quickly did to Maximo what she had wanted; and as soon as I did it to her, to Maximo, the whore, immediately I mounted my horse and went to the girl (his wife)."[51] Predictably, Digenes is then overtaken by remorse for his action, which the author of the Grottaferrata version, always more interested than the Escorial in defining sexual crimes, calls "adultery." The definition is not precise in legal terms, for he was really guilty of fornication and the seduction of a virgin, but we have seen that there was confusion in the common usage of the terms adultery and fornication since Roman times. The Escorial version is less interested in defining the crime and more involved in showing the total defeat of Maximo both in battle and in sexual terms—here is a woman who lost both her valor and her virginity: "After seducing Maximo, three injustices I did to her: first that I had her, second that she was shamed, and third and worst, that she lost her valor."[52]

The hero's conscience bothers him, especially after he has spoken with and lied to his wife. In the Grottaferrata version, he becomes enraged, goes back to Maximo, and "having caught her I slew her ruthlessly, after adultery performing the sorry murder."[53]

Neither version of the poem condones Digenes' actions in this episode, and neither explicitly states that Maximo, rather than Digenes, was the most culpable. But it does not take a very sophisticated reader to realize that, in the end, the blame falls primarily on the woman. It is she who declares her intention, honorable at first, to be sure. Her desire, or consent, to marry Digenes is taken to extend to a desire, or consent, to have sex with him. At

---

[51] E 1565–68: Κ' ἐπέζευσα τὸν μαῦρον μου καὶ λύω τ' ἄρματά μου/ καὶ τὸ ἐπεθύμα ἡ Μαξιμοῦ γοργὸν τῆς τὸ ἐποῖκα· / κ' ἀπῆτις τῆς τὸ ἔκαμα ἐγὼ τῆς Μαξιμοῦς τῆς κούρβας,/ εὐθὺς ἐκαβαλλίκευσα κ' ἐπῆγα εἰς τὸ κοράσιον.

[52] E 1586–88: Μετὰ τὸ φθείρειν τὴν Μαξιμοῦν τρία κακὰ τὴν ἐποῖκα· πρῶτον μὲν ὅτι εἶχα την, δεύτερον ὅτι ἐντράπη, τρίτον καὶ περισσότερον ἔχασε τὴν ἀνδρειάν της.

[53] I have changed somewhat Mavrogordato's translation (p. 215).

another level, she bears responsibility because it is her beauty and "her sweet words" that seduce the hero. In legal terms, Digenes is guilty of the seduction of a virgin with her consent, which would carry punishment for the man but not for the woman. In literature, the man emerges relatively unscathed, but the woman is punished very severely. Is she punished for her consent, or because she was polluted and therefore cannot be allowed to survive in her former role as a warrior virgin?[54] At still another level she is, of course, punished most severely because, having broken every code of female behavior, she is outside the pale.[55]

Some parallels with literature emanating from a religious or monastic milieu, namely, saints' lives and morality tales, are immediately obvious. The most obvious parallel lies in the fact that woman, with her beauty and wiles, leads man into temptation and cannot be held innocent for his crimes, whatever the law might say; equally, the woman is punished in some way, whether her punishment is self-inflicted or not. A more striking parallel has been brought to my attention by Alexander Kazhdan. The Synaxarion of the Church of Constantinople relates the story of the hermit Iakovos and the daughter of a rich man. The girl was possessed by a demon, who made her call out the hermit's name. Her parents brought her to Iakovos to be healed. After expelling the demon, the hermit began to be attacked by desire (πολε-μεῖσθαι). He was defeated (ἡττηθείς) and slept with the girl, whom he subsequently killed. Such was his remorse that he buried himself in a grave and, through repentance, was so purified of the pollution (τοσοῦτον διὰ μετανοίας ἑαυτὸν καθῆρε τοῦ μύσους) that he was able to perform a miracle, assuring his sanctity. Thus his sin was corrected, and his saintliness increased. The girl's own punishment, for an unstated sin, was as irrevocable as that of Maximo who had transgressed in a number of ways.[56] Neither this story nor the story of Maximo can be taken as representing what people actually did; but they are powerful indicators as to the attitudes that suffused the legal system, especially in the implementation of the law, and influenced profoundly the lives of people.

[54] Note, however, that in the Escorial version that is precisely how she survives; she goes away "shamed."

[55] Cf. Galatariotou, "Structural Oppositions," 59–62.

[56] *SynCP*, 128–30. The date of the story unfortunately is not known, although it is placed in Samaria; the Synaxarion dates from the 10th century. The attitude reflected here is older and is preserved by the church and, it seems, by secular literature.

The literature of the twelfth century, on which we have concentrated, is, on the surface, a celebration of young love that conquers all; it is, further, a celebration of desire, most frequently the desire of the two young lovers for each other, but also desire *tout court*. However, our investigation has shown that this surface picture is painted on a sturdy canvas of quite a different texture. What is truly valued is virginity in the woman and a proper marriage for the two young people; transgressing the boundaries makes for a tense plot, but the resolution is always the same, and thus people do not challenge the norms, they affirm them. In my view, the clearest illustration of this is the story of the abduction of Digenes' bride. The poet covers every base, so he can have it all: the excitement of a seeming abduction and the clear understanding that no laws were truly broken, and the marriage stands perfectly valid in the end. So intent is the poet, especially of the Grottaferrata version, that one is tempted, despite all that has been said above, to seek here the reflection not of a common practice of abduction but of a particular event, a cause célèbre of its day, of which we now know nothing. But that, of course, is rank speculation.

The issue of consent is inscribed within this context. The consent of the woman is always present when there is an abduction/elopement; and it is always absent when the hero tries to persuade the girl to engage in premarital sexual relations, so these do not take place, except perhaps in an erotic dream.[57] It is her consent that legitimizes the abduction and the eventual marriage, but the consent is greatly circumscribed by that of the families. In *Digenes Akrites,* explicit consent to various illicit sexual relations is not an important factor in differentiating between crimes, or in establishing the punishment of the hero, which is always internal; it does, however, and significantly, play a telling role in the punishment of the virgin who willingly allows herself to be seduced.

[57] See one of Ysminias' erotic dreams, in which he presses the resisting girl with some force: Hercher, II, 185 ff.

Conclusion

This examination of the role of consent to sexual relations in the Byzantine legal system and in Byzantine society has shown that there were several different positions, conflicting at some points, agreeing in others. Consent was both a factor creating legal categories and an issue which was recognized by the church and by society. Its importance in establishing legal categories derives from Roman precedents, but the treatment of consent acquired greater clarity and therefore force in the Byzantine period, certainly since the eighth century. The consent of the woman served as the differentiating factor that created the category of rape. The emphasis on the importance of consent for the punishment of the man and the fact that the law, with very few exceptions, did not punish a woman who consented to illicit sexual intercourse outside marriage, create a situation that seems favorable to women, on the one hand; on the other, it reduces the woman's responsibility for her own actions. The emphasis on consent also led, in practice, that is, in the law courts, to the development of external criteria which created presumption of force. I would argue that the insistence on objective criteria, as these were defined in Byzantium, also served as a protection for the woman.

The other side of this argument is that subjective criteria for establishing consent or its absence functioned negatively for the woman in Byzantine society. As we have seen, subjective criteria were discussed primarily by the canonists, and in terms that bring out the complexities of the position of the church. The issue of personal responsibility, regardless of gender, looms large in the thinking of the church, and so, necessarily, does consent. The sinner, whether male or female, is punished, the punishment serving to expiate the sin. At the same time, the probing of the issue of internal consent, which at times becomes almost a psychological investigation, necessarily brings to the surface concepts regarding the true nature of women as well as ideas regarding purity and pollution. The canonists' efforts to investigate the deeper aspects of consent sometimes leads them to a position which almost considers immaterial the outward, visible signs of absence of consent on the part of the woman. There is, thus, a contrast between the acceptance of consent as the factor which establishes responsibility, culpability, punishment (as it does in civil and canon law) and the position that consent, particularly the consent of the woman, is irrelevant, since it is the action itself that is important. That second position is taken by some ecclesiastical and some literary sources. It is predicated upon a complex of ideas regarding shame, honor, and pollution which were shared by society generally and which serve to attenuate the importance of consent. A later text, which I have not discussed here, presents in a somewhat ghoulish fashion a farfetched logical conclusion of the attitude that focuses on pollution. It is a secular text, the treatise *On the Laws* of George Gemistos Plethon, and the severity of its provisions regarding the punishment of sexual crimes is closer to Western Renaissance societies than to Byzantine attitudes.[1] Those (males) engaging in homosexual activities, those guilty of bestiality, the adulterers, and those guilty of rape are to be burned, or "cleansed by fire" (πυρὶ καθαίρειν). Furthermore, they are to be burned not in the common cemeteries, but in special ones, designated for the most odious and polluting (ἐναγέσι) criminals. The only time the question of consent enters is in the case of consensual sex with an unmarried girl or woman who is still under a guardian's authority: the man is still to be burned, but he will be buried in the common cemetery.[2]

The importance given to φθορά by civil and canon law stems, undoubtedly, from such attitudes and from the value placed on virginity. Marriage, as we have seen, functions as a remedy to both seduction and elopement, and even to abduction if a formula can be found to make abduction resemble elopement. Marriage regularizes irregular situations and restores the honor of the family. The relative paucity of Byzantine (as opposed to late Antique) legislation regarding abduction may have the same causes as the somersaults of the canonists who tried to squeeze abduction into the more acceptable suit of elopement: the concern was less to maximize prosecutions for abduction, an irremediable crime, and more to allow as many cases as possible to be remedied by marriage. It should be reiterated, however, that although mar-

---

[1] For Western Europe, see, among others, Guido Ruggiero, *Boundaries of Eros: Sex, Crime and Sexuality in Renaissance Venice* (New York, 1985), and R. Carrasco, "Le châtiment de la sodomie sous l'Inquisition (XVIe–XVIIe siècle)," in A. Corbin, ed., *Violences sexuelles* (Paris, 1989), 53–69; for Dubrovnik in this period, see B. Krekić, "Abominandum Crimen: Punishment of Homosexuality in Renaissance Dubrovnik," *Viator* 18 (1987), 337–45.

[2] C. Alexandre, *Pléthon, Traité des Lois* (Paris, 1858), 124–28.

riage is vigorously promoted as a remedy for a number of illicit sexual relations, both partners must be willing to give their consent to it. And here the issue of the limits of individual consent becomes central, since it was always circumscribed by the interests and desires (and formal consent) of the family, the state, and the church, three institutions whose relative weight in regard to the control of marriages varied according to historical period and social class.

In this study I have tried to investigate the various parameters of the complex and sometimes contradictory Byzantine attitudes toward the issue of consent. The importance of this topic for social history and the history of women has, I hope, become evident in the text. Perhaps one more word may be said about a particularity of the subject treated here. If one were studying the role of individual consent in marriage or in property relations (for example, the alienation of land) one would have to address, in the first instance, the limitations placed upon the desires of the individual by the interests of others who must consent to his/her action in order for the action to be valid: the consent of the parents in marriage, the consent of neighbors and others in the sale of land. In the case of consent to sexual relations, the focus is different: what is at issue is less the limits placed on the individual by other interested parties, and more the question of the effects of certain actions upon the actors themselves. Hence the question of personal attitude, responsibility, culpability is paramount. Guilt is not merely legal guilt but a moral failure, stemming from the individual and reflecting on the family as well; and a crime is also a sin. While this may be the case with other crimes, for example, murder, it is most pointedly true of sexual activity, a fact which explains the ambiguities and the richness of the response to both actual and theoretical or fictitious situations.

Dumbarton Oaks/Harvard University

Part Three

The Medieval West

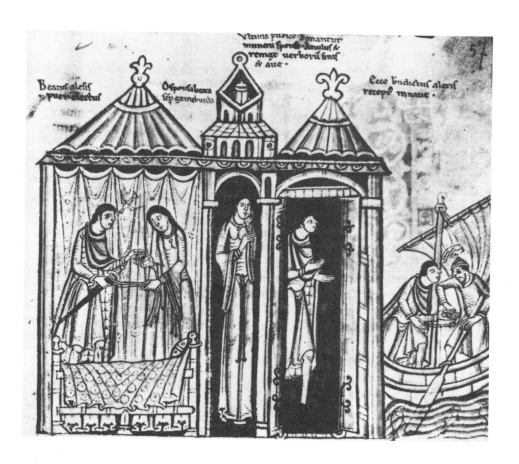

Prompted by the Holy Spirit, St. Alexis abandons his spouse before the consummation of their marriage. He returns the ring, leaves her in distress, and takes ship for the Holy Land. Page 57 of a psalter brought together ca. 1119–23 at St. Albans for Christina, anchoress of Markyate, to whose enforced and unconsummated marriage the Alexis miniature may allude (Otto Pächt et al., *The St. Albans Psalter* [London, 1960], 136). The manuscript is now in the Cathedral Library, Hildesheim. (*Courtesy of the Warburg Institute, London*)

Consent and Dissent to Sexual Intercourse in Germanic Societies from the Fifth to the Tenth Century

SUZANNE F. WEMPLE

> One falls rapidly in love with a beautiful girl, says a certain scholar, and it is difficult to guard her that many men love.
> Isidore of Seville, *De ecclesiasticis officiis*, 2.20.9 (PL 83: 812)

Isidore of Seville was certainly right in defining the extremely difficult task of the guardian in barbarian societies. By the end of the sixth century, the Germanic tribes had organized themselves into states in Western Europe: the Anglo-Saxon, Frankish, Lombard, and Visigothic states. These peoples were governed by Germanic laws. With the exception of the Anglo-Saxon kingdoms, large Roman populations lived on their territory. To rule these, Roman law was applied. Although the Germanic and Roman laws influenced each other, their application differed in one very important aspect. The Roman law was a territorial law, and everyone living in a Roman province was generally under it. The Germanic laws were not territorial but personal laws, and each female followed the law of her father or, if she was married, the law of her husband, regardless of where she was located geographically.

Our earliest knowledge of Germanic sexual mores dates from the late first century account of Tacitus, who commended the Germanic honor of the family and the chastity of women. While noting that there was polygamy among those of high rank, Tacitus described the humiliating penalties for adultery which were applied to unfaithful wives and to their partners in crime.

In this paper, the behavior of girls and widowed women will be discussed: not their comportment in engagement and marriage, but their abduction, rape, and molestation, the sexual misdeeds of betrothed and married women, in particular adultery, concubinage, and prostitution, and the lot of consecrated women who fornicated. In each instance, I will describe the punishment of the men who committed or shared in the crime.[1] The elements of consent or dissent in the proscribed acts will be obvious.

Primitive Germanic customs were reflected in the Salic *Pactus* and the *Book of Salic Laws* issued by Clovis between 507 and 511, reissued with additions between 511 and 513, and again revised from 567 to 596, and the *Ripurian Law* compiled in the seventh century. Roman influences appeared in the laws of the Burgundians and Visigoths issued in the fifth century, as these tribes had been in contact with the Romans for centuries, and to a lesser extent in the laws of the Bavarians and Alamans, which were compiled in the eighth century on the model of the Burgundian or Visigothic compilations. The Lombard *Code* consists of *Rothair's Edict*, almost entirely Germanic custom, and of four different law codes issued in the late seventh or eighth century and containing more advanced laws than *Rothair's Edict*. The Anglo-Saxon dooms show very slight influence of Roman practice and were written in the vernacular. To understand the extent to which the laws were obeyed, I have supplemented the analysis of the laws with narrative sources.

All the sources state that prior to marriage a woman was under the power of her family. Under the Visigothic and the Roman laws, however, she was under her father's or guardian's protection only until she reached the age of majority, twenty or twenty-five as the case may be.[2]

---

[1] The best account is James A. Brundage, *Law, Sex and Christian Society in Medieval Europe* (Chicago, 1987). See also Katherine Fischer Drew, *Law and Society in Early Medieval Europe* (London, 1988), and Suzanne Fonay Wemple, *Women in Frankish Society: Marriage and the Cloister* (Philadelphia, 1981), and "Les traditions romaine, germanique et chrétienne," in *Histoire des femmes,* ed. Georges Duby and Michelle Perrot, II, *Le Moyen âge,* ed. Christiane Klapisch-Zuber (Paris, 1991), 185–216.

[2] *Lex Romana Burgundionum* 37.2, Monumenta Germaniae Historica (= MGH) (Leipzig and Hannover, 1825–), *Legum,* sectio I, 2/1, 145; and Paul David King, *Law and Society in the Visigothic Kingdom* (Cambridge, 1972), 299.

The father retained the right of making matrimonial arrangements for his daughter, a right that passed to his widow, or if she died or remarried, to her brother or her paternal uncle, or to a guardian. The consent of the woman to a marriage was not required, unless her protector was someone other than her parent or brother.

If she married, the father's right of protection passed to her husband, except in *Friedelehe* (free marriage) or in *Raubehe* (marriage by capture), because in neither case did the husband purchase her or her children's *mundium,* the "right of protection," that remained with her own family. Betrothal was as binding as marriage. Usually girls married very young, aged twelve to fourteen, with the groom between fifteen and sixteen.

Rape, Abduction, and Fornication

The laws made a distinction between an unmarried free girl and a betrothed woman. The Salian *Pactus* as well as the *Book of Salic Laws* states that if a group of men abducted a free girl from her home or her workroom, each man had to pay a compensation of 5 solidi; if they had arrows, each one owed an additional 8 solidi, and the abductor was liable for her bride-price, 62 ½ solidi.[3] The same penalty fell upon the man if the girl had been placed in the king's protection. If the abductor was a servant of the king or a half-free man, he had to pay with his life or was given as a slave to the girl's family.[4] If the girl voluntarily followed, she lost her own freedom.[5] He who raped a free girl, and this was proved against him, owed the bride-price, that is, 62 ½ solidi.[6] But if he had intercourse with her approval in secret, he had to pay only 45 solidi.[7] The laws do not state who was to receive these payments. We can only assume that it was her family or guardian. That rape was considered one of the most serious offenses is apparent from King Childebert's decree that the rapist "shall suffer loss of life" or be outlawed if he sought refuge in a church.[8]

---

[3] *The Laws of the Salian Franks,* trans. with an intro. by Katherine Fischer Drew (Philadelphia, 1991), XIII: 1–4, pp. 77–78; and XXIII [XIV], p. 189.

[4] Ibid., XIII: 6–7, p. 78; and XXIII [XIV] 6, p. 189.

[5] Ibid., XIII: 8, p. 78; and XXIII [XIV]: 7, p. 189.

[6] Ibid., XV: 2, p. 80; and XXIII [XIV]: 13, p. 190.

[7] Ibid., XV: 3, p. 80; and XXIII [XIV]: 14, p. 190.

[8] Ibid., "Capitula," VI, II: 2, p. 157.

According to Alaman law, the man was to pay 40 solidi if he abducted a free girl but did not rape her before returning her to her family. He was liable to render her wergeld (the price of her life, 400 solidi), if he wanted to keep her.[9] If the woman died before he acquired her *mundium* protection, he was also responsible for compensating her family with 400 solidi. If he begot children and these died before he possessed their mother's protection, he had to compensate the mother's father with their wergeld.[10] If he fornicated with a girl, he was liable to pay her 40 solidi, but if she was an adult woman, twice that amount.[11] The Bavarian code stated that if a man abducted a virgin against her will or that of her relatives, he had to give her 40 solidi. If he raped a poor widow with children, he was to compensate her with 80 solidi.[12] The same code punished with 12 solidi the man who fornicated with a free woman whom he did not want to marry.[13] He had to pay the same amount if he persuaded someone that he wanted to marry her and dismissed her on the way to marriage.[14]

The Lombard law approved any punishment a family would mete out on its free daughter who fornicated willfully. If her partner agreed to marry her, he had to pay her bride-price (*meta*), plus 20 solidi to compensate her family for the illegal intercourse, and 20 more to avert a feud. If he would not marry her, he was liable for 100 solidi, half of it to her family and half to the king. If her relatives failed to punish the girl, the king decided her fate.[15] If a man violently seized a woman and made her unwillingly his bride, he was to pay a compensation of 900 solidi, half to the king and half to her relatives. If she did not have relations, then all would go to the king. The woman, moreover, had the right to choose who would have protection over her and her property. In addition to the compensation, the man had to pay her the price of her protection. If she died before he became her guardian, he had to pay to her relatives her wergeld.[16]

---

[9] *Laws of the Alamans and the Bavarians,* trans. with intro. by Theodore John Rivers (Philadelphia, 1977), XXXII: 1–2, p. 55.

[10] Ibid., LIII: 2, p. 84.

[11] Ibid., LXXX: 1, p. 84; and LVI: 2, p. 85.

[12] Ibid., VIII: 6–7, p. 139.

[13] Ibid., VIII: 8, p. 139.

[14] Ibid., VIII: 17 p. 141.

[15] *The Lombard Laws,* trans. with an intro. by Katherine Fischer Drew (Philadelphia, 1973), Rothair 188–89, p. 87.

[16] Ibid., Rothair 186–87, pp. 86–87.

In the Visigothic kingdom, if the abductor sought refuge in a church with the girl, presumably a safe place, they had to be separated and handed as slaves to the girl's relatives. Only if rape was not perpetrated could the relatives arrange a betrothal. Killing a ravisher was allowed under Visigothic law.[17] All the codes were severe with an abductor and rapist, but the Visigothic *Code* was the harshest. King Childebert's decree alone was similar in its intent. The Burgundian *Code* was also strict regarding seizure and rape. The penalty was nine-fold payment of the girl's wergeld, plus a fine.[18]

There were lesser crimes which the codes recognized. In Burgundy when the girl was returned uncorrupted to her parents, the abductor was responsible for six times her wergeld. If the girl sought the man out voluntarily and he had intercourse with her, he had to pay her marriage price three-fold. But if he did not have sexual relations, he was not to be blamed for anything.[19]

That these laws were heeded is apparent from the chroniclers. Gregory of Tours, in the *History of the Franks,* described how the former count of stables to King Chilperic did not manage to carry off as his bride the daughter of the late Bishop Le Mans. The girl's mother heard of his plan and defended her daughter. Although the former count escaped, he was discredited and several of his men were killed.[20]

The law codes tried to persuade the parents and the girl not to consent to marriage by abduction. A Visigothic girl lost her inheritance if she married without her father's or guardian's consent while she was under age.[21] Gregorio di Catino, in his *Regesto di Farfa,* wrote of an eighth-century case of abduction. A young man, Rabenno, the son of Count Rabenno of Fermo, was engaged to Halerana, but the armed Hermifrid abducted the girl and had intercourse with her. We do not know whether they had agreed, but the story seems to indicate that it was not a case of rape. Rabenno took the matter before the ducal court, and both the girl and the abductor were arrested. They were turned over to Rabenno, who placed the girl in a convent and gave the

[17] *Leges Visigothorum,* ed. Karl Zeumer, MGH, *Legum,* sectio I, T. 1, 3.3.1–2, 3.3.6–7, p. 142.

[18] *The Burgundian Code,* trans. Katherine Fischer Drew (Philadelphia, 1972), XII: 1, p. 31.

[19] Ibid., XII: 2–4, p. 32.

[20] Gregory of Tours, *The History of the Franks,* trans. with intro. by Lewis Thorpe (Harmondsworth, 1974), X: 5, p. 553.

[21] King, *Law and Society,* 231.

man his freedom. At a later date, Rabenno changed his mind, killed Hermi-frid, and married Halerana. The property of Hermifrid and half of the pos-sessions of the girl were taken away and went to the king. The king gave all to the monastery of Farfa, to which Rabenno withdrew at a later date, pre-sumably sending his wife once again to the convent.[22]

The virtue of the semi-free man and the slave was also well protected. According to the *Salic Laws,* a free man who had intercourse with a slave girl owed 15 solidi to her lord. If she happened to be the king's slave, he was liable to pay 30 solidi. If a slave had intercourse with someone else's slave girl and the girl died, the slave had to give 6 solidi to the girl's lord or be castrated. If the slave girl did not die, the slave would either receive 300 lashes or pay 3 solidi to the girl's lord. If a slave married another lord's slave girl without his consent, he was held to the same punishment, rendering him-self to lashing or 3 solidi.[23] He was considered to have committed fornication. Under the *Salic Laws,* women were subjected to the same punishment as men if they were caught with a slave. A free woman who married a slave of someone else was to remain in servitude with him, and all her property would belong to the master whose slave she married.[24] Later, the *Formulae* mitigated this harsh order with exemption for the slave's wife and for her children from the laws of slavery. If she had intercourse with or married her family's slave, she could be killed.

Amalasuntha, orphaned daughter of the Ostrogothic king Theodoric, ig-nored the advice of her mother, Audofleda, the sister of Clovis, to marry a king's son, and took as lover one of her own slaves called Traguilla and eloped with him to a neighboring city. Her mother begged her not to disgrace the royal blood, but she would not listen. The mother then sent a band of armed men who killed the slave and returned Amalasuntha to her. Amalasun-tha put some poison into her mother's cup from which she was to take com-munion. Audofleda drank from the cup and dropped dead. The Italians sum-moned Theudat, king of Tuscany, to judge and punish her. When he heard the deed of this woman, he had a very hot steam bath prepared for her and or-

---

[22] Gregorio di Catino, *Il regesto di Farfa,* 144, 148, ed. I. Giorgi and U. Bal-zani, 5 vols. (Rome, 1879–1914), II, 121–22.

[23] *The Laws of the Salian Franks,* XIII: 9–11, p. 78; also XXIII [XIV]: 11,15, p. 189.

[24] Ibid., XXV: 4, p. 87; also in "Capitula," VII, III, p. 164.

dered her inside with one of her maids. As soon as she entered, she fell on the floor and died from the steam.[25]

The *Code* of the Alamans and that of the Bavarians were more lenient. The man who had intercourse with someone's chambermaid against her will had to compensate her with 6 solidi. The same fine was imposed on the ravisher of the supervisor of the textile workshop, but only 3 solidi if he had sex against their will with the other maids of lesser position. If he fornicated with a manumitted servant, he was to pay 8 solidi either to her relatives or to her lord. In case she was a virgin maidservant, he owed only 4 solidi.[26] If a slave fornicated with a free woman, his master had to turn him over to her relatives, who could punish him with death. The slave-owner did not have to pay anything more; he was sufficiently punished; the people hated not only the slave but him as well.[27]

In Britain, the code of Aethelbert of Kent provided for fines to be paid by the fornicator to the woman's protector: 50 shillings for a serving maid in the royal service, 20 shillings for a noble man's serving maid, 12 shillings for a noble man's servant, 6 shillings for a small landowner's maid, 50 sceattas to a slave woman of the second class, 30 sceattas to a slave woman of the third class, and 30 shillings for "a free woman with long hair" (a distinction of freedom). But if he took a widow, the penalty was doubled.[28]

In Lombardy, if an *aldius*, a semi-free man, fornicated with a free woman with her consent, his lord had to render to her relatives 50 solidi and the price of her *mundium*. The relatives were responsible for her punishment, which was frequently death or slavery, with her possessions divided.[29] Quite interesting is the law which shows that the Lombards cared less for the Roman slaves than for their own. Commission of immorality with a Roman slave was only 12 solidi, whereas with a Lombard it increased to 20 solidi.[30]

Being brought up in these circumstances, it was small wonder that girls

[25] Gregory of Tours, *History*, III: 30, pp. 187–88.

[26] *Laws of the Alamans and the Bavarians*, LXXXV: 1–3, p. 94; VIII: 11,13, p. 140.

[27] Ibid., VIII, 9, p. 139.

[28] *English Historical Documents*, I (ca. 500–1042), ed. Dorothy Whitelock (New York, 1955), 29; 10, 14, 16, 73, 76, pp. 357–59. A sceatta was a coin of which 3 later became worth a shilling.

[29] *The Lombard Laws*, Liutprand, 60.VII, p. 169; 24, VI, p. 155.

[30] Ibid., Rothair 194, p. 86.

came to resist their ravishers. The young women from Cividale, Paul the Deacon tells us, "put the flesh of raw chickens under their breasts," probably held in place by clothing or by straps, to resist Avars who were leading them from their homeland as captives. As a result, the Avars, when they wanted to touch them, could not endure the smell that they thought was natural to the women and moved away from them, cursing, saying that all Langobard women had a stench. Afterwards, the young girls were sold throughout various regions and secured noble marriages on account of their high birth. One of them is said to have wedded the king of the Alamans, and another a prince of the Bavarians.[31]

If her guardian consented to his female ward's abduction, according to Lombard law, he had to pay her wergeld to the treasury and the man who took her was fined 600 solidi. If the guardian did not give his consent, he got half of the 600 solidi.[32] According to Visigothic law, if the brothers of a girl contributed to her abduction, they were to pay the same amount that the ravisher paid, but they could not be killed. If their father was dead, they lost half of their property to their sister and received fifty lashes.[33]

Betrothal

The engagement of a girl in the barbarian kingdoms was as binding as marriage. The girl under no circumstances could avoid the marriage, but the man could renege with the payment of a penalty. According to Salic law, if a girl was with her attendants, proceeding to marriage, and she was attacked by a man who married her, he had to pay 62 ½ solidi to her family or guardian and 15 solidi to the man to whom she had been promised. If the man did not want to marry her but only had intercourse with her, he was liable to pay 200 solidi to her family or betrothed.[34] Not a word in these laws that perhaps the girl welcomed the attention she was receiving. Another law concerned one who became engaged to a girl and then changed his mind. The law stated that whoever was guilty of this had to pay 62 ½ solidi.[35] The Alamans had a

---

[31] Paul the Deacon, *History of the Lombards,* trans. William Dudley Foulke (Philadelphia, 1974), XXXVII, pp. 183–84.

[32] *The Lombard Laws,* Liutprand 30.I, p. 159.

[33] *Leges Visigothorum,* MGH, *Legum,* sectio I, T.1, 3.3.4, p. 142.

[34] *The Laws of the Salian Franks,* XIII: 12–14, p. 79; see also XXIII [XIV]: 8–10, p. 189, and also "Capitula," VI, 7, p. 162.

[35] Ibid., LXVa, p. 126; also XXV [LXX] p. 191.

similar law: if anyone dismissed his betrothed and took another girl, he would have to pay 40 solidi and swear with eleven oath-takers that he found no fault in her but had loved another.[36] The same *Code* legislated that if a man took another's betrothed, he had to dismiss her and compensate the other man with 200 solidi; if he did not wish to return her, he had to pay 400 solidi, even if she died.[37]

We read in the Burgundian *Code* that a widow, who had committed herself to be remarried with the consent of her parents and had received part of her wedding-price, broke her pledge and had sexual relations with another man. For this she was to be punished with the "pouring forth of her own blood." However, the punishment was reduced to a heavy fine because the execution would have been inflicted on a holy day. The woman had to pay her wergeld, "300 solidi," to the wronged man. The man with whom she committed this crime was also punished. He had to pay 150 solidi, unless he took a public oath with eleven others that he was unaware that the woman had been pledged to another.[38]

Adultery

Adultery was defined as an act of sexual intercourse between a married woman and a man who was not her husband. Her partner could be married or not. In the case of adultery, the Visigoths gave the right to the woman's father or brother to kill the partner.[39] The Alamans, on the other hand, were quite liberal with the male partners in the offense, and asked the man to return the woman to her husband and compensate him with 80 solidi. If he did not wish to or could not return her because she died, "let him pay 400 solidi."[40] The Bavarians also gave her wergeld to her husband. If the male partner in crime was killed while in the act, the husband had no further recourse. If a man tried to commit adultery and was rebuffed by the wife, he had to pay 15 solidi for the attempt.[41] If he laid with another man's married maidservant, he owed her lord 20 solidi.[42] If he laid with a married free woman, he had to

---

[36] *Laws of the Alamans and the Bavarians,* LII, pp. 83–84.
[37] Ibid., LIII: 1–2, p. 84.
[38] *The Burgundian Code,* LII: 1–5, pp. 59–60.
[39] *Leges Visigothorum,* MGH, *Legum,* sectio I, T.1, 3.4.5.
[40] *Laws of the Alamans and the Bavarians,* L, p. 83.
[41] Ibid., VIII: 1, p. 138.
[42] Ibid., VIII: 12, p. 140.

compensate her husband or her relatives with 40 solidi.[43] If a slave was caught with a married free woman and both were killed, the master of the slave had to pay the wergeld of the wife to the husband, minus 20 solidi. If the slave was not killed, his master, who did not impose any discipline on him, had to return him to the man whose wife he disgraced.[44]

The Frankish codes demanded more money from the male partner in adultery. He was to pay 200 solidi to the husband.[45] In England, the punishment was lighter; the adulterer had to pay her husband the marriage-price.[46] The *St. Gall Penitentiary* laid out the penalties in case of adultery ranging from twelve years for a bishop, ten for a priest, seven for a monk, and five for a layman or clerk in minor orders. Finding a husband in fornication with an unmarried or widowed woman did not create great sensation.[47] The Lombard *Code* contains a rule that damned a woman who had sexual relations with a married man in his own home. She lost all her property to the king and to her relatives, and all the blame was imputed to her.[48]

Paul the Deacon related with good humor the amorous behavior of King Cunincpert. The king's wife, in an attempt to amuse him, reported on the beauties of one Theodote, a noble Roman girl she had seen in the bath. Her description so aroused Cunincpert's sexual passion that he summoned Theodote, had relations with her, and sent her to a monastery in Pavia which was named for her.[49]

Lechery

The women's honor was also guarded from lechers. Anybody who uncovered a virgin's head or raised her clothing to her knee compensated with 6 solidi according to the law of the Alamans. Those who raised her dress to expose her buttocks or genitalia or lustfully seized a virgin's hair compensated with 12 solidi.[50] The law of the Franks was more severe. A man who touched the

---

[43] Ibid., VIII: 10, p. 140.

[44] Ibid., VIII: 2, p. 138.

[45] *The Laws of the Salian Franks,* XV: 1, p. 80; see also VII: 4, pp. 164–65.

[46] *English Historical Documents,* 31, p. 358.

[47] *Sangallense tripartita,* 1.4, ed. Hermann Joseph Schmitz, *Die Bussbücher und die Bussdisciplin der Kirche,* 2 vols. (Mainz, 1883–98), II, 179–80.

[48] *The Lombard Laws,* Grimwald 8, pp. 134–35.

[49] Paul the Deacon, *History,* XXXVII, pp. 240–41.

[50] *Laws of the Alamans and the Bavarians,* LVI: 1–2, p. 85.

head, arm, or finger of a free woman owed her 15 solidi; if he touched her elbow, 30 solidi. But he who touched a women's breast or cut it so that blood flowed was liable to pay 45 solidi.[51]

It was not enough not to touch a woman. A man could not call her a prostitute; if he did, he had to pay 45 solidi according to the Salic *Pactus*.[52] The Salic law punished those who called her a witch or a harlot with a fine of 82 ½ solidi.[53] Moreover, the guardian who plotted against the protected girl's life, gave her a husband she did not want, or accused her of adultery, witchcraft, or harlotry lost his care over her. She could return to her relatives or commend herself to the court of the king, according to Lombard law.[54] A man who placed his hand on the bosom of someone else's consenting wife paid her wergeld to the husband. The wife had to undergo the husband's discipline, but she could not be killed or mutilated.[55]

Women's Behavior

Calling her names, touching a woman, and exposing her to sexual encounters encouraged her bad habits. In the early Middle Ages, it was a general principle that women were evil creatures, the inheritors of Eve's sexual sin. To overcome this sin, women had to be chaste and dutiful virgins, obliging mothers, and spotless widows. Paul the Deacon tells the sad story of Rosemund, daughter of Cunemond, king of the Gepidae. She was taken in marriage by Alboin, king of the Lombards, after he had killed her father in battle. Out of Cunemond's skull, Alboin had a drinking cup made, and some years afterwards he ordered Queen Rosemund to drink from it. At this point, she resolved to avenge the death of her father. She conspired with Helmichis, the king's armor bearer, who told her to get Peredeo, a strong and clever man, to advise them. She was able to get Peredeo's help by tricking him into sleeping with her instead of her maid. They killed the king. With Alboin dead, Helmichis married her because he coveted the throne. The Lombards, however, would not raise him to royalty. Rosemund, fearful for their lives, sent a letter to Longinus, prefect of Ravenna, to send a ship, and the couple fled at night to Ravenna with the whole treasury. Once in Ravenna, Longinus began to

---

[51] *The Laws of the Salian Franks,* XX: 1–4, p. 84; also XXII [XXII]: 1, p. 188.
[52] Ibid., XXX: 3, p. 94.
[53] Ibid., XXVII: 2, p. 199.
[54] *The Lombard Laws,* Rothair 195, p. 89.
[55] Ibid., Liutprand 121.V, pp. 197–98.

urge Rosemund to kill Helmichis and marry him. Rosemund was no longer the innocent princess Alboin fell in love with. She remembered that Alboin used force to wed her, that she committed a sexual offense to murder Alboin, that Helmichis took her as his wife to gain regal status, that the Lombards hated her also, and that to be the wife of the prefect of Ravenna was not a deplorable situation. She therefore prepared a poisonous beverage for Helmichis. After drinking from it, Helmichis realized that it was fatal and made her consume the rest.[56]

The same chroniclers also tell us that not every married woman was of this caliber. For example, the Lombard Adalulf suggested a love affair to Queen Gundeberga, wife of King Charoald. The queen vigorously refused and spat in his face. Thereupon, Adalulf accused her of having a love affair with Duke Taso, and stated that she wanted to place Taso on the throne and murder the king. Charoald took these accusations to heart and shut the queen up in the fortress of Lomello. But King Chlotar of Frankland sent a delegation to inquire why King Charoald had humiliated his kinswoman, who was the daughter of King Ago and Theolinda, an Agilolfing princess. Persuaded by the delegates, Charoald ordered that the matter be decided by a "single combat," during which the representative of the queen killed Adalulf. Thus the queen was reinstated after three long years of exile.[57]

Concubinage

Concubinage was quite common in Germanic relationships. Queen Fredegund was initially a concubine of King Chilperic, succeeding to the throne after she had persuaded him to have his wife, Galswinda, murdered.[58] Dagobert had so many concubines that the chronicler, Fredegar, declined to name them for fear of making his volume too bulky.[59] Concubinage was usually between a free man and a slave girl. Gregory of Tour's history is replete

---

[56] Paul the Deacon, *History,* I: XXVII, II: XXVIII–XXIX, pp. 49–51, 81–85; also "Origo" V, p. 319.

[57] Fredegar, *The Fourth Book of the Chronicle with Its Continuations,* trans. and ed. J. M. Wallace-Hadrill (Westpoint, 1981), pp. 41–42.

[58] Gregory of Tours, *History,* IV: 28, pp. 222–23.

[59] Fredegar, *The Fourth Book of the Chronicle,* pp. 49–50; see also *Gesta Dagoberti* 22, MGH, *Scriptores rerum Merovingicarum (= Script. rer. mer.),* 2, 408.

with stories of counts taking maidservants as their concubines. Only if he had intercourse with someone else's servant did the man have to be careful. With his own slaves, he could do as he pleased. The church was powerless to stop this behavior. For example, the Roman synod of 863 insisted that a girl must not become a concubine, even if her parents wanted it.[60]

Prostitution

Prostitution flourished in the Germanic kingdoms. We do not know the names of the prostitutes, but there are sufficient notices that testify to their existence. Taking a bath in mixed company called for a year of fasting, according to St. Hubert's penitential.[61] In a case of brutality by a man of high rank, Gregory of Tours reported that Eulalius, count of Auvergne, neglected his wife Tetradia for harlots, beat her, and squandered her jewelry and gold.[62] St. Columban would not bless the children of King Theuderic II (612–613) because they were begotten by harlots.[63] St. Boniface complained that Anglo-Saxon nuns who went on pilgrimage to Rome often ended up in the houses of prostitution that lined the road. "There are very few towns in Lombardy, or Frankland, or Gaul where there is not a harlot of English stock," he wrote to the archbishop of Canterbury. "It is a scandal and a disgrace to your whole church."[64] In the ninth century, Jonas of Orléans lamented that sons of the nobility had taken peasant women and prostitutes to initiate them into sexual pleasures.[65] A capitulary of Louis the Pious, entitled *De disciplina palatii Aquisgranensis,* used the word *meretrix* to warn men not to associate with

---

[60] Synod of Rome (863), c. 7, in J. D. Mansi, *Sacrorum conciliorum nova et amplissima collectio* (Florence and Venice, 1759–98; Paris, 1901–27) (= Mansi), 15, 655.

[61] Saint Hubert 47, in Friedrich Wilhelm Hermann Wasserschleben, ed., *Die Bussordnungen der abendländischen Kirche nebst einer rechtsgeschichtlichen Einleitung* (Halle, 1851), 383.

[62] Gregory of Tours, *History,* X: 8, 554–55.

[63] Ionas, *Vitae sanctorum: Columbani* 1:19, MGH, *Scriptores rerum Germanicarum in usum scholarum* (= *Script. rer. germ.*), 188.

[64] Boniface, *Epist.* 62, 78; Ephraim Emerton, trans., *The Letters of Saint Boniface* (New York, 1940), p. 140.

[65] Jonas of Orléans, *De inst. laicali,* 2.2, ed. J.-P. Migne, Patrologia Latina (Paris, 1844–64) (= PL) 106, col. 170D.

women of uncertain behavior.[66] Even more important than prostitution were acts of lesbianism and masturbation. The women charged with the crimes were considered to be as guilty as men who raped a widow or a virgin. The punishment for all three crimes was the same: the offender had to fast for three years.[67]

Religious Women

In the march toward sanctification, the church placed great emphasis on virginity and chastity. Secular laws accorded equal place to safeguarding the virtue of religious women. The Bavarian laws, for example, stated that if someone abducted a nun from a convent and took her as his wife, the bishop, with the consent of the king or the duke, could demand her back. The man was to return her and pay 400 solidi for stealing the bride of Christ, twice the amount due for abducting someone's betrothed. If he did not wish to return her, he was expelled from the province.[68] The Lombard *Code* was even stricter; it punished not only those who abducted nuns from convents but also those who abducted females living at home not yet consecrated by a priest, who had donned the veil, or the religious habit, or who had been dedicated to God by their relatives. If such a woman left her home with a man, he had to pay 600 solidi, and she lost all her property and was to be judged by the king. If a female devoted to religion committed a sexual act, the man paid 200 solidi. If she was not yet consecrated, the penalty to the man was 100 solidi, and all her property was confiscated. If she was a slave girl in religious garb, who was taken by her lord to a sacred place, and subsequently a man abducted and married her, they had to be separated; he was to pay 40 solidi, and she was to be returned to her former habit.[69] In England, the *Laws of Alfred* stipulated that if anyone "in lewd fashion seizes a nun either by her

---

[66] *Capitularia de disciplina palatii Aquisgranensis* (ca. 820), 3, MGH, *Capitularia regum francorum* (= *Capit.*), 1: 298; *Capitula Francia* 8, MGH, *Capit.* 1: 334, forbade prostitutes from bringing cases in court and testifying.

[67] John T. McNeill and Helena M. Gamer, *Medieval Handbooks of Penance* (New York, 1990), 185 (the Penitential of Theodore), and Wasserschleben, *Die Bussordnungen der abendländischen Kirche*, 401 and 474 (the Penitentials of Merseburg and of Cummean).

[68] *Laws of the Alamans and the Bavarians*, I: 11, p. 122.

[69] *The Lombard Laws*, Liutprand 30.I, p. 157; 76.VII, pp. 176–77; 95.XII, p. 185.

clothes or her breast, without her leave, the compensation is to be double than that we have established for a lay person."[70]

Despite the legal prohibitions, councils lamented and deplored the fact that monasteries of women were houses of prostitution. The Council of Aachen in 836 held that unchaste nuns might be killed, as the Romans had done with unchaste Vestal Virgins.[71] Indeed, under Abbess Aebbe of Coldingham, according to Bede, decline was so far advanced at the monastery that Cuthberth of Lindisfarne had a long list of complaints. He wrote that

> even the dwellings, which were built for praying and reading, are now converted into places of revelling, drinking, conversation and forbidden doings; the virgins who are vowed to God, laying aside all respect for their profession, whenever they have leisure, spend all their time in weaving fine garments with which they adorn themselves like brides, to the detriment of their condition, and to secure the friendship of men outside.[72]

Notwithstanding the accuracy of these reports, there were many young women who resisted the marriage proposed by their parents. The legend of St. Mildred, who lived around 670, illustrates this. She was sent to Chelles as a young girl, and the abbess Wilcome asked her to marry her kinsman. When she refused, she was cast into a furnace from which she emerged unharmed, and she escaped to England where she founded a settlement in Kent. Her escape from the burning furnace is clearly legendary but perhaps illustrates the heroic attachment that women had to virginity in the early Middle Ages.[73] Self-mutilation—cutting off a nose or an ear to become ugly and unattractive to men—is well illustrated in an article by Jane Tibbetts Schulenburg.[74] I would like to call attention to the Merovingian and Carolingian

---

[70] *English Historical Documents,* I, no. 18, p. 376.

[71] Council of Aachen (836), 2.12, Mansi, 14: 682. It is repeated in Rabanus Maurus' letter from the bishop of Würzburg, *Epist. Fuldiensium fragmenta* 6, MGH, *Epistolae,* 5: 525.

[72] Bede, *Venerabilis Baedae historiam ecclesiasticam gentis Anglorum,* IV, 25, ed. Carolus Plummer (Oxford, 1896), p. 269.

[73] Lina Eckenstein, *Women under Monasticism* (Cambridge, 1896), 86–87; Early English Text Society, *The Lives of Women Saints of Our Countie of England,* ed. Carl Horstmann (London, 1886), 64.

[74] Jane Tibbetts Schulenburg, "The Heroics of Virginity," in *Women in the Middle Ages and the Renaissance,* ed. with intro. by Mary Beth Rose (Syracuse, 1986), 29–72.

saints' lives, among which we find many examples of spiritual resolution. Young virgins of not more than twelve to fourteen years of age defied their parents to avoid wedlock. The father of St. Burgundofara dragged her from a basilica where she had hidden when he wanted to betroth her. The legend surrounding Austroberta follows the same pattern. Apprehensive that her father would force her to get married, Austroberta fled, taking her young brother with her. The courage and inventiveness of these young girls and others like them earned the respect and the sympathy of churchmen.[75]

Other ladies developed psychological illnesses to fend off marriage. For example, St. Gisla, the sister of Charlemagne, terrified that her parents would want to betroth her, developed a fever and swelling of the lymph nodes around the neck.[76] St. Ulphia, an eighth-century recluse, feigned insanity to avoid marriage. In the ninth century, women were more willing to please their parents.[77]

Conclusion

Women were more heavily penalized, even for minor sexual offenses, under the Germanic laws. Sexual acts with the permission of women were punished with exile, slavery, and death. The loss of virginity was a grave sin which detracted from marriageability. Foremost was the consideration that any woman who failed to keep herself chaste, pure, and mindful of conventions that attached to maidenhood, marital status, motherhood, and widowhood, committed a grave social error. Men were allowed to lose their virginity, keep concubines, have sexual adventures even when married, cavort with harlots, and take baths with females. They were punished only if they infringed upon another man's rights. Ideals about sexual purity took shape in the early Middle Ages and dominated the social and intellectual scene of medieval and modern times. It was the duty of the female to uphold and practice the sexual restraint that distinguished the two genders. If they did so, they were praised; those that did not were condemned.

---

[75] Ionas, *Vitae sanctorum: Columbani* 2.7, MGH, *Script. rer. mer.* 4:1, 122; and J. O'Carrol, "Sainte Fare et les origines," in *Sainte Fare et Faremoutiers* (L'Abbey de Faremoutiers, 1956), 4–35. *Vita s. Austrobertae* 7, *Acta Sanctorum* (Paris, 1863–1931) (= *AS*), 10 Feb.; 2, 420.

[76] *De s. Itisberga virgine, AS* 21 Maii; 5, 46b.

[77] See, for example, *De s. Ulphia, AS* 31; Jan. 3, 738.

Rape was a crime, as it is now. A woman had difficulties denouncing the rapist, but her male relatives did not. Even if the abduction was an elopement, that is, it had the girl's consent, her kinsmen could treat the case as a rape. For example, St. Rictrud's brothers, her ninth-century biographer tells us, killed her husband several years after the abduction that was done, I assume, with her agreement, even though by that time the union had produced several children.[78] In a formula drawn up by Marculf, the husband acknowledged that he had endangered his life by uniting himself with his wife by means of a rape against the wishes of her parents.[79] The "Capitula" of King Childebert began with rape. But then it was added that if the woman consented, presumably to fornication, both the man and the woman should be sent into exile.[80]

There were many young women who preferred a female monastery or living at home, a life devoted to God. Women who gave their consent to fornication and adultery were usually married women or widows. If a free woman was attacked by a semi-free man or slave, the man was punished severely. The woman who consented to such an act could remain in servitude with him or could be killed. A man enjoyed his own slave girls and also those of others, if he was willing to pay a relatively small payment. He could also escape an engagement if he had found another girl. If he was powerful, he could humiliate the woman.[81] No such opportunities were available to women. She was regarded as a secondary creature and chattel to men.

For women living in those days, life was not easy. The sexual laws stressed the role of dissent in their lives, but they did not prevent women from finding fulfillment in a variety of sexual and functional roles.

Barnard College

---

[78] Hucbald, *Vita S. Rictrudis,* 1.11, *AS* 12 Maii; 3, 83. Although Rictrud died in 668 and her life was composed in 907, L. Van der Essen, in his *Étude critique et littéraire sur les Vitae des saints mérovingiens de l'ancienne Belgique* (Louvain and Paris, 1907), 261–62, accepts it as reliable.

[79] *Marc. form.*, 2.16; *Form. Salicae Lind.* 16, MGH *Formulae,* 85, 277.

[80] *The Law of the Salian Franks,* "Capitula," VI, II: 2, p. 157.

[81] Paul the Deacon relates in his *History* VI, XXII, that King Aripert caused the wife of Ansprand, Theodorada by name, to be seized. When she boasted with her woman's willfulness that she would get to be queen, she was disfigured in the beauty of her face, her nose and ears being cut off. The sister of Liutprand was also mutilated in this manner.

Implied Consent to Intercourse

JAMES A. BRUNDAGE

When two people consent to marry each other, does this necessarily imply that each of them also agrees to have sexual relations with the other? This question no doubt seems absurdly simple and the answer self-evident.

Lawyers, however, have a knack, which the rest of the world sometimes finds intensely annoying, for discovering problems where everyday common sense might suggest either that none existed or that none ought to exist. And so it is with this question.

If marital consent necessarily implies consent to intercourse, then is that consent unconditional? If not, what limits can one party justifiably impose upon the other's lusts and passions? Is consent to intercourse, in fact, an essential element of marriage at all? Is an unconsummated marriage really a marriage? And if a marriage has been consummated, can one party subsequently deny sexual access to the other without rupturing the marriage agreement? Can a husband lawfully demand sexual favors from his wife at any time, in any place, under any circumstances? If not, when is the wife justified in refusing to have sex? If the wife denies her husband sexual relations, does he then have the right to force her to submit to his attentions against her will? If so, does the law set any limits to the brutality he may employ? Can he hit her with his fists? What if he uses a club? Or ties her down with his belt? And how far can the wife lawfully go in resisting his attack? Is it acceptable for her to scratch his eyes or kick him in the groin? What if she uses an axe? Or a butcher knife? Or a .44 magnum? These questions may be, and in real

245

life all too often are, terrifying, immediate, dangerous, and sometimes deadly.

Solutions to these issues are by no means obvious or self-evident, nor have all societies at all times agreed upon what answers seem most appropriate. My aim is to explore some solutions to questions of this kind that a few eminent medieval lawyers hammered out in the high Middle Ages, during the classical age of Western canon law. I shall restrict myself to the canonists, since for numerous reasons they were the jurists who concerned themselves most often and most explicitly with these problems. The problems seem worth exploring for two principal reasons: first because the answers may respond to some important issues in the history of Western society and social values during the Middle Ages. And second because they may also tell us something about our own society, which is descended from that one and which, as children have a way of doing, is at once quite different from, and yet bears an uncanny resemblance to, its forebears.

The question of whether consent to marriage necessarily implies consent to sexual intercourse lies close to the heart of the difficulties that medieval canonists experienced when they tried to define what marriage was and how a marital union came into being. In the mid-twelfth century, just after the appearance of Gratian's *Decretum* (ca. 1140) and the *Sententiae* (1155–58) of Peter Lombard (d. 1160), three views on the formation of marriage were current among Western jurists. The first, taught by the Bolognese (or Italian) school, insisted that marriage was a two-stage process that began with consent and was completed by physical consummation. According to the Bolognese way of thinking, then, coitus was an essential element and without sexual union there was no binding marriage contract.[1] This was Gratian's own position on the matter, and the Bolognese decretists who commented on his text championed the master's views.[2]

---

[1] The central texts occur in the *Decretum* of Gratian at C. 27 q. 2; this and the rest of the *Corpus iuris canonici* will be cited throughout from the standard edition in 2 vols. by Emil Friedberg (Leipzig, 1879; repr. Graz, 1959). For a more extended analysis of the Bolognese teaching, see James A. Brundage, *Law, Sex, and Christian Society in Medieval Europe* (Chicago, 1987), 235–39.

[2] Notably Paucapalea, *Summa* to D. 17 q. 1 pr. and C. 27 q. 2, ed. Johann Friedrich von Schulte (Giessen, 1890), pp. 112–14; Rolandus, *Summa* to C. 27 pr. and q. 2 c. 5, 16–17, 33–34, 50, ed. Friedrich Thaner (Innsbruck, 1874), pp. 114, 127, 129, 131–33; and Rufinus, *Summa* to C. 27 pr., ed. Heinrich Singer (Paderborn, 1902; repr. Aalen, 1963), pp. 430–32.

The Parisian (or French) school, in contrast, adopted the views of Peter Lombard, who taught that consent alone created marriage and that the contract was complete and valid the instant a couple exchanged present consent. In this scheme of things, therefore, sexual consummation was almost a tangential issue, irrelevant to the existence of a valid marriage.[3]

A third view, held by Master Vacarius (d. ca. 1205) and the anonymous author of the *Summa Coloniensis,* rejected both of these theories. Instead, Vacarius and a few others held that the essential element in marriage was neither consent nor consummation, but rather the physical delivery (*traditio*) of the bride to the groom.[4] This third theory of marriage, however, failed to find much favor in the law schools and soon faded from view.

The legal elite of the Western church continued to debate the merits of these differing theories about the formation of marriage during the 1150s, 60s, and 70s until ultimately a decretal of Pope Alexander III (1159–81) in a marriage case that arose around 1180 seemed to put an end to the matter. Alexander's decision came down on the side of the Parisian school. In the decretal known from its opening words as *Veniens ad nos,* the pope ruled that

---

[3] Peter Lombard, *Libri IV Sententiarum* 4.27.2–5 and 4.28.3, 3rd ed., Spicilegium Bonaventurianum, vols. 4–5 (Grottaferrata, 1971–81), II, 422–24. One of the earliest canonistic commentators to adopt the Lombard's view was the anonymous author of the *Summa Parisiensis* at D. 34 c. 19; C. 30 q. 5 pr.; C. 32 q. 2 pr.; C. 32 q. 7 c. 18, ed. Terence P. McLaughlin (Toronto, 1952), pp. 33–34, 237, 241, and 248. See also the glosses of a commentator known simply as "The Cardinal" (*Cardinalis*) to C. 27 q. 2 d.p.c. 39 v. *uel effectum;* C. 27 q. 2 c. 35 v. *quam confirmat,* ed. Rudolf Weigand, "Die Glossen des Cardinalis (Magister Hubald?) zum Dekret Gratians," *Bulletin of Medieval Canon Law* (hereafter *BMCL*) 3 (1973), 76, 78, 80. In addition, Johannes Faventinus, *Summa* to C. 27 q. 1 pr. and C. 27 q. 2 pr., in London, British Library (hereafter B.L.) MS Royal 9.E.VII, fol. 131vb and 134ra; Sicard of Cremona, *Summa* to C. 27 pr., in B.L. MS Add. 18,367, fol. 53v; and the glosses of Gandulphus to C. 27 q. 2 c. 17 v. *nuptiale ministerium* and C. 27 q. 2 pr., ed. Rudolf Weigand, "Gandulphusglossen zum Dekret Gratians," *BMCL* 7 (1977), 28, 32.

[4] Vacarius, *Summa de matrimonio,* ed. Frederic William Maitland, in *Law Quarterly Review* 13 (1897), 133–43, 270–87, at 270–71, 276, 278, 280. The marriage sections of the *Summa Coloniensis* have not been published, but see Maitland's introduction to his edition of Vacarius' *Summa* at 137, as well as Stephan Kuttner and Eleanor Rathbone, "Anglo-Norman Canonists of the Twelfth Century: An Introductory Study," *Traditio* 7 (1949–51), 279–358 at 300, reprinted in Kuttner's *Gratian and the Schools of Law* (London, 1983) with identical pagination, and Adhémar Esmein, *Le mariage en droit canonique,* 2 vols. (Paris, 1891; repr. New York, 1968), I, 114 note 3 and 118 note 1.

couples could contract valid marriages in two equally valid ways. Either they might freely and voluntarily agree to marry at once, in which case the pope held that they were married the instant that they exchanged mutual consent couched in the present tense, or else they might freely and voluntarily agree to marry at some future time, in which case their marriage became effective the next time that they had sexual intercourse, which in effect ratified the earlier exchange of verbal consent. In either situation, Pope Alexander held, consent was the essential element in the marriage, and, once a couple had firmly consented to marry, they were bound together in matrimony so long as both parties lived.[5]

Pope Alexander's decision in *Veniens ad nos* became the ruling authority in Western marriage law throughout the rest of the Middle Ages and to the close of the Council of Trent in 1563.[6] But the decretal left numerous important issues unresolved, among them the role of sexual consummation in the creation of marriage and the questions that I wish to address here, namely, whether marital consent necessarily implied consent to sexual intercourse and whether that consent, once given, was irrevocable.

Although Pope Alexander held in *Veniens ad nos* that marital consent was the crucial element in determining whether a couple was validly married or not, some of his other decretals showed that he nonetheless considered that sexual consummation involved important legal consequences. Thus Alexander ruled in other cases that when fundamental changes in the relationship between a couple occurred after they had exchanged consent but before they had consummated their union, church courts might declare the contracted but unconsummated marriage null and void.[7]

---

[5] X 4.1.15. This decretal unfortunately is undated. It is addressed to Bishop John of Norwich and must therefore have been written after 26 November 1175, when John of Oxford was elected bishop of Norwich, and before 11 August 1181, when Alexander III died. See also Charles Donahue, Jr., "The Dating of Alexander the Third's Marriage Decretals: Dauvillier Revisited after Fifty Years," *Zeitschrift der Savigny-Stiftung für Rechtsgeschichte,* Kanonistische Abteilung 68 (1982), 70–124 at 81, 105–15.

[6] Indeed, it endured in many regions long after 1563; in England, for example, until the Marriage Act of 1753, and in many regions of the United States until late in the 19th century; see my study "Roman Law, Canon Law, and the Law of Marriage in the United States," forthcoming in *Aufstieg und Niedergang der römischen Welt.*

[7] X 4.11.2 and 4.13.2. See also my further observations in "Marriage and Sexuality in the Decretals of Pope Alexander III," in *Miscellanea Rolando Bandinelli Papa Alessandro III,* ed. Filippo Liotta (Siena, 1986), 59–83.

Such a situation might arise, for example, if one of the marriage partners contracted leprosy. In a case in which a husband had contracted leprosy after consummating his marriage, Alexander III held that his wife was bound to remain with him and to minister to him "with marital affection," a phrase that certainly implies that sexual relations were to continue.[8] Likewise in another case, where the wife became a leper, Alexander also ruled that her husband must go with her to the *leprosarium* and must continue to give her sexual solace on demand.[9] In both of these leprosy cases, however, the pope clearly indicated that the obligation to remain with the stricken spouse arose because the couple had consummated their marriage and thus owed each other the conjugal debt.

The conjugal debt doctrine was theologically based upon St. Paul's injunction to husbands and wives that each must pay the other what was owed to them, and the Apostle's further observation that each partner had power over the other's body (1 Cor. 7:3–4). When twelfth- and thirteenth-century jurists contemplated these statements, they sought to fit them, naturally enough, into the context of the Roman law of obligations.[10] Gratian and later canonists accordingly elaborated a complex doctrine of marital debt in order to specify quite precisely the sexual rights and duties of married couples.[11]

The conjugal debt came into being, according to Gratian, the instant that a couple consummated their marriage. Prior to that, the parties had no sexual obligation to each other and in Gratian's view the exchange of marital consent was insufficient in itself to create such an obligation. Once sexual intercourse occurred following the exchange of consent, however, a mutual obligation of continuing sexual service sprang into being. Thenceforth each spouse was bound to render sexual service to the other upon demand. This obligation,

---

[8] X 4.8.1. On the notion of marital affection, see John T. Noonan, Jr., "Marital Affection in the Canonists," *Studia Gratiana* 12 (1967), 479–509.

[9] X 4.8.2.

[10] *Debitum* and *obligatio* are not necessarily the same, and early Roman practice apparently distinguished between them. The classical jurists with whom medieval canonists were familiar, however, did not draw this distinction, which had become obsolete long before their time. See W. W. Buckland, *A Text-Book of Roman Law from Augustus to Justinian,* 3rd ed. rev. by Peter Stein (Cambridge, 1966; corrected repr., 1975), 406–7; Barry Nicholas, *An Introduction to Roman Law* (Oxford, 1962; corrected repr., 1975), 159.

[11] See particularly Elizabeth Makowski, "The Conjugal Debt and Medieval Canon Law," *Journal of Medieval History* 3 (1977), 99–114.

Gratian believed, was absolute: it made no difference, at least in principle, where, when, or under what circumstances the demand was made—the spouse from whom the debt was required had to comply.[12]

The decretists, that is to say, the teachers who sought to explain Gratian's text to law students, felt bound to accept the teaching of the authorities whom Gratian cited on this matter, but also attempted to explore the implications of marital consent doctrine more fully. They often examined hypothetical situations in order to do this—a favorite strategy of law teachers, then and now. Thus, for example, if one spouse, say the husband, demanded payment of the conjugal debt on a day when church law forbade marital intercourse (during Lent, for instance), did the spouse who complied with the request (in this case, the wife) commit a sin by doing so? Answers differed. The majority concluded that the spouse who complied did so under duress—the wife, in my example, might reasonably fear that she would offend God in either case, but that if she refused, then not only God but also her husband would be angry with her—and this, they reasoned, excused her from the guilt she might otherwise have incurred by having sexual relations during the penitential season. The husband in this situation surely sinned by making the demand, but the wife was guiltless for complying with it.[13]

Other decretists, however, took issue with the majority position. Master Rolandus (ca. 1150?)[14] went so far as to credit the partner who rendered the debt at the other's request with a positively meritorious action, but none of his peers seemed prepared to adopt that position.[15] Johannes Faventinus (d. ca. 1187) expressed a more common view when he held that rendering the

---

[12] Thus C. 27 q. 2 d.p.c. 26 and d.p.c. 28; C. 32 q. 2 d.p.c. 2; and C. 33 q. 5 d.p.c. 11.

[13] Thus, e.g., Rolandus, *Summa* to C. 27 pr., C. 28 q. 1 c. 15 v. *prima coniugii fides,* ed. Thaner, pp. 114, 140–41; Rufinus, *Summa* to C. 27 q. 2 c. 9 v. *a prima fide desponsationis,* ed. Singer, p. 450.

[14] Contrary to common opinion, this Master Rolandus was almost certainly not Rolandus Bandinelli, the future Pope Alexander III; John T. Noonan, Jr., "Who Was Rolandus?" in *Law, Church, and Society: Essays in Honor of Stephan Kuttner,* ed. Kenneth Pennington and Robert Somerville (Philadelphia, 1977), 21–48; Rudolf Weigand, "Magister Rolandus und Papst Alexander III.," *Archiv für katholisches Kirchenrecht* 149 (1980), 3–44.

[15] Rolandus, *Summa* to C. 33 q. 5 c. 1 v. *pro sanctificatione perfecta,* ed. Thaner, p. 197: "Quasi diceret: non solum non punieris, sed imputabitur tibi ad coronam."

marital debt did not confer positive merit, but simply avoided the penalties that refusing it would entail.[16] Huguccio (d. 1210) stood at the opposite end of the spectrum of opinion on this issue when he asserted that in our hypothetical situation both parties sinned. The husband who demanded sex sinned mightily: not only was he seeking something that by its very nature was sinful, but in addition his sin was compounded by the circumstance of seeking intercourse during Lent. Further, his wife also sinned, although only venially, by acceding to his demand because, as Huguccio saw things, sex was always pleasurable and the experience of pleasure must invariably be sinful.[17]

Discussions of the matter by the twelfth-century decretists established a core of doctrine concerning marital consent whose central tenets remained unchanged for roughly three-and-a-half centuries. That discussion, moreover, has left a lasting imprint on subsequent marriage law throughout the Western world.

The consensus that had emerged by about 1200 centered the formation of marriage on free consent by the parties to an agreement to live together and to share property and other resources between themselves for the balance of their natural lives. This agreement further created an implied obligation on each party to refrain from sexual activity with any third party.

But while consent alone created a marriage bond between the spouses, it did not by itself create sexual rights. Sexual rights at that stage were separable from marital rights. It took a completed act of sexual intercourse between the parties subsequent to the exchange of marital consent to create the conjugal debt, from which sexual rights arose. Once the marriage had been consummated, then (but not before) each party acquired virtually unlimited rights to demand and receive the sexual services of the other. Failure to perform on demand could in principle, and sometimes in practice as well, subject the defaulter to sanctions in the ecclesiastical courts.[18] It is in fact not

---

[16] Johannes Faventinus, *Summa* to C. 32 q. 2 d.p.c. 4 v. *non datur presentia sancti,* in B.L. MS Royal 9.E.VII, fol. 142vb, quoted in Brundage, *Law, Sex, and Christian Society,* 283 note 116.

[17] Huguccio, *Summa* to D. 13 pr. v. *item aduersus,* in Vat. lat. 2280, fol. 12ra–b, and Cambridge, Pembroke College MS 72, fol. 124va–b, quoted in Brundage, *Law, Sex, and Christian Society,* 283 note 117.

[18] Thus Simon of Bisignano, *Summa* to C. 27 q. 2 in B.L. MS Add. 24,659, fol. 29va–b: "Item queritur si sponsa sponso debitum reddere compellatur, et dicemus eam non cogi ad soluendum debitum antequam fit, secus una caro effecta. Primo ergo

uncommon to find in the records parties who come before canonical judges to petition for restoration of conjugal rights, which certainly included availability for sexual service on demand.[19] It seems highly likely, however, that in many, perhaps most, of these cases the underlying issue was desertion, rather than denial of sexual service, and that suits for the restoration of conjugal rights provided a procedural method for securing a court order requiring the wandering spouse to return. By the late fourteenth century even spouses formally separated from bed and board (*a mense et thoro*) by court order might be required to treat each other with marital affection and to pay the conjugal debt. Thus a canonical court decreed in one separation order: "We hold the defendant bound to pay the conjugal debt to the plaintiff in her father's house one night each week and to keep this obligation faithfully, until we shall order otherwise."[20]

It may seem inconsistent with the view that the marriage debt arose only in consequence of consummation that canonical judges nevertheless granted annulment of marriages when one party complained and was able to prove to the judge's satisfaction that consummation had never taken place because of the incapacity of the other party to engage in sexual relations. In impotence and frigidity cases, the issue of implied consent to sexual relations comes sharply into focus.

It is obvious that the theory of marriage formation championed by Gratian and the masters of the Bolognese school would render an unconsummated marriage incomplete and imperfect.[21] Marital intercourse, in their

---

coitus gratie est, non debiti. . . . A fide uero carnalis commixtionis debent sibi mutuam seruitutem corporis, unde postquam fuerunt una caro effecti, nullus sine consensu alterius potest uel seruare continentiam uel ad religionem transire. . . ." See also Bernard of Parma, *Glossa ordinaria* to X 2.13.8 v. *et ab eo cognita*. The *glos. ord.*, i.e., the standard interpretation of passages in the various books of canon law taught in medieval law faculties, is cited here from the printed edition of the *Corpus iuris canonici* in 4 vols. (Venice, 1605).

[19] For some examples see Richard H. Helmholz, *Marriage Litigation in Medieval England* (Cambridge, 1974), 67–69.

[20] "Dicimus ream teneri ad reddendum debitum coniugale actori in domo patris una nocte semel in hebdomada adhibita fideli custodia quousque aliter ordinabimus." Quoted in Anne Lefebvre-Teillard, *Les officialités à la veille du Concile de Trente*, Bibliothèque d'histoire du droit et droit romain 19 (Paris, 1973), 199 note 265.

[21] Gratian, C. 27 q. 2 c. 19–26 and d.p.c. 26.

view, was an essential element in creating a marriage and hence any exchange of marital consent necessarily implied consent to physical consummation. If one party became impotent following consummation, the marriage nonetheless remained binding. If, however, one partner proved from the outset incapable of sexual relations and it could be proved that in consequence the marriage was never consummated, church courts could pronounce that union void and the partners (or at least the partner who was not sexually incapacitated) could then remarry.[22]

For the masters of the Parisian school, however, and all later canonists who had to work within the framework established by *Veniens ad nos,* the matter was more complex. In apparent contradiction to the marriage formation doctrine embodied in *Veniens ad nos,* Alexander III ruled in other decretals that incapacity to consummate rendered marital consent null.[23] The Parisian decretists had, in fact, anticipated the difficulty of reconciling a consensual theory of marriage formation with the well-established practice of treating marriages that could not be consummated because of impotence as invalid. Stephen of Tournai (d. 1203) reasoned in his *Summa* (ca. 1160) that the grounds for nullifying such marriages must be that consent to them had been predicated upon an erroneous belief that the impotent spouse would be able to have sexual relations. Since consent had been based upon a faulty assumption, he argued, discovery of the error invalidated marital consent and hence the marriage could be canceled.[24] Johannes Faventinus agreed and added the further possibility that deliberate deceit could also be a factor in such cases.[25] Huguccio's analysis of the problem was more nuanced, since he took into account situations where impotence arose from mental incapacity

---

[22] Gratian, C. 27 q. 2 d.p.c. 28, c. 29 and d.p.c. 29.

[23] X 4.2.9; 4.15.2–4; and see above, note 7.

[24] Stephen of Tournai, *Summa* to C. 33 q. 1 pr., ed. Johann Friedrich von Schulte (Giessen, 1891; repr. Aalen, 1965), pp. 245–46.

[25] Johannes Faventinus, *Summa* to C. 27 q. 2 d.p.c. 28 v. *uel his qui aduersariis,* in B.L. Royal 9.E.VII, fol. 135vb: "In frigidis autem alium erat et aliud putabatur. Nam si qua mulier ei quem posse reddere debitum crederet, cum reddere non posset, deciperetur et erraret et immo matrimonium a principio non constaret quo ad deum; et si ignoranter castrato nupsisset mihi uidetur hec ratio potius esse contra eos quam pro eis." See also *Quaestiones Cusanae,* no. 16, ed. Gérard Fransen, "Les Quaestiones Cusanae: Questions disputées sur le mariage," in *Convivium utriusque iuris: A. Dordett zum 60. Geburtstag* (Vienna, 1976), 215–16.

or age, rather than some innate physical inability to engage in sex.[26] In dealing with physical incapacity, both congenital and acquired, however, he followed the reasoning of the Parisian decretists and defended declarations of nullity in these situations on the grounds of error of consent.[27]

A few writers, to be sure, expressed reservations about the practice of declaring marriage to an impotent spouse invalid. Laurentius Hispanus (writing ca. 1210–15) and Tancredus (d. 1236), for example, denied that the pope had the power to terminate unconsummated marriages and maintained that decretals that claimed to exercise such a power were in error.[28] Theirs, however, proved to be the minority position. Other writers, such as Alanus Anglicus (fl. ca. 1210), Vincentius Hispanus (d. 1248), John of Tynemouth (fl. 1188–ca. 1221), and Johannes Teutonicus (writing ca. 1215), viewed papal power over unconsummated unions more benignly, and their position finally prevailed. All of these authors agreed that the pope could, indeed, properly declare unconsummated marriages invalid and permit one or even both parties to enter a new union in which they might be able to have intercourse successfully with a new partner.[29] None of these writers, however, explicitly stated that consent to marriage necessarily implied consent to intercourse.

Writers who adopted the majority position probably felt uneasy at the prospect of grounding their conclusions, at least overtly, on a theory of implied consent to sexual union because that would conflict with another traditional canonical teaching, well-attested in Gratian's work: that married couples could, under some circumstances, separate and abandon their mar-

---

[26] Huguccio, *Summa* to C. 33 q. 1 pr., in Admont, Stiftsbibliothek, MS 7, fol. 381ra, quoted in my study "Impotence, Frigidity and Marital Nullity in the Decretists and Early Decretalists," in *Proceedings of the Seventh International Congress of Medieval Canon Law,* ed. Peter Linehan, Monumenta iuris canonici, Subsidia 8 (Vatican City, 1988), pp. 407–23 at 416 note 36.

[27] Huguccio, *Summa* to C. 32 q. 7 c. 18 and C. 33 q. 1 pr., in J. Roman, "Summa d'Huguccio sur le Décret de Gratien d'après le manuscrit 3891 de la Bibliothèque Nationale, causa XXVII, questio II," *Revue historique de droit français et étranger,* 3rd ser., 27 (1903), 763, 765, 783.

[28] Tancredus, *Apparatus* to 2 Comp. 3.20.2 v. *contumelia* and Laurentius, *Apparatus* to 2 Comp. 3.20.2 v. *et liber aditus,* both quoted by Rudolf Weigand, "Unauflösigkeit der Ehe und Eheauflösungen durch Päpste im 12. Jahrhundert," *Revue de droit canonique* 20 (1970), 44–64 at 58–59.

[29] All quoted by Weigand, "Unauflösigkeit," 54–55, 62.

riages in order to enter the religious life. Writers of the Parisian and Bolognese schools differed, however, over what those circumstances might be. The Italian school held that so long as the marriage remained unconsummated, one party could unilaterally decide to terminate the marital relationship in order to embrace the religious life.[30] If the marriage had been consummated, according to these authors, both partners must agree to part ways; in addition, both must agree to take vows of chastity and enter a religious community.[31] The French school of thought, on the other hand, was prepared to permit unilateral separation only following the exchange of future consent and prior to consummation. After the exchange of present consent, or alternatively after the consummation of a future consent marriage, mutual agreement to part ways became essential and both partners must vow continence.[32]

The canonistic texts thus show that both the French and the Italian schools assumed that when a couple married and consummated their union physically through an act of sexual congress, consent to that first act of marital intercourse implicitly carried with it unconditional consent to future intercourse at the will of either party through the remainder of their natural lives. This implied consent to future intercourse, moreover, could be revoked only by mutual agreement, followed by the entrance of both parties into religious life or at the very least by vows of perpetual chastity.

Modern common law and civil law traditions have both inherited these teachings from the medieval canonists in slightly modified form. The traditional doctrine that marriage entails virtually unlimited rights to the sexual services of the spouse and that those rights cannot be revoked so long as the marriage endures underlies and justifies what we now call spousal rape. In most parts of the United States, for example, marriage between the parties provides defendants with an affirmative defense against charges of rape and most other kinds of sexual abuse. A handful of states—among them California, Delaware, Florida, Iowa, Minnesota, New Jersey, and Oregon—have

---

[30] Gratian C. 27 q. 2 c. 27–28 and d.p.c. 28.

[31] Gratian C. 27 q. 2 c. 19–26 and d.p.c. 26; Paucapalea, *Summa* to C. 27 q. 2 c. 34, ed. Schulte, pp. 114–15; Rolandus, *Summa* to C. 27 q. 2 c. 19–26, ed. Thaner, p. 130; Rufinus, *Summa* to C. 27 q. 2 pr., ed. Singer, pp. 440–41.

[32] Stephen of Tournai, *Summa* to C. 27 q. 2 and to C. 13 v. *ad matrimonium*, ed. Schulte, pp. 236–37; Gandulphus, gloss to C. 27 q. 2 d.p.c. 26 v. *ecce* and to c. 19 v. *prohibuit*, in Weigand, "Gandulphusglossen," 29, 33.

explicitly repealed this so-called spousal exclusion by statute. Elsewhere, however, the doctrine that marriage implies practically unlimited sexual access by each party to the body of the other has continued in force.[33] This remains, in my view, one of the less fortunate residues of our heritage from medieval canon law.

University of Kansas

[33] For details see the survey of rape law in *Women's Rights Law Reporter* 6 (1980), Supp. 3.

Consent and the Marital Debt:
Five Discourses in Northern France
around 1200

JOHN W. BALDWIN

In an influential study Georges Duby evoked the *History of the Counts of Guines* by Lambert d'Ardres to construct a model of aristocratic marriage for northeastern France in the twelfth century.[1] Noble families like the counts of Guines and the lords of Ardres employed the institution of matrimony to assemble, preserve, and transmit the lands upon which their political and social power rested. Because of these patrimonial preoccupations, the marriage of all women in the family was strictly arranged by the eldest males of the clan, be they fathers, uncles, or sons without fathers. The ultimate goal was to engender legitimate children through whom property could be retained and transmitted within the family. A son could occasionally assume the initiative and obtain a bride on his own by means of abduction or seduction. Although daughters and other women pertaining to the family were permitted a semblance of consent to the arrangements of their menfolk, their underlying

---

[1] Georges Duby, *Medieval Marriage: Two Models from Twelfth-Century France*, trans. Elborg Forster (Baltimore, 1978), 83–110. Subsequent versions in *Le Chevalier, la femme et le prêtre: Le mariage dans la France féodale* (Paris, 1981), 269–300; English translation by Barbara Bray, *The Knight, the Lady, and the Priest: The Making of Modern Marriage in Medieval France* (New York, 1983), 253–84.

duty was nonetheless to submit to these decisions. In the presence of a large crowd in her father's house, for example, the bride of the count of Guines "expressed her willingness by the happy expression on her face." Students of gender have characterized these arrangements of male dominance as "sexual asymmetry."[2] Before marriage and after the death of their wives, aristocratic men were free to indulge in numerous extramarital liaisons, producing, in the case of the counts of Guines, at least five bastards. All women, however, were closely surveilled to protect their virginity before marriage and their chastity thereafter. Duby's source did not permit him to describe the sexual relations within marriage, but in view of masculine predominance over all other marital decisions, it would be surprising if the wife was not expected to submit unreservedly to the sexual appetites of her husband. The countess of Guines died exhausted on the birth of her tenth recorded child. This gender asymmetry of the aristocratic family could be further exacerbated by other disparities of age, wealth, and social status. It is not my intent to assess the historical validity of Duby's model, but its underlying functions nonetheless seem to be plausible for aristocratic society.

Against the powerful forces skewing the balance between the sexes, churchmen attempted to introduce elements of gender symmetry into the Christian definition of marriage. James Brundage has recounted the efforts of the canonists to define the essence of matrimony not as consummation but as free consent given by both spouses. Jenny Jochens shows that female consent became the distinctive hallmark of Christian marriage in the newly converted world of the Norse.[3] The canonists may have chosen consent over consummation because the former was more susceptible to proof in a court of law than the latter and thereby facilitated the certifying and legalizing of individual marriages. (*Verba de presenti* publicly exchanged before witnesses could be better demonstrated than sexual intimacies performed privately.) Whatever the reason, however, the insistence on mutual consent introduced a patently artificial symmetry into the pervasive asymmetrical relations between the sexes in early medieval Europe.

---

[2] For some examples of the use of the concept of gender symmetry/asymmetry, see *Sexual Meanings: The Cultural Construction of Gender and Sexuality,* ed. Sherry B. Ortner and Harriet Whitehead (Cambridge, 1981), ix; Gerda Lerner, *The Creation of Patriarchy* (New York, 1986), 16–18; and Joan Wallach Scott, *Gender and the Politics of History* (New York, 1988), 4.

[3] For Brundage see above, pp. 245–56; for Jochens see below, pp. 271–89.

In canonist doctrine, moreover, matrimony, once consummated, created a second and discrete set of mutual obligations called the marital debt (*debitum*), whereby married partners were required to respond fully to each other's sexual demands. Falling equally on husband and wife, these obligations could be abrogated only by mutual agreement. Characteristic of the legal métier, the lawyers' discussions became absorbed with possible exceptions to this regime caused by unusual circumstances such as impotence, disease, and religious vocation, because such peripheral matters were those that invariably appeared in their courts for adjudication.[4] In fact, however, the canonists had constructed a second symmetrical relationship between spouses that resisted the imbalance of patriarchal society, but it was less clear how the factor of obligation to engage in sexual relations affected the consent of both partners.

I would like to focus on how the marital debt might have been understood to operate under normal conditions for most couples (those who rarely appear in court) and how it conditioned the canonistic norm of mutual consent. Proceeding beyond the ratiocinations of the lawyers, I shall inquire into the perception of the marital debt in other discourses. In particular I propose to recapture a historical moment around 1200 in northern France when five discourses (three in Latin, two in the vernacular) converged, each with a prominent spokesman articulating a discrete tradition. The five consist of: (1) theologians at Paris such as Peter the Chanter and his students Robert of Courson and Thomas of Chobham, who represented the Augustinian tradition and closely approximated the position of the canonists; (2) the physicians of the *Prose Salernitan Questions* of northern France and England who adopted the medical doctrines of the ancient authority Galen revived at Salerno since the eleventh century; (3) the enigmatic Andreas Capellanus and the anonymous author of the vernacular commentaries to Ovid who carried on the Ovidian Latin traditions established in the clerical schools; (4) the vernacular *romancier* Jean Renart from northeastern France who wrote courtly romances, a genre recently created by the Tristan legend, Marie de France, and Chrétien de Troyes; and (5) the authors of the vernacular *fabliaux* who had begun to reduce to writing stories perhaps derived from more ancient folkloric traditions. Although the contemporary Jean Bodel of Arras is the earliest of the *fableors,* his corpus is too limited to suit our purposes. I shall therefore

---

[4] In addition to Brundage (above), see Elizabeth M. Makowski, "The Conjugal Debt and Canon Law," *Journal of Medieval History* 3 (1977), 99–114.

turn to other similar and near contemporary *fabliaux* that address our questions.[5]

Although it is unlikely that any individual from these five sets of spokesmen knew the others, they were contemporary neighbors and shared a common historical culture. Speaking for different traditions, they also addressed different audiences. The theologians and physicians wrote for the clerics of the schools learned in Latin as well as the clergy at large. Andreas Capellanus and the anonymous translator and commentator of Ovid bridged the span between the classical traditions of the Latin schools and the recently emerging vernacular literature of the aristocratic courts. The writers of vernacular romance, although possibly clerics themselves, also wrote for these distinctly aristocratic audiences. The *fableors* faced much more diverse audiences ranging from the lower aristocracy through the bourgeoisie. Until our period the Latin of monks and clerics had been the sole medium for discussing matters pertaining to marriage and sexuality. Now for the first time in Western Europe we are able to breach the linguistic barrier between the clergy and the laity and to hear distinctive lay voices. Indeed, for the first time we are able to listen to the laity themselves talking about marriage and sexuality—that function which defined them socially and lay at the heart of their identity.

Unequivocal gender symmetry received its most forceful expression in the original Pauline text of 1 Cor. 7:3–4: "The husband should give to his wife her conjugal rights (*debitum*), and likewise the wife to her husband. For the wife does not rule over her body, but the husband does; likewise the husband does not rule over his body but the wife does." Even the formulation of the passage served to emphasize the principle of complete reciprocity. The place of the husband in the first sentence is exchanged for that of the wife in the second. Glossing this text, Peter the Chanter elaborated further: "In this the man and woman are equal, even though the husband's lordship is not thereby eliminated."[6] In other words, sexual relations constituted a privileged

---

[5] For an introduction to the five discourses and a sketch of a larger project investigating sexuality and gender in northern France around the year 1200, see my "Five Discourses on Desire: Sexuality and Gender in Northern France around 1200," *Speculum* 66 (1991), 797–819.

[6] Commentary to 1 Cor. 7:3: "In hoc enim pares sunt vir et mulier nec in hoc tollitur viro dominium in muliere sed vicium." Peter the Chanter, Paris, Bibliothèque Mazarine, MS lat. 176, fol. 180rb.

realm within the normal regime of dominance of husbands over wives. Thomas of Chobham explained that wedlock was called *matrimonium* rather than *patrimonium* because in generating, carrying, and nourishing children, the mother bears more burdens than the father. Most properly, however, the institution should be called *coniugium* because it pertains equally to men and women.[7] Like the canonists, the Chanter and Robert of Courson accepted the four Augustinian reasons for which sexual intercourse was justified in marriage: progeny, the marital debt, avoiding incontinence, and fulfilling sexual desire. Unlike the canonists, however, the Parisian theologians had no doubts that the marital debt along with progeny could be served without any sin whatsoever.[8] So absolute were marital rights that Robert, unlike the canonists, did not hesitate to give them precedence over compromising circumstances. If a wife, for example, sought to have intercourse on Easter or Good Friday—an extreme case because these were the two days on which abstinence was most strictly enjoined—the husband could not refuse her request, even if it were only suggested by gesture or the tone of voice.[9] James Brundage has argued that, according to canonist theory, when couples consented to marry and had consummated their union, the initial consent implied un-

---

[7] Thomas of Chobham, *Summa confessorum,* ed. F. Broomfield, Analecta mediaevalia Namurcensia 25 (Louvain, 1968), 145.

[8] For Peter the Lombard's assembling of Augustine's statements on the "final causes" of marriage, see *Sententiae in IV libris distinctae,* 4, 30, 3; 4, 31, 5; 4, 32, 1; ed. [Quarrachi], Spicilegium Bonaventurianum 5 (Grottaferrata, 1981), II, 441, 446–47, 451–52; ed. J.-P. Migne, Patrologia latina, cols. 918, 920, 922. For a discussion of the theologians preceding and including the Lombard, see Hans Zeimentz, *Ehe nach der Lehre der Frühscholastik,* Moraltheologische Studien, Historische Abteilung 1 (Düsseldorf, 1973), 147–62. Prominent among the canonists was Huguccio, who believed that the sexual act could never be immune from sin. See James A. Brundage, *Law, Sex, and Christian Society in Medieval Europe* (Chicago, 1987), 281–82.

[9] "An peccabit vir in festivis diebus vel noctibus si cognoscat uxorem, et si uxor petat instanter in die pasche vel passionis dominice, debet ei denegare debitum. . . . Solutio . . . Sed tamen si aliter uter instanter petat debitum vel voce vel signis sed relitus est ydoneus vel potest reddere, non potest ei quod suum est negare iuxta illud apostoli [1 Cor. 7:4]. . . . Si autem illa dissentiat et debitum petat, non est in potestate vir negare." Robert of Courson, *Summa* XLII, 31, 32, Paris Bibliothèque Nationale MS lat. 14524, fol. 155vb, 156ra. Compare this with the canonists cited by Brundage (note 8).

conditional consent to all future intercourse. The theologians at Paris did not explicitly treat the effects of the marital debt following consent in their discussion, but by insisting on complete reciprocity they assumed, in all likelihood, that the mutuality of the marital debt did not debilitate the original consent to marry.

The absolute symmetry of the theologians' doctrine of the marital debt received positive reinforcement from the contemporary physicians. The *Prose Salernitan Questions* accepted the Hippocratic-Galenic theory that women, as well as men, possessed testicles which produced seed necessary for reproduction. The emission of seed, moreover, depended on the experience of sexual desire, both for women and for men. In perfect reciprocity, conception could not take place unless the man and the woman felt desire and emitted seed which joined to produce the fetus.[10] The *Questions* defined coitus as "the natural and voluntary union of a man and a woman in which sperm is emitted, a fetus produced, to the accompaniment of great delight."[11] Added to the reciprocity was the explicit term "voluntary," which confirmed the element of mutual consent.

Implicit in the physicians' two-seed theory was the simultaneous emission of both male and female seed to bring about conception. Since desire was requisite to the emission of seed, both partners had to become aroused at the same time. Although the *Prose Salernitan Questions* were little interested in sexual techniques, they did take note of the advantages of simultaneous climaxes in coitus as they dealt with the humoral complexions of women. (The context of this discussion was provided by prostitutes of whose sexuality the physicians were best informed.) After showing how women with cold and moist complexions needed to be warmed by vigorous lovemaking, the discussion passed to coital techniques. If the task (*officium*) of each partner is exercised and completed at the same time (*simul*) so that neither anticipates or delays the climax (*celebratio*), such delight follows that sex is repeatedly and frequently sought. To the symmetry of the reproductive anatomy in the male-female testicles and of the physiology in the two seeds the physicians added the necessity of simultaneous sexual arousal and climax to effect con-

---

[10] *The Prose Salernitan Questions,* ed. Brian Lawn, Auctores Britannici Medii Aevi 5 (London, 1979), 6, 93.

[11] *Prose Salernitan Questions,* 9.

ception. This achievement was normally accomplished by consenting partners.[12]

Although the physicians provided the physiological rationale for sexual techniques, Ovid remained the acknowledged authority for lovemaking in the twelfth-century schools. When the poet finally brings his lovers together in bed at the end of Book II of his *Ars amatoria,* he closes the door to their chamber, but not so tightly as to prevent him from coaching the pair in erotic techniques. As they proceed with murmurs and caresses, Ovid advises them not to hurry but to encourage each other with deliberate delays. "Do not unfurl your sails to leave the other behind; finish the line at the same time (*simul*). Pleasure (*voluptas*) is fullest when a man and woman lie equally (*pariter*) vanquished."[13] As Ovid's translator and commentator rendered the Latin text for his French audience, he transformed the poetry and euphemisms of the antique master into the lexicon of the *fabliaux*. Those parts of the female anatomy that Ovid evoked indirectly are now glossed with the direct locutions of *mamelles* and *con*. Approaching *jouissance* is signaled by shouts of *harou* and frenzied dog bites, but the advice for lovers remains identical to that of the ancient master: "try to finish together if you can, because, as the *chanson* says, 'the game is good and beautiful when love comes together' (*vient d'ambedeux*)."[14]

These expressions of gender symmetry and free consent in the theologians, physicians, and Ovidians were transformed into a prescribed ideal by the writers of romance. The negative exemplar against which subsequent *romanciers* reacted was provided by the Tristan legend. Since the love of Tristan and Iseut was the product of drugs, free consent was thereby vitiated. When Iseut was forced to marry King Marc, their relationship could not become reciprocal. In an early lyric, Chrétien de Troyes protested that unlike Tristan the poet never imbibed a potion. Love was not forced upon him but came freely through the eyes.[15] In similar fashion, Chrétien's young couple Erec

[12] *Prose Salernitan Questions,* 7. The exception was, of course, rape, which could also produce pregnancies.

[13] Ovid, *Ars amatoria,* ed. E. J. Kenney (Oxford, 1961), 2, vv. 704–28, pp. 168–69.

[14] *L'Art d'Amours: Traduction et commentaire de l' "Ars Amatoria" d'Ovide; Édition critique,* ed. Bruno Roy (Leiden, 1974), 222–25.

[15] Chrétien de Troyes, *D'amours qui m'a tolu a moi,* ed. Wendelin Foerster, *Kristian von Troyes: Wörterbuch zur seinem sämtlichen Werken,* Romanische Bibliothek 21 (Halle, 1914), 208.

and Enide explicitly rejected Iseut's example on the night of her wedding to King Marc, as they themselves consummate their love on their own nuptial night. Fired by looks, consumed by mutual desire, and exchanging kisses and embraces, they willingly—Chrétien uses the term *volantiers* twice in two lines—render to each member its debt (*lor droit randent a chascun manbre*),[16] in full compliance with the theological formula. But how can two individuals be thus one in heart and body? Chrétien answered this paradox in his second romance, *Cligès,* where the hero's desire (*volonté*) passes to his beloved Fenice. The mystery can be compared to different people singing in harmony.[17]

Following Chrétien's lead, Jean Renart composed two romances in which the love of two young couples comes to fruition in marriage. In *L'Escoufle,* Guillaume, the son of a French count, was born at the same time as Aelis, only daughter of the German emperor. Raised together in the same nursery, the two children soon fall in love. Like Daphnis and Chloe, they explore together their developing sexuality, masking their status as *ami* and *amie* with the names of brother and sister.[18] In the *Roman de la Rose,* Jean's second romance, the couple is composed of Conrad, emperor of the Germans, who falls in love with the belle Lïenor, sister of a lowly knight from Dole.[19] In the first romance, the emperor intends to unite the young pair in matrimony and make Guillaume his successor. In the second, Conrad plans to marry Lïenor and produce an heir to the imperial throne. In both, the marriages are opposed by the great princes of the empire who object to the flagrant *mésalliance* resulting from the disparity of social status, but in the end mutual love triumphs over all obstacles. In *L'Escoufle,* Jean frequently compared Guillaume's and Aelis' love to that of the youthful Tristan and Iseut, but he has Guillaume protest that, unlike the legendary couple whose tragedy was caused by the potion, their love was never the result of compulsion (*force*).[20]

---

[16] *Les Romans de Chrétien de Troyes: I, Erec et Enide,* ed. Mario Roques, Les Classiques français du moyen âge (Paris, 1970), v. 2036.

[17] *Les Romans de Chrétien de Troyes: II, Cligès.* ed. Alexandre Micha, Les Classiques français du moyen âge (Paris, 1957), v. 2805.

[18] Jean Renart, *L'Escoufle,* ed. Franklin Sweetser, Textes littéraires français (Paris, 1974), vv. 1978–91.

[19] Jean Renart, *Le Roman de la Rose ou de Guillaume de Dole,* ed. Félix Lecoy, Les Classiques français du moyen âge (Paris, 1979).

[20] Jean Renart, *L'Escoufle,* vv. 6352–59.

In fact, throughout both romances, so reciprocal are the desires of the two pairs that it would be difficult to distinguish between the partners. As in Chrétien's *Erec et Enide* and *Cligès,* matrimony is the befitting reward for mutual love that presumably prolongs the couple's happiness into the future. In a remarkable way the romance dream of Chrétien de Troyes and Jean Renart aestheticized and reinforced the fundamental sexual reciprocity inherent in the theologians' marital debt, the physicians' two-seed physiology and mutual desire, and the Ovidian technique of simultaneous orgasm. Although space does permit entry into details, such sexual reciprocity also characterized the thousands of couplings represented in the *fabliaux* where men and women abandoned themselves with pleasure and enthusiasm both within and without matrimony.[21] Explicitly or implicitly, this gender symmetry was undergirded by the presumption of mutual consent for both partners.

Other voices, however, were less persuaded of this last assumption. Early in the twelfth century, the precocious and perceptive Heloise isolated and identified the constraints endemic in matrimony. In her celebrated first letter to Abelard, she rejected the title of wife (*uxor*) with its coercive bonds (*vinculi nuptualis, matrimonii foedera*) for the name of *amie,* concubine, strumpet, or even whore under which designation she could express her unconditional love for Abelard without compulsion.[22] Andreas Capellanus agreed with the conclusions of Heloise's analysis in the equally celebrated letter that he attributed to Marie, countess of Champagne, and which announced that "love cannot exist (*extendere*) between two married people." Beyond the problems of jealousy and other practical matters, Marie noted that wedded couples are "yoked together" (*duos iugales*), compelled by the marriage obligation to submit to their mutual will (*mutuis tenentur ex debito voluntatibus obedire*), and in no way able to deny themselves to each other (*et in nullo se ipsos sibi invicem denegare*).[23] Elsewhere, Andreas declared that couples were permitted no other solace (*solatium*) beyond the theological categories of progeny and the marital debt.[24] Among the vernacular *roman-*

---

[21] To take some examples from Jean Bodel, *Li Sohaiz desvez,* vv. 201–6, in *Jean Bodel: Fabliaux,* ed. Pierre Nardin (Paris, 1965), p. 107; *Le Vilain de Bailluel,* vv. 86–92, p. 82; and *Gombert et les deus clers,* vv. 152–57, p. 92.

[22] Ed. J. T. Muckle, "The Personal Letters between Abelard and Heloise," *Mediaeval Studies* 15 (1953), 70–71.

[23] *Andreas Capellanus: On Love,* ed. P. G. Walsh (London, 1982), 1,6, p. 156.

[24] *Andreas Capellanus,* 1, 6, p. 150.

ciers, it was Marie de France, however, who was best able to articulate this matrimonial bondage. Although she esteemed the mutually shared felicity of lovers such as Lanval and his fabulous lady, Marie nonetheless sketched the figures of at least two wives unhappily imprisoned in marriage. In *Yonec,* a young spouse who was unable to fulfill her matrimonial duty of providing heirs for her rich husband is emblematically locked in a tower guarded by an old sister-in-law. Similarly, in *Guigemar,* another wife of an aged and jealous husband is closely watched by a castrated priest. Both women escape their matrimonial confines by accepting and reciprocating solace from young lovers whose names entitled Marie's stories.[25] It is undoubtedly significant that it befell the feminine voices of Heloise and the two Maries to articulate the constraints that matrimonial obligation placed upon the consent of spouses. Despite the similar conclusions, individual differences may be discerned within these three analyses. Undoubtedly all three included the element of indissolubility among the coercive bonds of Christian marriage, but at least Marie de Champagne judged these burdens to weigh equally on husband and wife. To Marie de France it was the young women who suffered most.

Not only was consent endangered by the matrimonial bonds, but an additional asymmetrical element was introduced into the marriage paradigm. Although the physicians had postulated symmetry in their two-seed theory, they also distinguished an important difference between the two sexes. Guillaume de Conches, followed by the *Prose Salernitan Questions,* noted that although women are cold and humid by complexion, they are more fervent in desire than men. The heat of female desire resembles wet wood, which catches fire less readily but burns longer and more strongly. Men are like the ignition of straw, quickly aroused but quickly receding. The composition of the female uterus is more like iron which warms slowly but holds its heat longer. Since the uterus is cold and the male semen is hot and dry, the uterus rejoices to receive it. Whereas a man experiences pleasure only in the emission of his own seed, a woman has a two-fold delight (*duplex delectatio*), in both the emission of her seed and the reception of the man's.[26] The vernacular commentator to the *Ars amatoria* of Ovid recited a comparable physiological

---

[25] *Lanval, Yonec,* and *Guigemar* may be found in Marie de France, *Lais,* ed. Alfred Ewert, Blackwell's French Texts (Oxford, 1976).

[26] [Guillaume de Conches], *Dragmaticon* (Strassburg, 1567), 238–39. *Prose Salernitan Questions,* 4. Franz Redeker, *Die "Anatomia Magistri Nicolai phisici" und ihr Verhältnis zur Anatomia Chophonis und Ricardi* (Leipzig, 1917), 59.

difference between men and women. Female desire is like burning coals covered with ashes. They burn with greater heat, intensity, and duration than the more open passions of men. Rather than alluding to the medical theories, however, the glossator cited Ovid's well-known story of Tiresias found in the *Metamorphoses*. When Jupiter and Juno had failed to agree as to whether men or women derived greater pleasure (*voluptas*) from sexuality, they chose as arbitrator the wise man Tiresias who had observed the mating of serpents and spent eight years of his life as a woman. Loyal to his own sex, as could be expected, Tiresias granted the decision to Jupiter, who had argued for the greater pleasure of women. Although Ovid's version was susceptible to nuanced and ambivalent interpretations, the vernacular commentator merely concluded that women are hotter (*plus chaut*) than men.[27] The physicians' conclusion about female desire, reinforced by Ovid, was accepted as one of the standard articles in the traditional litany of misogyny. In Book III, the violent palinode of the *De Amore*, Andreas Capellanus, for example, followed the arguments against love with an equally long catalogue of the ills of women. Included was a brief recitation of innate feminine lust (*luxuria*). No matter the social disparity, a woman will always rut after a potent man, but no man, whatever his virility, will be able to satisfy a woman.[28]

When the gender asymmetry created by greater female desire is melded with the symmetry required in the reciprocity of the marital debt, inordinate stress is applied to the element of consent. This is precisely the situation exploited in the thirteenth-century *fabliau, La Dame qui aveine demanoit pour Morel sa provende avoir* (The Lady who asked for Dobbin to be fed his oats). This lady and a *vallet* loved each other with great abandon of heart and body, a passion that remarkably continued even after their marriage, as both according to the biblical command loved each other equally as one is loyally obligated (*car chascuns . . . ama son per tant com il dut loialment*). This is evident because their two wills were one. More than Tristan and Iseut they make love without cease, day and night, in bed and on the ground. To facilitate their couplings the husband proposes that the wife summon him with the mating call: "let Dobbin have his oats." Dobbin's hunger, however, persists unabated by the week, day, hour. . . . In fact, there is no barn large enough

---

[27] Ovid, *Metamorphoses*, 3, 316–38, ed. Frank J. Miller, Loeb Classical Library (Cambridge, Mass., 1984), I, 146–48. *L'Art d'Amours*, 102–3.
[28] *Andreas Capellanus*, 3, p. 318.

to store oats to satisfy Dobbin. Unable to extinguish the devouring fire—to shorten a story whose conclusion is already evident—the husband falls sick, his bones drained of marrow. After a short reprieve revives him, the wife recalls him once more to his duty (*devoir*). Reduced to desperation at this point, the *vallet* turns his backside to her lap and discharges his bowels. "Here, take the bran; . . . the oats are finished." Thereafter, the wife takes what she can without forcing the rest, whereas the husband serves her as he can, but whenever he pleases. "I do not say," interposed the narrator, "at her wish but at the will of her husband." The moral for the married, he concluded, "is to do it in measure whenever you see the time and place." [29] When the symmetry of sexual relations is destroyed by the imbalance of female desire, the reciprocity of the marital debt prescribed by the theologians is no longer possible. The dominance of the man must replace mutual consent and restore the equilibrium.

After delineating the aristocratic model of marriage in twelfth-century France, Georges Duby demonstrated how it first came into conflict and finally accommodated itself with the opposing ecclesiastical model. This investigation into the five discourses prevailing in northern France at the turn of the century reveals a remarkable congruity on the subject of sexual relations and consent. The theological enjoining of married partners to reciprocate fully the marital debt found corroboration in the medical theories of the male-female testicles, of the resultant two seeds and mutual desire, and the Ovidian instruction in simultaneous orgasm. We may note that even if the theologians may not have dared to reveal interest in the erotic techniques suggested by the physicians and exhorted by the Ovidians, their doctrine of the reciprocal marital debt allowed them little cause for objection. The vernacular romances addressed to the lay aristocracy also dreamed of mutual love leading to rapturous matrimony. It is true that family strategies of marriage do lie at the background of Marie de France's unhappy young wives and of Jean Renart's two emperors who must marry to perpetuate the imperial succession but whose choice of spouses are opposed by the princes on the grounds of patrimonial interests. Marie and Jean nonetheless advocate to their audiences both

---

[29] *C'est de la dame qui aveine demandoit pour Morel sa provende avoir,* ed. Anatole de Montaiglon and Gaston Raynaud, *Recueil générale et complet des fabliaux des XIIIe et XIVe siècles* (Paris, 1872), I, 319–29.

the freedom to choose one's marriage partner and the reciprocity of sexual relations. All of these constructions of gender symmetry implied, if they did not overtly enunciate, full consent of both parties. Seldom has a theological pronouncement received such sympathetic ear from competing discourses. Other important issues on the ecclesiastical agenda, such as the definition of sexual desire as concupiscence, the interdiction of extramarital relations, and the duty of engendering progeny, did not elicit the same unanimity among the five discourses.[30]

Despite this general consensus, however, voices of women did express doubts about the consensual nature of the matrimonial bond and physicians entertained theories that imputed greater sexual appetite to women than to men. The consequence of this asymmetry was enregistered in at least one *fabliau* which articulated the misogynist fear of the voracious appetite of female sexuality.

The agreement achieved over gender symmetry around 1200 soon came under sharp attack. During the first decade of the thirteenth century the metaphysical and natural treatises of Aristotle were cited at Paris through Latin translations of Arabic versions. The *Quaternuli* of David de Dinant, for example, rehearsed the characteristic Aristotelian themes that only the male emits sperm, that the female merely produces menstrual blood for nourishing the embryo, and that it is unnecessary for the female to experience pleasure in order to conceive. Female delight was likened to that of a prepubescent boy, because, in Aristotle's famous dictum, "a female is essentially an imperfect male, just as is a boy (*femina est mas imperfectus, quamadmodum et puer*)."[31] This physiology merely exemplified Aristotle's underlying theory on gender that the male is the efficient cause conferring form, the female the material contributing only matter. The former is active, the latter passive.

---

[30] For the inability of the theologians to enlist agreement on their doctrine of concupiscence, see Baldwin, "Five Discourses," 813–15. The only unequivocal accord among the five discourses was a shared antipathy toward homophilia.

[31] David de Dinant, *Quaternulorum fragmenta*, ed. Marianus Kurdziałek, Studia Mediewistyczne 3 (Warsaw, 1963), 23, 31. See also Gabriel Théry, *Autour du décret de 1210, 1: David de Dinant*, Bibliothèque Thomiste 6 (Le Saulchoir, 1925), 7–12. For a comprehensive study on the history, significance, and influence of the Aristotelian theories on gender, see Prudence Allen, *The Concept of Woman: The Aristotelian Revolution 750 B.C.–A.D. 1250* (Montreal, 1985).

These Aristotelian paradigms directly contested the assertions of gender equality derived from the Hippocratic-Galenic doctrine of the two seeds and the concomitant theories of the five discourses around 1200. David de Dinant and the newly discovered Aristotelian treatises were condemned by the theologians in a provincial council at Sens in 1210, to be confirmed by Robert of Courson as papal legate in 1215, but during the course of the thirteenth century they were rehabilitated by the Parisian theologians, most notably Albertus Magnus and Thomas Aquinas. This eventual acceptance of Aristotle had momentous consequences for both the science and philosophy of gender relations thereafter. The physiological basis for gender symmetry derived from reciprocal contribution and desire was dismantled. As the female contribution to conception was devalued and her need for sexual pleasure was denied, the woman's sexual role was increasingly perceived as passive and her right to consent attenuated.

Johns Hopkins University

"Með Jákvæði Hennar Sjálfrar": Consent as Signifier in the Old Norse World

JENNY JOCHENS

During a meeting of the Icelandic Althing set in the middle of the tenth century, Egill Skalla-Grímsson was approached by Hǫskuldr, a fellow chieftain, who requested the hand of Egill's daughter Þorgerðr in marriage to his own son Óláfr. Although favorable to the match, Egill replied that he wanted to discuss the matter with his daughter before giving a final answer, because "no man shall marry her against her will." Seeking out Þorgerðr, Egill presented her with the proposal, and, without hiding his own approval, assured her that the decision was hers. A lively discussion ensued between father and daughter. Þorgerðr argued that Egill's desire for the match opposed his often professed love for her, and her principal objection was Óláfr's illegitimate birth, although the young man admittedly was handsome and well dressed. Even the disclosure that, through his slave-mother, Óláfr was the grandson of an Irish king, was insufficient to persuade her. Egill had to report his failure to Hǫskuldr who in turn informed his son.[1]

---

[1] *Laxdæla saga,* ed. Einar Ól. Sveinsson, Íslenzk Fornrit, V (Reykjavik, 1934), ch. 23: 63–64. In the following, references to the sagas will be given in the Íslenzk Fornrit edition (abbreviated ÍF), indicating volume, chapter and page. Most sagas exist in English translations. For a recent comprehensive list, see Donald K. Fry, *Norse Sagas Translated into English: A Bibliography* (New York, 1980).

This episode is by no means unique. Like þorgerðr, several heroines in the Icelandic family sagas were given the opportunity to accept or refuse a proposed suitor.[2] Taking this right for granted, others became angry if they were not asked. Married against her will at the age of fifteen, Guðrún "let it be known that she was displeased," and, predictably, the marriage lasted only two years.[3] Other women presented conditions to be fulfilled before agreeing to their suitors' proposals. Assured by her uncle that her refusal would be sufficient reason to call off the negotiations initiated by Njáll on behalf of his foster son, Hildigunnr demanded that the young man obtain a chieftainship before according her consent. Once the condition was met, three years later, they were married.[4] Widows were often free to remarry according to their own wishes. When a new suitor courted Guðrún after the death of her second husband, her father reminded him that "Guðrún is a widow and can answer for herself." Paternal and fraternal persuasion made her enter this marriage against her better judgment, however. But after this husband's death, she managed to deflect and exploit the marital interest of a new admirer before taking his rival as her fourth spouse.[5]

More striking illustrations of female consent in marriage can scarcely be found, but, remarkably, these episodes allegedly occurred during the tenth century when Iceland was still heathen.[6] When we look closely at the marriage arrangements in these narratives, however, we discover that pagan marriage was primarily a commercial contract that regulated the transfer of property from two parental families to the household of the new couple. In due course the young people's productive efforts were expected to augment these

---

[2] For good overviews of some of the genres of Old Norse literature dealt with in this essay, see the chapters by Carol J. Clover (Family sagas), Theodore M. Andersson (Kings' sagas), and Marianne Kalinke (Chivalric sagas) in Carol J. Clover and John Lindow, eds., *Old Norse-Icelandic Literature: A Critical Guide,* Islandica XLV (Ithaca, N.Y., 1985).

[3] *Laxdœla saga,* ÍF V, 34: 93–94. See also Sigríðr's displeasure at her brother's marital arrangements on her behalf: *þórðar saga hreðu,* ÍF XIV, 4: 183–84.

[4] *Njáls saga,* ÍF XII, 97: 241–47.

[5] *Laxdœla saga,* ÍF V, 43: 129–30; 60: 179–81, 65: 193–96, 68: 199–202. In the same saga, see also the remarriage of þorgerðr, V, 7: 15.

[6] The depiction of women in the family sagas has been treated by Rolf Heller, among others, in *Die literarische Darstellung der Frau in den Isländersagas* (Halle, 1958).

assets, while their sexual and reproductive activities were to result in a new generation. The initial financial arrangements of the new *ménage* were arranged entirely by men—normally the male guardians of the two young people, although the future husband could act on his own behalf—but, as we have seen, they were apparently willing on occasion to let the woman have free choice in deciding on her future husband, the normal definition of consent.[7] Since, as we shall see, consent was unusual in pagan marriages and normally associated with Christian nuptials, the question of its appearance in this heathen context imposes itself.

The relatively few occurrences of female consent do not tell the full story. Completing the spectrum of available female responses, the family sagas also show women, who, if asked, demurely and passively agreed to their fathers' candidates.[8] In the overwhelming majority of marriages, however, the woman's response was not reported. Given the fact that men often negotiated these arrangements in the absence of women, for example, at meetings of the Althing, we can conclude that normally a woman was not asked for her opinion of her future spouse and was not informed until later, at times not until the moment of the wedding.[9]

Upon closer inspection, even the cases of purported female consent look suspicious. In the first place, whether the women showed anger, set conditions, or refused the proposal outright, eventually they all married the men chosen for them. Furthermore, the marriages contracted against the specific wishes of the women invariably ended in death, injury, or divorce—all dis-

---

[7] The marriages already mentioned included property arrangements. For a more detailed account, see the financial transactions preliminary to the marriage of Hrútr and Unnr: *Njáls saga*, ÍF XII, 2: 7–9.

[8] To stay with the women in *Laxdœla saga*, when Hrefna's father and brother presented her with Kjartan's request for her hand, she "did not refuse and asked her father to decide." Likewise, the young þórdís' response to the spokesman for her suitor was that "she would rely on her father's judgment"; ÍF V, 45: 137 and 70: 206.

[9] Married without consultation were þórdís in *Gísla saga*, ÍF VI, 5: 19, and her daughter þuríðr, by then a widow, in *Eyrbyggja saga*, ÍF IV, 29: 77. The widow Helga's new marriage was arranged at the meeting of the Althing (*Heiðarvíga saga*, ÍF III, 15: 259), as was þorgerðr's (*Hávarðar saga Ísfirðings*, ÍF VI, 4: 303 [her name is revealed in 7: 314]). Steingerðr was not informed about her impending marriage to Bersi until she was taken to the wedding (*Kormáks saga*, ÍF VIII, 7: 225–27). After her husband's death, a woman admitted that she would rather have married his brother in the first place (Ingibjǫrg to Gísli in *Gísla saga*, ÍF VI, 1: 5).

asters for the men.[10] In other words, it appears that the few alleged cases of free choice in marriage were not typical. On the contrary, women were normally not asked for their approval, and, as we shall see, those episodes describing consent may carry the authors' hidden agenda. It is obvious, nevertheless, that the family sagas—written in the thirteenth century but purporting to portray the pagan period—were familiar with the notion of female consent. From where did it come?

To explore the alleged appearance of consent in the pagan period we shall first turn to the legal evidence. The Icelandic law code *Grágás* shares with the family sagas a double legacy from pagan and Christian traditions.[11] With oral roots in Norwegian and Icelandic pagan society and recited orally at the Althing for generations, the law was eventually written down at the initiative of Bishop Gizurr beginning in 1117, and the process continued under the leadership of other churchmen.[12] Replaced by *Jónsbók* in 1281, *Grágás* is normally seen as describing the twelfth century, but its span is much wider as several features reflect pagan conditions and the earliest manuscripts have been dated to the middle of the thirteenth century. In both Norwegian and Icelandic law, marriage was placed in the context of property. The Norwegians embedded the rules in the so-called *Kaupa bálkr* or Merchant Law found in various provincial versions, whereas the bulkier Icelandic text devoted a full chapter to the so-called *Festa þáttr* or Engagement Section.[13]

During the first half of the twelfth century, the growing influence of ecclesiastics enabled them in both countries to promulgate the so-called Christian Laws that were appended to the secular legislation. In Iceland the

[10] The cases are listed in Jenny Jochens, "The Medieval Icelandic Heroine: Fact or Fiction?" *Viator* 17 (1986), 35–50, note 84.

[11] The various manuscripts have been published by Vilhjálmur Finsen: *Grágás: Konungsbók,* 2 vols. (Copenhagen, 1852); *Grágás: Staðarhólsbók* (Copenhagen, 1879); and *Grágás: Skálholtsbók m. m.* (Copenhagen, 1883). The three volumes are used in the reprint edition (Odense, 1974) and cited as *Gg* Ia, Ib, II, and III, followed by page references.

[12] *Íslendingabók,* ÍF I, 10: 23–24.

[13] For Norway, see *Norges gamle Love,* ed. R. Keyser and P. A. Munch, I (Christiania [Oslo], 1846), 27, 231 (hereafter *NgL*). For Iceland, see *Gg* Ia, 222; Ib, 29–75; II, 152–209.

process was started in the period 1122–33.[14] For our investigation it is of interest to note that, despite keen interest in the subject, churchmen did not succeed in moving the marriage rules from the secular to the Christian laws. Furthermore, in the oldest versions of these laws, consent is not mentioned.

Reinforcing the impression from the saga narratives and corroborated by legal evidence from continental Germanic tribes, *Grágás* stressed the overwhelming commercial character of the marital arrangements. The negotiations were entirely dominated by men. Speaking for himself, the future groom would indicate to the woman's guardian the price he was willing to pay for the bride.[15] Fixed by law at a certain minimum, this *mundr* was often much higher in reality. If the father found the offer satisfactory, he would in turn reveal the *heimanfylgja,* or dowry, the woman's share of the paternal inheritance that he would hand over to the couple on their wedding day. When the two parties had reached an agreement, witnesses were called in, the two men repeated the conditions, and shook hands on the bargain. Since the woman received no mention, it appears that neither her presence nor her agreement to the conditions or the candidate were needed.

As a widow, the woman had the right to be consulted about her second marriage, but if her father was still alive, he remained entirely in charge. In this case a scribe inserted into one of the manuscripts an addition stating that a father was not allowed to force into marriage a daughter who wanted to become a nun.[16] Suggesting at best a belated respite for the few women who could be accommodated by the two Icelandic nunneries, this statement leaves an overwhelming impression that paternal coercion of daughters was pervasive and normal in marital matters.

We have seen that the oldest laws and the family sagas, the only two genres that possibly might convey authentic information about pagan conditions, differ on the issue of consent: non-existent in the former, it is found in several episodes in the latter. In what follows we shall maintain this bifurcated approach, as we first search for the introduction of Christian consent into the ecclesiastical charters and laws and then as we look for reflections of this legislation in the narratives outside the corpus of the family sagas. In the

[14] *Gg* Ia, 36–37; II, 45–46.
[15] *tina mundarmál; Gg* Ib, 29; II, 155.
[16] *Gg* II, 156.

process we shall attempt to resolve the problem presented by the divergent legacy from the family sagas and the law.

Despite ancient Roman roots, consent in marriage—interpreted not as parental consent but as that of the young couple—was fully formulated as Christian doctrine only by the middle of the twelfth century by Peter Lombard.[17] Already by the 1180s the doctrine was propagated by churchmen in Norway and Iceland. This is clear from a letter written by Archbishop Eiríkr of Niðaróss (Trondheim) to the two Icelandic bishops, in which he declared that full matrimony was established as soon as a man in the presence of witnesses had betrothed a woman *með jákvæði hennar sjálfrar* (literally: with her own yes-word).[18] This audible female consent became a hallmark of Christian marriage legislation in the North. The clergy's insistence on this feature grew from their desire to extend to women the freedom in matrimonial matters that Germanic law gave to men and of which churchmen approved. Female consent accommodated and facilitated two basic ideals held by churchmen: gender equality and the extension of the Christian family beyond inherited tribal and social restrictions.

Not content to have this rule articulated only within the church, clergymen successfully incorporated consent into Christian legislation at the provincial and national level. In Norway it can be found already in the oldest existing versions of these laws, as, for example, in the so-called Older Borgarthing Christian Law. According to this text, a man wanting to marry should first seek the advice of the woman's relatives, but next he must inquire into her own opinion. In this stumbling and cumbersome way, the text explains how witnesses representing both the future groom and the bride were to listen whether "the woman says no to the request for marriage or yes. If she says yes or is silent, the marriage can be concluded according to both lay and ecclesiastical law. . . . But if she says no to it, the marriage cannot be concluded legally."[19] Although Norwegian historians have dated this law to the first half of the twelfth century, this well-developed concept of consent

---

[17] James A. Brundage, *Law, Sex, and Christian Society in Medieval Europe* (Chicago, 1987), 235–78.

[18] *Íslenzkt Fornbréfasafn: Diplomatarium Islandicum,* I (Copenhagen, 1857–76), 287 (hereafter *DI*).

[19] *NgL,* I, 382.

suggests that the particular passage was included later.[20] It is nonetheless clear that the passive role traditionally attributed to women in matrimonial arrangements made churchmen willing to accept a bride's silence as a performative answer.

In the Older Frostathings Law, normally thought to be slightly later, the obligation to ascertain the woman's response was placed on her guardian.[21] The passage interpreting the woman's silence as a positive answer is also found here, suggesting that it was not only an accommodation to shy women but also an attempt to attenuate the radical idea of consent, undoubtedly accepted with greater reluctance by the woman's parents than by the groom himself.

Christian laws in Norway dating from the middle of the thirteenth century were phrased more elegantly. No longer retaining the need to consult with the woman's relatives, the law instructed the suitor to go directly to the woman he wanted to marry. Assuming that ecclesiastical impediments did not prevent the union, he should take her hand in the presence of witnesses, mention her name, and declare that he betrothed her in accordance with the law of God. The witnesses were to hear the woman's "*jáyrði* (yes-word) because it is prohibited according to God's law that a man should marry a woman or a maiden against her will (*nauðga*)."[22]

Brought to this radical conclusion, the feature of consent validates the secret marriage of young people, an undesirable development for propertied parents anywhere.[23] The total absence of reference to the woman's relatives was apparently not acceptable, since they were reinstated in the next version of the Norwegian Christian Law written by Archbishop Jón in 1277.[24] Although intended for all of Norway, this law was probably never implemented,

---

[20] See the article "Kristenrettar" in *Kulturhistorisk Leksikon for Nordisk Middel-alder* IX (Copenhagen, 1964), 297–306 (hereafter *KLNM*). On the speed with which Gratian's ideas became known in Norway, see Erik Gunnes, "Erkebiskop Øystein som lovgiver," *Lumen* 13 (1970), 127–49; reprinted in Claus Krag and Jørn Sandnes, eds., *Nye middelalderstudier: Kongedømme, kirke, stat,* Norske historikere i utvalg VI (Oslo, 1983), 94–109.

[21] *NgL* I, 155.

[22] *NgL* II (Christiania [Oslo], 1848), 299–300, 319, 333.

[23] On this problem in the late medieval period, see Steven Ozment, *When Fathers Ruled: Family Life in Reformation Europe* (Cambridge, Mass., 1983), 25–49.

[24] *NgL* II, 367–68.

but it remained an important model for other legislation. Both this and the local Christian Laws promulgated a generation earlier also included the requirement that banns be read by priests on three consecutive Sundays, a measure instigated by the Fourth Lateran Council to combat incest and bigamy and prevent secret marriages.[25]

Similar steps were taken in Iceland. In 1269 Archbishop Árni Þorláksson (1269–98) introduced new rules for the church service that included brief references to both the reading of banns and female consent.[26] Further elaborated and including references to consultation with the woman's kin, these rules also became part of the so-called New Christian Law accepted by the Althing in 1275.[27] According to both this and Bishop Jón's Christian Law for Norway, the formal engagement where witnesses heard the woman give her assent could not take place until after the banns had been read, but the man had also to consult with the woman before arranging the banns with the priest. In other words, the law specified two occasions on which the woman should be consulted by her suitor.

Secular laws were also revised during this period. The control of ecclesiastical laws over marriage was not exclusive, because secular legislation still regulated property. As in the older secular laws, the "Inheritance Section" constituted an important part of the varied versions issued by Norwegian kings for Norway and Iceland. Here the old rules of the family's control over a daughter's marriage remained intact. The Christian notion of gender equality was acknowledged, not for the bride, however, but for her mother. While the older laws accorded only men the right to arrange the marriages of their female relatives, the new laws stated that "father and mother shall decide on the marriage of their daughters."[28] No mention was made of the bride's consent, and, in fact, the laws stated specifically that if a woman married without her kin's advice, she forfeited her inheritance to the next in line who would assume her share.[29] Surely this must have been a powerful deterrent for any

---

[25] *NgL* II, 319, 300, 368. See the article "Lysing," *KLNM* XI (Copenhagen, 1966), 24–32.

[26] *DI* II (Copenhagen, 1893), 29.

[27] *NgL* V (Christiania, 1895), 36–40.

[28] *NgL* II, 227; *Jónsbók,* ed. Ólafúr Halldórsson (Copenhagen, 1904; repr. Odense, 1970), 70.

[29] *NgL* II, 75, 227–28; *Jónsbók,* 71.

woman inclined to follow her own wishes, but it may have been deemed necessary because of the new freedom offered her by ecclesiastical legislation. The idea was undoubtedly so radical that lay society felt compelled to create protection against unwanted consequences.

In Iceland the inherent conflict between lay and ecclesiastical perceptions came into the open in 1281 when *Jónsbók,* the new secular law, was presented at the Althing by the representative of the Norwegian king. With the Althing's acceptance of the New Christian Law only a few years earlier, which, as we recall, included consent, Bishop Árni now claimed that only the bishop had jurisdiction over matters dealing with marriage, and he protested against *Jónsbók*'s regulations concerning "marriage of women . . . and the inheritance of those women who had been seduced at home as well as those who marry secretly."[30] Despite the bishop's protest, however, *Jónsbók,* patterned on Norwegian models, was accepted. The divergent views among lay and ecclesiastical authorities on the issue of women's self-determination in marriage continued to raise conflicts for individual families in both countries.

These legal prescriptions for marriage can be placed against descriptions of real or imagined marital events in the saga narratives.[31] To determine whether the age-old arranged marriages continued among Nordic people or whether the theoretical consent in the laws was followed by social implementation, we turn to the genre of the so-called contemporary sagas, narratives depicting Icelandic aristocracy and Norwegian royalty written shortly after the described events and therefore treating the period during which churchmen were actively promulgating consent. In the case of Iceland, this involves looking at the saga complex known as *Sturlunga saga,* which brings to life the turbulent society of the twelfth and thirteenth centuries. Reporting countless marriages, it does not include a single case in which the woman's wish was taken into consideration. Men arranged the marriages of their available

---

[30] *Árna saga biskups,* ed. Þorleifur Hauksson (Reykjavik, 1972), 77; *Biskupa sögur,* I (Copenhagen, 1858), 718. The bishop's concern for gender equality caused him not only to envision secret marriages of women but also "men who marry against the advice of their kin."

[31] For a fuller discussion, see Jenny Jochens, "Consent in Marriage: Old Norse Law, Life, and Literature," *Scandinavian Studies* 58 (1986), 142–76.

womenfolk according to their own economic and political advantage, favoring in particular reconciliations between formerly feuding parties. Widows and divorced women were not given any say in the choice of second husbands, even when it was evident that they did not favor the matches.[32]

The civil wars in Norway during the twelfth century depicted in the genre known as the Kings' sagas, afforded unusual opportunities for the victor to reward his followers with spoils, including women, although they were awarded not as slaves and concubines, which was still the case in foreign wars, but as wives, whose opinions, nonetheless, were not solicited. The more peaceful thirteenth century reduced the opportunity to reward martial valor with rich marriages. Ample evidence still remains that fathers decided on their daughters' marriages, accompanied by little indication that the women were asked about their wishes.[33]

Only in a few cases involving prominent women from royal families was female consent sought, but it was done under the explicit auspices of churchmen. These cases, therefore, are more indicative of ecclesiastical wishes than widespread social practice. Furthermore, churchmen used consent as a means of manipulating the women according to their own interests.[34] In a few cases, however, astute and articulate women were able to use the absence of consent to obtain a divorce in a marriage that had not worked out.[35]

Despite this initial resistance, it is clear that consent eventually worked its way into Nordic society. The first response to the new doctrine was not immediate social implementation, but echoes and images in authors' minds as they constructed more or less reliable historical accounts of the past or let their imagination roam freely in fictitious stories. Among these, the so-called Kings' sagas provide a rich historical source. Written prior to the family sagas, they deal with the history of the northern world, particularly Norway, from mythical times to the middle of the thirteenth century. They are, of

[32] Jochens, "Heroine," 43.

[33] Jochens, "Consent," 145–46; eadem, "The Politics of Reproduction: Medieval Norwegian Kingship," *American Historical Review* 92 (1987), 327–49.

[34] For illustrations, see Jochens, "Consent," 147–50.

[35] See the case of Cecilía Sigurðardóttir who obtained permission to remarry from the Norwegian archbishop by arguing that she had not consented to her first marriage; Jochens, "Consent," 142–43.

course, more trustworthy as historical evidence the closer the distance between their time of composition and the period they describe. They include a number of marriage accounts among which we have already noticed that consent occurred only in a few contemporary marriages arranged by churchmen. We shall now turn to the marriages within the Kings' sagas that are placed in the distant past and thereby included pagan as well as Christian settings. These accounts will not, of course, be reliable as historical sources, but they will tell us something about the contemporary outlook of their authors.

Not a single case of consent exists from the pagan and mythical era of Scandinavian history. The cases that do appear are found only from the end of the tenth century, when Christianity first became known in the North. A closer analysis of these situations reveals two interesting features: first, the idea is applied anachronistically. According to the Kings' sagas, consent—absent during paganism—already existed in the North at a time when it had not yet been incorporated into Christian laws anywhere else. Second, if the same event is treated by several authors, the later versions are more likely to include consent than the earlier. In other words, writing during the time when church leaders were propounding consent, the authors of the Kings' sagas clearly understood the connection between Christianity and female consent. Although they were mistaken as to when the idea was first promulgated, their writings reflect the growing propriety of consent for Christian women.[36]

If the Kings' sagas thus suggest the chronological and conceptual origins of consent, an exploration of other genres, sometimes grouped together under the label of "the lying sagas," provides a clue to the Nordic perception of the notion's geographic spread during the Middle Ages.[37] Starting with a Norwegian translation of *Tristan* in 1226, a handful of poetic French texts were reworked into Old Norse prose. In turn, these narratives inspired a body of native stories with settings and subject matter taken from the distant past. The

---

[36] A particularly interesting case concerns the four sisters of King Oláfr Tryggvason. Described in narratives dating from the end of the 12th to the beginning of the 14th century, their marriages were arranged by their brother in the last decades of the 10th century. The oldest account contains no reference to consent, but, according to the most recent version, all four sisters enjoyed this right. For details on this and other cases, see Jochens, "Consent," 151–58.

[37] Jochens, "Consent," 159–65.

bulkiest and, formerly, most popular of Old Norse literature, these "lying sagas," in most cases written later than the other genres, have traditionally been divided into two groups according to their geographic setting. When the arena is the larger European world, they are known as the *riddarasǫgur*, or the chivalric or romantic sagas, whereas the *fornaldarsǫgur*, or legendary sagas, include stories in which the action is limited to the North. The common term "lying sagas" captures the fantasy permeating both genres.

No longer satisfied with this taxonomy, recent scholarship has identified a distinct genre of bridal-quest romances of special interest for our concern.[38] Encompassing narratives within the translated stories, original *riddarasǫgur*, and native *fornaldarsǫgur*, they share an aura of romance with other *Brautwerbung* stories from around the world, as they depict a male hero's quest for a wife.[39] The story's interest and length increase with the obstacles he encountered, but—often of a fantastic nature—these do not ordinarily include the woman's refusal, and the problem of consent is not prominent.

It is obvious that resistance from the desired woman would add a special twist to a story focused on a hero's search for a wife, but only in Iceland was this potentiality developed. A sub-genre of the traditional bridal-quest romance is centered on the *meykongr*, or maiden king. Added to the normal attractions of unmarried youth and beauty was her position as single ruler of a country.[40] Most often without kin and family, a maiden king would naturally answer suitors' requests for marriage herself, but even when her father was still alive she had wrested this privilege from him.[41] Since she knew that if she married she would no longer be a *meykongr* but merely the *dróttning* (queen) of her husband who would take over her role as *kóngr*, she

---

[38] See Hermann Pálsson and Paul Edwards, *Legendary Fiction in Medieval Iceland*, Studia Islandica 30 (Reykjavik, 1971).

[39] See Friedmar Geissler, *Brautwerbung in der Weltliteratur* (Halle, 1955); Kalinke (above, note 2); and Marianne E. Kalinke, *Bridal-Quest Romance in Medieval Iceland*, Islandica XLVI (Ithaca, N.Y., 1990). Focusing on the male protagonists in the latter work, she deals only intermittently with consent.

[40] See Kalinke, *Bridal-Quest*, 66–108.

[41] On the former, see Ingigerðr in *Sigrgarð's saga frœkna, Late Medieval Icelandic Romances*, V, ed. Agnete Loth, Editiones Arnamagnæanæ, Series B, vol. 24 (Copenhagen, 1965), 3: 54–55, and on the latter þornbjǫrg in *Hrólfs saga Gautrekssonar*, in *Fornaldar sögur Norðurlanda*, IV, ed. Guðni Jónsson (Reykjavik, 1954), 4: 63.

was staunchly misogamous initially, resisting marriage as long as possible. Whether refusing or, in the end, accepting a suitor, a maiden king thus represented the most extreme version of a woman's consent as she decided on her marital fate without any interference from her natal family. The man's first move remained firm, however, and not even a maiden king would initiate a marriage.

Often more fantastic than the other "lying sagas," the maiden king romances will obviously blur the general picture of consent within these narratives. To be sure, these tales do not carry great credence as historical sources, but in the traditional grouping of *riddarasǫgur* and *fornaldarsǫgur*, they can still serve as indicators of how foreign concepts were reflected when Nordic minds tried to envision the distant past at home and abroad.

An analysis of the two dozen original chivalric sagas reveals that on the issue of consent the authors pictured Europe as divided into two large sections: a northern area stretching roughly halfway down the European continent and including England and Ireland, and a southern circle reaching around the Mediterranean coastline and encompassing such distant places as India, also considered Christian. In the North, the marriage of a woman was most often decided by her male kin. The few northern women who were asked demurely accepted the decisions of their male relatives and only occasionally murmured about the suitor being too old, or suggested that they consented because a refusal would arouse their fathers' anger.[42] In the South, women were not only asked in a perfunctory manner but were given the opportunity to express opinions about their suitors, often in elaborate speeches, and many were completely free to choose.

This geographic distribution was applied with such finesse that authors would let the same saga illustrate both the northern and southern model as the action shifted geographic center.[43] As a general rule it seems that the

---

[42] This was not only a literary *topos*. A charter from 1429 has captured the moving vignette of a woman who obtained a divorce from one of the Icelandic bishops by declaring that "the little yes" that had created her marriage had been forced out of her "by persuasion of others and fear and dread of her father"; *DI* IV (Copenhagen, 1897), 394.

[43] For illustrations, see Matthildr and Erminga in *Mágus saga jarls* and Ríkilàt and Herborg in *Jarlmanns saga ok Hermanns*. For references and other illustrations, see Jochens, "Consent," 159–64.

farther the action in these stories was removed from the Nordic authors' homeland, the more firmly was the doctrine of consent established. Moreover, female approval of a marriage candidate was perceived as pertaining to countries where Christianity had a long history.

Only one narrative with a northern setting at first appears to contradict this rule. In *Bærings saga,* Vilfríðr, daughter of King Pippinn of Paris, was asked in marriage by the emperor of Greece. The archbishop advised the union, and her father was prepared to agree, assuming it were her wish also. When she expressed her willingness, the two were engaged. At that moment the hero of the story, the irresistible Bæringr, entered the hall. Falling in love immediately, Vilfríðr regretted her consent and escaped marriage in the only way acceptable to churchmen—by pretending that she preferred to enter a nunnery.[44] With an archbishop present at negotiations for a marriage involving a groom from southern Europe, consent was in order for this northern young woman.

To probe the problem of how consent was understood in Scandinavia's distant past, we turn to the legendary sagas. From the roughly two dozen narratives in this group, almost one hundred marriage arrangements can be identified. Of these, two-thirds were negotiated by male relatives who paid no attention to the women's wishes. In the remaining cases, some familiarity with the idea of consent was evident. Deeply rooted in pagan times, these tales cannot, of course, explicitly show the influence of churchmen. It is not excluded, however, that the striking cases of consent in the pagan setting of the family sagas, by then well known to the authors of the legendary sagas, inspired these to postulate similar situations in their own stories. In other cases, a father's plausible reason in permitting a daughter to express preference was his own inability to choose between two equally qualified contenders or his fear of a particular suitor.[45]

[44] Text in Gustav Cederschiöld, ed., *Fornsögur Suðrlanda* (Lund, 1884), 85–123, esp. 97–98.

[45] For illustrations, see Ingibjǫrg in *Hervarar saga ok Heiðreks* and *Ǫrvar-Odds saga* and Húnvǫr in *Þorsteins saga Víkingssonar*. In the latter case a man with the frightening name Hárekr járnhauss ("Iron Skull") asked not only for Princess Húnvǫr in marriage but also wanted her father's kingdom for which in return he promised merely to refrain from killing the king. No wonder that the latter's measured reply was: "I think it would be a good idea to find out what she will answer." For references and further details, see Jochens, "Consent," 165–67.

Although female consent was inserted into the ecclesiastical law books, the contemporary sagas resist the conclusion that it was, in fact, implemented. The Kings's sagas as well as the chivalric and legendary sagas nonetheless indicate that the concept had become part of the general discourse, as authors applied it liberally to those historic and geographic settings they found suitable. Although their chronological and geographic details were occasionally incorrect, their overall vision that consent was a Christian phenomenon, spreading from the South toward the North, was consistent with the actual development.

How, then, can we explain the cases of consent in the pagan setting of the family sagas? Without additional evidence of oral tradition from myth, poetry, or law, this feature must be ascribed solely to the thirteenth-century authors of the family sagas. Often with a thorough clerical training, they were more exposed to ecclesiastical propaganda than ordinary people. As a consequence they took consent so seriously that they included it in their constructions of those parts of their ancestors' lives for which they had little information, thus making it an integral part of the pagan marriage contract. Not even churchmen would expect pagans to live according to Christian norms, of course, but the authors undoubtedly hoped that on this issue their stories would be understood as models worthy of emulation. This didactic quality also clarifies the curious phenomenon that the marriages contracted against the expressed will of the women ended in disaster. Warning that merely asking the women did not suffice, these stories demonstrated the dire consequences when their wishes were not heeded.

So far, we have culled the references to consent in the family sagas from such classical narratives as *Laxdœla saga* and *Njáls saga*. It is worth taking a look at *Víglundar saga,* a little-studied story written probably during the second half of the fourteenth century. Although still firmly anchored within the genre of the family sagas through subject matter, history, and geography, this narrative is also influenced by the atmosphere and vocabulary of the chivalric sagas and the *fornaldarsǫgur*.[46] Set in Norway during the reign of Haraldr hárfagri, as are so many other family sagas, an episode involving the

---

[46] On this issue, see Torfi H. Tulinius, "Landafræði og flokkun fornsagna," in *Skáldskaparmál* 1 (1990), 142–56. The saga has been analyzed by Marianne Kalinke, "*Víglundar saga:* An Icelandic Bridal-Quest Romance," in *Skáldskaparmál* 2 (forthcoming).

beautiful Ólof and the equally handsome Þorgrímr is of interest for our study.[47]

The couple fell in love at first sight and Ólof received Þorgrímr's proposal of marriage positively, assuming her father would agree. He refused the match, however, but the young people swore an oath of faithfulness to each other (*bundit sitt eiginorð*). Nevertheless, while Þorgrímr was away, Ólof's father engaged her to an older man, Ketill, although she gave neither *jáyrði . . . né samÞykki* (literally: yes saying . . . nor approval). Arriving back just in time for the wedding, Þorgrímr interrogated Ketill about the negotiations, asking him whether he had *keypt* Ólof (bought or obtained her legally). Responding to Ketill's positive answer, Þorgrímr further insisted on knowing whether the arrangement had been done with Ólof's approval (*ráð*). In conformity with the old system, Ketill answered that he assumed her father could decide (*eiga at ráða*) in these matters and that the paternal settlement therefore was legal. Articulating the new rule of consent, Þorgrímr revealed his and Ólof's sworn oath according to which she should not marry any man but himself. When she confirmed this, Þorgrímr argued with perfect logic that "it seems to me that I have the woman," and he proceeded to abduct her.[48] Settling in Iceland, the couple lived a long and happy life.

In contrast to the few cases from the classical family sagas in which the incipient notions of consent became stifled as the women eventually married the candidates proposed by their fathers, the author of the late *Víglundar saga* portrayed two women, Ólof and later her daughter-in-law Ketilríðr, who chose their husbands according to their own inclinations, in the process repudiating the choices made by their families. Furthermore, unlike the heroines in the classical stories, they proceeded to live happily with their husbands. Writing in the second half of the thirteenth century, the authors of *Laxdæla saga* and *Njáls saga* were intrigued by the notion of consent, but its novelty prompted them to present the idea hesitatingly. A century later, how-

---

[47] Text in ÍF XIV, 63–116. The passage of interest is found in 5: 70 and 6: 71–74.

[48] Þorgrímr extinguished all lights in the hall in order to facilitate the abduction. The same theme, albeit in magical disguise, was used by the author of *Reykdæla saga* as Þóra was being abducted by Vermundr at the moment of her wedding to Helgi. After a battle between the two suitors, Þóra was married to Helgi (ÍF X, 14: 191–92). In this older story, no mention is made of consent nor of the woman's feelings for the two men.

ever, the concept's wider acceptance allowed the author of *Víglundar saga* to articulate it with greater confidence.[49]

We can probe the author's understanding of consent by paying close attention to the statement that the young couple had *bundit sitt eiginorð* (literally: tied their marriage).[50] Compounded from the adjective *eiginn* (own) and *orð* (word), *eiginorð* has at least three different, related meanings. Reflecting the oral character of property transactions, the word can simply mean "property" (that which is transmitted or received through "one's own word"). In the law it is used in this sense about meadows, stranded whales, and sheep and in the narratives about land.[51] Given the close connection between property and marriage, it is not surprising that the word can also mean the institution of marriage.[52] For our purposes the most interesting feature is that it can be used specifically about the wedding ceremony. Giving a man who was marrying a woman already in possession of a household the option of deciding at the *eiginorð* whether he wanted to move his Thing attachment and residence to her domicile or hers to his, the law identified in the next sentence the *eiginorð* as the *brullaup* or *brúðkaup* (wedding).[53] In another passage, the law allowed a person to retrieve the money given a woman at her wedding if she later died childless, provided it had been stipulated at the *festamál* (engagement) or *eiginorð* (wedding).[54]

---

[49] Mutual consent is also found in another late narrative, *Gunnars saga Keldugnúpsfífls*. The twelve-year-old Gunnarr killed Helga's two brothers, but before he left Iceland he and Helga swore an oath never to marry anyone but each other, "if they could decide." During Gunnarr's absence, Helga's father died of grief; when the young man returned after several years, he and Helga were married (ÍF XIV, 7: 76; 11: 378).

[50] It was used in the same sense in the following generation about Ólof and Þorgrímr's son Víglundr and his neighbor and foster sister Ketilríðr, as they assured each other of their undying love (7: 76). Although going through more prolonged and more titillating difficulties—provided by Ketilríðr's mother in an interesting switch of gender, with the woman playing the antagonistic role normally reserved for men— than Ólof and Þorgrímr, this young couple was eventually also married.

[51] See *Gg* Ib, 86, 129, 156; II, 23, 449, 459, 494 and *Egils saga*, ÍF II, 65: 211. On the meaning of the word, see *Gg* III, 600.

[52] In the legal context, see *Gg* Ib, 58, 243; II, 188, 189. In the narratives, see *Kormáks saga*, ÍF VIII, 8: 232.

[53] *Gg* Ia, 139; II, 275. *Brúðkaup* is found in the second text.

[54] *Gg* Ia, 222; II, 65–66. The word is also used in a paragraph outlining the procedure for the groom if he became sick and unable to attend his *eiginorð* (*Gg* Ib, 31; II, 158).

Eiginorð never became a common term, however, but the documentary evidence suggests that during the late Middle Ages it was used about the wedding ceremony with increasing frequency.[55] It is likely that the author of *Víglundar saga* intended the oath with which the two generational couples strengthened their *eiginorð* to be precisely that "one's own word" implied in the concept of consent and which churchmen considered the only performative act of marriage. In other words, "consent" should be included among the possible nuances of *eiginorð*.

The evidence for social implementation of consent in the medieval North is clearly far slimmer than for its presence in prescriptive, fictitious, and imaginary discourse. In time, however, women were eventually allowed to decide on their partner in marriage in the Nordic world as elsewhere within the Western tradition. In order to envision the process by which this happened, we need to speculate on the unknown people whose marriage arrangements were not recorded. The father for whom the right choice of a future son-in-law was important belonged to the class with wealth and power. Naturally concerned about the qualifications of his future son-in-law, through whom he hoped to gain important new kinsmen and to whose offspring part of his own accumulated riches would pass in the next generation, such a father would be reluctant to concede the choice to his daughter, especially if he feared she might have in mind a candidate different from his own. For the less endowed population, however, we may assume that fathers would do their best to find for their daughters men who would become suitable husbands. Even if it seems clear that fathers legally did not have to and probably only rarely discussed such matters formally with their daughters, we are probably correct in guessing that they knew their daughters' preferences and in most cases respected them. When consent became the law of the land, such ordinary men were willing to turn the decision over to their daughters. The visual and performative difference between the old and the new order, emblemized in the ceremonies, must have been startling; in the pagan context, the passive and silent woman was being transferred from her father to her husband as a piece of property, whereas the Christian bride publicly and loudly declared her willingness to share her life with her husband.

---

[55] For examples, see *DI* IV, 392, 430, and 463.

The conclusion that a majority of marriages eventually included female consent can be corroborated from linguistic evidence, to which we shall finally turn.[56] The traditional Old Norse vocabulary expressed the pagan marriage transactions in terms that made the woman the passive object and the man the active subject. She was *fǫstnuð* (betrothed) or *gefin* (given) to the man, while he would *taka* (take) or *fá* (get) her. In the thirteenth century, however, a new word, *púsa*, appeared, used as a verb meaning to espouse, as a noun connoting the marriage ceremony, and—most interesting for our purpose—as nouns in either feminine or masculine form, *púsa* or *púsi,* designating the bride and the groom respectively. Based on Latin *sponsa,* from which also the French *épouse* and *époux* originated, these two words, from the same root and with identical meaning, reflected churchmen's concern for the equality of the spouses as they entered marriage.

It is interesting to note, however, that the new words appeared in discourse first through the translated French literature and shortly after in the native chivalric sagas. Only when they were firmly established in literature and, very likely, in common parlance, did churchmen incorporate them into their legislation. Indicative of a change in marriage customs, the new vocabulary was at the same time instrumental in bringing about that change in a clear illustration of the power of language and literature to cause social change. A father to whom it did not greatly matter whether his daughter was consulted or not may easily have been persuaded by his priest to accept both the new doctrine and the new vocabulary, thereby fully acceding to the idea. In the meantime churchmen had been able to establish female consent in a few spectacular cases among Norwegian royalty. The two movements eventually coalesced, rendering female consent generally acceptable in the North. Although the new vocabulary eventually went out of fashion, the doctrine remained. Sponsored by Christianity, consent became a fundamental right for women throughout the Western world, in sharp contrast to, for example, Asiatic cultures where marriages have been arranged for both men and women until the present.

Towson State University

---

[56] For references and details, see Jochens, "Consent," 167–69.

Index